With Best Wishes

Anne Collins Walker
and Roadrunner

THE GIFT SHOP
THE RICHARD NIXON LIBRARY & BIRTHPLACE
Yorba Linda ★ California USA

CHINA CALLS

Paving the Way for
Nixon's Historic Journey to China

With Best Wishes

*Anne Collins Walker
and Roadrunner*

THE GIFT SHOP
THE RICHARD NIXON LIBRARY & BIRTHPLACE
Yorba Linda ★ California USA

CHINA CALLS

Paving the Way for
Nixon's Historic Journey to China

by

Anne Collins Walker

Edited by

John Eastman and
Elizabeth C'de Baca Eastman

NIXON LIBRARY BOOKS

Madison Books

Co-published by Nixon Library Books

Madison Books
4720 Boston Way
Lanham, Maryland 20706

3 Henrietta Street
London WC2E 8LU England

Distributed by National Book Network

The paper used in this publication meets the minimum
requirements of American National Standard for
Information Sciences—Permanence of Paper for
Printed Library Materials, ANSI Z39.48–1984. ⊗™
Manufactured in the United States of America.

Library of Congress Cataloging-in-Publication Data

Walker, Anne Collins, 1939–
China calls : paving the way for Nixon's historic
journey to China / by Anne Collins Walker ; edited by
John Eastman and Elizabeth C'de Baca Eastman.
p.   cm.
Includes index.
1. Nixon, Richard M. (Richard Milhous), 1913–
—Journeys—China.   2. Visits of state—China.
I. Eastman, John.   II. Eastman, Elizabeth C'de Baca.
III. Title.
E856.W34   1992
951.05'7—dc20   92–27899 CIP

ISBN 0–8191–8619–8 (cloth : alk. paper)

TO ROADRUNNER

FOR ALWAYS SHARING

IN MEMORY

OF THESE MEN WHO MADE HISTORY

AND HELPED FURTHER THE CAUSE OF PEACE

Ollie Atkins
Mac Collins
Joe Gancie
Ronald L. Jackson
John Mitchell
Robert Taylor

CONTENTS

viii

FOREWORD

Through the often deceiving eye of television, a foreign trip by a President of the United States looks almost effortless, as though it is all smiles and handshakes, leisurely arrival and signing ceremonies, and clinking champagne glasses. The real work is done behind the scenes, by the leaders themselves in their private meetings, and by the men and women the leaders depend upon to get them to their meetings on time—the advance men.

The requirements of television have made good advance work all the more important in politics, because so much depends, for better or for worse, on how an event looks rather than what the candidate says. But there is and always has been more to advance work than pretty pictures, especially in the foreign affairs realm. Negotiations, often delicate ones, must be undertaken with the other side over the schedule, which can involve anything from the length of key meetings to the location of various staff members' hotel rooms. Arrangements must be made for the care and feeding of a President's large and highly demanding contingent of traveling reporters, producers, and technicians. Vehicles, aircraft, supplies, and hundreds of medical and military support personnel have to be arranged so that everyone and everything are in place precisely when they are needed.

Good foreign advance work is complicated enough with the full range of communications and other services available at our embassies. But when I announced on July 15, 1971 that I would visit the People's Republic of China, I knew that to make the arrangements for this unique visit to a mysterious land, I would need a man with very special organizational and diplomatic skills.

The United States and China had had no direct relations for over two decades. We had no embassy there, and no diplomatic personnel whatsoever. A telephone call between Peking and Washington was unthinkable. Despite the often unrealistic optimism in the media about the prospects for my discussions with the Chinese leaders, I knew that the distrust between us after years of hostility would not be easily overcome and indeed that it would probably manifest itself in the early discussions between our representatives and those of the Chinese government.

Our man would have to be a skilled, culturally sensitive diplomat who could avoid needlessly offending the Chinese and yet ensure that our interests were always protected. He would have to be self-confident and stable enough so that the scores of other aides and technicians on the team could come to him with their problems. He would have to be supremely patient because then, as now, the Chinese were justifiably known as masters of bureaucratic gamesmanship. He would have to be a man who could make the tough decisions when the right time came, who would force the issue when it had to be forced, who could speak sharply without losing his temper, who would stay cool when others got hot.

Ron Walker, the head of the White House Advance Office and later Director of the National Park Service, was my first and only choice. This story, assembled by Anne Collins Walker, is about the behind-the-scenes trips to China by Walker and his tightknit band of colleagues and friends that made my own trip to China possible. Because of her unique role both as observer and, in a way, participant, Anne Walker has written a story with equally rich political, diplomatic, human, and frequently humorous dimensions.

While I was known for bringing many very able and very young men and women into the White House, some eyebrows were undoubtedly raised in both capitals when I designated a 34-year-old as head of the advance party. My decision was vindicated not only by the success of the visit but by the seasoned judgement of Han Hsu, who, as Chinese chief of protocol, was Ron Walker's opposite number in 1972. Han later became Ambassador to the United States. When I first arrived in Peking, he told me how impressed he was by our young advance men and particularly by Ron Walker, whose straight-talking style must have been a shock to Chinese officials accustomed to argument by indirection.

Indeed I believe Ron Walker's work directly increased the prospects for a successful Presidential visit, which is why I am so pleased that the Richard Nixon Library & Birthplace is publishing this insider account of one of modern history's last true expeditions into the unknown.

Richard Nixon
Park Ridge, New Jersey
July 1, 1992

PREFACE

This is a true story. It happened because President Richard Nixon wanted to extend his hand in friendship to eight hundred and fifty million people. The transcripts of the satellite communications between the advance team on the ground in China and the White House, contained in these pages, tell only part of the story, however. It is also a story about friendship: unlikely friends, new friends, true friends.

Unlikely friends. The Chinese and the Americans had no basis from which to begin, except that their leaders had agreed to meet. Both groups desperately wanted to make the trip a success. They worked hard to get to know one another, struggled daily to understand one another, and eventually grew to rely on one another.

New friends. Realizing the importance of their mission, the Americans overcame political differences, overlooked turf battles, forgot job descriptions, and became a team.

True friends. Trusted colleagues developed an uncanny ability to communicate without having to speak with words that might be offensive to others listening.

Friendship was the glue that made the enterprise a success. It may not be evident to future researchers, but to me, knowing each the people involved, it is the very heart and soul of this story.

The transcripts are taken from the actual recordings of the telephone calls between Peking and Washington, as the book's title indicates. They have been preserved by the White House Communications Agency. Without them, much of this story would have been lost. Through them, the frustration, laughter, tension, and exhaustion felt by the men advancing this important historical event are evident. Through them, too, one recaptures the sense of excitement that captured the nation in the winter of 1972, before Watergate made other White House tapes the butt of late night television monologues.

It is a story that needed to be told. So many negatives have been written about the Nixon years that the hard work, the dedication, and above all, the friendship, have sometimes been overlooked. The nation knew in 1972 that President Richard Nixon had opened a new era in international relations. In hindsight, it does seem ridiculous that the United States had been isolated for so long from so many people. God bless the bravery, far-sightedness, and leadership of Richard Nixon for hearing his own China call.

Roadrunner was thirty-four years old when he took one hundred Americans to the People's Republic of China twenty-one days in advance of President Nixon's visit. This is his story.

Anne Collins Walker
Potomac, Maryland
February 21, 1992

ACKNOWLEDGEMENTS

Acknowledgements in books are boring . . . unless you find your very own name. So first, let me say that if you bought this book, I am terribly thrilled because you are helping to support an outstanding facility and the only Presidential Library that operates solely on private funding.

I want to express my appreciation to John Taylor, Executive Director of the Richard Nixon Library and Birthplace, for the idea of publishing books directly related to the Nixon Presidency and for choosing *China Calls* as the first in the series. It is my hope that this effort will prompt others to write their stories of the Nixon years.

My deep appreciation also goes to John and Elizabeth Eastman for an outstanding job of editing and for their enthusiasm about the project. They are responsible for the involvement of Madison Books.

As I look back on the five years I spent on the exciting project, my heartfelt thanks goes to my wonderful parents and brother for always making me think I could succeed; to daughters Lisa, Marja, and Lynne for always listening to my latest writings; to my pals Susie Chapin, JoAnne Jackson, Marcia Howard Schoenbaum, and Dick Howard for encouraging me to write; to former colleague Malcolm Barr for telling me I could write; to former boss Commerce Secretary Malcolm Baldridge for assuring me it was the week that changed the world and citing the Baldridge-related trade figures with the PRC to prove it; to Ron Thompson for helping me find vintage equipment; to Bill Livingood, U.S. Secret Service, for his valuable cooperation; to President Nixon for going to China; to Ambassador Han Hsu for inviting Ron and me back to China in 1978; and to my husband, Roadrunner, for always sharing.

Acknowledgement also goes to the several individuals and organizations who have granted permission to reprint lyrics, newspaper articles, maps, and cartoons: MCA Music Publishing and Don McLean; Mike Curb and the Mike Curb Congregation; United Press International; the *Washington Post*; the *Los Angeles Times*; Time Warner, Inc. (copyright 1972); U.S. News & World Report (copyright 1972); and Newsweek, Inc. (copyright 1972). All rights are, of course, reserved by the original publishers.

EDITORS' NOTE

White House transcripts form the core of this book. They tell a story that is concise because the time was so intense. Occasional commentary is provided, where necessary, and is set off from the actual transcripts by brackets. Editing of the transcripts has been kept to a minimum so that the excitement of the trip, and the countless details and frustrations of advance work, would come through. We have removed most of the radio jargon ("over" and "roger") and on occasion deleted exchanges of pleasantries at the beginnings and ends of conversations and also portions that were garbled because of transmission difficulties.

The careful reader will note the use of outdated spellings for certain Chinese places and names (e.g. Peking instead of Beijing, Han Hsu instead of Han Xu). We have retained the usage that was common in 1972.

Finally, we would be remiss were we not to praise Anne Walker's ability to flavor the transcripts with the wonderful personal stories that bring the transcripts to life. On many occasions one could hear sounds of laughter coming from our office as we read of Roadrunner's latest ice cube escapade.

John and Elizabeth Eastman
West Covina, California
July 4, 1992

VOICE CALL SIGNS
WHITE HOUSE COMMUNICATIONS AGENCY

THE PRESIDENT	SEARCHLIGHT
NIXON, MRS. PATRICIA	STARLIGHT
COX, MRS. PATRICIA	SUGARFOOT
COX, MR. EDWARD	SEMINOLE
EISENHOWER, MRS. JULIE	SUNBONNET
EISENHOWER, MR. DAVID	SAHARA
THE VICE PRESIDENT	PATHFINDER
AGNEW, MRS. JUDY	PHOTOGRAPH
THE WHITE HOUSE	CROWN
GUAM RELAY STATION	CARNATION
ATKINS, MR. OLLIE	HAWKEYE
CHAPIN, MR. DWIGHT	WATCHDOG
COLE, MR. KEN	SPECTATOR
EHRLICHMAN, MR. JOHN O.	WISDOM
EISENHOWER, MRS. MAMIE	SPRINGTIME
ELBOURNE, MR. TIM	SNAPSHOT
HALDEMAN, MR. H.R.	WELCOME
HIGBY, MR. LARRY	SEMAPHORE
HUGHES, BGEN JAMES D.	RED BARRON
KISSINGER, DR. HENRY A.	WOODCUTTER
KLEIN, MR. HERBERT G.	WITNESS
LUKASH, DR. WILLIAM M.	SAWHORSE
MACGREGOR, MR. CLARK	WHIPCRACK
TIMMONS, MR. WILLIAM	WINDOWPANE
TKACH, DR. WALTER	SIGNATURE
WALKER, MR. RON	ROADRUNNER
WOODS, MISS ROSE MARY	STRAWBERRY
ZIEGLER, MR. RON	WHALEBOAT

THESE CALL SIGNS ARE CURRENTLY AUTHORIZED.
DESTROY ALL EARLIER DATED CALL SIGN CARDS.

2 AUGUST 1971   /S/

ALBERT REDMAN, JR.
GENERAL, USA
COMMANDING

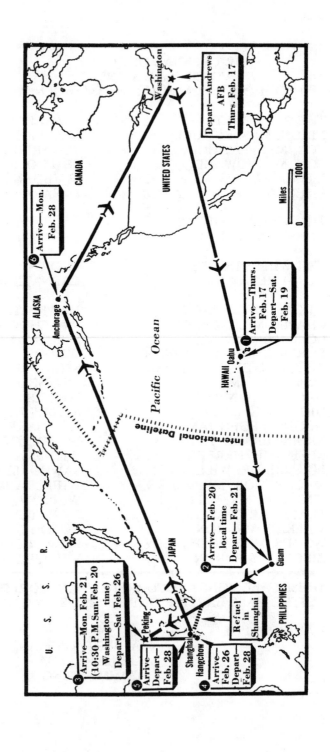

CHINA CALLS

CHAPTER 1

DESTINATION: CHINA

JULY 15, 1971

"Roadrunner, Roadrunner, this is the Signal board, sir. Watchdog requests that you report immediately to the Western White House."

Roadrunner's heart began to race when his radio crackled with the message. It meant the President of the United States was about to leave the Western White House, La Casa Pacifica. The rare, quiet moment relaxing in the sun by the swimming pool at the San Clemente Inn was over.

Roadrunner was the radio communications code name for Ron Walker, staff assistant to the President of the United States and Director of the White House Advance Office. Watchdog was Dwight Chapin, deputy assistant to the President and the appointments secretary. Signal was the White House military switchboard, manned by the U.S. Signal Corps.

They met in the Staff Mess at the Western White House, and were joined that morning by Bob Taylor, head of the Presidential Protection Detail of the Secret Service, General Al Redman, Commander of the White House Communications Agency, Tim Elbourne, the staff press advance man, and Nell Yates, Dwight's secretary. The purpose of the meeting, like so many that had

3

occurred before, was to make arrangements for the President to address the nation, this time from the NBC studio in Burbank. Little did the advance team know, however, that the President's announcement was about to change the world.

The meeting was short. The members of the advance party hurried to the helicopter pad at El Toro Marine Station, about fifteen minutes from the Western White House, to fly to Burbank. One of the first priorities was to clear a parking lot immediately adjacent to the studio for the President's helicopter, Marine One. A mundane-sounding task, perhaps, but one that was never as simple as just announcing over the intercom system that everyone needed to move their cars, immediately. Wreckers eventually had to be summoned to haul vehicles off the lot. The irate owners would be dealt with later.

Inside NBC, the holding room was chosen, the press filing area set up, the studio was identified and preparations for the speech were begun, all in a few hours. Arranging the logistics required to move the President, his staff, and the huge press corps that always accompanied him was a difficult task. In between tasks, Roadrunner couldn't help but wonder what important statement the President was going to make.

"Roadrunner, Roadrunner, this is Signal. Searchlight has departed. ETA your location in approximately twenty-five minutes. Will advise at five minutes to wheels down, sir."

"Roger, Signal, we copy and are standing by for arrival," Roadrunner radioed back.

The glistening, olive green, white-topped helicopter gently set down amid whirling dust and small particles of asphalt onto the just-cleared parking lot. The President looked relaxed and tanned. Henry Kissinger, his National Security Advisor who had just returned from a trip around the world, looked like the proverbial cat that had swallowed the canary. Ron Ziegler, White House Press Secretary, was laughing. Paul Keyes, a close friend of the President's and producer of the popular television show, "Laugh In," joined the group as they walked along the route Roadrunner had chosen and managed to get in a couple of jokes before they arrived at the building.

On the air, the President announced that while Dr. Kissinger was in Pakistan, where he was thought to have been confined to quarters, he had actually flown to the People's Republic of China and met with Premier Chou En-lai and other Chinese officials. The joint statement, issued simultaneously in Peking and in the United

States, read: "Knowing of President Nixon's expressed desire to visit the People's Republic of China, Premier Chou En-lai, on behalf of the Government of the People's Republic of China, has extended an invitation to President Nixon to visit China at an appropriate date before May, 1972."

Ron Walker, watching the TV monitor in the holding room, was stunned. "Oh my God, I am going to CHINA," he thought, feeling as though the wind had been knocked out of him. He fell backward onto the couch, mesmerized by the President's words and glued to the television. He realized an official party would go to China to make the preliminary arrangements, followed by an advance team to prepare for the first visit to the People's Republic of China by an American President.

Thus began the first step toward normalization of relations with a country the size of the United States and with a population four times as large. The thought of the task ahead was mind-boggling. International trip preparation for the President was exacting work. As Nixon's chief advance man, Walker had planned many.

"But China?" Walker said to himself. "We don't know much about it. As kids we thought if we dug a hole deep enough in the playground we would end up there. We saw movies about being shanghaied. We read Pearl Buck's *The Good Earth*. President Nixon was going to China, and dear God," Walker thought wildly, "we don't even have an embassy there!"

CHAPTER II

WHITE HOUSE BRIEFING

JANUARY 25, 1972

Six months of preparation and three trips to China were needed to prepare the way for President Nixon. In October 1971, Henry Kissinger led a small group to Peking to set the agenda for the upcoming trip. Kissinger described this trip, code named Polo II, in his book, *White House Years*:

> Exchanges with Peking leading to my second visit were not without their testy moments. For one thing, even in the millennia of their history the Chinese had never encountered a Presidential advance party, especially one whose skills had been honed by the hectic trips of a candidate in the heartland of America and disciplined by the monomaniacal obsession of the Nixon White House with public relations. When I warned Chou En-lai that China had survived barbarian invasions before but had never encountered advance men, it was only partly a joke.

Polo II was followed by yet another trip, in early January 1972. As Kissinger wrote, "The Chinese were astonished by the size of what we called an advance party for the Presidential trip, and the fact that it would need to be followed by a third visit by a yet larger technical

7

The advance team meeting in the White House bomb shelter.

team." The so-called "Haig trip," named for its ranking official, Deputy National Security Advisor Alexander Haig, included key members of the White House Advance team, led by Ron Walker, who would return to China a full three weeks before President Nixon's arrival to make final preparations for his trip.

Back at the White House, Walker and his Advance Office staff spent the rest of January preparing manifests, schedules, personal requests, the list of the press corps who would travel with the President to China, flight schedules, and the countless other details associated with an international trip. The advance office conference room in the Old Executive Office Building adjacent to the White House became their command center. Daily meetings were held with representatives of the Secret Service, the Military Aide's Office, the White House Communications Agency, the Press Office, and the Advance Office. Finally, on the eve of their departure, a send-off briefing, recorded by the White House Communications Agency (WHCA), was held for the departing advance party in the family theater at the White House.

GENERAL ALEXANDER HAIG: I just want to say a word about what this visit is all about and what your particular role in it is going to be. This trip is the event upon which the building blocks are going to form . . . our relationships with China in the decade ahead and maybe beyond that. The whole tone of our relationships with China are going to evolve from the atmospherics, if you will. The arrangements, the personal contacts, the working relationships that evolve between our representatives and the representatives of the People's Republic. So that makes advancing it, the substantive nitty gritty work, far more sensitive than any kind of a presidential trip we can conceive of.

In other words, these people are taking the measure of America . . . and the future potential for any kind of communication with us is focused right on the individual contacts that each of you have over there in China. It becomes doubly hard because they are no longer virgins and we're no longer virgins. It's very easy for Henry Kissinger to flash in and out of there in July, again in October, and talk some graceful substantive things. Abrasiveness, or things that don't work well, are overlooked. But now we've had a series of visits there. Each of you are down to the nitty gritty things that in some instances are very difficult for these people to accept and absorb. They are watching you as people. They are beginning to take the measure of each of you. As we are of them. It's harder to maintain that kind of . . . what I call the visceral flow of the juices, to keep your tact and to keep your cool and to keep your patience and to keep this very, very essential facade of professionalism that you've just got to maintain in every contact you have. Your patience level gets thinner. Theirs gets thinner. You're going right into a very tough session that's prolonged, under very difficult conditions, but quite frankly, it's even far more important than the earlier visits in the context of the overall results that we will achieve from the President's visit there. That is, can we communicate with these people? Is it worth their while trying to communicate with Americans? Is there some hope in the future that there's going to be productive results? There are no results right now. This is going to be damn, damn difficult.

Having just spent a week there, I know what kind of tensions build. I know conditions under which you live and have to operate, dealing with people who are just not used to our ways. They just don't understand them, and they are principled to the point of being quite stubborn on occasions. So it's here that you have to be so patient and so careful. We've been very careful about selecting the key guy for this thing. That's why we have Ron set in that position. Because he's been there. He knows the problems. He knew the last time that he was going to have to take this problem. There has to be total control and there has to be central control. So I think it's very, very essential that you be as aware as the President is of Ron's responsibility. And as the Chinese are, because when we left we made it very clear to them that if problems develop our people are going to bring them to Ron and he has got to be the focal point. You've got to understand that, too. So keep that in your mind as you go through these next twenty-one beautiful days.

We're past the point of talking about things, dealing with principles and making broad arrangements. . . . Now we've got to produce the baby. When you do that, that's when the real frictions develop. So I can't think of anything more important than what you all are going to have to do. Because I am confident that if we have a problem with the trip, it's going to occur during this period, not the earlier periods, but this period. And if we don't do it right, then the trip itself is going to suffer, essentially the success of the whole initiative. This is the way the whole thing will evolve. Their assessment of us, their assessment of their ability to work with us is the key substantive part of this whole Peking summit.

Now, let me give you one further word of advice. I have watched the evolution of our visit to China very carefully. The first visit that Henry made was extremely formal, very few what I call man to man type conversations. Everything was programmed to a tee. Few exposures to the people and to the lower level officials. It started to get a little more graceful the second trip and by our last trip, by the time we left, I looked down the runway where our people were saying goodbye to their counterparts and I wasn't quite sure it wasn't a college fraternity saying goodbye for the summer vacation. Some warm relationships had developed between counterparts.

You're going to be there twenty-one days. Never lose sense of the fact that these people are measuring you. They're measuring your toughness. They're measuring your dedication, and they're measuring your ability to get your interests conveyed the right way. The social side is a very disarming aspect of Chinese hospitality. They work hard and they have their banquets and their dinners and their social occasions. They like to have their whiskey. They are measuring you every minute. When I saw Chou En-lai after the banquet the third night, he knew exactly how many snorts Mr. Chapin had, how many I had, and how well we handled it. So be very, very careful. Don't let your guard down. Keep your poise. Keep your gentleness. They are a gentle people. They don't react well to brusqueness. In fact, they will freeze right up on you. So you have to be gentle and patient, but that doesn't mean that you're a push-over. You can't do that either. Keep your tentacles out all the time. If in any one of your particular areas you see a problem developing, don't let it fester. When you sense a problem developing, get it right in to Ron, so he can assess it in terms of the whole.

The last technical point is very, very critical for all of us to understand. That's this. The size of our party has been negotiated, honed and re-honed, at the top level. Right up to Chou En-lai himself. He knows precisely how many people are involved in this operation, what they're doing, and he personally has approved everything. That is a centralized operation over there. No one here, on his own, can make a demand which requires further people or a drastic change in the arrangements already worked out. He just cannot do it. He's got to bring that requirement, if it's an inescapable one, into Ron, and Ron quite frankly knows he's going to have to come back here. This is not a technical arrangement, it's a diplomatic issue. It's a major political issue.

That's the point I'm trying to make in the whole talk. Everything we're doing is essentially substantive and essentially critical to this visit. That's why each of you has been selected very carefully, not just for your professional skills but even more than that, our confidence and the President's confidence in your ability to handle what is going to be a very, very tough job. After twenty-one days and beyond that I'm quite sure you'll agree with me in spades. Never loose sight of what you are doing there. These are tough, dedicated, doctrinaire people. Their interests are not ours. They're not dedicated, for example, to furthering the interest of the United States of America. You've got to understand that. I think all of you do. This is a tough diplomatic role you're playing, in addition to your technical and professional role.

I would like to express to you, what I know is the President's gratitude for what you're doing. This is not a big pat on the back exercise, and all you ever get in the business you are in is a kick in the teeth if something goes awry. The simple fact of it is, it's the heart and soul of this visit and of the success this visit will have. Good luck to you. I envy you in a lot of ways; in some I don't. (laughter)

RON WALKER: I know there is an arrival ceremony [for the President] soon and some of you will have to leave, but I just want to back up for one minute. We have worked very hard, everybody in this room, for three years on all Presidential advances. We started out a long time ago, when I was new and green behind the ears, and everybody helped me. It was team work. There is not a person in this room that I haven't worked with, personally, and I look forward to working with again. There's no way in hell that I'm going to be able to do this job without the support of each one of you in your own specific areas. In no way will I step into a security ring or Timmie's [Tim Elbourne, White House press advance] press arrangements unless I can be of some assistance. I will guarantee you that the advance men in the other two stops [*Shanghai and Hangchou*] will do the same thing.

There's an awful lot of work that's gone on behind the scenes, for a long time, in preparation for this trip. Dwight started some three months ago in the bomb shelter with a small, hard-core group of people trying to figure out the best way to approach that first visit the advance team made. There has been an awful lot of give and take transpire. Everybody is cut down to the bare minimum. There will be people doing jobs that they wouldn't normally do and the only thing I refuse to do is carry a gun for Livingood [*Wilson "Bill" Livingood of the U.S. Secret Service*]. It's going to be that kind of team work that is going to pull this trip off. We don't have the normal support that we usually do for an international advance for the President. The Chinese feel very strongly that they can provide an awful lot of support that we normally rely on an embassy for when we travel about the world. In all three cities it is imperative that we work closely together, stay together, keep the team work together, and keep our sanity together.

One of the biggest jobs we're going to have in all three locations is helping Elbourne keep a rein on, not only the press, but the technicians and ground support people. We don't know them as well and we don't have the controls we'd like to have. We know you people and you know us. Each person in this room has been approved personally. I'm not going to kid you. It's going to be a rare experience spending twenty-one days prior to the President's arrival in China.

I'm sure you've been told there is not a whole lot to do. We are making arrangements to provide certain types of entertainment, recognizing that certain other types of entertainment will not be available. So . . . (laughter) we're going to take in some movies. (laughter) I would imagine that everyone would like to put in a box of crackers and some squeezie cheese, because after two or three banquets and breakfast, lunch or dinner of Chinese food, it's going to get a little old. It got a little old for a week. And . . . those are the things we have to look forward to.

I think one of the most difficult things is going to be working closely with the Chinese, and to re-emphasize what General Haig said, they are a very charming people. It's like having an advance man for every person on a trip. You come off an elevator and they will meet you. There are the pleasantries. It gets a little difficult to always exchange those same pleasantries.

It is going to be absolutely essential that each of you, and the people that are with you, remember you are not anything except

Americans and everybody is equal. There won't be any distinction except by responsibility. They are going to look at you just like they look at anybody in the official or unofficial party. That's what you are representing.

When a decision is going to be made, it is categorized in one way. Period. And that is a point of principle. It is a point of principle that the President of the United States will not ride in an American car in China. It is a point of principle that the President of the United States will not, will not, fly in his American plane inter-theatre. These are some of the points that they feel very strongly about.

One thing that General Haig did not mention that will probably ring in my ears for the rest of my life, is what Chou En-lai said the night we met with him. He was most gracious to receive us and he said, "You are a relatively old country." We are two hundred years old where they are only twenty years old. We think of China as a country with an ancient civilization. They see themselves as a young communist country. This is going to be a rare experience. We are going to be able to pull this off. We can't afford an incident. If something happens, it could blow the trip out of the water.

Timmie, would you like to say a few words? I know you have to go to this arrival.

TIMOTHY G. ELBOURNE: I really don't have too much to add to that, except we're sure as hell going to be depending on each of you for help and support in your particular area. As Ron mentioned, these technicians going over there have no idea what they are walking into. A very Spartan kind of a life which they are not used to. What? Yeah. Well, I am more used to it than they are. (laughter) These guys are pulling down thirty, forty, fifty, seventy, one hundred thousand dollars a year and all of a sudden they go in to a country where they can't buy everything they want. To illustrate Ron's point of principle here, the Chinese consider all of us guests in their country. We are their guests. They won't let us pay for one thing. They won't let us pay for rooms, food, or anything. The technicians are guests, coming in as technician advisors to the Chinese. And I think this is pretty much the way the Chinese are looking at all of us, really--advisors to them, giving our country's view of how they might handle the President's activities and movements. This is a little bit different from how we've ever worked before.

Accordingly, I'm sure going to depend on WHCA an awful lot because they're going to be working with these technicians. To reiterate General Haig's remark, if you see any kind of a problem developing with a technician at the transmission center or out at the airport and I'm not around, I sure would appreciate if you would relay it back to Fred Swift or me or whoever the trip officer is and that would come back up to Ron and we'd work it out that way. I think we can't emphasize the control, the central control for all of our movements, enough. The Chinese will not deal in these principal matters with fifteen or twenty different people. They will deal with one individual. All of this information has got to come back up to Ron so he can weigh it. We have guaranteed to the Chinese, the dignity and decorum of the press group that's coming with us. Why the hell we did that I don't know, but . . . we had to.

Please. Any help you can give us, with any problem, we surely would appreciate.

BILL LIVINGOOD: . . . I'd like to say that when you are there, your conversations among yourselves in your rooms, if you are going to say something about the Chinese, wait till you come back here to the United States. They have the capability to monitor everything you are saying. I'm not saying they are monitoring. We don't have any idea and you won't have any idea, but if you are going to say something derogatory (about your counterpart, about the Chinese, about their customs) . . . wait until you get back here to say it. Do not say it out in public, in your rooms, or in the hallways. Remember this. . . . Now on security, the only thing I'll say there is, if you notice anything unusual, make sure you bring it to our attention. . . . We have a good complement and I feel there is no security problem, but if you see anything that you can help us with, or you think should be brought to our attention, make sure you do. Even if it's a minor thing. We will evaluate it and make a decision. I think the trip is of the utmost importance. I think from a security standpoint it looks very good. I don't think we're going to have any major security problems, or any security problems. That's about all I have to say. Don't let professionalism wane as days wear on.

LT. COL. VERNON C. COFFEY, JR.: [*United States Army Aide to the President*] . . . There's no question about it, we are going to show them how professional we can be. That's got to be foremost in your mind all the time. Yes, we've got to do these social things, we've got to be nice, and we should never run in to them with our hurry, hurry, hurry American attitude and we've got to have it right now. Everything moves in a much slower, measured pace. When they decide to talk business, then you've got to be ready to focus on that. But up to that point, do the social things, make the nice comments, and compliment the flowers or the tea or whatever it might be. As General Haig said, this thing will go on years and years after all of us have left the White House and gone on to other jobs. . . . Once you get down to business, I urge you to try to use common words. Do not use slang. They don't understand slang at all. We said "back-up plane" and that completely lost them. Now "reserve plane" is a common term they understand. . . . "Sweep aircraft" just won't wash. So you've always got to focus and think about it before you say it. Don't use big words out of the dictionary which you know they will have a hell of a time translating.

The other thing is the Chinese do not react to any show of anger or any enthusiasm. They are very measured. The rah rah, go out and get 'em guys, the sock it to 'em, just won't make it. This is something you've got to be aware of down at the lowest level. Even their workers, they aren't house boys because they are all workers, and be sure that everyone understands you can't push these people, and don't try because you'll just create problems. That's where the problems are going to be. Not the people at Ron Walker's level or Timmie's level. It's going to be someone in your activity, out at the airport or at the guest house, who's doing something, who hasn't gotten the word and he starts this little thing and it gets bigger and bigger and before you know it, it shows up at the top and we've got a major problem.

Something else that was mentioned earlier, this is going to be a tough trip. . . . If we really get wrapped up in our jobs and do our jobs, I think the time will go so fast we won't think about it. . . . Yes, it will be hell if you don't like Chinese food, because you are going to have Chinese food coming out your ears. But, I don't recall a meal being served when they didn't serve something you could live with and tolerate. I'm saying have an open mind. If you don't like it you don't have to eat it. But taste it and if you like it, dig into it. You'll find that the meals can be enjoyable. Yes, when we got back, everybody wanted a big hamburger. You're not going to see any hamburgers there, but they've got something that's just as good. (laughter) Don't know if you heard that in the back. Tim Elbourne said sparrow. Yes, we did have sparrows at one meal. We also had a lot of people chirping when we got on the airplane. (laughter)

The last thing I'd like to say is, being the Military Aide on the trip, our primary concern is to back up Ron with logistics, military support and everything else it involves behind the scenes. Although that is my interest, I'm going to help Ron, or Tim, or Bill, or anyone I can in any other area. We are not taking as many people as we'd like to take and it's going to require everybody to go further than your area. We would like to take a thousand people, but we can't. Already we are being slashed in many, many areas. But we still have to provide some very, very basic services to the President and the Presidential party if this is going to be a successful trip.

RON WALKER: OK, I'm going to wrap this thing up very quickly. Not being an expert in the national security field, I'm going to try and remember what Dr. Kissinger said on this. Chairman Mao is more of a religious leader than anything else. He is the founder of the new revolution that has emerged in the last twenty-two years, since he started the Long March. We don't really know, at this point, what exposure there will be to Chairman Mao. We are anticipating that the President will meet with the Chairman, but we don't know. If it happens, it will happen. We may be told long enough in advance to make some preparations for it, but at this point we are going to play that very close to the vest. Chairman Mao's picture is everywhere. Chairman Mao's sayings are everywhere, mainly in Chinese, but you don't have to worry about it. The running dog signs and things that are anti-imperialist and anti-American, for the most part, I think, have been removed. We did see one in the Hangchou train station, but we saw it on the way in and it wasn't there when we came out. So, I think there is a great effort being made on their part.

I'm going to say this, because it is my own personal opinion, the majority of people you are going to deal with are most gracious, but they are hard-line communist. Communism is a religion. Dr. Kissinger explained to us that it's unlike the Soviet bloc countries, where they have become fat bourgeoisie communists with the rich things in life and the good things in life. They are a dedicated people. You go to a commune and you can see this. They are hard-line communist. As a result of that, in my mind, and I think most of the people who were on the two previous trips will agree, at this point in time they are our enemy. We will never experience that, but we should never forget it. I think each one of these men that are heading the various portions of this organization, said it perfectly.

The Prime Minister is another subject. He will meet with the President, and will probably have a great deal of exposure.

When it comes to the balloon drops, I will handle that, so don't worry about it. OK? (laughter)

The schedule is going to be very flexible. We're going to do things differently than we've ever done them before. It may be that the night before, when the President is on the ground and we're scheduled to go to the Great Wall the next morning, they'll say there is a possibility of snow, so tomorrow we're not going to the Great Wall. We're going to have to be extremely flexible in whatever the President does. There are portions of the schedule that you are not going to have to worry about inclement weather alternates. We will have these contingencies, and each individual of this team that will be on the ground prior to the President's arrival will know exactly what is involved in those various movements of the President and his party.

Mrs. Nixon will have her separate schedule, but will accompany the President for the most part, other than the head-to-head meetings. There will be an awful lot of time in meetings, and those will transpire, at least in Peking, at the Great Hall of the People (which, by the way, was built in ten months). They built Timmie's transmission center in less than two months and we didn't even know they were going to do it.

You will have an opportunity, I think, to have some freedom of movement, in the three cities where we will be located. We don't know to what degree. Last time they told us we did, but we never really did. It was all in a controlled environment.

I'll re-emphasize two things before we close. That's the teamwork aspect, recognizing of course that we have no embassy, and it is unlike anything we've every attempted to do, at least in our administration. And the positive attitude and helping everybody keep up the good morale.

Are there any questions?

QUESTION: What are the guidelines on questions from the press?

WALKER: I know everyone, with their passion for anonymity, understands this, because we encounter it here on every trip. But, if you could instruct all your people, even in Hawaii and in Guam. If something transpires where there is a camera or an interviewer, they should simply say, "No comment." We are looking forward to our trip and that's it. Don't be obnoxious so that the story comes out from that standpoint.

I was approached by a Japanese correspondent. Thank heavens a Chinese moved in very rapidly and I had not given him my name. There are very few westerners and the ones that are there do not have freedom of movement. There are very few correspondents, but there has just been a *Los Angeles Times* U.S. correspondent admitted. The first one.

It is the first time we have gone as a group with technicians. They are news people. So they are going to see an awful lot of our moves. I think that's going to be a challenge on all our parts to do the job that each of you do so well, but yet do it with that in mind, always. Those times that we get together and have shooter, they will probably be with us because we will all be staying in the same hotel in all three locations. Be friendly and pleasant with them and don't

Advance team in the White House conference room.

give them the cold shoulder. We can't do that, but they are going to
know that we are going to have to watch our moves and our
conversations. They are, for the most part, good people. At least the
ones we were associated with, they are all good men. We know that
they too are conducting these kinds of meetings, stressing the
seriousness of the visit.

The next time we will all be together, everybody, including the
technicians and the Comsat and ground station people, will be in
Guam. We will have a general meeting to update everybody on
where we stand at that point. The second wave will come in for
Shanghai and Hangchou, arriving Shanghai on the eleventh. Although
we're hoping they will let certain individuals move inter-theatre, we
don't have real concurrence on it yet. An awful lot of things that
we're assuming, I think will transpire, but we are going to once again
ask permission to do these things.

We are hopeful that Timmie and Bill and I will be in Shanghai
to brief those coming in on the eleventh and have signs and a crowd
for you. (laughter).

Just to answer one more question, we don't know whether there
will be any crowds anywhere. But to give you a sidelight, the crowd
estimates for some heads of state during this twenty-two-year history

of revolutionary China, is between 250,000 and a half a million people on the twenty-five-mile drive into Peking. So, with a few hand bills we ought to be able to pump that up to a million. Oh! John [*John Thomas of the State Department*], by the way, would you bring a printing press? We may have to do our own handbills. [*Handbills were distributed throughout an area to generate a crowd for a political rally.*]

Thank you everybody.

CHAPTER III

SURVIVAL SUITCASE

JANUARY 26, 1972

Roadrunner was a master packer. A four year stint at an American Missionary School in India made packing for long periods of time a necessity. Third class travel on the trains of India taught him early on to keep everything in close proximity to his person at all times. The warning "Snooze, you lose" must have originated on a train rumbling toward the station in Madras or Calcutta.

His first advance trip to China in January was a chance to learn some important lessons for the long stay preparing for the President's visit. It was almost impossible to read anything by the light of the thirty watt bulbs furnished in all Chinese hotel rooms, but every room, every day, at every moment, had a thermos of steaming hot water on a table. It was replenished three times a day, so it seemed logical to take along some of those tasty instant packets which only needed some hot water: instant coffee, oatmeal, tea (Lipton is better than jasmine), hot chocolate, and cup-of-soup. And good old G.E. light bulbs would make one hell of a difference!

For practical purposes, ice did not exist in the People's Republic of China. But since they were going to be there in the middle of winter, why not just take along a couple of ice trays? Roadrunner could make his own ice cubes on his hotel window sill. Everyday items, which we take for granted, needed to be taken in abundance: toothpaste, Kleenex, deodorant, shaving cream, Rolaids, Alka Seltzer, aspirin, Pepto-Bismol, Kaopectate, and cigarettes (Marlboros are better than Chunghwas). And Chinese toilet paper almost defies description; its texture is somewhere between wax paper and sand paper.

What about snacks? Familiar tastes that one would most likely miss after a couple of weeks--peanut butter, jam, crackers, Coca-Cola, Gatorade and squirt cheese--were added to the shopping list. What better way to unwind at the end of a busy day than with a cocktail and something to snack on before dinner? Chinese food may be delicious, but every day for breakfast, lunch, and dinner?

Roadrunner's family went to the Giant Food Store a couple of days before his departure to buy everything for his "survival suitcase." They had talked a great deal about what should go in it and his girls did not want to miss the adventure of putting this assortment together. They waited until the last minute to be sure the important things like the Snickers and the Fritos would be really fresh. The check-out clerk was appalled at the junk food the woman with the three little girls was buying. She could hardly contain herself as she rang up bag after bag of chips, pretzels, peanuts, marshmallows (for the hot chocolate!), cans of bean dip, and powdered and freeze-dried everything. The $264.59 grocery bill did not include anything fresh or perishable, but it did include six 150-watt light bulbs and six four-packs of squeezably soft toilet paper!

John Thomas, the State Department bag man, had given Roadrunner "recreational money." When they landed on Guam to refuel, he went into the post exchange and spent his recreational money on cases of whiskey, scotch, vodka, bourbon, cordials, and brandy. The plan was to set up a "commissary." On most international trips, a room of this type would have been organized by the American embassy. Because there was not an embassy in Peking, Roadrunner was going to provide his own support system for his men. It turned out to be a great idea and one that would prove invaluable to the camaraderie of the group. They would gather after long, difficult days and interminable working dinners for a relaxing drink and discuss the difficulties and frustrations that they were experiencing.

The master packer also took movies to provide entertainment in the evenings, and since this was before the existence of the VCR, a projector and screen had to be taken along as well.

The departure day was at hand. Roadrunner had insisted they travel via commercial airliner as far as Guam because he was convinced that the drafty and always freezing military aircraft made everyone sick. This trip was too important to risk starting out on the wrong foot. The families of the men going on the trip went out to Dulles Airport in the Virginia countryside to see them off. It was an exciting time. The historical significance of the mission was apparent to everyone. The uncharted territory that the men approached made those left behind experience some degree of anxiety.

On the next trip to the allergist, something Roadrunner's children did every Wednesday after school, Marja asked her mother, "Why did that man step out from behind the tree and take a picture of our car?"

Was it a coincidence, or was someone watching the families of the men who went to China?

CHAPTER IV

Red Carpet Arrival

February 1, 1972

Roadrunner was on the first C-135 aircraft to touch Chinese soil. They flew in over the heart of Shanghai, and Roadrunner could almost feel the teeming millions of people below. The coastal waters were lined with seagoing vessels, and traditional Chinese junks and fishing vessels bobbed on the sea among submarines and Japanese rocket launchers.

Although Roadrunner had been to China only three weeks earlier, he was as excited and nervous as everyone else on the plane. They had worked hard to prepare for this trip and all seemed acutely aware of their contribution to this historic visit. Roadrunner was proud of them. They were a good group of men. Their President was going to be the first American President to visit the People's Republic of China and it was their job to make it happen.

Roadrunner had spent a great deal of time telling them what to expect when they arrived. He had tried hard to paint an accurate picture of the working conditions ahead of them, the good and the different, the difficult and the funny. He had told them about Mr. Whu, an animated man who was never without a cigarette. His hands were only used to strike a match and light the cigarette. From then on the thing lived in his mouth. He talked and gestured with gusto, and the cigarette spewed ashes and sparks in all directions. He coughed often and gulped air between coughs, and the cigarette neither went in or out. It was actually quite a fascinating spectacle to watch. His clothes were covered with ashes and pock-marked by burnt spots. When Mr. Whu talked, one had to try very hard not to appear rude by flicking the ashes off one's own clothes and tie. It was very hard to know what to do when talking or listening to Mr. Whu.

Roadrunner had really perfected his imitation of Mr. Whu and assured everyone that they would know him immediately. They had laughed about this and prodded Roadrunner to tell the story again and again. They lit Marlboros and practiced and joked that they were getting ready to meet the famous Mr. Whu.

At the airport, there were security guards every hundred yards up and down the runway. Large billboards with huge Chinese characters could be seen in all directions. The Chinese people, in the distance, were three and four deep watching the strange aircraft arrive in Shanghai. The greeting committee consisted of responsible members of the Chinese ministry, led by Mr. Chu, the Deputy Chief of Protocol, who would become Roadrunner's counterpart. Once again the Chinese clothing was startling at first glance--the long overcoats with Mao buttons over the heart and the caps with the same button above the short bill. Mao buttons were everywhere and on everyone. And sure enough, there was one man who needed no introduction--Mr. Whu, the one covered with ashes and hundreds of little burnt spots. The Americans were secretly pleased that he was there and his familiarity helped ease their nervousness. They somehow felt more prepared for the tasks that lay ahead.

Roadrunner introduced the members of the American delegation and Mr. Chu welcomed them to his country. Then Mr. Whu took over as the host and invited them to enjoy some tea and Chinese cigarettes. They sat on huge, overstuffed sofas and spent about ten minutes exchanging pleasantries (and watching Mr. Whu). He was even better than Roadrunner had promised. It was hard for the Americans to keep their composure and Bill Livingood would later recount that he nearly swallowed his tongue as he gulped tea to keep from laughing. The Chinese love their tea and slurp it loudly to show how good it tastes. Roadrunner, ever a quick study, slurped often and loudly. The hosts seemed to appreciate this early sign of friendship and cooperation from this young man who had been designated "the responsible person" for all the Americans.

They moved into the airport dining room where they were served a nine course meal, complete with "gombays," toasts with the national drink called mao-tai, a sorghum-based, fiery and foul tasting

Han Hsu welcomes the advance party at the Peking airport.

liquor that the Chinese use for ceremonial occasions. Roadrunner noticed that most of the Americans managed their chopsticks surprisingly well, except for peanuts and the slippery mushrooms. He wondered if they had been practicing at home.

Mr. Chu, a radio technician and a navigator accompanied the Americans on the nearly two-hour flight to Peking. The C-135 aircraft is very loud and this seemed to be nerve-wracking to the Chinese.

They touched down in Peking, and were met by another delegation that included the Director of Protocol, Mr. Han Hsu. It was quite a sensation to step out of that aircraft into the bitter cold and onto a red carpet. That universal symbol of welcome reserved for special guests was another jolting reminder of the importance of their mission. Formal introductions were made. Interpreters interpreted. Counterparts began to identify each other and to form fast first impressions.

A motorcade was eventually lined up, but there appeared to be a great deal of confusion over the luggage and the gear that was on the airplane. Did the Chinese think that the Americans had brought too much with them? It was clear that there were not enough vehicles to transport everything. Finally, leaving some of the luggage behind, they began the forty-five minute drive to the Hotel of the Nationalities, where they would live and work for the next three weeks. Roadrunner rode in the car of honor, number 81, with Mike Schrauth, a White House advance man. Mr. Yu, an interpreter from the Foreign Ministry, rode in the front seat with the driver. Fresh snow about three inches deep had left the streets clean and the countryside white and beautiful. All along the roadway there were gigantic billboards with huge Chinese characters that seemed to scream their messages. Instinct silenced Roadrunner's desire to ask what was written on them.

They turned onto East Chang Avenue (the avenue of the long countryside), ten lanes wide and decorated with hundreds of Chinese flags and another flag that Roadrunner recognized as the flag of Pakistan. He realized that President Bhutto of Pakistan was visiting the city. Thousands of flags decorated Tienanmen Square and the face of Mao was everywhere. It was quite a sight. Banners were stretched across the streets and Roadrunner was surprised to see, written in English, "Long live the friendship between the Afro and Asian countries."

They arrived at the Hotel of the Nationalities, a huge, staid and flat-faced building. Their rooms were in a far wing with spectacular views of East Chang Avenue and Tienanmen Square. Roadrunner's corner room adjoined a large sitting room, with Schrauth on the other side of the sitting room. It was much more comfortable and spacious than the accommodations on the previous visit. The Chinese obviously wanted the Americans to be as comfortable as possible. Tim Elbourne and Bob Manning, from the White House press office, had a similar suite across the hall, overlooking the north portion of Peking.

The sitting room was filled with big, puffy, square furniture with white crochet doilies on all the arms and backs. The suite soon became the focal point of the advance team's activities. The desks had the predicted thirty-watt lamps, a bottle of ink, two pencils, paper, envelopes, and a green telephone. The beauty of the fresh fruit laid out made them wonder where it was grown in the middle of January.

Mr. Chu, it was clear, was to be Roadrunner's counterpart. All of the other Chinese counterparts were watching him for guidance. He was a serious man, but his quiet politeness helped to soften his stern manner. Roadrunner hoped that they could form an effective working relationship, so he asked Mr. Chu if he would be so kind as to arrange a meeting that afternoon to discuss the schedule for the next several days. Mr. Chu responded that it was to be a free

View from Roadrunner's hotel room.

afternoon for everyone and the evening would be for rest.   There
would be no working or meetings scheduled that day or the next.   A
banquet in their honor, hosted by the Director of the Office of the
Foreign Ministry, Mr. Hu Hau (just returned from the United Nations
in New York), and co-hosted by Mr. Han Hsu, Director of Protocol,
was planned for the next evening.

Roadrunner wasn't very pleased about the delay in getting
started, but he unpacked the contents of his "survival suitcase."   He
filled the ice trays with water and put them out on the window sill.
It was bitterly cold in Peking and he smiled at himself for bringing
plastic ice cube trays all the way to the other end of the earth.   He
wondered what the Chinese would think when they saw them outside
his window.

He fell asleep, this first night in China, thinking about tomorrow.
The suitcase satellite would be hooked up and he could talk to
Washington.   It would be a very busy day, but he made a mental note
to tell Snapshot that the ice cubes would be ready to have with their
scotch at the end of their first full day in the People's Republic of
China.

CHAPTER V

AN UNFORGETTABLE SOUND

FEBRUARY 2, 1972

Roadrunner awoke with a start. A strange sound filled the air, a sound he would remember for many years to come. It was a melodious sound with an endless echo that did not fade in and out like a siren, but remained constant as it engulfed his room. He was not exactly sure what it was, but it was coming from outside. He jumped out of bed at the Hotel of the Nationalities and hurried to look out of the window. He was mesmerized by the sight on the street below: a weaving, snaking display of movement in the early light of dawn, countless darkly clad riders on an endless parade of bicycles. "The sound," he realized with a smile, "was bicycle bells!" It was like a tapestry in motion, with its lovely sound that proclaimed the absence of vehicular traffic.

He dressed hurriedly and went to inquire about a ride to the airport to call Washington from the telephone on the C-135 plane. The forty-five minute drive was long and Roadrunner was already tired. "After all," he reminded himself, "it was a thirteen hour time change from Washington. Everybody at home was still asleep."

He studied the countryside and the starkness of the scene passing by his car window. There was no color. The sky was gray and cloudy, the trees bare. The black or dark blue trousers and

31

jackets that the people wore almost never matched, as if to purposely prevent the impression that they were wearing suits.

The car wound its way around a wagon with a huge load and Roadrunner strained for a glimpse at the faces of the Chinese sharing the road with him. The wagon driver hid his face from the cold wind. A farmer on foot was almost doubled over with the strain of a gigantic, burlap-wrapped load on his back. They passed very few cars, and except for some military vehicles, most of the traffic was either on two or four legs.

Roadrunner hoped that he would not have to make this drive too many times. As he prepared to call Washington from the C-135, he vowed to get the suitcase satellite hooked up as soon as he got back to the hotel.

The conversation with Washington from the airplane was not recorded, but on the drive back to Peking an anxious Roadrunner wondered whether the suitcase satellite would actually work. It was a modest-looking metal suitcase, bigger than a briefcase but smaller than a standard piece of luggage. It was unbelievably heavy, as the entire inside was a very sophisticated radio. "It's absolutely state of the art," everyone who was in the know and accustomed to this sort of thing had told him over and over. At a quarter to ten that night, Roadrunner assembled the antenna, then beamed the dish, which reminded him of his children's snow saucer, outside his hotel room window toward heaven. Lo and behold, just like magic, he was talking to the other side of the world. In Washington, it was eight forty-five in the morning.

RADIO OPERATOR: Gentlemen, per your request, this telephone conversation is recorded by the audiovisual branch of the White House Communications Agency. Please go ahead with your conversation.

ROADRUNNER: Roger, be advised I am talking to you via the suitcase satellite. Everything seems to be working well. We have had a few problems, nothing to write home about.

WATCHDOG: OK. When will you be able to use the TWX there? [*A TWX was a way of sending messages via a punched tape that sent sound over the telephone and reproduced type on the other end. It was also capable of being scrambled.*]

ROADRUNNER: I do not know, repeat, I do not know, we have been trying to get a time and date but have had no success.

WATCHDOG: Roger, but you are using the suitcase satellite right at this time?

ROADRUNNER: That's a roger, I am speaking through it right now.

Roadrunner on speakerphone hookup to the satellite suitcase.

WATCHDOG: Roger, but doesn't the TWX machine just plug into the suitcase satellite?

ROADRUNNER: Negative, repeat, negative.

WATCHDOG: OK. . . . Well, that is our next problem to conquer because we have, as you can well imagine, quite a bit of material that is beginning to stack up here that we cannot get into over the telephone. Do you understand?

ROADRUNNER: That's a roger. I understand. I also have a considerable amount for you that I cannot give over the telephone. Hopefully we will have it tomorrow, but I can't say yes or no.

WATCHDOG: Ah, roger, I understand. (pause) Is everybody OK?

ROADRUNNER: That's a roger. Everybody from the White House support area, but be advised there is one technician who possibly has pneumonia. I have just visited with Director Han Hsu and it was determined that we would leave him in the hotel. They wanted to put him in the hospital, but we'll make a decision tomorrow whether he will leave on the C-141 or is in good enough shape to stay.

WATCHDOG: OK. Should we start another one on the way via commercial carrier just as a backup or can you get along without him for a while?

ROADRUNNER: Ah, negative. We'll call for that in our next conversation if that is the decision. Right now we have made no decision. Over

WATCHDOG: OK, I understand. Do you have any other points you would like to make?

ROADRUNNER: Yes, I do. Be advised that since our conversation from the plane this morning, we have made considerable progress as you can well imagine from this telephone conversation. I have received, as have other members of our party, numerous repeat, numerous, apologies for the inconvenience that was caused with the off-loading. The PRC was embarrassed at not being properly prepared to receive us. I have made it very clear it could have been just as much our problem for not letting them know what our requirements would be. So, at this point I think that everything is tracking fine. Did you copy?

WATCHDOG: I copy and I understand completely and perhaps we should have provided more information there.

ROADRUNNER: Roger, I am in agreement. Also, be advised I met with my counterpart today, and this afternoon we had a tour of the summer palace and did a survey for Starlight [Mrs. Nixon]. Tomorrow morning we will visit the Great Hall of the People for a complete survey of all areas there.

WATCHDOG: That's good, I understand, and glad to hear you are moving off on that.

ROADRUNNER: Roger, I feel extremely good now and I think everything is going well. This evening, the Vice Chairman of Security was the host at a reception and then the Director of Foreign Affairs and the Director of Protocol hosted a banquet for us. There was an exchange of toasts and I didn't screw it up.

WATCHDOG: Good for you! OK! That's sensational and I understand Mr. Han Hsu was there, is that correct?

ROADRUNNER: That's a roger. I did not have a chance to talk to him because I was at the opposite end of the table but I feel, after seeing him just now that things are OK. The way the men handled themselves last night and the dinner this evening, with my toast, may have helped the situation. [The Americans and Chinese were feeling each other out and getting to know one another. Very important first impressions of everyone concerned were being formed.]

WATCHDOG: OK, I understand, that's good. Do you have anything else?

ROADRUNNER: Negative. This is Walker at this end, and I have no other information. If that is all I'll sign off.

WATCHDOG: Roger, I will sign off too. Be advised, I expect to hear from you in twelve hours.

ROADRUNNER: That's a roger. I will call you at . . . let's just talk for one moment. I have to be at the Great Hall of the People at 8:30 so we'll leave here, just a moment . . . Watchdog, this is Roadrunner. How would 7:30 A.M. Peking time and 6:30 P.M. your time sound to you?

WATCHDOG: That's better, let's do that this time. 6:30 P.M. Eastern time, 7:30 A.M. Peking time will be the next call.

ROADRUNNER: Roger, roger, I will call you at 7:30 Peking time tomorrow morning.

WATCHDOG: OK, very good. That's all I have. Out.

ROADRUNNER: OK. Thank you. This is Roadrunner, out.

WATCHDOG: Bye.

Whew! It had been a long day. The formal banquet and the diplomacy of the toasts had made everyone feel very tired indeed. Roadrunner thought they had made some progress. He *HOPED* they had made some progress. Why did it seem so difficult? He needed to unwind. He needed to talk to Snapshot. "Let's have a scotch. The ice!"

He hurried to his room and thought again about how smart he was to have brought plastic ice cube trays to the People's Republic of China. He hung up his jacket and went to open the window. He leaned out over the sill, far above the hundreds of workers now riding their bicycles home from work. Bells tinkled incessantly as they threaded in and out on the wide Peking street below. He marveled again at the sound and sight and then picked up the tray of ice.

Roadrunner couldn't believe his eyes. The frozen cubes were absolutely black, black with the coal soot that polluted the wintry air in this huge Chinese city.

"Damn it," he said out loud.

Snapshot arrived and they cussed about the filthy, black ice cubes and poured scotch over them and sipped carefully. They slurped the liquid through their teeth to strain out the soot. They showed each other the biggest pieces and worried about what breathing this stuff must be doing to their lungs. It felt good to laugh a little.

They lounged comfortably on the overstuffed furniture, feet up. By the second drink, they were seeing which one could spit the Peking pollution particles the farthest onto the Chinese carpet. They assured each other that it didn't even taste so bad anymore.

CHAPTER VI

RATTAN FURNITURE AND THE RED DETACHMENT OF WOMEN

FEBRUARY 3, 1972

Roadrunner again awoke to the rhythm of bicycle bells that began with the first light of dawn. He was climbing out of bed when the hall attendant came in with a fresh thermos of steaming hot water. "Great timing," Roadrunner thought, but he was really wondering at the coincidence. "Had the Chinese been listening for the first signs of movement?"

He made some instant coffee, another of the pleasures from the survival suitcase. He savored the smell as he sipped it. As far as he was concerned, Chinese tea just did not start the day like a good cup of American coffee.

At the designated time, Roadrunner greeted Mr. Chu in the hotel lobby. "Did you have a pleasant rest?" Mr. Chu asked.

"Yes, thank you. I had a very pleasant rest," Roadrunner assured him. "I trust you did as well."

"Oh yes. Very pleasant. Thank you," Mr. Chu responded.

"And is your family well?" Roadrunner politely inquired.

"Oh yes, very well. I am very fortunate," Mr. Chu said.

Entering the Great Hall of the People, across from the Forbidden City.

"I will tell you about the Great Hall of the People," Mr. Chu began as they left the hotel. "It is to the west of Tienanmen Square, across from the main gate to the Forbidden City. It has three stories of stone and marble and was built in ten months. It has three main sections. The middle part is the Hall of Ten Thousand People, where the People's Congress meets when they are in session. The east wing contains over twenty-eight large provincial rooms, named for the provinces, and each one has examples of the finest Chinese carpets and scrolls and jade carvings and the finest treasures from all over China. The west wing is a beautiful gold and white colonnaded banquet hall that can seat five thousand people. In the People's Republic of China, all of the most important diplomatic meetings take place here, including the one with your President in a very few short weeks."

"He is looking forward to it," Roadrunner responded.

"It is indeed a very large building, covering over 51,520 square meters, or 560,000 square feet," Mr. Chu said.

Roadrunner's eyes glazed over, but he lowered his head so that Mr. Chu would not notice. "We are very honored to be able to meet with your leaders in this magnificent building, and I look forward to seeing, once again, your very beautiful Chinese art work," he said as they started their survey of the Great Hall of the People.

They spent a long time in the Hall, walking in and out of the dozens of meeting rooms and through the vast and ornate banquet facilities.

In the afternoon they toured the Peking Hotel kitchen, a possible site for one of Mrs. Nixon's tours. After dinner, the advance party went to see a preview of the modern revolutionary ballet, "The Red Detachment of Women," presented by the China dance and drama troupe, which was being considered as an evening of entertainment for the President and Mrs. Nixon.

Roadrunner read from his English version of the program:

On Hainan Island, during the Ten-Year Civil War

Prologue. Night. In a dark dungeon in the manor-house of the despotic landlord Nan Pa-tien (Tyrant of the South). Wu Ching-hua, daughter of a poor peasant, is chained to a post. Lao-szu, the landlord's running dog, has orders to sell her. Filled with pent-up hatred, Wu Ching-hua suddenly kicks him to the ground and flees.

Act One. Late in the night. In a pitch dark grove of coconut palms. Wu Ching-hua, having escaped from the landlord's den, fights the pursuing blackguards desperately. She is beaten black and blue and faints away. As a rainstorm is imminent, Nan Pa-tien, thinking Ching-hua dead, hurriedly departs with his henchmen. Hung Chang-ching, a Red Army cadre, and his messenger Hsiao Pang, on the scout, enter in disguise. They rescue Ching-hua and, on enquiry, get acquainted with her story. With profound proletarian feelings, they direct her to the Red Army Base Area. . . .

Act Six. Dusk. . . . The Red Army liberates Palm Grove Manor. The despotic landlord is shot. The laboring people whose families have been subjected to oppression for generations see day light. They are determined to carry the revolution through to the end. Ching-hua, who has gloriously joined the Party at the front, carries on as Party representative. The broad revolutionary masses flock to join the Red Army amidst resounding battle songs. Forward, forward, under the banner of Mao Tse-tung, forward to victory!

As they filed out of the ballet, Roadrunner was troubled by what he had seen. It had been a harsh piece of Communist propaganda. Communist Party praises had been combined with folk art and dance stories of peasants and the triumphs of the People's Liberation Army. This had now become China's national culture. He knew that Chiang Ching, Chairman Mao's wife, was the one pushing for the President and Mrs. Nixon to see this performance. Mao had allowed her to take total control of cultural affairs and she insisted on purely socialist Chinese art, untainted by any trace of Western influence or by remnants from earlier Chinese society. The world would later learn that on this very day, when Roadrunner was troubled by such militant propaganda, hundreds of people, including China's last emperor, were enduring solitary confinement, torture and humiliation because of the cruelties of the cultural revolution and people like Chiang Ching.

While Roadrunner found the ballet to be long and somewhat redundant, he was rather taken with the musical score. When he returned home, he entertained his family and friends by playing the records that he had purchased, performing his version of the ballet, complete with flying red flags and leaping pirouettes. His performances were very much in demand, until one exceptionally robust rendition resulted in knee surgery and the end of his revolutionary ballet dancing.

He hurried back to the hotel for the conference call. It was only 9:15 in the evening, China time, but to Roadrunner it seemed much later. The call came in at 9:39; it was 8:39 in the morning in Washington.

ROADRUNNER: Be advised, we do not, repeat, do not have permission to set up our telex yet. There was a meeting that transpired this afternoon that became a little touchy in that I explained it was vitally necessary to have this facility in order to properly discuss the business that is at hand.

WATCHDOG: Roger, I understand. What were the reasons given for not having the facility at this time?

ROADRUNNER: It is maintained that the request was never made specifically and it apparently stems from a misunderstanding and they have taken it to their source and are hopeful of having a rapid approval.

WATCHDOG: OK. I understand. I believe the item was covered when you were present during the train ride from Hangchou to Shanghai.

ROADRUNNER: That's a roger. I concur, repeat, I concur, as does Major Swift. However, here we are.

WATCHDOG: OK. I understand and I hope that the People's Republic understands that this facility would be used only for administrative traffic in getting the arrangements for the visit worked out.

ROADRUNNER: Believe me . . . I repeat . . . *Believe me*, I have made that abundantly clear and put it on official note this afternoon. Mr. Chu, my counterpart, I believe understood and told me he would take it under his immediate consideration.

WATCHDOG: OK. I understand and I know that you've put it forth as we would. Let me ask you, did everything go OK at the Great Hall of the People this morning your time?

ROADRUNNER: That's a roger. Let me assess and I will break occasionally so that we can be sure you're copying me. We started this morning at 9:00 A.M. with a very small group that included the four technicians and a limited number from White House support. We started at the Great Hall to walk through everything with the exception of our reciprocal banquet. I was extremely pleased with the results of our meeting. It was very, very productive and many, many of our earlier questions have been resolved in my mind. (pause) We started at the east entrance of the Great Hall of the People where Searchlight will arrive for the first meeting. . . no, negative, negative, . . . for the cultural show with Starlight. We walked through every movement, we saw how the official and unofficial parties would be handled and how the cultural show would be conducted. The cultural show itself will be approximately two and one half hours with an intermission one hour and fifteen minutes into the program where they will break and the Prime Minister will accompany Searchlight to a holding room for tea and then return for the conclusion of the concert. At that point they can depart. Did you copy?

WATCHDOG: Yeah, I copy, Ron, can I ask you a question?

ROADRUNNER: Roger, go ahead.

WATCHDOG: Do you want me to ask Nell to take down the details of the handling of the official and unofficial parties and where the President and Starlight would move, etc., or do you want to wait and TWX it to us later? [*Nell Yates was Watchdog's secretary and had been working at the White House since the Eisenhower administration.*]

ROADRUNNER: Roger. I would like to wait at least until tomorrow night before we start going through that kind of detail because I have made it very clear that it is very difficult to talk by voice communication on these details and that is the reason that we are so anxious to receive that facility in order not only to give you the information that you need but also to receive information from your end that is so vitally necessary to the movement of our activities here.

WATCHDOG: OK, now I understand. Make sure though that as we go through this step by step that you're getting that typed up with the steno so that it's ready to roll through the TWX as soon as we get the thing established.

ROADRUNNER: Roger. I understand that and be advised that is exactly what we have done and we are ready to roll, once we're in a position to do so.

WATCHDOG: OK, I understand. Go ahead from the point after you had the tea with the Prime Minister. You go back in and then when the banquet's over you return to the guest house, right?

ROADRUNNER: That's a roger. That's a roger. It looks like they plan on moving the official and unofficial parties in the same motorcade. We have not talked motorcades at all yet. But they are planning on moving them together.

WATCHDOG: OK, I understand.

ROADRUNNER: Roger. The next move that we made was to the north entrance of the Great Hall of the People where we backtracked through the arrival for the first evening at the Prime Minister's banquet. The President and Mrs. Nixon will be met by a responsible member of the People's Republic of China . . . maybe. [*While this seemed very logical, the Chinese were not saying and thus Roadrunner did not know for sure.*] They will then be escorted into the north hall and up that long staircase, I'm sure you will recall. Presently it looks like the Prime Minister will receive Searchlight and Starlight at the top of the stairs and at that point there will be a small receiving line for the official and unofficial parties. Once they have moved through the receiving line they will move to the large mural, which I am hopeful you will recall at the very top of the staircase, for an official photograph.

We talked at great length about camera positions and it is felt at this point that there is a good possibility that the recommendation will be made that it be live. Repeat, live television coverage of the arrival for the first banquet. Did you copy?

WATCHDOG: Roger. I read you loud and clear and I do recall the mural. Go ahead.

ROADRUNNER: Roger. There will be a camera that will cover the Searchlight movement up to the top of the stairs and then through the receiving line and the official photograph. I have also received permission that any time the PRC official photographers do anything they will include our official photographers, both still and reels. That was given to me this evening. . . . It is no problem.

Once the official photographer has taken the pictures, the President and Starlight will proceed to their right, down a very short corridor, to Peking Hall. I am going to recommend that only, repeat,

罗纳德·沃尔克先生

MR. RONALD H. WALKER

Roadrunner's banquet seating card.

only, the official party go into Peking Hall. The rest of the party, to include all the Americans, would proceed on into the banquet hall.

There will be tea and informal, impromptu remarks in Peking Hall and shortly after that the Prime Minister will escort Searchlight and Starlight into the main banquet hall.

At the Great Hall of the People, they refer to the hall only as the Banquet Hall. Once they arrive in the Banquet Hall, they will again be picked up on camera and there will be a long U-shaped receiving line comprised of both the members of the PRC and those Americans attending the banquet. Once they have moved through the receiving line, they will then move to table number one, directly in front of the large stage, and begin the banquet. Did you copy?

WATCHDOG: Yes, I understand. That was pretty close to the way we understood it would work anyway, isn't it Ron? (pause) Yoo, hoo, over.

ROADRUNNER: Yes, Watchdog, that is correct. There were some changes that were picked up today which I have documented and are in a schedule ready for transmission. Did you copy?

WATCHDOG: Yes, I did. Go ahead.

ROADRUNNER: Roger. Then the banquet proceeds. It is possible that there will be anywhere from ten to twenty people at table number one. It will be flanked by either two other tables or four other tables. Making a total of three or five. My present thinking is, they will probably take the official and unofficial parties and put them on the red carpet at all five tables with officials and dignitaries from the PRC. Did you copy?

WATCHDOG: Roger, I understand and that becomes important in terms of the toasting.

ROADRUNNER: Yes, that's correct. I continue . . . at the conclusion of the meal itself . . . of all the courses . . . the Prime Minister will move a very few steps to his rear. At the front of the stage there is a double staircase . . . with five steps on either side that lead to a stand-up mike. At that point the Prime Minister will propose his toast with phrase translation. Repeat, phrase translation. At the conclusion of his translation, and the conclusion of the toast, he will more than likely move to table number one and then go to each of the official and unofficial tables and go through that routine. Did you copy?

WATCHDOG: Yes sir, I understand. Go ahead.

ROADRUNNER: OK. Shortly thereafter, but I am really not positive when because there may be a fish course in between the Prime Minister's toast and Searchlight's toast, but in any event, the President would move to the same position. My recommendations are that the PRC interpreter be used and that he do a phrase translation also. It is also being recommended that this be covered by television and it appears at this time that presents no problem. At the conclusion of Searchlight's toast, I would also recommend that he go through the same routine . . . to return to table number one and shortly thereafter, the Prime Minister will accompany him and Starlight to their motorcade and bid them goodnight.

WATCHDOG: OK. I understand.

ROADRUNNER: Roger. Then the next event that we went to . . . we went to the North Hall again, the entrance to the North Hall, and moved to a room which I have no name for, but it is the room that Woodcutter, repeat Woodcutter, met in previously. I have a suspicion that will be the site for the first meeting. We talked plenary session and quite obviously they had received the information that you had transmitted and they, without full agreement, thought that was a good idea . . . to set the scene for a week-long period of time and talks. Did you copy?

WATCHDOG: Yes, I know what you're saying. Let me ask you if that room is the room where they have kind of the rattan furniture or is it the room where we went and sat down when we met with the Prime Minister on our visit? [*"He must be kidding!" Roadrunner thought. "The whole country has rattan furniture! Sure! And the room where we drank tea in little cups with lids!"*]

ROADRUNNER: Negative. It is neither of those rooms. It is another room. I will recommend that if you have a question and you want that answer, talk to either Winston Lord or Dr. Kissinger himself because they will remember. It was very, very close to the main entrance from the North Hall. [*Winston Lord, National Security Council staff, later became the American Ambassador to the PRC.*]

WATCHDOG: OK, I understand.

ROADRUNNER: From that point on we visited . . . well first of all, do you have any questions about the Great Hall?

WATCHDOG: No, I have no questions.

ROADRUNNER: I understand it is very difficult to discuss the arrangements this way and I have tried to make that abundantly clear to my counterpart. I think he appreciates the problem and hopefully we will have it resolved very soon and we can go about our business in a better fashion.

At 2:00, 2:00 P.M. our time this afternoon, we were able to go to the Peking Hotel and be received by the management and the cook and had the opportunity to go through a Chinese kitchen which you had asked Director Han Hsu to find. I believe we looked at it only as an alternative for Mrs. Nixon and will look at a University later this week. I think we will probably have anywhere from six to eight events that we can choose from. Did you copy?

WATCHDOG: I did copy and I have some additional information regarding the First Lady's requests and I will forward that as soon as the TWX is up.

ROADRUNNER: Roger, I understand.   OK.   Presently, this is our time schedule. We will do a survey of everything that Searchlight will do. It will be a very thorough survey, similar to the one at the Great Hall of the People today. Then Livingood can return with his men, Elbourne can return with our technicians plus the many Chinese technicians and Swift can return with his people. This is much more acceptable to the Chinese now than it was when I first arrived because time is getting short and they understand that we must split our forces in order to accomplish the task at hand. Mr. Schrauth will start moving out tomorrow totally on Starlight's activities along with McFarland, who is the agent from her detail.

We will depart Peking on the ninth, repeat the niner, niner, for Shanghai. We will do a survey of Shanghai on the ninth, and have an opportunity to visit with the personnel coming off of the plane on the tenth, receive the plane for Hangchou on the eleventh and they have granted us permission to ride the C-141 into Hangchou. I have issued the invitation to the PRC to ride with us. Problem. We may have to increase the number of seats on board that C-141 to arrive on the eleventh by as many as fifteen in order to handle our party as well as the guests that we have invited to ride with us. I will have that answer tomorrow. Colonel Coffey informs me that's enough time to configure that C-141. Do you copy?   Over

WATCHDOG: I have copied that and Duval is here and has copied and we'll work with the Military Aide's Office on that particular part.

ROADRUNNER: That's going to be a very important factor if we need those seats. The next thing, once we have received the advance party on the eleventh, we will go into Hangchou and do a complete survey there and then depart on the twelfth. I am not sure what facilities will be made available for us to move from Hangchou to

Peking. Therefore, problem. We have John Thomas arriving and I think we need to know what amount of equipment he is going to have or what amount of equipment needs to be moved from either Shanghai or Hangchou into Peking.

WATCHDOG: We understand on that and will put together an item on that which we will be able to send on the TWX to you. Over

ROADRUNNER: Roger, roger, thank you. The next thing. This is off the subject quickly. Don't be alarmed, but Colonel Coffey is relatively ill at this point. He is confined to his room. We have a number of men who do not feel very well. I think it's more influenza than anything but I am not concerned at this point. If we have more problems by tomorrow I'm going to be *very* concerned.

WATCHDOG: OK. I understand and I won't get alarmed, but one thing that I want you to do is get plenty of sleep and the same for Schrauth. Do you understand?

ROADRUNNER: Yes, Dwight, I understand.

WATCHDOG: Ron, one other point. Basically you're going to be out of communications with me from the ninth to the twelfth. Is that correct?

ROADRUNNER: We are attempting to establish some means . . . we will have the C-141s and we are hopeful that we can make arrangements for each of those aircraft to facilitate in the same manner as they did here when we first arrived.

WATCHDOG: Roger, I did that and we'll make sure from this end that they have the proper radio gear on those C-141s in order to make SURE that we can communicate. Over

ROADRUNNER: Roger, roger. Thank you. Do you have anything else?

WATCHDOG: Hang on a quick second. Ron, do we have it worked out so that on the twenty-first the only things that will take place will be the arrival and the meeting in the afternoon plus the banquet in the evening? That's the only thing for both Searchlight and Starlight? [*They thought so, but in fact the President was swept away to meet with Chairman Mao.*]

ROADRUNNER: Roger, that's correct. That's the program that I have presented to the PRC and they have no problems.

WATCHDOG: OK, thank you. That's good.

ROADRUNNER: Roger, I have one other request, that is, that the PRC has requested from me a protocol order list, repeat, protocol order, of the entire American party to include press, technicians, flight crews, everything . . . all 390. I would like some help back there. Unfortunately we're relatively cramped, the xerox doesn't work and we've just got a few problems. So if they could start to work on that we could finish it up.

WATCHDOG: Roger. We'll put together an order for the number-less American party. *[Watchdog didn't want a specific number mentioned.]*

ROADRUNNER: Roger, Dwight, and I think the best thing to do is take the few people that are the leaders and put the rest of them in alphabetical order.

WATCHDOG: That's a good idea and we will follow that advice.

ROADRUNNER: Roger. Thank you. Wait one. Wait one . . . . . Watchdog, Roadrunner, would you please give me the status of what the invitations are for our banquet. Am I to provide you with any information regarding that or what is the status?

WATCHDOG: Roadrunner, we will be doing the printing of the invitations here. We have a mock up that's going in to Haldeman *[H.R. Haldeman, White House Chief of Staff]* this morning. Then we will print. We are going with a 7:30 time. Is that OK? *[There was a problem with old Chinese characters. The Americans did not know the current usage of the language and realized too late, and to their embarrassment, that they should have had them printed in China. The Chinese actually laughed when they saw them!]*

ROADRUNNER: Yes sir, I don't have any problem with that and my counterpart does not either. They have very graciously agreed to assist in our banquet. Be advised that I did not bring up the champagne yet. *[The Americans wanted to use Schramsberg, a California champagne, for the toasts at the reciprocal banquet.]*

WATCHDOG: OK. That's fine. I'm sure they realize that we would like to put a couple of American touches on it and we'll proceed accordingly unless we hear otherwise from you.

ROADRUNNER: Roger. Be advised, I did not sense any problem and actually I feel they are very appreciative.

WATCHDOG: Roger, Roadrunner. Let me go back to one point if I can for a minute. Besides Colonel Coffey, how many other men are you talking about? *[That is, people who were sick.]*

ROADRUNNER: Right now I know of exactly three, possibly four, including Abel Araiza *[the stenographer]* and you can see what that's doing to us.

WATCHDOG: Roger. I understand. Is Dunn taking care of them?

ROADRUNNER: Yes, he's providing very good attention but, be advised, he's not a doctor.

WATCHDOG: OK, I understand. The one point I was going to make to you I think you've already covered, about having the official photographer, both still and reels, able to have separate opportunities for photographing other than the ones with the press corps. But I think that's in hand, isn't it?

ROADRUNNER: Roger, roger. At this point, I have raised the question and it was accepted as a good idea, and they thanked me for recommending it and they're making arrangements. Over

WATCHDOG: OK. Hang on one second. (To the room: "Does anyone here have anything?") That's all that we have here at this end. Do you have anything else?

ROADRUNNER: No, be advised that both Schrauth and I are in good health, repeat, good health. We are getting a lot of rest. We were very fortunate this evening that the People's Republic of China made available the "Red Women's Detachment" and we were able to watch that along with our Chinese colleagues and it was very enjoyable.

WATCHDOG: OK, I understand. I'm glad to hear that you're in good health. Be advised, today is bridge day and you're the topic of conversation, along with Mike, and I will advise the girls that everything is OK. [*A group of White House staff wives met regularly to play bridge, volunteer for organizations and events, and provide a support system for their stressful, political lifestyles.*]

ROADRUNNER: Roger, roger, I appreciate that. It's nice to know you're thought about at home.

WATCHDOG: That's all I have, Ron. I'll be ready for your call tonight.

ROADRUNNER: Roger, roger, nice talking to you, give my best to everyone. Schrauth sends his also. This is Roadrunner out.

It had been another long, stressful day, but maybe (hopefully) progress had been made. Roadrunner wondered where Snapshot was. It was time to get the scotch and check the ice.

After the polluted, black cubes of last night, Roadrunner thought he had solved the problem. Before setting off in the morning, he had filled the ice cube tray and very carefully wrapped it in a bath towel before setting it out on the window sill. He was very excited. He was going to have clean, crystal clear ice tonight! He gave Snapshot the high sign and hurried to his room.

Everything looked fine. The hall attendant had straightened up and probably read everything on his desk. He'd done the old "hair on the briefcase" trick and had confirmed that the Chinese were checking things out, but just knowing this somehow made it easier to deal with.

He opened the window and retrieved the towel-wrapped tray of ice. "Good," he thought, seeing the filthy towel. He set the bundle on the desk and uncovered it. There were no cubes in the tray. "What?" he exclaimed as he did a double take. He looked at the towel. There they were, twelve little cubes, two by two in neat little rows, hanging on the towel. "Damn! Frozen fast to the threads of the terry cloth!"

Snapshot arrived. They cussed, then laughed and laughed. They poured the scotch over the fuzzy cubes. They were now experts at straining stuff through their teeth and besides, lint was probably healthier than coal soot.

The next morning, Roadrunner and Snapshot were up early. They checked on their men, savored a cup of Folgers Instant, and were ready for the conference call at 7:20. It was 6:20 P.M., Eastern Standard Time, in Washington, D.C.

ROADRUNNER: I have Snapshot with me. We had a long and peaceful rest. I have a medical report this morning. Presently it appears we might have gone through the same situation that we went through on our last trip, because there are six people on our sick call. Five of them are feeling much better this morning. Colonel Coffey is still resting and we have not bothered him this morning. He will require three or four more days to rest up according to the Chinese doctors.

WATCHDOG: That is encouraging. We will not worry. One thing we have is a suggestion Bob Haldeman made that perhaps we should request bringing in a regular doctor on the plane on Friday just as a measure that it would be best for both our countries. [*They needed to be careful. "Regular" meant an American doctor. Roadrunner thought such a move would cause the Chinese to lose face.*]

ROADRUNNER: Roger, I will relay that to my counterpart. I would like to talk to him about it and get back to you this evening.

WATCHDOG: Roger. We will wait to hear on that tonight.

ROADRUNNER: Watchdog, it would be helpful if I knew what doctor. Can I assume that it would be Dr. Ward? [*Chet Ward, United States Army doctor*]

WATCHDOG: That's a possibility, but we have no assurance.

ROADRUNNER: Roger, I understand. I have one comment and it's the same one I make every time. I'm sure that C-141 ride did not help any of these people. Those of us that came our way all seem to be in very good health. [*Roadrunner insisted on traveling as far as possible, Guam, on commercial carrier, and then via C-135 rather than the cavernous, time consuming, windy and always freezing, cold C-141.*]

WATCHDOG: That's a good point. We appreciate that answer.

ROADRUNNER: I have talked to our people and we are all in very strong agreement.

WATCHDOG: We may start sending the C-141s into Guam earlier and let them spend some time there to recoup. [*Washington was still insisting on the military rather than commercial carrier.*]

ROADRUNNER: Roger, sir, I understand. That may also be helpful. I have two things, very quickly. The People's Republic of China has asked that we make available fifteen, repeat fifteen, sets of luggage tags and the luggage tag decals we will use in all three cities. I have two sets with me and I know that Duval and Thomas are bringing additional sets, but I am not sure they will bring that number for each city. They would like to have fifteen sets for each city. Did you copy?

WATCHDOG: Roger, I copy. Do you want fifteen sets . . . total . . . or fifteen sets for each city?

ROADRUNNER: They have asked for fifteen sets for each city. That would be a total of forty-five sets.

WATCHDOG: OK Ron, I understand. You should be advised that I have you on my speaker phone and I have Henkel and Duval here with me. [*Bill Henkel and Mike Duval were both full time members of Roadrunner's White House advance office.*]

ROADRUNNER: Roger, roger. Give my best to both of them, please. Also, the other thing is that Livingood had a set of pictures of the three support pins for the official and unofficial parties, for the press, and then for the technicians. We need twenty sets of those for each city.

WATCHDOG: Roger, for a total of sixty. We understand.

ROADRUNNER: Roger, roger. They were very pleased and very appreciative that we had taken that extra measure and had responded so rapidly. It will help them greatly.

WATCHDOG: OK. I understand.

ROADRUNNER: Roger, I do not know what our schedule will be today. If they suggest we go to the guest house, I am not in a position to go to the guest house until I have received information from you by telex. Therefore, we will not see the guest house today for sure. [*It was time to get hard-nosed about the telex.*] Did you copy?

WATCHDOG: Yes, Ron, I copy.

ROADRUNNER: Wait one, please. (static) Watchdog, Snapshot was wondering if it would be possible within the next fifteen minutes to get Whaleboat to a phone [*Whaleboat was the code name for Ron Ziegler, Press Secretary*]. I am assuming you are in the Advance Office conference room and it may be too long a wait getting him to this phone. If we have to go off the air before we have finished our conversation we will have Snapshot call Whaleboat as soon as they have concluded their test on the satellite in New Mexico.

WATCHDOG: Roger, I understand. Be advised that Searchlight has just departed for Andrews en route Key Biscayne and Whaleboat is with him and will be aboard the Spirit of '76 and therefore will probably be unreachable.

ROADRUNNER: Roger, roger, Snapshot requests you pass this information along to Whaleboat. He did try to reach him this morning. He will attempt to do so this evening or will place a call tomorrow morning.

WHALEBOAT: Roger. We will tell Ziegler that. Now Ron, when I talk to you, can everyone in the room there hear me or are you on an instrument?

ROADRUNNER: Be advised, we have made every effort to get a speaker phone. There is a speaker box that comes out of the suitcase satellite, however, it is very, very difficult to hear unless you are right on top of it. But we are doing OK.

WATCHDOG: OK, I understand. Tomorrow when we talk to you, in the room with me, there will be Scowcroft, Redman, Taylor, plus the regular men . . . Henkel, Duval, John Thomas and then Dewey and Foust, and I want you to be advised we're all going to be listening to what you say and we thought it would be helpful if everybody on your end could hear our conversation. [*Brent Scowcroft, Military Aide's Office, and Jon Foust and Dewey Clower from the advance office.*]

ROADRUNNER: Roger, I understand and that's a good idea, thank you. I'll make arrangements to have all their counterparts available for a phone conversation tomorrow morning.

WATCHDOG: Where do we stand on the TWX?

ROADRUNNER: Well, be advised that I have heard nothing since my meeting with the members of the People's Republic of China yesterday afternoon. So far this morning there has been no contact.

WATCHDOG: OK, Roadrunner, now, be advised that the high frequency communication will be available on both the C-141s arriving in Shanghai and Hangchou February 10 and 11 and the Aide's Office will coordinate the arrangements for continuous service and messages.

ROADRUNNER: Roger, roger. That's very, very, helpful. Thank you. That will keep us in constant communication.

WATCHDOG: Roger. Now, have you asked the Chinese government for permission for the above communications, yet?

ROADRUNNER: Negative. I have not. Negative. I will take it up with them today. Over

WATCHDOG: OK. The C-141 departing Shanghai for Hangchou February eleventh, currently has twelve seats available. If twelve seats are not sufficient, we can put on six additional seats. Just advise us.

ROADRUNNER: Roger, roger. I will advise you *now*. Go ahead and put those six seats on.

WATCHDOG: OK. That's what we'll do. We are working on the PRC's request for a master protocol list and we will cable those suggestions to you once we have them.

ROADRUNNER: Roger, roger, thank you very much. Now, let me back up for a moment. We have not received permission to have that C-141 come straight from Hangchou into Peking. I have asked, but have not heard yet.

WATCHDOG: OK. I understand what you're saying. Thank you. We need to get some word as soon as possible. I am sure you understand Mr. Ziegler's problem on this regarding the January 27 memorandum which you delivered to Mr. Han Hsu on arrival. [*This memo explained why they needed to increase the size of the press corps that would accompany the President.*]

ROADRUNNER: Roger, sir. Both Snapshot and I are very much aware of it. Be advised, I have not been told that memorandum was approved. I thought possibly they were going through back channels and letting you know first.

WATCHDOG: Say it again.

ROADRUNNER: I said, we are assuming they are going to approve the request you made January 27. However, I have a feeling that they will probably approve that through back channels directly to you and Ron Ziegler before we know.

WATCHDOG: OK, I understand what you are saying. Now, let me go to another point here. We do have some changes in the official and unofficial party. Minor alterations in terms of where people fall in the lineup and I will TWX those to you once the equipment is up.

ROADRUNNER: Roger, roger. You say they are minor?

WATCHDOG: That's correct. Mainly it's placement.

ROADRUNNER: Roger, I understand. That's very important as you can well imagine. [*The slightest changes were seen as major changes in the points of principle originally discussed.*]

WATCHDOG: Yes sir. We understand. Hang on a minute. (lots of static)

CROWN: Roadrunner, Roadrunner, Crown.

ROADRUNNER: Crown, this is Roadrunner, Go.

CROWN: Roger, when you have finished with this conversation would you please put Swift on for Redman? Go ahead.

ROADRUNNER: Roger, roger. Crown, be advised you do not have much time. We've only got about four minutes until we've been requested to break down this call so New Mexico can work on that satellite.

CROWN: Roger, Crown understands, use your best judgement as to who should get the time. Go ahead.

WATCHDOG: Roadrunner, this is Watchdog. Since we're evidently almost out of time, why don't you and I end. I don't have anything of any importance to pass on to you at this time other than our good luck for a successful day, today.

ROADRUNNER: Roger sir, be advised that control in New Mexico has just advised us that they are not going to need that down time. Crown, please pass on our thanks to New Mexico. Watchdog, Snapshot would like to talk to you for a moment. Wait one.

SNAPSHOT: Watchdog, watchdog, Snapshot.

WATCHDOG: Hello Snapshot, welcome to the world.

SNAPSHOT: How are you sir? Is your health good? [*Adopting the Chinese habit of exchanging pleasantries before discussing business.*]

WATCHDOG: Yeah, go ahead. [*Not willing to do the same.*]

SNAPSHOT: We have requested, that because of the ability now to go to Shanghai and Hangchou and back to Peking on our aircraft, that the three executive producers come in on the airplane on the tenth so that they can see those two cities. The PRC feels this is a good idea, so you might want to alert Whaleboat to have those people meet that airplane in Guam in order to come in on the tenth. [*Raymond Lockhart, Robert Wussler, and Walter Pfister.*]

WATCHDOG: OK, Tim, did the Chinese agree with that?

SNAPSHOT: They have agreed in principle to this. I am sure that they will get back to us on this when they approve or disapprove the twenty-seventh memorandum. I have talked in detail with them on that memorandum and we are just waiting for word now. Once we get that word, I would also request that the two photo technicians come in on the tenth airplane. That's an additional five people, that we would like to have come in on that airplane.

WATCHDOG: OK. I understand. The three executive producers plus the two photo technicians. Naturally, the only thing we've got to be sure we do is make sure the People's Republic is totally informed as to what we would prefer to do and get their concurrence.

SNAPSHOT: OK. That's a roger, Dwight. That's the only major thing I have right now. I think we're going along very, very well and getting marvelous cooperation.

WATCHDOG: OK. Very good, Tim. I'll relay that to Ron.

SNAPSHOT: OK. That's a roger. We have Major Swift here. Would you like to talk to Roadrunner or Swift?

WATCHDOG: I have no reason to talk to Swift, let me have Roadrunner a minute.

SNAPSHOT: That's a roger.

ROADRUNNER: Watchdog, this is Roadrunner. Go.

WATCHDOG: Hey, Roadrunner, have a good day and we'll talk to you tonight, your time. It will be 9:30 your time and 8:30 tomorrow morning our time.

ROADRUNNER: Roger, roger sir. Have a pleasant rest. Be advised, we are making arrangements this evening for one of our movies and we have invited many people from the People's Republic of China to be our guests to watch *Butch Cassidy and the Sundance Kid.*

WATCHDOG: Very good. That ought to be a lot of fun. Duval and Henkel say good night, er . . . good morning and we're off for tonight.

ROADRUNNER: Roger, roger. Thank you very much. I realize it is very difficult to communicate this way. I am very hopeful that by this evening we will have sent telex material between both our locations.

WATCHDOG: Yes. We're starting to get extremely concerned here about the amount of material that's piling up and the importance of getting it to you so you people can get your work done.

ROADRUNNER: Yes sir, we understand and agree fully. I would like to ask you one favor. That is, at your convenience, would you please check with General Redman about a letter that was supposedly put in one of our pouches. It is dated January 12, 1972, from the White House Communications Agency, and the subject is communications support in the PRC. Did you copy?

WATCHDOG: Roger. I'm familiar with that letter and we feel that it laid it out.

ROADRUNNER: Yes, sir. We are in extreme agreement, however, it is our feeling and it is definitely Major Swift's feeling that his counterparts are completely unaware of it.

WATCHDOG: OK. Hang on just a minute, Roadrunner, while I look at something.

ROADRUNNER: Roger. Roadrunner's waiting for Watchdog . . .

WATCHDOG: OK, Roadrunner, be advised that I am looking at a rough transcript of the conversation on the train when we went from Hangchou to Shanghai and I remember that Miss Chang, the interpreter, was on that train trip and took extensive notes. I think if she looks at her notes she will find our whole discussion regarding this communications situation with the TWX and that it may help them to understand our problem. The main thing being that Miss Chang participated in a conversation with General Haig and I think that the words make it quite clear as to what our problem is.

ROADRUNNER: Roger, roger, sir. I understand that. We have suggested that. That was very much in evidence during our conversation with the PRC last night. And I made that specific point. As you will recall, I was in that meeting. But, we have not seen Miss

Schrauth, Livingood, and Roadrunner at the Forbidden City.

Chang. [*They did not know what had become of her and questions were met with polite non-answers.*] However, I will make that suggestion. I am going to follow through until about noon to see what kind of response I get before I start moving again.
WATCHDOG: OK. That's all I have, do you have anything else?
ROADRUNNER: Negative, negative. Schrauth sends his best and have a pleasant rest and we'll talk to you this evening.
WATCHDOG: OK. Thank you.

Roadrunner gathered up his papers and sorted through the documents that they had used during the conference call. Snapshot was muttering about something and Roadrunner realized he had not been listening when he half-heard Snapshot say, " . . . and see if I care if those horse's ass executive producers ever get any closer to China than the Guam Holiday Inn." Then they both had to laugh.

The advance party and their Chinese counterparts set out from the hotel to do a survey of the Forbidden City, so named because only emperors were allowed to live there. This home of the Ming and Ting emperors was in the heart of Peking and was now the Old Palace Museum. The Chinese officials showing the Americans around were quick to point out the rich and wasteful lifestyles enjoyed in the days of the emperors. Figures were quoted to show how many workers the old extravagant ways would feed today.

"Because of the wise leadership of the Helmsman," one guide said, "we no longer prepare delicacies for the Emperor to smell. Today all the people of China are fed and no one is allowed to go hungry."

The wood carving was magnificent in the Hall of Complete Harmony and the ornate pillars and furniture in the Hall of Preserving Harmony were masterpieces of workmanship. Roadrunner knew that the President and Mrs. Nixon would be very taken with the beauty they would see here.

Next they surveyed the Temple of Heavenly Peace, where the emperors prayed for rich harvests. The cone-shaped building with its beautiful blue tiled roof was an engineering feat. No nails or metal were used in the construction. Trees from the Yunnan forest provided the twenty-eight columns that were the main support beams. The four in the center represented the four seasons, the next twelve referred to the months of the year, and the remaining represented the hours in the day.

There were no cross beams supporting the tile roof, only arches. Because of this, the outside wall formed an echo chamber where the sound was reflected and could be heard anywhere around the wall. Snapshot knew this would be an intriguing place for the American party to stop, a natural photo opportunity.

CHAPTER VII

EYEBALL TO EYEBALL
WITH THE RED CHINESE

FEBRUARY 4, 1972

It was past nine o'clock when they settled down for the evening's conference call with Washington. Roadrunner was very distressed with the lack of communication from the Chinese. "But," he thought to himself, "they seem to be night people and I'll probably hear from them just about the time I am ready to crawl into bed and pull the covers up under my chin." In Washington, it was 0819 hours.

WATCHDOG: Let me ask about the health question first. How is everyone feeling?
ROADRUNNER: Be advised that we have four, repeat, four people who are presently on the sick list. Colonel Coffey is still running a considerable temperature and the Chinese doctor who called on him this evening said that in the event he is not better tomorrow morning they will put him into the hospital for other treatment. Did you copy?
WATCHDOG: Roger, will you repeat, what doctor called on him?

ROADRUNNER: Roger, Dr. Lee, repeat the famous Dr. Lee, from one of the Chinese hospitals. [*The Chinese always referred to him as the famous Dr. Lee, perhaps to let the Americans know that Colonel Coffey was getting the best medical treatment available.*]

WATCHDOG: OK, Ron, go ahead with the other three.

ROADRUNNER: Roger, be advised that Sergeant Araiza and Sergeant Collins are also bedridden at this point. [*Army Master Sergeant Abel Araiza and Marine Gunnery Sergeant Mac A. Collins were both support personnel.*] They were not in good health last night and they are in worse health this evening.

WATCHDOG: Roger. Did you raise the subject with your counterpart of bringing in a doctor, perhaps this weekend?

ROADRUNNER: That is a negative. I will give you a status report on how our day went and I think you will understand. Did you copy?

WATCHDOG: Yes I did. Let's do that. Why don't you run through a general report of the day. Don't go into the specifics of any particular event but just give us an overview of everything that you have covered.

ROADRUNNER: That's a roger. We received word at approximately 8:30 this morning that we would be going to the Forbidden City at 9:00. A group of the survey personnel spent approximately three hours at the Forbidden City. We learned that the PRC is expecting Mrs. Nixon to do a second, repeat, a second visit to the Forbidden City during her stay here in Peking. We returned, I did have my counterpart with me during that survey, to the hotel, and were informed we would be going to the Temple of Heavenly Peace. I did not raise any subjects this morning based on the circumstances that I observed. I was hopeful that during the course of the afternoon I might be able to raise the number of questions that are pending. However, my counterpart did not show for the visit to the Temple of Heavenly Peace. Upon returning, I asked for a private meeting and was informed he was involved and would not be available. I have to this point not heard from anyone.

WATCHDOG: I understand. Let me ask, is the Pakistan Prime Minister still in town? (static, click, click, static)

ROADRUNNER: Watchdog, Watchdog, Roadrunner, you will have to say again, you were broken badly.

WATCHDOG: I repeat. Is the Pakistan Prime Minister still in Peking?

ROADRUNNER: That is a negative. Negative. He left the day before yesterday, repeat, day before yesterday on the second of February. [*"Good try Dwight, but this is not why they aren't talking to us," Roadrunner thought. "I wish it were that simple."*]

Schrauth on a site survey.

WATCHDOG: Roger. I understand. What else did you do after you went to the Temple of Heavenly Peace this afternoon?

ROADRUNNER: Be advised that I personally did absolutely nothing. I worked on my paperwork. However, be advised that Schrauth and a Mrs. Nixon survey team did in fact survey the glass factory.

WATCHDOG: OK. Good. I understand. You have had no further communications though in terms of the TWX facilities, for example?

ROADRUNNER: That is a negative. I asked status of it earlier today and was informed that I would be advised, and I have not been advised and neither has Major Swift. One critical point, Major Swift has not, repeat, has not seen his counterpart all day.

WATCHDOG: Roger, I understand. What progress has been made by the communications people in terms of putting up equipment?

ROADRUNNER: You are presently listening to the only set-up we have been able to put forth at this point. However, be advised that the technicians are apparently moving with some degree of success.

WATCHDOG: Roger, I understand. Do you have a work day schedule put together by which you can log how tight a situation you are getting yourselves into by being unable to put up this equipment?

ROADRUNNER: That's a roger. We do. Every day it becomes shorter and shorter and much more critical.

WATCHDOG: OK. I think that if you do not hear something within another hour or so that you ought to put in a phone call, through whatever source you can, to Mr. Han Hsu and register strongly our concern over the developing situation.

ROADRUNNER: Roger, I understand and fully have intentions before the evening is out of making that call again.

WATCHDOG: OK. Do you have anything else in regard to reporting what's happened today?

ROADRUNNER: Watchdog, wait one.

SNAPSHOT: Watchdog, this is Snapshot. Let me give you just a little re-cap on how the technicians are doing.

WATCHDOG: Roger, go ahead, Snapshot.

SNAPSHOT: They have made very good progress in the transmission center at this point. However, they ground to a halt this afternoon because they are having problems getting permission to set up their microwave equipment which is so vital. They also cannot set up their radio equipment. Further, they were informed today that they could not turn on any of their equipment for transmission until the President's plane touches down.

WATCHDOG: Roger, let me make sure I understand. They will not be able to turn on their equipment until the moment that the President's plane touches down and this is a decision made by their government and is understood by the technicians to be a decision made by their government.

SNAPSHOT: Watchdog, Snapshot, I can't . . . . it's impossible. [*It was unbelievable that the Chinese were this naive about the communications equipment.*] We have to do testing before the President touches down as you are very well aware. I think this can be cleared up at a future meeting, if we can get one. Further, be advised that about five minutes ago one of the people from the information office told me that we would meet sometime tomorrow afternoon and that he will have the answers to many of our questions. So, I am looking forward to tomorrow afternoon.

WATCHDOG: Roger. I understand, because . . . if that rule of theirs holds, perhaps we cannot ensure in any way that the facility will work properly.

SNAPSHOT: That's a roger, we are prepared with many back up materials to document that.

WATCHDOG: OK. I understand. Do you think, in your meeting tomorrow they'll have some answers to the January 27 memorandum? [*There were two memos dated January 27, 1972 on the subject of personnel. One to Png-hua, Deputy Director, Department of Information, from Ron Ziegler and John Scali explained that adjustments in the basic press list of eighty were necessary because of intense interest in the United States about the President's trip. While recognizing that the PRC desired to keep the traveling press corps as small as possible, Ziegler was nevertheless concerned that additions were necessary to avoid charges of favoritism in the U.S. He wanted to increase the number of press without increasing the overall party of 389. The second memo, from Watchdog to Han Hsu, stated that the Americans would accommodate Ziegler's request for four additional press personnel by eliminating one logistical assistant, one chef, and two support personnel. Actually, it was a more complicated request, because Ziegler wanted to replace Frank VanderLinden of the Nashville Banner with Richard Wilson of the Des Moines Register because Mr. Wilson was a personal friend of the President and had traveled with him on all of his foreign trips over many years. It was also important to replace three writer-producer technicians with processing-transmitting technicians, William Achatz of AP and Fred W. Lyon, Jr. of UPI, to work in the press center and Mrs. Fay Wells of Storer Broadcasting to cover Mrs. Nixon. The additional reporters who would replace staff would be Tom Ross, Chicago Sun Times; William Sprague, Voice of America; William F. Buckley, Jr., National Review; and Joseph Kraft, Publishers Hall Syndicate. He also wanted permission for three television executive producers, Robert Wussler, CBS; Raymond Lockhart, NBC; and Walter Pfister, ABC; to enter China seven days ahead of the President, and for Achatz and Lyon to be permitted to enter with them. It was no wonder the Chinese were not able to respond immediately.*]

SNAPSHOT: I feel we might get some answers to that tomorrow based on what I was told a few minutes ago. It seems that certain portions of that were immediately favorable, others were debatable. So, I think we will just have to wait and see what they come up with on that.

WATCHDOG: OK. We understand. Do you have anything else, Tim?

SNAPSHOT: Ah, yes, that's a roger. I think the memorandum could be one of the problems in the holdup here on our radios and all of the other answers we have to get. I think they're studying that and will not let us have anything until a decision has been made on that.

WATCHDOG: OK, Tim, I understand. Hang on a second. Al Redman has a question. [*General Al Redman, head of White House Communications Agency.*]

SNAPSHOT: Roger, Swift is here.

REDMAN: Tim, this one's for you. Could you give me a reading on what Siegenthaler's [*Bob Siegenthaler, ABC pool producer.*] comments have been on the RCA installation? I've had meetings with the RCA people here in Washington and they have assured me that Siegenthaler, whom they had been in touch with prior to his departure, is considering live hook up through their facilities. Do you know anything about this?

SNAPSHOT: Redman, Snapshot. No, I do not know anything about that. I have talked with Siegenthaler. He cannot make a judgement until we get to Shanghai and see that facility. However, be advised that the PRC says the user, the user, will have to make application to Intelsat [*International Telecommunications Satellite Organization*].

REDMAN: Snapshot, Redman. That's a roger. Be advised that the application has been made by RCA to the Intelsat Corporation and they will not act until their regular meeting on the twenty-third. If this is the case, it will be the twenty-fourth before the system will be up on the air in Shanghai.

SNAPSHOT: Redman, Snapshot. I understand that. Be advised, we cannot make a determination on the use of that equipment until the survey is made in Shanghai.

REDMAN: Snapshot, Redman. That's a roger. I have nothing further, does Swift have anything for me?

SNAPSHOT: Redman, Snapshot. That's a roger. The PRC has not given us any information regarding the earth station other than to say that RCA has been contacted and told us there were twenty-four voice channels available, video capability, and that is all, that's all they told us.

REDMAN: Snapshot, Redman. Would you ask Swift, when he feels that the Western Union earth station will be able to test with Jamestown? [*Communications went from Peking to Intelsat to Riverside, California to Jamestown to the Pentagon to the White House.*] And also, have they provided diesel fuel for the generators?

SWIFT: Redman, Swift. That satellite station of ours here in Peking, has been on the air testing. They have plenty of diesel fuel and everything is on schedule as far as they're concerned.

REDMAN: That's a roger, but as far as I understand it, they will not allow us to bring up any of the White House voice channels. Is that correct?

SWIFT: That is correct because the switchboard is still packed away in the boxes and there are no lines between the airport and town, as far as our use is concerned. So that is the reason we can't have any circuits.

REDMAN: That's a roger.

SWIFT: I have a meeting with my counterpart tomorrow morning and they have promised to discuss all of the questions we have proposed to date and hopefully we will get some answers at that time.

REDMAN: Good luck.

WATCHDOG: Roadrunner, Watchdog.

ROADRUNNER: Go, Watchdog.

WATCHDOG: OK. What else do you have? Anything?

ROADRUNNER: Not very much. I have a schedule for tomorrow. Schrauth will go to the commune at 9:00 with those people who are involved with Mrs. Nixon. The rest of the party concerned with Searchlight will depart at 9:30 for the gymnasium. In the afternoon at 2:00, Schrauth will go to the children's hospital, and at 2:30 the remainder of the group responsible and concerned about Searchlight will go to the airport for a survey.

WATCHDOG: Sounds good. When will you try and get your meeting? Tonight or tomorrow morning?

ROADRUNNER: I have asked, twice, for a meeting this evening. However, I have received no word as to the availability or to the prospects of a meeting. I personally feel that since everyone, repeat, everyone from the PRC has been pretty much out of pocket this afternoon, that there has been some discussion transpiring, regarding everything that has been discussed to date.

WATCHDOG: I think you are probably right. I know what you are saying.

ROADRUNNER: Roger, roger. Did you in fact receive information from Howe, repeat, Howe, that the memorandum that was dated 1/12/72 regarding communications for the advance team was in fact dispatched? [*Jonathan Howe was with the National Security Council.*]

WATCHDOG: We're going to double check that this morning.

ROADRUNNER: That's a roger.

WATCHDOG: Bob Taylor is here, does Bill have anything for Bob?

LIVINGOOD: Negative. I just went along with Roadrunner on the survey and sent McFarland with Schrauth. McFarland is going separate ways for Mrs. Nixon's schedule. I have not heard anything on the question we had asked earlier. I had not brought it up, actually, because I have not met with my major counterpart. I thought we might hear through you. [*Secret Service had requested that they be permitted to provide an armored limousine for the President.*]

WATCHDOG: Roger, we're just waiting on that one, Bill.

LIVINGOOD: I thought it better to just not say anything yet, and wait.

WATCHDOG: Roger, is there any indication yet on the matter we sent through channels prior to your departure?

LIVINGOOD: That's what I have been talking about. Negative, I have not brought it up. I will probably get an answer or you will get an answer through channels.

WATCHDOG: Roger, Bill, I'm sorry, I'll pay attention. Is Timmie there?

LIVINGOOD: Roger, wait one.

SNAPSHOT: Party calling Snapshot, go ahead.

WATCHDOG: Snapshot, this is Watchdog. Jack D'Arcy is here, but across the room, so I'll ask the question. We have the replacement for Mark Richards. His name is Joe Keating, K-E-A-T-I-N-G, and he is now on the press list there, and you can find him on the list. We need to know when you want him to come in?

SNAPSHOT: He should come in on the aircraft coming seven days in advance. That's the C-141 bringing the mobile units.

WATCHDOG: OK. Tim, one more thing now. He will be replaced, Keating who is on the list of the press people to come in the day before, will be replaced by Tim O'Brien, that's O, then B-R-I-E-N of ABC.

SNAPSHOT: Why do they have to do that? That's just f---ing stupid! They just don't realize how that complicates things. (pause) [*Snapshot was furious! They cannot start making changes on things we don't even permission to do!*] (Sigh) We'll do if it's necessary.

WATCHDOG: You mean you would rather leave Keating on and have O'Brien come early?

SNAPSHOT: Negative. If that is what they want we will just have to live with that. What is O'Brien's first name?

WATCHDOG: His name is Tim, T-I-M, Tim.

SNAPSHOT: OK, that's a roger, I'll try and work with that one.

WATCHDOG: Hang on a minute. (To the room: "Why are we doing it this way? No, why in hell don't we send O'Brien early and send Keating in when he was scheduled to go? Christ!") [*Now Watchdog was furious for the same reason.*] OK. Is Roadrunner there?

ROADRUNNER: Roger, this is Roadrunner, go.

WATCHDOG: Here is one of the more important things of the day. You're an uncle again! The Chases had an eight pound, two ounce boy. [*John Walker Chase was born to Roadrunner's sister, Beverly Jeanne Walker Chase and John P. Chase in Philadelphia, Pennsylvania, February 4, 1972.*]

ROADRUNNER: OH! Very good! Thank you. I appreciate that. That's very exciting.

WATCHDOG: Everybody is in good health, there, I guess. Now hang on just a minute. (pause) Roadrunner, is your Xerox still broken?

ROADRUNNER: Negative, negative, the Xerox is working fine, I just wish we had something that would go into it.

WATCHDOG: Yeah, I understand. How are you doing on your steno support? You must be cramped there, too.

ROADRUNNER: Not very good, repeat, not very good. We have been unable to receive any support today from them at all. However, the White House Communications Agency has volunteered their help tomorrow and I'm sure they'll come through with flying colors.

WATCHDOG: OK. Well, when you talk to Mr. Han Hsu, hopefully tonight, I hope you let him know that from my standpoint things sound a little pessimistic on the communications set-up, and that I am very concerned over the materials we have here and the need to move this along if we are going to have the successful meeting we have talked about so often.

ROADRUNNER: I understand. Be advised that it's almost impossible, repeat impossible, to pull off what you've asked. [*Director Han Hsu was just not available for them to speak with.*]

WATCHDOG: OK, I understand. If you can't do that, then relay it as appropriate.

ROADRUNNER: Thank you for understanding, that's exactly what I am attempting to do. Unfortunately, to this point it has been very unsuccessful. I am hopeful that I will be able to see the person involved this evening, but if not then we will have to make arrangements tomorrow and then we will have lost another day.

WATCHDOG: Well. I am to give Dr. Kissinger a complete report on where this matter stands, immediately after our next telephone call, because he is personally concerned over this. [*Name-dropping would send a still stronger message to the Chinese!*]

ROADRUNNER: Roger. Be advised, that in the event I am successful in meeting this evening, I will initiate another call at the conclusion of that meeting.

WATCHDOG: That would be ideal and we would appreciate that very much. We will be available all day, today.

ROADRUNNER: Other than that, everybody in the room here is in good health and I will check to see if anyone has a last message.

WATCHDOG: Roadrunner, while you're checking, we're getting the answer on this January 12 memorandum.

SNAPSHOT: Watchdog, on that C-141 going to Hangchou, if there is any way to put on additional seats we would be benefitted by that. If the PRC wants to put people on it we will be in serious trouble.

So if you can put additional seats on that 141, it would be appreciated.

WATCHDOG: Check with Roadrunner right there. I think we covered this last night. We have eighteen seats, presently. Isn't that right, Ron?

SNAPSHOT: That's a roger, but we have re-evaluated and we are asking for at least six more seats.

WATCHDOG: OK. We will have to work on that one and get back to you.

SNAPSHOT: That's a roger, I understand. Watchdog, is Whaleboat patched into this conversation, by any chance? [*Wishful thinking on Snapshot's part!*]

WATCHDOG: Negative. You're going to have to give him a separate call. I would suggest you do it as soon as we hang up.

SNAPSHOT: I will do that. It's too bad that he wasn't patched in. [*It would have been so much more efficient to have everyone involved with the trip a part of the conference calls.*]

WATCHDOG: OK. Hang on one minute. Tim, be advised that Bill Small wants to come in seven days ahead of time and you may want to raise that subject with Ziegler when you talk to him.

SNAPSHOT: That might be a little bit difficult at this time. We are still waiting for their answers to the memorandum of January 27, and I would like to get the answers to those before I start raising additional requirements. [*Why was this so difficult for Washington to grasp?*]

WATCHDOG: I understand, and I think this is the important part involving the TWX and everything else. We have a lot of questions and a lot of requests that have to be considered and we've got to get the facility established so they can be sent forward to the government.

ROADRUNNER: Be advised that I wholeheartedly agree and concur in what Snapshot relayed a few moments ago regarding the memorandum of January 27. I have not, repeat, have not talked about any additional personnel, including the steno for Hangchou. I feel it is a problem and once we have reached some foundation we will be able to start talking about any additional items. It appears to me that any changes we have asked for since our arrival has done nothing but confuse the People's Republic of China [*So much so that they were now hiding from and ignoring the Americans.*] and very much hindered our successful movement throughout our operation. [*"Now," Roadrunner said to himself, "we not only do not get answers to our questions, we cannot even do our basic jobs!"*]

WATCHDOG: Roger, I understand. Hang on a minute, now.

REDMAN: This is directed to Mike Schrauth and Swift. I just talked to Jonathan Howe. He indicates that in the packet that Schrauth took over there is a memo which was sent to the People's Republic of China, along with the manifest. However, the 12 January memorandum did not go. Howe says that Swift discussed this with him and they sent a reduced version of the January 12 memorandum. The memorandum that did go in the packet, along with the manifest, Mike Schrauth has a copy of. It was acknowledged as being acceptable.

ROADRUNNER: General Redman, thank you very much. We have a copy of that memorandum that was sent by Commander Howe and we are very appreciative. However, I would like you to be advised that the memorandum that was sent made no reference whatsoever to telex facilities being available specifically as had been indicated in Major Swift's memorandum initially. Commander Howe saw fit to change that memorandum and listed it as "communications center" in applicable hotels. I feel personally that is the problem, because it was not spelled out. Do you copy?

REDMAN: That's a roger. Howe mentioned that he had discussed the modified version with Swift and that he sent it after Swift concurred. Is this a roger?

SWIFT: That's not quite the way I recall it, General. Howe called me at home one night, we discussed it, and he said he was going to send out the first paragraph. The first paragraph covers all the way to subparagraph B which was the communications center being moved to the guest house forty-eight hours prior to the arrival of the President. And the second page, which is what I understood was going to be dropped, was a simple two paragraph discussion of the pros and cons of locating a switchboard in the hotel versus the guest house.

REDMAN: Swift, that's a roger. Then you're telling me that you did not see the memorandum that was finally sent by Jonathan Howe. Is that correct?

SWIFT: Yes sir. That is absolutely correct. I did not see it until today when Mr. Schrauth showed it to me.

REDMAN: That's a roger.

WATCHDOG: (To the room: "Well, that's the problem.") Roadrunner? [*No wonder the Chinese were huddled trying to figure out what they were talking about!*]

ROADRUNNER: Go, Watchdog.

WATCHDOG: OK, obviously that's what the problem is. Now, do you want us to start something through channels at this end just as a backup on this whole thing?

ROADRUNNER: Sir, at this point I would accept anything, however if you send it through channels, it is going to take a fair amount of time. I think we have established the need for these facilities. I am very, very confident that the PRC has considered all the information we have given them and I am very hopeful that in a relatively short period of time that we will have these facilities.

WATCHDOG: OK, Roadrunner, I understand, and if you want to get back to me later today, I'll be available. We will sign off unless you have something.

ROADRUNNER: Roger, roger, Watchdog, have a very nice day. Everything here is fine. [*SURE! Just great!*]

WATCHDOG: OK. We all send our best. Hope you have a meeting and then get a good night's sleep. Everybody here is fine, your family is fine and so is everyone else's families.

ROADRUNNER: Roger, roger, it would be very, very nice if there is someone in the office who would call the families represented here and tell them we are all in good health.

WATCHDOG: It will be done.

ROADRUNNER: Thank you very much. Have a nice day and I'll hopefully talk at you in a few hours. If it takes all night, it's worth it.

WATCHDOG: Roger, I understand and good luck, Ron.

ROADRUNNER: Thank you, good night.

Roadrunner was really down. Snapshot looked tired and grumpy and depressed and everything else that was bad. What were they going to do? Why wouldn't Mr. Chu talk to him? They were wasting all this time when they had so much to do!

As he walked into his room, his hotel phone rang. Mr. Chu informed him that Director Han Hsu would like to see him. Could they please come to Mr. Walker's room in a few minutes?

Roadrunner yelled at Snapshot, "Timmie, that was Mr. Chu. He's bringing Han Hsu up here. They want to talk."

Snapshot came rushing into the room with Manning on his heels. Their expressions were a mixture of trepidation, surprise and excitement. "What do you think they want?" Snapshot asked.

"To talk, and hopefully, to get things moving," Roadrunner said. Listen, I've got an idea. Let's open that transom above this door and maybe you two will be able to hear the conversation from your side. I can use all the help I can get at this point."

"Great idea," Snapshot laughed, rubbing his palms together.

Roadrunner hurried in to the bathroom and splashed cold water on his face. He brushed his teeth; somehow that always made him feel a little refreshed. He opened his door that led to the hotel hallway. Snapshot and Manning had already opened the transom and were huddled on the other side of the double doors that led to their suite.

The Chinese arrived. "Good lord, they brought a damn army," Roadrunner thought as he jumped from his chair to greet Director Han Hsu and the men who accompanied him.

"Good evening, Mr. Director, it is an honor to see you," Roadrunner said as he shook hands with Han Hsu.

"It is always a pleasure to see you, Ronwalker," Han Hsu said. As always, he pronounced Roadrunner's whole name quickly, as if it were one word.

After a few moments of exchanging pleasantries and the ordering of tea, Han Hsu came to the point. "We don't know who you are, Ronwalker. You must understand that we are very concerned. We are very troubled and worried about what you are asking us to do. We don't understand what you are asking us to do. You keep asking for this communication with your country. We don't know what it means. We want to study this request, because we do not know how it works. If you can talk to your country, you can talk to any place. We don't know where this information will go."

Director Han Hsu paused, and then added, "Perhaps the polar bear will be able to listen."

Roadrunner was shocked. He couldn't believe what he had just heard. "My god, he thinks I'm a spy or CIA!" Roadrunner realized. He fell back in his chair and took a deep breath. Then he leaned forward as far as he could and locked eyes with Director Han Hsu. "Sir, with all the time you have had to prepare for my arrival, you must know something about me. I am here as the President's representative. I am an advance man. I make arrangements for the President of the United States when he travels. It is as simple as that. I am not a diplomat. I am not an intelligence officer. I am here to do the very best job that I personally can so the President of the United States can come to your country and meet with your leaders. You and your people are asking many questions of me. I don't have all the answers to give you. I must receive guidance from my leaders at times. I need to be able to talk to them. They need to be able to talk to me. Then we can make sure that the visit of my President with your Prime Minister will go smoothly and make both of our countries very proud. And that is absolutely all I came here to do. You must believe that."

The two men stared at each other. No one spoke or moved. The tension in the room was terrifying. Han Hsu's face was flushed. Roadrunner thought for a moment that perhaps he was going to be asked to leave the country. Maybe the Chinese were going to ask all of them to leave. "Had they failed to accomplish their mission?" he asked himself. He could never face the President and tell him that he had failed.

After a long, tense silence, Han Hsu looked around the room for a moment and then said, "Is your room comfortable, Ronwalker? Do you have everything here to make you comfortable?"

"Oh, yes sir. The room is very comfortable. The hall attendants and everyone in the hotel have been most gracious and kind. All of the Americans are very grateful, Mr. Director."

Then all of the Chinese men smiled. Roadrunner smiled back and told Mr. Han Hsu how much he appreciated his being frank with him on this important matter. Han Hsu stood up to leave, and they exchanged innocuous pleasantries while everyone departed. Roadrunner closed the door behind him and leaned against it. His heart was pounding. His head and neck ached.

Snapshot and Manning came flying through the double doors. "Holy shit, they think we're spies," Snapshot said. "That was a hardcore, heavy-duty session, wasn't it?"

"You should have seen his face, Timmie. Now I know why they are called red Chinese. He was either really mad or he was embarrassed that he had to ask that question. It was really a frightening face."

They all slumped into the chairs and thought about what they had just witnessed. They were scared. They were worried. But somehow they knew that it was a turning point. They thought that Han Hsu must have believed that Roadrunner was leveling with him. Han Hsu just *had* to believe it.

Roadrunner, with Snapshot and Manning on his heels, hurried to the suitcase satellite to call Watchdog. It was approaching midnight in China. In Washington it was 10:45 in the morning.

ROADRUNNER: I explained to them, that I was involved in no activity that could be counterproductive to the President's visit. I was informed that they were conducting a study as to how these facilities could be used for any other activities, which I am sure you can pick up on.

WATCHDOG: I understand what you are saying and I understand what they are saying. [*Watchdog was stunned when he realized what Roadrunner was telling them.*]

ROADRUNNER: I explained to them that I personally was not involved in any other activities, and no one in our group was attempting other activities, but I appreciated their concern and understood their concern and thanked them for being very frank with me.

WATCHDOG: OK. I understand. I think that one of the principal points that we have got to impress upon Mr. Chu and Mr. Han Hsu is the fact that much of the information which we want to send from this end to you is information that we feel, for practical purposes, should not be talked about over the air waves which can be monitored by other sources.

ROADRUNNER: Roger, roger. I understand that. Please be advised that I did the best job I knew how in trying to explain just exactly that. I was informed that they would take it under consideration.

WATCHDOG: I understand, Ron, and believe me, you know that I realize that and I'm not questioning that at all. I'm just trying to make the point and make sure that it's made, that we can send and talk about information over this form of communication, but when we do, it's going to be instantly, public information.

ROADRUNNER: I understand. I will attempt to make that point. I simply stated that we had tried to make as clear as possible, the importance of receiving this facility as quickly as possible because of the information that would be disseminated between you and me, between Peking and Washington. Many, many answers that they had been pressuring me for could be answered. They feel it is their responsibility to take care of the President and his party, and we are here as a temporary means to provide any information that is necessary. Therefore, our needs are simply that of an advisory group. Are you copying me?

WATCHDOG: Yes, I understand.

ROADRUNNER: Right now I am on record that if they don't want us to use any facilities besides this suitcase until just prior to the President's arrival, they had best tell us. Right now we don't understand anything, because they aren't talking to us and they don't return our phone calls.

WATCHDOG: OK. Now in regard to the role being played by the men there on the ground, obviously from all of our talks with them we know that they are indeed the hosts and that we are there only to offer our advice and guidance as far as our country is concerned which will help to insure the success of the President's visit. We have no other intent at all.

ROADRUNNER: Roger, roger, I understand . . . uh . . . I understand. [*Roadrunner did not need to comment. Watchdog was talking to the Chinese, whom he assumed were monitoring the conversation.*]

WATCHDOG: The point that they make about other activities, of course, all we can do there is deny it and hope they realize the good intent of our mission.

ROADRUNNER: Yes, sir. I think that you can rest assured. I would hope that you would take me at my word that every member of this party has conducted himself accordingly and with great taste and dignity to this point.

WATCHDOG: Obviously, that's to be continued barring whatever problems are encountered, as you know. [*God forbid someone gets mad and tells the Chinese where to go.*]

ROADRUNNER: Yes, we understand that also.

WATCHDOG: OK. Well, I don't think that there is any more that we can say about this at the present time. We're just going to have to wait and see what we hear.

ROADRUNNER: Yes, sir. I understand that and I think they understand also.

WATCHDOG: OK. I will put together a rough draft of what we would propose that we release on the schedule for the President, and I guess if we can't talk tomorrow I'll run through that schedule over the air with you.

ROADRUNNER: I'm sorry for it to come to that point. However, I feel I have done the best job I know how and I have been told that they will take it under consideration. I do not feel that I can raise that subject again within any reasonable amount of time.

WATCHDOG: OK, well, let's wait and talk about that tomorrow. In regard to our next phone conversation, we plan on gathering tomorrow morning at 10:00 P.M. your time tonight which will be 9:00 A.M. tomorrow morning our time.

SNAPSHOT: Watchdog, could you see if Whaleboat could get patched into that conference tomorrow evening?

WATCHDOG: Roger, I'll talk to him about that.

SNAPSHOT: Roger. [*"But be sure to tell him not to strain himself!" Snapshot thought.*]

ROADRUNNER: Watchdog, that's all I have.

WATCHDOG: Take care. We've passed the messages on to the families.

ROADRUNNER: Roger, roger. And thank you very much. Good night.

It was past midnight in China. All the men were exhausted. Roadrunner and Snapshot both slumped back into the overstuffed sofa and exhaled loudly. Some of the men began to leave amid the "good nights" and "sleep wells" and "see you tomorrows."

Roadrunner was pooped but too pumped up to sleep. Then a thought jolted him upright. It had been such a long and hectic evening that he had forgotten to check the ice! He yelled at Snapshot, and they flew down the hall into Roadrunner's room and over to the window sill. A very long and busy day ago they had wrapped the ice trays in a pillow case from Roadrunner's bed. They had reasoned that this would keep the Peking soot out without leaving little cotton hairs in the water as it began to freeze. Now they would be able to pour their scotch over clear, clean ice.

Roadrunner looked out at the bundle on his window sill. As expected, the pillow case was filthy. He'd have to remember to ask the hall attendant for another. He reached outside and . . . Damn! the whole bundle was as stiff as a frapping board. It had absorbed all the water and was frozen stiff--as hard as a damned rock. There weren't any cubes at all. At least dirty or fuzzy ones were better than nothing.

They drank a couple of sips of scotch. Neat. They began to commiserate about their layers of frustration. Their co-workers were sick, and getting sicker instead of better. They had no steno support and neither of them could type worth a tinker's damn.

"Hell, you could try to type," Roadrunner told Snapshot, "at least your fingers work!" Roadrunner had cut his wrist as a young boy and had no feeling in two of the fingers on his left hand.

"And then what are we going to do with it after I type it, mail it to the White House?" Snapshot asked.

"Good point," Roadrunner muttered.

They had no telex because the Chinese feared they were spies, or might try to sabotage the trip in some way. "For Christ sake, we're advance men," Roadrunner declared. "We blew up balloons and built crowds during the 1968 campaign."

"I worked at Disneyland. Mickey Mouse is one of my very best friends," Snapshot responded.

"How come the Chinese don't know any of this?" they wondered. Roadrunner and Snapshot agreed that the Chinese must have had some kind of a dossier on them. "Hell, the Chinese probably invented spying, what with all those stories about Imperial Palace intrigue," Roadrunner exclaimed. "Everyone knows that all Communists are supposed to be spies, but now they won't even talk to us or return our phone calls."

"Think about how I feel. At least Watchdog talks to you," Snapshot reminded Roadrunner. "How would you like it if he was ignoring you, along with the Chinese?"

Snapshot paused a moment and then said, "I know Whaleboat's not *really* ignoring me. He is just very busy right now. He's got a really tough and demanding job. It's probably the hardest job in the whole White House, because he's got to know everything about every-thing. He is expected to be the expert on whatever the press wants to grill him on at the daily briefings."

"Snapshot, you are amazing," Roadrunner told him. "You are always defending the fact that he is often difficult to deal with and very hard on those around him. I've seen him scream clear across a room at you and demand a package of Marlboros. I'd have hit him right in the mouth, just for starters, to make sure I had his attention, before I told him what to do with his damn cigarettes."

"I know, and I've said a few choice words under my breath, too, but making sure he's prepared is part of my job."

"Well, it's obvious he hasn't decided to concentrate too much on China until he absolutely has to. Besides, Whaleboat is too important to talk to us until the very last minute," Roadrunner said. "Then he'll panic and yank our chain and ask us fifty million questions so he won't be caught with his pants down in front of the American press corps."

They sipped and pondered this for a minute. Somehow, blowing off steam complaining about the White House big shots made them both feel better, and they laughed and went off to bed smiling. Roadrunner was so tired that he fell asleep immediately and didn't even notice that he didn't have a pillowcase on the lump of ticking under his head.

But Snapshot couldn't get to sleep. He tossed and turned and worried. He really did need to talk to Whaleboat. At three o'clock in the morning he got up and tiptoed out to the suitcase satellite.

"Crown, this is Peking calling Whaleboat," he told the White House Signal operator a few minutes later. It was two o'clock in the afternoon in Washington, and after a brief pause, Snapshot was actually talking to Whaleboat.

The next morning, Roadrunner was sipping Folgers, staring at the suitcase satellite, and waiting for Watchdog to come on the line. His dreams during the night had been about spies. Spies who really didn't know what they were doing, all alone in strange bars, trying to convince the bartender, who only spoke in unknown tongues, that they desperately needed to have ice cubes in their drink. It was 8:05 in Peking when the call came in. In Washington it was after seven in the evening.

WATCHDOG: Roadrunner, Watchdog.
ROADRUNNER: Watchdog, this is Roadrunner. Good evening.
WATCHDOG: Good morning, how are you this morning?
ROADRUNNER: Very fine, sir. Had a pleasant rest. I trust that you've had a nice day at the office. [*After only three days in China, Roadrunner was already picking up the Chinese habit of exchanging pleasantries before getting down to business.*]
WATCHDOG: That's correct and we're still here. Let me ask you, do you have a steno in there with you?

ROADRUNNER: That's a negative, they are both in bed this morning with a fever.

WATCHDOG: OK. I hope that we'll go slow so that you can take some notes as we get into all of this, but we need to obviously get them up to par in order to be able to transmit any of this material over the radio. Let me start by saying that Bill Henkel is with me, we have you on a speaker phone. Be advised that Duval has departed for San Francisco and on the circle in order to get to your location.

ROADRUNNER: Roger, roger, I understand, and I hope he has a good journey and takes care of himself.

WATCHDOG: We have made it emphatically clear that he is to do so and so are the others, as best we can, to avoid situations such as you've run into there.

ROADRUNNER: That is a roger. I am convinced in my own mind that is why those of us that came the way we came are in such good health. [*Another pitch for commercial airline travel.*]

WATCHDOG: OK, Roadrunner. Let me ask you since the last time we talked around midnight your time, whether or not there have been any developments.

ROADRUNNER: Watchdog, that is a negative. I, shortly thereafter, went to bed and everything has remained the same throughout the evening.

WATCHDOG: The only point I want to make right now is that I understand that around 2:00 in the afternoon our time, which would be 3:00 in the morning your time, that Timmie was talking to Whaleboat. I think you ought to talk to him about making sure he stays up on his sleep.

ROADRUNNER: I understand exactly what you're saying. Be advised that he did remain at the hotel yesterday afternoon and rested and through the course of last evening did a considerable amount of work. I have not seen Snapshot this morning.

WATCHDOG: OK. I have talked with General Haig and we have come up with an idea which may be helpful to your situation there regarding our transmission of various documents and I would like to describe that. OK?

ROADRUNNER: I trust that General Haig is in good health and please give him my regards. I am waiting for any suggestions.

WATCHDOG: We feel that perhaps we should set up a joint communications room with the People's Republic of China for the purpose of working out the various logistical details of this trip. This would be an office where we have communication to prepare and receive cable traffic so both countries will know what is going back and forth and what the various problems are. We feel that we could transmit rooming lists, names and passport numbers and all of these details working in conjunction with the Chinese government in a joint facility. [*In other words, they were inviting the Chinese to openly monitor all communications.*]

ROADRUNNER: Roger sir, I would like to repeat and have you confirm your last transmission. The transmission was that I approach my counterpart and offer a joint communications center, where we could receive traffic and send our traffic, with them monitoring. Did you copy?

WATCHDOG: Roadrunner, I would say that it is a joint communications room for the purpose of working out the logistical arrangements.

ROADRUNNER: I understand. I am attempting to get Major Swift. As I understand it, the communications center may be the only way we can receive the equipment that we so vitally need. At some point in time, we could pull back the communications center and use it for the President as we normally do when traveling and carry on our normal work activity at a determined point just prior to Searchlight's arrival. I will attempt with Major Swift to sell that very early this morning.

WATCHDOG: Ron, I understand and I would say that immediately prior, to whatever date you agree to, to the President's arrival, it shifts, and it serves the function as it normally does, as a Presidential communication center rather than a joint countries communication center.

ROADRUNNER: I am talking to Major Swift, and he has raised a point that it would be a non-secure circuit and would be non-crypto. Did you copy?

WATCHDOG: I copy on that, but I think that what we could do is use the crypto with both parties reading the messages coming in, that way at least between your party, the government there and the White House here, at least we would have communication and can pass information more securely than we can over the air waves. As far as we are concerned, that would solve a problem and we have nothing, I repeat, we have nothing at all to send to you that we would not want the People's Republic to read.

ROADRUNNER: That's a roger, sir, I understand. I have made that point. However, I have not made the offer that you have just suggested of a joint communications center.

WATCHDOG: OK. Well, I would make that approach, and I think they would understand that it is different than any individual country operating their own facility separate from something the People's Republic of China is involved in.

ROADRUNNER: I have just ascertained from Major Swift that we can set that TELEX up without the crypto equipment, and operate in a normal fashion and incur no problems, repeat, no problems with the PRC. [*Swift meant no technical problems.*]

WATCHDOG: OK, you mean you already know that from them?

ROADRUNNER: I'm sorry, say again, please.

WATCHDOG: Have you already been told that from them?

ROADRUNNER: No, sir, I have not made that approach to the PRC.

WATCHDOG: You just said, Major Swift told you that you could set this up and not incur a problem. Do you already know that for a fact?

ROADRUNNER: That's a negative, sir, we do not know if it will be a problem for them. I have not raised the subject.

WATCHDOG: OK, I think that when you talk to the People's Republic, you are better off using the crypto with their knowledge and their understanding, and then we will share all of the information.

ROADRUNNER: We will have a direct circuit from our communications center, minus the cryptographic equipment, directly to the comm center at the White House Communications Agency there at the White House. I see no problem. With your permission and with General Redman's I would like to approach it in that manner today.

WATCHDOG: OK. Go ahead on that. Let's move off and see if they are agreeable.

ROADRUNNER: OK, I am ready to go with anything else you've got.

WATCHDOG: Roadrunner, let me say, I have a lot of information here that goes on and on in terms of names of people and the airplane numbers. I can either give that to you now if it will be helpful or we can wait and see if maybe it would work to TWX it tomorrow, or late tonight your time.

ROADRUNNER: Major Swift says that he feels his counterparts from the communications side will be very anxious to work hand and hand with him and his people along those lines. If that is the case, my first gut reaction is, I think that I can sell that also. Therefore, realizing we are going to possibly lose another day, it will save time, because we have to leave here at 9:00 for a survey. I will try to sell that first thing this morning and then hopefully, by morning your time, we will be able to receive that traffic.

WATCHDOG: What we will do is leave all of these names and numbers at our communications center here, so that if during the day you get your facility operating, they can send it to you during our nighttime.

ROADRUNNER: I copy. That's very good. I hope it works!

WATCHDOG: Roadrunner, we have reviewed our numbers extensively. We keep ending up, in all of our addition, with three, repeat, three more people total than our original list.

ROADRUNNER: We have continued to update and check our figures. Mike is sitting with me now and we feel that we're in good shape. We have a total right now of 390. Do you copy?

WATCHDOG: I copy and I think we come out with 393, so we've got a discrepancy either on your end or our end, and we will leave it up to you to sort out there because you know more about it than we do. I admit that I'm confused on it and I'll leave it to you to work out.

ROADRUNNER: Yes, sir, I understand. I will do that. Anything else?

WATCHDOG: Yes. Do we know yet if the PRC will permit three executive producers and two photo technicians to arrive in Shanghai on the tenth?

ROADRUNNER: That is a negative. Snapshot has been working on that problem, along with my help, and at this point we have not gotten final approval.

WATCHDOG: We need an answer by tomorrow if we are to alert them in order to make their travel arrangements.

ROADRUNNER: Yes, sir, I understand that, however, be advised I cannot guarantee that answer in that period of time. My advice would be to put those men on a plane, similar to what we did with Chief Dunn, and hope that we get word somewhere en route.

WATCHDOG: OK. We would like to add Bill Small to that group.

ROADRUNNER: Yes, sir, we're aware of that. But be advised that it's extremely difficult.

WATCHDOG: OK. Well, we're just going to go ahead and pack them up and send them, and if they have to wait, then they have to wait.

ROADRUNNER: Yes, sir. I understand. Be advised that Snapshot has been working on that problem and he has been discussing it with Whaleboat.

WATCHDOG: I can run very quickly through the rooming assignment list for the Peking guest house where the President will stay and give you a new set of room numbers in case you are going to go out there today.

ROADRUNNER: Thank you. That would be very helpful, because I have been hesitant in accepting that invitation, as you can well imagine.

WATCHDOG: OK. Let's run through it and I'll go slow and I'll stop to ask, periodically, if you have any questions.

ROADRUNNER: Yes, I understand, thank you.

[*What followed was a lengthy exercise in futility as the President's appointments secretary and his premier advance man attempted to agree on a list of names and room numbers through the static of their satellite linkup.*]

ROADRUNNER: Watchdog, this is Roadrunner, you're fading in and out very badly, as well as breaking, and there is a great deal of interference.

WATCHDOG: Roadrunner, I will say it slowly that in room 201 we will put Taylor.

ROADRUNNER: Was that room 101 would be Bob Taylor?

WATCHDOG: Negative, that's 201.

ROADRUNNER: Roger, roger, I copy, 201 for Taylor.

WATCHDOG: OK. That's correct. That would take care of the President's villa. That is building 18.

ROADRUNNER: Watchdog, you will have to say again, please. [*The difficulty of trying to pass numbers and names over the satellite was frustrating for both men. Finally, Watchdog cried, "Uncle."*]

WATCHDOG: OK. We have other material that we can very easily TWX and I think we just ought to hold up. We will leave all this TWX traffic with the situation room in case you get your communications up. If that does not get started, you should plan on having a steno, if possible, for the phone call tomorrow morning.

ROADRUNNER: Yes, sir, I think I understand. If we are not successful today that we will have to go through that material over the phone, similar to this, tomorrow morning.

WATCHDOG: That is correct. Our feeling is that we would have one of the girls in the advance office give it to a steno.

ROADRUNNER: I understand. Thank you for thinking of me.

WATCHDOG: Can you tell me how Coffey is?

ROADRUNNER: Colonel Coffey had a pleasant night's rest, and as I understand it, there is a little improvement in his condition this morning. So I think that he'll be OK.

WATCHDOG: I have not contacted Sarah on purpose. [*Sarah Coffey was Vern's wife.*]

ROADRUNNER: I understand. I will ask him if he wants us to tell Sarah. I would think it would be better to wait until tomorrow morning.

WATCHDOG: We will do that. I think that Anne Walker went to Philadelphia. [*To see the new nephew!*]

ROADRUNNER: Yes, sir, I understand.

WATCHDOG: OK. I just wanted you to know where she was.

ROADRUNNER: Thank you very much. OK, how is everybody there?

WATCHDOG: Everybody's fine. Everybody in the White House keeps asking about you men all the time.

ROADRUNNER: Thank you very much. I'm sure that everyone is very appreciative of that.

WATCHDOG: We don't have anything else, Ron, I think we better let you get to work, hadn't we?

ROADRUNNER: Yes, sir, that would be very nice. I am hopeful that we'll have something to do.

WATCHDOG: Roger, I understand. Our best to all of the Americans and to our Chinese friends, and we will talk to you tomorrow morning.

ROADRUNNER: Yes, sir. Get a good night's sleep, give my best to your lovely wife and your family.

WATCHDOG: Let me add a personal note here now. If in the middle of the night our time if something would break or you need a question answered, don't ever hesitate to call either Bill or me. [*Dwight was famous for answering late night phone calls by lifting the receiver and immediately letting it drop back down, perhaps without waking up. So he was letting Roadrunner know he was getting ready for a late China call.*]

ROADRUNNER: Roger, I understand that. Thank you. However, to this point that has not been necessary.

CROWN: Roadrunner, Roadrunner, Crown.

ROADRUNNER: Crown, this is Roadrunner.

CROWN: We have you loud and clear yet. Is there anyone else there with traffic for this station, go ahead.

ROADRUNNER: Negative, Swift says negative. Thank you very much for your help this morning.

CROWN: Roger. Thank you very much. We'll be standing by for the next call.

ROADRUNNER: Roger, roger, we'll talk to you tonight.

CROWN: Roger, have a good day.

"That was nice," Roadrunner thought to himself. "Now even the dispatchers were dropping their always professional facade and telling him to have a nice day." Everyone seemed to be feeling the importance of this mission. It made Roadrunner proud to realize the men in China were being supported by their colleagues back in the White House. That thought was a great help to him as he and Fred Swift sat down with the Chinese and attempted to explain and sell the idea of a joint communications center.

Roadrunner had purchased several picture postcards, and using his book of Chinese phrases, he had written messages on them in Chinese characters. He stopped at the desk in the hotel lobby to buy some postage stamps so he could mail the cards to his daughters and his office. The desk clerk was very surprised to see that the postcards were written in Chinese. "Did you do that?" he asked Roadrunner.

"Yes, I wanted to send the message to the United States in Chinese," Roadrunner assured him.

The desk clerk studied the postcards a moment, and then he told Roadrunner, "You must have very smart parents."

Roadrunner was very taken with the clerk's remark. "Only in China," he thought to himself. "In America, people would have praised the one who had written it, but here in China, my smart parents get all the credit." He couldn't wait to tell his Mom and Dad.

CHAPTER VIII

COLONEL COFFEY IS STILL IN THE HOSPITAL

FEBRUARY 5, 1972

Roadrunner noticed that the Chinese were all wearing their "we are honored to have you as our guests" masks when he broached the subject of a joint communications center. He thought they were receptive to the idea, but it was almost impossible to tell what they were really thinking. He wondered if the gracious face of Mr. Chu would always remain in place. He vowed to watch them all very closely for signs of slippage. Perhaps he would get a lucky glimpse behind one or two, if they ever thought he was thinking of other things and not really watching them.

After a day surveying the gymnasium and the airport and a meeting at the transmission center, Roadrunner and Snapshot were ready for the conference call at ten o'clock that evening. It was nine in the morning in Washington.

WHALEBOAT: This is Ziegler on the line. [*He was patched in from the President's residence in Key Biscayne.*]

SNAPSHOT: Whaleboat, Whaleboat, this is Snapshot! [*Snapshot couldn't believe his good fortune. A real live Whaleboat on the line!*]

WHALEBOAT: I copy you, Snapshot.

SNAPSHOT: Whaleboat, let me go over a few things with you here while we are waiting. I just now walked out of a meeting with our counterpart and we have been advised of the following things. Do you want the good news or the bad news?

WHALEBOAT: I don't know if we should be talking now; they are trying to pipe this other thing up.

SNAPSHOT: That's a roger, we'll wait. (sigh!)

CROWN: Carnation, Carnation, Crown.

CARNATION: Crown, Carnation, go ahead.

WATCHDOG: Good evening, Ron, I want you to be advised that we have everyone here in Washington again this morning, plus we have Ziegler on the line in Florida.

ROADRUNNER: Snapshot was just speaking with Whaleboat. Our regards to Whaleboat.

WATCHDOG: Let me ask you first off for a medical report.

ROADRUNNER: The two stenographers are in better condition this evening. Colonel Coffey is still in the hospital, and we have had one additional person admitted to the hospital this evening. He is with the Hughes earth station, his name is George Thiede.

WATCHDOG: Does Vern Coffey want General Scowcroft to call Sarah and advise her of his condition?

ROADRUNNER: General Tkach is making that contact. [*Walter Tkach, the President' doctor.*]

WATCHDOG: OK. Ron, do you have any dermatological problems? [*A rash from poisonous sumac lacquer on the hotel toilet seats that came to be known as "Baboon Syndrome."*]

ROADRUNNER: That is a negative, we have had no problems.

WATCHDOG: OK, Roadrunner, I think the next thing we would like to do is get a report of your day.

ROADRUNNER: After our conversation, we had a meeting with my counterpart and Major Swift. We proposed the offer that we had discussed early this morning. I believe they were receptive. They asked a lot of questions. Major Swift was able to provide information for them. They realize the sense of urgency.

We were due to depart at 9:30 for the gymnasium. My counterpart was not available when we left for the gymnasium. We did the survey, along with the technicians and Mr. Livingood and his men. In the meantime, Schrauth went to the commune and did that survey on behalf of Mrs. Nixon. At 2:00 Schrauth left for the hospital, and at 2:30 we left for the airport to do a survey of the arrival, repeat, the arrival only.

We then had an opportunity to go by the transmission center and meet with some of those people there. That is it for the most part. Elbourne has met with his people and I believe he wants to talk to Whaleboat, at a convenient time.

WATCHDOG: We will let that call follow immediately after this call. Now, going back to the meeting you had after our call this morning your time, we have had no further word from the PRC, is that correct?

ROADRUNNER: That is *absolutely* correct. I have not seen Mr. Chu again. I have received no word all day. I do have a piece of information that shortly after my meeting this morning, with my counterpart, he was seen leaving with Mr. Han Hsu.

WATCHDOG: You do feel that they understand the arrangement and perhaps will be agreeable?

ROADRUNNER: (pause) I think the answer to that is yes. I don't know when.

WATCHDOG: OK. I understand. We want to make one point if you talk to them on that particular subject. That we go to the secure facility, the crypto portion, the day that Searchlight [*The President*] would depart Washington, because of the fact that traffic may start coming in which will be confidential and would have to be held for Searchlight or Woodcutter [*Henry Kissinger*] or Welcome's [*H. R. Haldeman*] arrival.

ROADRUNNER: I appreciate you bringing that to our attention. However, it's extremely difficult to even get the facility, much less start putting ground rules on it.

WATCHDOG: But in terms of laying out the points of principle and determining where we can and we cannot be flexible, I think perhaps you should introduce that subject when appropriate and as early as possible so they can be considering it.

ROADRUNNER: I understand what you are saying and I will keep that in mind.

WATCHDOG: Now, we were going to release the press list on the seventh, but we are now going to move that to the ninth, and we want you to be so advised so that Snapshot can advise the counterpart there. I do not believe that has changed. Is that correct, Ziegler? (pause) Let's just move ahead and make sure Tim checks that point with Ziegler. In terms of the C-141 that's going to loop over from Shanghai into Hangchou, we told you last night that you had eighteen seats there and you asked for six more. That is going to be very difficult, and we need to know who, and why you need those seats, and how desperately you need them.

ROADRUNNER: Well, to be specific, the reason we need them is because we are taking half of the technician corps with us. Watchdog, be advised that Snapshot is getting us a list. The Chinese guests will be no more than three to five people. Right now Snapshot is planning on taking somewhere in the vicinity of ten and twelve people, counting himself.

WATCHDOG: Well, I would say that we should work to get that list lower, perhaps, or we would work on having them go by some other means of transportation, such as the train which we took.

ROADRUNNER: I understand.

WATCHDOG: We will hold with eighteen and you see what you can work out within that and then advise us if you see that is absolutely impossible. Then we will have to meet here again and see what we can do.

ROADRUNNER: I understand the problem. I will talk with Snapshot and see if we can stay within the eighteen seats.

WATCHDOG: Now, after this phone conversation, and after Whaleboat talks with Snapshot, we want to relay to you quite a bit of information, in terms of people and passport numbers and airplane numbers, and so forth, and we can put Julie [*Julie Rowe from the advance office*] on the phone to give it to someone on that end. Who do you have to take it down?

ROADRUNNER: Well, we'll find someone.

WATCHDOG: OK. Well you might want to have someone get to work on that so we can follow up before it gets too late over there. Our concern here is sending people into Shanghai and into Hangchou and leaving them without any form of communication, and this is something we will talk about at this end over the next day or so and determine whether or not we should be leaving aircraft on the ground or what we should do until we get some kind of communication with those people.

ROADRUNNER: I'm going to put Major Swift on. He also had a meeting with his counterpart at great length today. He has been assured of certain things and I'll let him cover those points.

SWIFT: Be advised, in my meeting with the counterparts, they did agree to have one voice circuit and one teletype circuit available from Shanghai and Hangchou to Peking upon arrival of the advance party.

WATCHDOG: Thank you. Now General Redman has a question.

REDMAN: Swift, Redman, who's equipment is this to be? Is this to be our equipment, one teletype and one voice, or equipment to be provided by the PRC?

SWIFT: I assume at this end in Peking it will be our equipment, and hopefully it will be our equipment at that end, but nonetheless I think the voice, even if it is an instrument for openers, will suffice.

REDMAN: How about extending this then from Peking back to Washington? [*Swift thinks "extending this" means the suitcase satellite hook-up they are now using.*]

SWIFT: Yes, that is the idea. From Shanghai back to Washington it would be extended through Peking and from Hangchou it would be extended through Shanghai and Peking back to Washington.

REDMAN: When can we set up the Peking to Washington circuit?

SWIFT: We are talking on it right now.

REDMAN: I am talking about the teletype.

SWIFT: I don't know. This was the meeting that we had this morning, which Mr. Walker was referring to earlier, where we proposed the joint operation, and as yet, as he already said, we have not had a reply.

REDMAN: I'm confused. I thought earlier you indicated that the PRC had agreed to one teletype circuit and one voice circuit from Hangchou to Shanghai to Peking. Is that correct? [*For communications experts, Redman and Swift sometimes seemed to have trouble communicating.*]

SWIFT: That is correct. They agreed that there will be one voice circuit and one teletype circuit available from those two cities to Peking, upon arrival of the advance party. The arrival of the advance party is a week from now.

REDMAN: But do they also acknowledge that there would be one teletype and one voice back to Washington, at the same time?

SWIFT: That is a negative. I say again, they agreed to have one voice circuit and one teletype circuit from Shanghai and Hangchou to Peking upon arrival of the advance party in those two cities. And that is all they agreed to.

WATCHDOG: Well, at least we know you can talk among yourselves there, and I think that should be done in a cooperative effort with the People's Republic just as we wish to do between Washington and Peking.

SWIFT: I feel quite certain that by the time we are in Shanghai and Hangchou with our advance parties that we will have both our teletype and voice working back to Washington.

WATCHDOG: Yep, Fred, I hope you are absolutely right, but I hope we get it much sooner than that, as I am sure you do.

SWIFT: I couldn't agree more.

WATCHDOG: Roger, can we hear for a moment, is everything going OK as far as Livingood is concerned?

LIVINGOOD: This is Livingood. I have not really had many meetings with them. We discussed a few things today and asked for a brief explanation of security at the airport and was really refused

much information. They just said they would take care of it. I have
not heard on my end the ones that we wrote to them about.

WATCHDOG: We understand, Bill. Be advised that Keiser is here
this morning and he noted that. [*U.S. Secret Service agent, Dick
Keiser.*] OK, Roadrunner. Going back to the original conversation
that we had about the possibility of a doctor coming in this weekend:
Our advice here seems to be negative on that and to leave all the
matters with Chief Dunn and in the good hands of the Chinese
doctors. Are you agreeable? [*They were afraid it would be a huge
insult to the Chinese, if the Americans asked to bring in an American
doctor.*]

ROADRUNNER: Yes sir, one hundred percent. I have not even
raised the question.

WATCHDOG: OK, fine. Do you have any points that you wish to
raise?

ROADRUNNER: We have, up to this point, prepared eight scenarios
[*detailed descriptions of events from the President's arrival to departure*]
that I am in a position to discuss at great length with the People's
Republic of China. I am going to request any suggestions they have
regarding these scenarios. They are very sketchy. The information is
predicated on our survey and with very little input from their side, so
most of the information is nothing more than a site survey and a
guess and a by golly on our side.

WATCHDOG: OK, I understand and we are structuring the schedule
material with the fact in mind that we just may not have all of the
details prior to our arrival.

ROADRUNNER: Yes sir, I'm informed that by the time Searchlight
arrives everything will be in shape and everything that the President
needs will in fact be done.

WATCHDOG: Are they aware of our departure date from Washington and the need to have materials ready prior to departure?

ROADRUNNER: Sir, I have tried very hard to make that point, and
have been told that everything will be in order for the President. I
am confident, as is everyone in this room, that there is going to be
no problem when the President arrives. And Livingood points out
that his counterpart asked him the status of any security support for
the Secretary of State?

WATCHDOG: Are they amenable to an addition for someone to
handle that?

ROADRUNNER: That's a negative. We have not even approached
that question at this point.

WATCHDOG: Roger. Right now we have, as you know, with the
Secretary, one aide, we would like to put in close proximity to him at
the various guest houses where he will stay. By close proximity I

mean across the hall or as adjacent as possible, to a bedroom for two of our men that are working with Livingood so that if there were a need at least somebody would be near by but it would be unofficial in terms of strict coverage.

ROADRUNNER: Roger, I have asked Livingood that and he says he understands, but it would not be their primary responsibility.

WATCHDOG: We understand. The Secretary is aware of our decision on this and concurs and has asked that we do our best to place his aide, and the three people acting as interpreters as close to him as possible and I think we have that accomplished looking over the rooming assignments.

ROADRUNNER: Is it still contemplated that you will bring three interpreters?

WATCHDOG: Yes it is and we have their names for you which we will relay to you during the 11:00 phone call your time tonight, and we will give you passport numbers for two of them. The third we should have the start of next week.

WHALEBOAT: Chapin, Whaleboat, do you read?

ROADRUNNER: Whaleboat, this is Roadrunner, you are almost un-readable. We are going to try and place this call again, and it will come through in a few minutes. If you are there, fine. If not, we'll go ahead and discuss the information with the other people and continue on with the other phone calls. This is Roadrunner out.

WATCHDOG: Whaleboat, Watchdog.

WHALEBOAT: Elbourne has some information he wants to pass to me. I can read him loud and clear and can take that. I am anxious to get the decisions he has.

SNAPSHOT: Number one point, the three producers have been approved to enter the People's Republic of China on the tenth.

WHALEBOAT: The three producers have been approved to enter the PRC on the tenth.

SNAPSHOT: Whaleboat, it is the wrong time this evening to bring up the other party. [*The request to bring Bill Small in early.*]

WHALEBOAT: That is a roger. Do you have answers on the wire service technicians?

SNAPSHOT: That is a negative. We have asked about that several times today. Roadrunner has asked about it, I have asked about it several times. They indicate that the decision will come to us in due course.

WHALEBOAT: Have you informed Siegenthaler of the third country matter you have just explained?

SNAPSHOT: That's a negative, I just got out of the meeting and wanted to talk to you on this patch.

WHALEBOAT: You should get to him soonest on that.

SNAPSHOT: I will, but I did want to talk to you.

WHALEBOAT: Do you have anything else?

SNAPSHOT: Let me continue. You might inform the networks that the PRC will allow each network two vehicles only, one mini bus and one car, per network.

WHALEBOAT: Repeat that whole message, Tim.

SNAPSHOT: The PRC will allow the networks two vehicles per network. The two vehicles will be composed of one mini bus and one automobile.

WHALEBOAT: Roger.

SNAPSHOT: On the President's toast at the banquet, I indicated that we have no objection to having the toast broadcast or filmed or taped. Is that correct?

WHALEBOAT: I will have to get back to you on that. [*Snapshot is surprised by this response.*]

SNAPSHOT: I would like to reconstruct. That's the impression you gave them the last time we were here.

WHALEBOAT: That's a roger.

SNAPSHOT: I'd like that soonest, Ron. They are making a decision currently on that. Also, we will have only four press vehicles in motorcade.

WHALEBOAT: Roger.

SNAPSHOT: There will be four people per automobile.

WHALEBOAT: Roger.

SNAPSHOT: They will make necessary provisions for press staff to travel in the motorcades.

WHALEBOAT: Roger.

SNAPSHOT: Major point, and the last point I have. There will be no, repeat no, absolutely no radio photo transmission from the airport. Over.

WHALEBOAT: Why?

SNAPSHOT: They indicate to us it is very difficult for them to perform this task, and we will have to hold the film until we get to the hotel where provisions have been made. It is an *absolute* no.

WHALEBOAT: Roger.

SNAPSHOT: This was a point that we approached very logically with them, they understood the point completely, and initially they sympathized with this point. However, this evening they said it was a firm no.

WHALEBOAT: Tim, have you been able to check whether or not we will have some courier flight service out of the PRC during the five days in Peking?

SNAPSHOT: I have not brought that up. I am waiting to see the situation in Shanghai and Hangchou.

WHALEBOAT: There is a need to have at least one courier flight, if possible, out of China, for the first five days, in order to ship color film.

SNAPSHOT: We will bring that up tomorrow. Can you give me a date you would like that courier to go?

WHALEBOAT: I will check. I would think we would want it on the fourth day.

SNAPSHOT: That's Thursday, the twenty-fourth in China, that would be in the United States, Wednesday the twenty-third.

WHALEBOAT: (pause) Roger.

SNAPSHOT: I will make that request. One thing more, Ron, I heard Dwight say that you had decided to release the press names on February 9. Is that correct?

WHALEBOAT: That is correct, but I need their answer.

SNAPSHOT: We will have to re-approach the PRC because we indicated the seventh as a result of the memo we received earlier.

WHALEBOAT: We are delaying because we do not have an answer from them.

SNAPSHOT: I understand. There is another problem as you know, Ron. It is important that these applications are processed properly or we'll be in deep . . . do you understand? [*The PRC required the press to complete applications containing their "personal particulars" that were signed seven days in advance.*]

WHALEBOAT: Do you have an answer for me on the question I raised yesterday regarding the applications?

SNAPSHOT: I do not have an answer, but the answer we received last time was seven days before would be fine.

WHALEBOAT: I asked yesterday if in some cases the application could be signed on arrival, but presented seven days ahead.

SNAPSHOT: I understand the request, Ron. However, I feel that it would be best, at another time, to raise those kinds of questions.

WHALEBOAT: That's a roger.

SNAPSHOT: I guarantee you that if we can do anything to reach the more difficult personnel in advance, to have them at least fill out an application, we would be way ahead of the game. [*Snapshot was worrying about members of the press corps giving the PRC a rough time.*]

WHALEBOAT: That's a roger.

SNAPSHOT: Well, that's about all I have right now. We are proceeding very well with the technical surveys; we have suggested camera positions to them, in drawing form; we have suggested press pools to them, in drawing form; and they will get back to us on their answers on these.

WHALEBOAT: That's a roger. I have two questions. Any word on Small?

SNAPSHOT: I said at the beginning of the conversation, this is the wrong time to bring up this point. [*Does the man ever listen?*]
WHALEBOAT: That's a roger, but the three executive producers will proceed.
SNAPSHOT: That's exactly right.
WHALEBOAT: I'll talk to you later. Whaleboat out.

Snapshot cast a discouraged look toward Roadrunner, who had overheard his exchange with Whaleboat. Roadrunner knew that Snapshot would have appreciated a "thank you" or a "great job" from his boss, but that was not Whaleboat's nature. The White House press secretary, efficient and loyal as he was, was not the world's most gregarious man under normal circumstances, and it was no doubt hard for the staff still in Washington to understand how isolated the advance team felt.

Roadrunner took it upon himself to perk his friend up. "Come on Snapshot. We've got an important experiment going on here and we've got to check it out," he said.

The sparkle came back into Snapshot's eyes. He knew immediately what Roadrunner meant. "You're exactly right," he said. "It is one of the more important aspects of our being in China."

That morning they had gotten some of the Chinese newspapers from the hall attendant and wrapped them around the ice tray. They thought the newsprint might keep out the pollution without drooping and absorbing all the water.

They hurried to the window sill and looked outside, hoping for clear, clean ice. Roadrunner reached out and pulled the newspaper-wrapped tray toward him. Water sloshed out and soaked his sleeve from wrist to elbow.

"Can you believe that?" he yelled at Snapshot. "It insulated the water from the cold and didn't freeze. After the whole damned day in this freeze-your-ass-off-cold!" Roadrunner was really mad now. There had to be a way to solve the ice problem.

Sipping scotch, neat, they vowed to find the answer. Maybe they couldn't control the Chinese, but by god they could figure out how to make ice, even if it harelipped Uncle Sam and Cousin Confucius! The reputation of American ingenuity was at stake now.

They headed off for bed and got a few hours of sleep before they were awakened abruptly. . . . The hotel was on fire!

CHAPTER IX

FIRE!

FEBRUARY 6, 1972

From the pitch black darkness of his hotel room, Roadrunner heard a strange voice. When he looked up he saw nothing but underwear.

He blinked his eyes and strained to see more clearly. He was looking at a T-shirt and boxer shorts towering above him. Then he heard the voice again and looked up at the white teeth talking to him. Chief Warrant Officer Ralph Douglas was telling him it was almost four o'clock in the morning and the hotel was on fire.

"Oh my God," he groaned as he jumped out of bed and ran to alert the other Americans on the floor. He yelled at Schrauth on the other side of the sitting room, "Mike, hurry, there's a fire." He ran across the hall to wake up Manning and Snapshot. Snapshot was not in his room. Where the hell was he at that hour?

He woke up Manning and ran back to make sure Schrauth was awake. He got there just as Schrauth was hurrying into the sitting room and watched him wedge the table leg squarely between the fourth and fifth toes of his right foot. Schrauth yelled, grabbed his toe and started to hop around on his other foot. The look on his face was a combination of pain and panic. The fact that he was in his skivvies made the slightly balding, former basketball player look

like something out of a Three Stooges movie. Roadrunner realized
that he really didn't have time to laugh. He hoped that the pain
would subside soon and Schrauth could quit howling and hopping
around and start thinking about getting the hell out of the hotel.

Roadrunner ran out in the hall to alert the other men. The hall
was completely engulfed in smoke. None of the doors were visible,
but he ran a short way, banging on the wall and then the doors as he
moved down the hall. After what seemed like a very long time, he
knew he had found the room where the fire had started. He ran into
the room and his toe hit a glass bottle. He bent down to pick it up
and realized it was an empty vodka bottle. He felt all around his feet
for more, and picked up a wad of hand-rolled cigarettes.

He quickly moved out of the room and realized he was sloshing
in water. Chinese voices, high-pitched and urgent, were all around
him. People were running, fire hoses had been removed from the
ancient wall racks and were everywhere. He tripped over a huge hose
as he tried to run back down the hall. He looked down at the fire
hose and became more horrified. It was a field of fountains. Water
was squirting out of it from hundreds of holes. Thin streams of water
were hitting his legs, his shoes and small rivulets were streaming down
the hotel walls. More people were coming into the hall and the
sounds of English began to mingle with the Chinese.

He had to hide the bottle and what he later discovered were
marijuana cigarettes. He had to get to the suitcase satellite. He had
to get word to Washington. The smoke was so thick in the hall that
he ducked into a room, took his handkerchief out of his pocket, wet
it and put it over his nose and mouth. He moved down the hall,
sloshing through the water and dodging the Chinese fire fighters who
seemed to be moving in all directions now. He thought about the
Chinese fire drill jokes and how this was not one bit funny because
it was not a drill. He entered the room where the WHCA team was
attempting to dismantle their equipment, and directed them to send
one last message to the White House. The satellite crackled to life
and he said, "This is Roadrunner. There is a fire in the hotel . . .
repeat, a fire in the hotel. We are evacuating immediately. This is
Roadrunner out."

Roadrunner ran back to his room and grabbed a suitcase. He
started to throw things into it and was surprised to find himself
thinking how useless some of his things really were. He packed
hurriedly and grabbed the heavy, quilted overcoat the networks had
given him. As he started to leave the room, he grabbed a bottle of
scotch. He could hear the sirens of arriving fire engines outside.
Inside Schrauth had quit hollering and was calling to him to hurry.
Manning went by, moving very fast. Roadrunner saw Snapshot arrive

and wondered again where he could have been. This was the second night in a row. He suddenly realized he was also very concerned about Snapshot.

Roadrunner grabbed the phone and tried to call Siegenthaler. There was no answer. The men were all moving out into the hall now. They all had suitcases and their jackets and as they reached the stairs, they found the double doors chained and padlocked! Roadrunner's mind began to race even faster, "My god! Is this the only fire escape? We're on the sixth floor. Are we going to perish in this fire? What will happen to the President's trip?" He took his suitcase and began to beat the door with it. The glass broke. He hit the door harder and harder. The cheap Sears suitcase was not made for this kind of abuse and it was falling apart, but luckily the wood began to splinter. Finally they were able to remove the chains and they pushed the doors open. They started down the staircase, dragging their belongings and climbing over the chairs and tables that were blocking their way. Roadrunner could not believe that the stairwell was evidently being used as a storage area for excess furniture. "I will have to voice a formal complaint," he thought to himself, "if we make it."

Suddenly, Mr. Fu, one of Mr. Chu's aides, was calling to him, "Mr. Walker, Mr. Walker, come with me please." Roadrunner told the other men to try and make it outside and get some fresh air. He went back up a few steps to the sixth floor and was escorted down the hall. The firemen were still moving back and forth, the fire hoses still squirting in all directions. The smokey haze gave the impression of an old black and white movie; the scene was chaotic and comical and unreal and frightening. They arrived at the room where the fire had begun. There was a fire marshall at the door, not letting anyone in or out, but he stepped aside when he saw Roadrunner approach with Mr. Fu. It was obvious that the fire had begun in this room and it had begun in the bed. It was a mess. Everything was sopping wet and charred: the pillow, the bedding, the chair, the desk, the walls, and even the curtains.

"Whose room is this?" Roadrunner asked. Then he saw Mr. Chu. They were both looking at the same horrible scene.

"One of the members of your American party. He has been burned," Mr. Chu said.

Roadrunner bowed slightly to Mr. Chu and said, "Please accept my sincerest concern for this terrible accident. The firemen and fire marshals have done an excellent job of extinguishing this fire in such a short length of time. They have been most efficient."

Roadrunner returned to his room and people began to gather immediately. Major Swift, Hank Gibbons, Schrauth, Livingood,

Snapshot, and the Chief Warrant Officer. Word had spread quickly that one of the Americans had been burned and they had hurried back to the sixth floor. Roadrunner learned that the burn victim had been taken to Chief Dunn's room. He also learned that all of the network people were down in the parking lot. As he always did when he traveled, Siegenthaler had conducted a fire drill the second day they were in the hotel. The reason he did not answer the phone when Roadrunner called was because he was already headed for the parking lot. The more Roadrunner got to know Bob Siegenthaler, the more he liked and respected the man.

Almost immediately, Roadrunner was summoned to the sitting room down the hall, where Director Han Hsu wished to speak with him. Roadrunner entered the sitting room and Han Hsu, with no initial exchange of pleasantries, asked that the burned American also join them. Roadrunner told him that the man was is in no condition to undergo an investigation. "I am very sorry, but that will have to wait until tomorrow." He could tell that they were very concerned, very upset and yes, probably scared. They asked Roadrunner to please go and talk to the burned man again and report back on his condition.

Roadrunner returned to Chief Dunn's room, where the injured man told him that he must have fallen asleep with a cigarette in his hand. When he awoke, there were flames in his eyes and he tried unsuccessfully to put them out with his pillow. The flames moved down to the ground and he ran out of the room.

Roadrunner took his notes and went back to the sitting room once again. He reported on his conversation and again expressed his deep concern about the fire and complimented the hotel floor staff, as well as all the firemen. Mr. Chu and Mr. Han Hsu expressed their concern as well, and Roadrunner realized they must have been staying in the hotel. There would not have been time to summon them from anywhere else. "That explains why he saw Mr. Chu and Director Han Hsu leaving together yesterday when he was buying stamps for his postcards," he thought.

Roadrunner returned to his room and more questions raced through his mind. "Where had the burned man gone when he ran out of the room and why had he not alerted the other Americans to the fire?" Roadrunner did not tell anyone that the victim had been drinking and smoking marijuana.

"Shit," he thought to himself. "Just when I was feeling so good about the way all the Americans have been conducting themselves. We do not need to give the Chinese one, single, solitary reason to stall or keep things from us, or instruct us on how to behave in their country."

Roadrunner suggested that everyone call their counterparts in Washington. He realized what his last transmission must be doing to them on the other side of the world.

Watchdog's pager went off while he was walking down M Street in Georgetown. It was a bitterly cold winter day in Washington, the kind when everything looks a dreary gray and people tend to feel the same way inside. It's hard to remember what green trees looked like and it seems as though it will never be sunny and warm again. He stopped at a phone booth and called the White House Signal switchboard.

"There is a fire in the hotel in Peking, sir. Roadrunner's message was that they were evacuating immediately," the signal operator told him.

Watchdog was stunned. "How bad is it? Oh dear God, keep those men safe," he prayed silently. He hurried back to the White House and waited.

When Roadrunner was able to reach Watchdog, he assured him that everyone was fine. The relief was evident in both their voices. They quickly agreed that the matter would not be discussed publicly. Too much was at stake. News of it could embarrass both countries.

When Roadrunner hung up the phone, Major Swift was waiting to tell him that Foreign Affairs Vice Minister Su Long was in the hotel and asking to see him. Roadrunner asked Bill Livingood and Major Swift to please accompany him to see the Vice Minister. The exchanges at the meeting were short and subdued, reflecting the seriousness which they all felt about the incident.

Roadrunner had only been back in his room for a few minutes when there was a knock on his door and Mr. Chu and Mr. Fu entered. They said they had come to express their concern and to say that no one should be alarmed about the Vice Minister's presence in the hotel. Mr. Su had come simply to express his concern and to look over the situation. Roadrunner was repeatedly asked not to be alarmed and to tell the other members of his party not to be alarmed. Mr. Chu and Mr. Fu also suggested that everyone involved keep this matter among themselves and not make a big incident of it. It would be unfortunate if it should become talked about in the International newspapers and on the television programs.

Roadrunner suddenly realized the incredible significance of this whole situation. Not only were one hundred Americans living in this hotel, but evidently so was Vice Minister Su Long and Director Han Hsu and probably hundreds of their deputies and staff assistants. All the officials who were making themselves so scarce when difficult questions arose were in fact under the Americans' noses all the time.

A short time later, Mr. Chu telephoned to say they would be changing the departure time to the Great Wall. They would now depart at 10:30 A.M. Since it had never been definite that they would be going to the Great Wall that day, it was quite an interesting phone call. "Incredible," Roadrunner thought. "Maybe the last few hours have made everyone realize just how much was at stake here. Maybe the fire did more than wake us up. It scared the hell out of me, and it looks like it did the same to just about everyone else in this damn hotel. Do the Chinese have any idea what a fire trap they have allowed this place to become? My God, if they had not been able to put that fire out so quickly, or if it had spread more rapidly, . . . no fire escapes, stairwells padlocked shut and filled with furniture, rotten fire hoses . . ." He forced his mind to stop racing. The thought of what could have happened was overwhelming. He shut his eyes and took a deep breath. "Stop it," he told himself. "It's over. Everyone is safe. We are going to the Great Wall today. Think of it, the Great Wall of China."

"OK, gentlemen, let's get to work!" he said out loud. "I am really looking forward to this trip to the Great Wall today. And is there somewhere I could stop and do some shopping? I need to buy a Chinese suitcase."

The Americans and their Chinese hosts set off for a long drive across the countryside to the Great Wall of China. There was great excitement. They were finally going to be doing something, going somewhere, making progress toward putting a schedule of events together for the President and Mrs. Nixon. It was as though the hotel fire earlier in the morning had jolted everyone into action.

The Chinese presented them with a huge box of Chinese shoes with crepe soles and large, heavy-quilted coats with thick, fur-like collars and matching hats. At a distance they looked just like everybody else in China, just a little taller (especially Schrauth!), and the sight greatly amused them. They had to stifle the urge to point at each other and laugh uproariously at the spectacle they presented. They couldn't wait to take pictures of themselves.

The countryside was bleak, stark, and naked. It was wintertime and there were no leaves on the trees. As Roadrunner watched outside his window, he thought, "Here I am in China, here I am on the way to the Great Wall, one of the old seven wonders of the world." He knew a lot of people who would love to be making this trip, but most people couldn't even travel here on a vacation. It was not a question of money; Chinese visas were required for entry into the PRC and simply were not available in many western countries. He wondered if the President's trip would change that. He tried to visualize Americans staying at his hotel and tour groups going to the

The Great Wall.

Great Wall. It was too far-fetched to think about. He imagined what it must have been like thousands of years before when the emperors ruled and the countryside was populated by feudal landowners and countless slaves. It must have been quite a sight. It must have been quite a land, this most ancient of civilizations.

As they approached the mountains, he strained to catch a glimpse of the Wall. A Chinese train was moving across the country-side. A great deal of work was being done on the road and the motorcade had to make many detours. He was hopeful that the preparation was for the President's approaching visit.

Then all of a sudden, like a sleeping dragon across the high cliffs and mountains, the Great Wall appeared. It was an awesome sight, and he could hardly conceive of the effort that had been required to build it. He was told forced labor, along with donkeys

Snapshot on the road to the Ming Tombs.

and goats, was used to carry one stone at a time up the sides of those mountains. The two-thousand-year-old wall stretches for fifteen hundred miles, weaving in and out of sight as it spans the sheer cliffs and the deep ravines of the Yinshan mountain range. It has a foundation of huge granite slabs that supports walls of large brick. Roadrunner remembered how impressed he had been that the astronauts could see this, the world's oldest and largest engineering project, from space.

As the motorcade came to a stop at the driveway to the Pataling Section, one of the main sections of the Wall that was rebuilt during the Ming Dynasty, the Americans suddenly felt like a bunch of caged animals set free, or schoolchildren let out for recess. They giggled and laughed. This first excursion outside Peking turned them into tourists. They took pictures of the Wall and of their Chinese counterparts. They even photographed themselves photographing each other.

Roadrunner, wearing his sand boots, scaled the steep wall with ease. The Americans who had worn their leather-soled shoes slipped and had to give up the climb. Even the Chinese were falling on some

The advance team inside the Ming Tombs.

sections of the steep incline. Roadrunner recalled the boyhood game, "king of the mountain," when he was the first to reach the summit and survey the surroundings. The Chinese told him that those who have been to the Great Wall are heroes.

Roadrunner tried to go up still another very steep incline to an additional sentry post, but was told to come back so the group could stay on schedule. He was testing the boundaries, and it did not take long to find that they were not very wide. The Chinese were still a bit staid and stand-offish despite the feeling of shared adventure between the two groups. The sizing up continued.

The Ming Tombs were about a forty minute drive from the Great Wall. Thirteen of the emperors who ruled China from 1368 to 1644 were buried there, surrounded by low, purple mountains. Huge stone animals straddled the road at the main entrance to the tombs-- elephants, camels, donkeys, monkeys, and giraffes. The Americans thought it was a great photo opportunity and again tumbled out to take pictures. Indeed it would become an important photo opportunity for the President and Mrs. Nixon and for many other presidents and dignitaries on visits to come.

The picnic that followed was the highlight of the trip thus far and a feeling of teamwork began to replace the apprehension of the last few days. Roadrunner was excited about being able to report this to Watchdog. On the drive back to the hotel he thought about the evening's telephone call to Washington and then about the ice cubes waiting on the windowsill. They had decided to tent the newspaper over the tray. They had reasoned that this would let the cold air circulate and still keep out the pollution particles. He smiled into the rapidly approaching darkness outside the car window. "It's getting dark. Why doesn't the driver turn on his headlights?" he asked Mr. Chu.

"Because it isn't seven o'clock yet," was the reply.

"Dear Lord, help me understand their reasoning," Roadrunner silently prayed.

The line of cars wound into Peking, and Roadrunner watched the bicyclists struggle against the cold darkness as they peddled their way home. They stopped by the hospital to see how Vern Coffey was doing. Roadrunner hated hospitals under any circumstances, but the Chinese hospital made him feel like he had travelled back in time. It seemed very primitive by American standards, and it smelled like formaldehyde. The cinder block floors and walls were unpainted, and they were constantly being wet-mopped in a dismal attempt to keep the dust under control. Patients were fed by members of their families who were huddled over cooking pots in rooms at the end of each hall. The combination of cooking odors mingled with the stench of sickness and formaldehyde was almost more than his stomach could stand. He noticed that windows were open to let in some fresh air, even though it was brutally cold outside. Bedding and clothes were drying in some of the windows and metal hot water pots were perched on most of the radiators. Each hall had a common bathroom, and there were no privacy screens to shield patients who were being bathed or using bed pans.

Vern looked tired. He was very anxious to get out of the hospital and Roadrunner could see why. "Please let me stay healthy," he thought to himself, "and get out of town before I have to come to this place!"

They arrived back at the hotel and the conference call came in at 10:35. It was 9:35 in the morning in Washington.

WATCHDOG: Roadrunner, this is Watchdog. Good evening.
ROADRUNNER: Good morning to you. We've had a very nice day. A very relaxing day. We went to the Great Wall and to the Ming Tombs and I cannot begin to tell you what a nice day it was. Be advised, there was a meeting scheduled for tomorrow morning at 9:00,

however after returning from the hospital this evening and seeing Colonel Coffey, we were informed that the meeting could be this evening at 9:00. It was outstanding. Everything we've been waiting for was in black and white and Mr. Chu went point by point through every area and we are off and rolling.

WATCHDOG: Well, that's great, Ron. Can you give me some idea of the various points?

ROADRUNNER: Be advised, and I'm sure Elbourne will be calling Whaleboat very shortly, they have agreed to the press corps announcement tomorrow the seventh your time.

Also, they have agreed to increase the press to eighty-seven. But they made it very strong that there had been an agreement at one point and that we had gone against that agreement. I cannot emphasize the degree with which they made that point. [*The Chinese could not understand why the Americans changed this number after an agreement had been reached.*]

WATCHDOG: I understand thoroughly exactly what you are saying.

ROADRUNNER: So the eighty-seven are approved and the PRC are expecting their names to be released tomorrow.

WATCHDOG: Roger, I understand.

ROADRUNNER: They have also agreed to the twelfth, repeat the twelfth of February for announcement of the official party and possibly the unofficial party. There is no problem, but they prefer the twelfth. The next thing is on the fourteenth of February, they are agreeable to talking about a draft release. They would like it to be in general form, not specifying days or dates, just in general what the rough itinerary of Searchlight and Starlight would be.

WATCHDOG: Well, of course that's almost next to impossible. We've done that, as you well know. Now, I have drafted a statement, which is very nebulous, it uses words like tentative, possible, and so forth, indicating that it could change. What I would like to do, if we can get the TWX thing working, is send it to you to read over with them and then let us know if it's OK.

ROADRUNNER: I'd like to point out one thing. They were emphatic, repeat, emphatic, that the names of counterparts in the plenary session not be used. They would like it only to read the leaders of the two countries will meet.

WATCHDOG: OK. That's fine. I didn't even get in to the meeting part of it, I just said that the President will be meeting with Chinese leaders.

ROADRUNNER: If you have an opportunity, change that to read the leaders of the two countries. That is their phrase.

WATCHDOG: OK.

ROADRUNNER: Also, be advised, we have received permission for our telex. It will not go up this evening because they can't work in the dark on top of this hotel, so the very first thing tomorrow morning you can betcha it'll be moving. WHCA's sitting on the sidelines ready to move.

WATCHDOG: Well, that is outstanding and it will be a very good thing for both of our countries to have this operating.

ROADRUNNER: The PRC will be assisting us in that installation. It was just a very good meeting. It seems that both sides were extremely happy. They were happy to be giving us this information and obviously we were happy to be receiving it.

WATCHDOG: That's great, it sounds like a very productive day.

ROADRUNNER: It was! Also, be advised that they have agreed to the first meeting, the plenary session at the Great Hall of the People to be covered as we have previously discussed. It's all agreed. [*Live television!*]

WATCHDOG: Very good, very good.

ROADRUNNER: OK. They have set a working date of February 15, repeat, February one-five, for us to start establishing the switchboard, the comm center and radio base station. It will go from there gradually into the President's visit.

WATCHDOG: OK. Is that workable as far as Swift is concerned?

ROADRUNNER: Yes, I think that is more than he expected. They also raised some points regarding television. They were very minor, and I believe Snapshot, for the most part, is pleased at this point.

WATCHDOG: Good. Let me ask if there is any basic change in the itinerary at all for Searchlight?

ROADRUNNER: I gave my counterpart the scenarios that we have been working on for the various events that we have surveyed. At the outset of our session this evening, he made it very clear to me that I had assumed times and dates when it may not be that way. I told him that I was very clear on that subject. However, the day that I arrived and on the aircraft between Shanghai and Peking, I had given him a rough summary schedule, and without any guidance during our six days stay it was necessary for me to use that as a working guideline since we had nothing else. He understood. But again, made it very clear to me that we would work on that schedule in detail in the days to come. Basically, that's all I've got. We've had a very nice day. The gentleman that was involved in the incident last night is fine today. A little concerned and still in a state of shock; however, I think he will be all right.

WATCHDOG: Roger, do we want to send any clothing for him from this location out on one of our planes?

ROADRUNNER: That's a negative. Everything is A-OK.

WATCHDOG: Let me ask you how Vern is?

ROADRUNNER: We had a chance to talk to the famous Dr. Lee this evening at the hospital, and he indicated that Colonel Coffey was running a fever in the evening and early morning and they are not able to break that fever. As a result, he will probably still be in bed a couple or three days.

WATCHDOG: How are Collins and Abel? [*The military stenographers.*]

ROADRUNNER: They rallied very well today, and got a lot of work out. We had one other technician, earth station type, admitted to the hospital this evening with the same virus. I must inform you that it is becoming a concern to our host government as to a possible epidemic. I was asked that we tell all our people to dress warmly and take care of themselves, and the PRC is taking their own precautions.

WATCHDOG: Roger. We'll do that. I talked to Walter Tkach earlier this morning, and we are going to ask everyone to also get a flu shot before they come in.

ROADRUNNER: It might not be a bad idea to have everyone get a physical. At this point, I would suggest again that those men headed for China be looked at by a doctor. I am going to ask that Chief Dunn be allowed to accompany us to Shanghai to receive those men after that long journey and administer any assistance that he might be able to.

WATCHDOG: That is a good idea, Ron. Now let me ask, do you have all of your scenarios stacked up and ready to put on the TWX once it's operating?

ROADRUNNER: Yes we do.

WATCHDOG: Do you send stuff by punching it on a tape and running it through the machine or do you type directly over the air?

ROADRUNNER: We have to poke that before we can send it, Dwight.

WATCHDOG: In other words you have to punch the tapes ahead of time, is that correct?

ROADRUNNER: That's a roger, repeat, that's a roger.

WATCHDOG: Good. Are the tapes punched yet?

ROADRUNNER: That's a negative, repeat, negative, we have been unable to get to the equipment and will not be able to do so until tomorrow morning when our hosts establish the room where that can be set up in the hotel.

WATCHDOG: That's fine. One thing I would like for you to send me on the TWX when you can, as early as possible, is a recap of each event and the extent of coverage, whether live, whether film, you know, exactly what it's going to be, because I need to review that with Searchlight.

ROADRUNNER: Be advised that we've been working quite heavily on that, Elbourne has done extensive surveys and we are prepared to include that in the information being telexed to you tomorrow.

WATCHDOG: Do you have any more material for me at this time?

ROADRUNNER: That's a negative, repeat, negative.

WATCHDOG: We are having some people over this afternoon and, you might want to call around 6:30 our time. [*Roadrunner's family was going to be having dinner at the Chapin's house!*]

ROADRUNNER: Roger, I will call and simply check in.

WATCHDOG: OK, good. Did you get the message that I left with the radio operator from Chapin and Ziegler regarding slapping a curfew on transmission there between the hours of midnight and 7:00 A.M.? [*An attempt to curb Snapshot's late night phone calls. He was frustrated at the lack of communication with Ziegler and could not sleep. He would prowl the halls and attempt to phone Washington.*]

ROADRUNNER: I received some type of information regarding that. We are taking it under advisement.

WATCHDOG: Roger. Well, we do not want calls coming over here at odd hours.

ROADRUNNER: I understand. We'll control that.

WATCHDOG: We're expecting that to be controlled.

ROADRUNNER: That's a roger, sir.

WATCHDOG: OK, Ron, well get a good night's sleep. Everything's fine here. I know you have not been able to have a news summary or anything, but there really hasn't been too much happening. [*It was horrible not to be able to get any news. They felt like they were living in a cave.*]

ROADRUNNER: We kind of feel like we are really out of it.

WATCHDOG: I know that you probably do. You should be advised that Henkel is putting together all of the news summaries and the various things that you wanted to have brought so you'll be getting those in just two or three days.

ROADRUNNER: I've only got a minute and a half before we have to close down this satellite. Our curfew goes into effect. [*It was almost midnight in Peking.*]

WATCHDOG: (laughter) Roger, OK! (laughter) Well, take care and we'll talk to you later.

ROADRUNNER: All right sir, good night.

February 6 was coming to a close in China, the best day so far despite the 4:00 A.M. fiery wake-up call. They could actually feel the events taking shape.

"Come on Snapshot, it's that very important moment," Roadrunner said. "Have we been successful? Will we have clean, clear ice with our scotch tonight?"

They hurried to the windowsill. The newspaper tent was intact. The freezing wind had blown off the Gobi Desert all day, but the tent had held. With great excitement, Roadrunner reached out and retrieved the newspaper and the ice tray. He pulled the paper away and he and Snapshot both let out a loud whoop.

"It's ice!" they cheered, slapping each other on the back and congratulating themselves.

"Yeah! We did it," Snapshot cheered. "You know, I think we passed two tests today," he said. "We passed the test the Chinese set for us and we passed the ice test we set for ourselves."

They made a ceremony out of filling two glasses with the precious cubes of ice, frozen by the Chinese wind. Roadrunner poured the scotch and held his glass up to his ear. "Listen," he said to Snapshot, "you can hear the Chinese wind . . . and the faint tinkling of bicycle bells."

They laughed, clinked their glasses together and toasted, "To the President."

It was 7:30 in the evening when the phone rang in the Chapin's home on Baltimore Avenue. It was cozy and warm inside the white, two-story house. A fire was blazing in the small living room and Neil Diamond's music was pulsing from the stereo speakers. Five small girls, two Chapins and three Walkers, were playing in the den while Dwight and Susie Chapin and Anne Walker discussed how they thought Roadrunner was getting along in China. Now they had a chance to hear his voice, and they would compare notes when the call was over. Watchdog and Roadrunner got right to business when the call came in.

WATCHDOG: Hello, Roadrunner, how are you tonight?
ROADRUNNER: Very fine, thank you. We have had a considerable amount of difficulty completing this call. The satellite is experiencing much difficulty this morning.
WATCHDOG: You're coming in strong.
ROADRUNNER: I can hear you but it's very difficult to understand.
WATCHDOG: OK, Ron. Let me hit a couple of points right off if I can, the first point being we need to know whether the three network men plus the two photo lab men and Bill Small have been approved?
ROADRUNNER: Everyone except Small, repeat, except Small. He has not even been requested.

WATCHDOG: We'll have everybody else ready to come in and could you move on the Small request?

ROADRUNNER: Snapshot is extremely reluctant, due to the touchy situation regarding the additional press corps and the agreement that had previously been made, to request any changes. Do you understand?

WATCHDOG: Yes, I understand. So what we really want to do is send in the three network men plus the two technicians and hold off on Small. Is that correct?

ROADRUNNER: That's a roger, sir. Snapshot and I concur. We'd like to play that as it comes along. We may be able to do it, but we would like to have you and Whaleboat understand. I know *you* understand that it's a very touchy situation.

WATCHDOG: Very touchy, and we understand why and I made a point of explaining to Whaleboat that they had approved the eighty-seven but felt that there had been a certain violation in the agreement.

ROADRUNNER: I can only further confirm that conviction this morning after thinking about it a great deal.

WATCHDOG: I know exactly what you're saying. Now, let me go to the Livingood matter, and let me assure you that had gone through channels and had been considered.

ROADRUNNER: Watchdog, this is Roadrunner. You were broken and very weak. Would you say again slowly.

WATCHDOG: Roger, I repeat Ron, that regarding the Livingood matter, that had gone through channels and had been explained and the people in the PRC should know exactly what we wanted.

ROADRUNNER: Roger, I understand, the communique from Taylor to Woodcutter did in fact come through channels and my counterpart should have that communique.

WATCHDOG: Let me state, though, that once again we are dealing with a point of principle and that we understand over here that is a point of principle and we know that the PRC is considering that as a point of principle.

ROADRUNNER: I am proposing, and Livingood concurs, that it will be necessary for him to sit down with his counterpart, hopefully today, and explain exactly what his stand is. I would like to make one comment. Everything that Mr. Livingood proposed last night was a point of principle from our side, for example, that in our hundred-year history of the Secret Service, they have always had an agent in the front seat of the car of Searchlight, for every President, no matter where they were around the world. However, the PRC in their twenty-year history has never had a foreign security agent in their head of state's car. So we have a point of principle on both sides. Do you understand?

WATCHDOG: I understand and let me say I feel that you should just stay there and we should wait to hear what they say. We have stated our case and once we hear back from them, you should report back to me. ["*Where else would he report?*" *Roadrunner thought.* "*To the polar bear like Han Hsu had wondered?*" *Good grief, he was beginning to think like the Chinese and he wondered if there had been other innocent comments that had made the Chinese suspicious.*]

ROADRUNNER: I believe what Livingood is going to do is request from Taylor that we receive a document as soon as our telex is up with all the pros and cons. Then he will once again approach his counterpart for a last ditch effort.

WATCHDOG: We understand their point of principle in terms of their guarantee of the security, and it just may be that we will have to look at it closely. [*Worrying about their honor.*]

ROADRUNNER: It is my personal feeling that this is the only point of difference that we have at this point. Everything else is in the course of being resolved, or has been resolved, and I believe there is good understanding and exceptional, repeat exceptional, cooperation.

WATCHDOG: That is outstanding and it is great to know that attitude is in existence.

ROADRUNNER: Let me make one point, I have not, due to the circumstances, requested an additional steno. I am hopeful I might do that today, however, I think the steno should proceed en route to Guam, and hopefully I will have an answer before they depart Guam.

WATCHDOG: OK. I wouldn't push on that any harder than you feel necessary.

ROADRUNNER: The only thing that bothers me is having an entire advance team in one of our spots with no clerical support. That bothers me because day after tomorrow I lose the second steno that I have here and it is only now that we begin the hard work.

WATCHDOG: OK. Let me ask you if in your room you are able to read these days?

ROADRUNNER: That is a negative. Mr. Thomas was gracious enough to make some equipment available to me; however, it doesn't work. [*John Thomas' reading lamp did not work and the GE light bulbs included in Roadrunner's survival suitcase did not fit. For Snapshot and Roadrunner, this was just another part of the Chinese torture.*]

WATCHDOG: We were just curious on that point. What have you been doing in the evening for entertainment, are you looking at the movies?

ROADRUNNER: We have had a movie the last three nights and a few of our hosts have been present. As you can well imagine, the men have enjoyed them very much.

WATCHDOG: Are there any supplies of any kind that you want to have sent to you?

ROADRUNNER: We have one critical item that we do not have and that is a paper cutter, repeat, paper cutter. [*Roadrunner wanted to be able to cut the paper for the small, pocket-size schedule books that would be given to the presidential party.*]

WATCHDOG: (Chuckles). We will send you a paper cutter.

ROADRUNNER: Other than that I think we are in good shape to make everything ready for you. It is going to be a little tight once you arrive as I am sure you are aware, because I see no change in their operations as far as Searchlight's visit.

WATCHDOG: That's a good point, and I appreciate your mentioning that and we will structure everything accordingly.

ROADRUNNER: I believe that per your advice, the way we structured the schedule while in Washington is going to be the best way. We can simply inform our people, probably late evening or early morning, who will go to the various places.

WATCHDOG: Good. I think that we can handle that fine, Ron, and we will condition all of our people here to be thinking that way.

ROADRUNNER: It is imperative that they understand that they will be handled beautifully.

WATCHDOG: In a moment I want you to say hello to Anne, but I want you to also tell Schrauth to call Henkel's home because Anne Schrauth is there.

ROADRUNNER: Roger, that's outstanding. He has tried twice. Unfortunately she has either had the children at swim team practice or been out of the house so he has not had a chance to talk to Anne.

WATCHDOG: That is where they are tonight.

ROADRUNNER: Thank you.

WATCHDOG: OK. Now, I am going to put Anne on to say hello.

ROADRUNNER: OK. Thank you.

ANNE: Hi, Ron. We had a nice chili dinner and we are all thinking about you. You are the main topic of conversation.

ROADRUNNER: That's encouraging, thank you. I am in good health, our hosts are treating us beautifully. We had a lovely day, yesterday, to the Great Wall and to the Ming Tombs, with a picnic. The weather was outstanding. They took our entire party, and it was a sight to behold, to see the way that our people were handled and moved. You have to realize that was almost a hundred Americans.

ANNE: That's great! I am so glad that you sound like you are in good spirits. I want you to know that all of your family is well, and we all miss you and we think about you a lot and we hope that everybody is healthy.

ROADRUNNER: Unfortunately, there has been a great deal of sickness. I am convinced that the reason some of us have been in good health is the way we travelled this time. I feel fine and have had no problems. I have been working very hard, as you can well imagine, but the time has gone very fast. It's hard to believe we arrived a week ago today. We had an outstanding meeting last night and received many answers. I think the relationship that we have developed over the last week is a good one, and I look forward to working with my counterparts in the success of Searchlight's visit.

ANNE: That's great. We are so glad. And we want you to know we are thinking about you, and everybody here is fine. Everybody is healthy. We had a nice visit in Philadelphia. We came back this afternoon in a snow storm, but there was really no problem. Everybody sends their best. We hope that those who have had problems with their health are now much better.

ROADRUNNER: I know they appreciate that thought. OK, love, I love you very much and give the children a big kiss for me, and we'll talk to you sometime in the next week.

ANNE: Is there anything, with regard to the package that we sent, that you would like replenished?

ROADRUNNER: No, that's a negative. I am in good shape and enjoying everything very much. It has helped a great deal.

ANNE: OK, well, I will sign off. Watchdog would like to say something to you now. Take good care of yourself. We are so glad to hear your voice.

ROADRUNNER: Roger, sweetheart, you give the little girls a big kiss for me, and it's awfully good to talk to you. You have a nice day and get a good night's sleep, OK?

ANNE: OK, we sure will and we love you! Here's Watchdog.

WATCHDOG: Roadrunner, Watchdog.

ROADRUNNER: Go Watchdog.

WATCHDOG: Everybody looks wonderful, and we have one of those wet and snowy Washington evenings, and everybody is fine.

ROADRUNNER: I wish I was there to share a little of that chili, but I wish you were here to share the food I am eating. I know how much you enjoy it.

WATCHDOG: Roger, I think you could survive the chili, but the Dao might be a little hard to take. [*Dao was a red wine from Portugal that was a particular favorite of the Walkers and Chapins.*]

ROADRUNNER: I understand.

WATCHDOG: OK. Let me ask you, who is in room there with you now?

ROADRUNNER: A radio operator for the suitcase satellite. That is all.

WATCHDOG: Good. How do we stand regarding the restriction on the radio traffic? Are we in better shape now?

ROADRUNNER: That's a roger. That was a very, very good move. It gave me the leverage that I needed with Snapshot. He felt very badly, and you know he is like a caged animal on occasions. I think he is in good shape . . . now, if I can just hold him down.

WATCHDOG: Just hang in tight on that.

ROADRUNNER: Yes, I understand.

WATCHDOG: OK. Roadrunner, we will talk to you tonight, which will be 8:30 tomorrow morning our time. Is that OK?

ROADRUNNER: Yes, sir. We have prepared to go with a conference call at 9:30 this evening. I think tonight's conference call could be very interesting because I think we will be able to talk about a lot of important things.

WATCHDOG: Ron, let me say that I think one of the great things, besides the fact that you seem to have such a good working relationship with the members of the PRC government, is the fact that you sound so well and everything seems to be falling in place. We are very proud and we are very happy that it is working out that way and we ask that you all take care of yourselves. We will plan on talking to you tonight your time, tomorrow morning our time, and make sure that everybody takes care.

ROADRUNNER: Yes, sir, thank you very much. I feel very good. There have been times when I wasn't so sure but I feel very confident going into this new week.

WATCHDOG: Well, you are not the only one. We feel the same way here, and the President is becoming very interested in all the arrangements. You can let the counterparts know he is looking forward to this visit with great anticipation.

ROADRUNNER: Thank you. One last thing, I have relayed messages to Mr. Han Hsu for his good health and long life. He would like to relay the same message to you and your family.

WATCHDOG: I understand, Ron, and thank you very much. If you can ever get him there, I would like to say hello.

ROADRUNNER: I have relayed that but have received no reply. Be advised, they have been extremely busy, as you well know.

WATCHDOG: OK, Ron. Well, have a very good day and a successful day and we will talk to you in the morning. OK?

ROADRUNNER: That's a roger. Thank you very much and I appreciate you taking care of Anne.

By Doug Sneyd

"Then, on the third day, we shall serve golden tree branches with century eggs, lily buds and minced pigeon, unless you think he'd prefer jade leaves with sea slugs, sharks fins and chicken baked in mud."

WATCHDOG: Our pleasure. We'll talk to you later.
ROADRUNNER: This is Roadrunner out.

On Baltimore Avenue, they poured another glass of Dao and sat down in front of the fire. They decided that Roadrunner was in good spirits and sounded very much in control. They assured each other that they would have heard something in his voice if things had not been going well.

"That was really a low blow to tell him we were drinking Dao," Susie told her husband. "And don't you know he'd kill for a bowl of your great chili?"

"I know," Dwight said. "He hates Chinese food. I never will forget how he ate this scary looking thing at the farewell banquet on the advance trip, while the rest of us just sat there looking at it and worrying about what it was. Finally, I couldn't stand it anymore and I asked them to tell me what it was."

"Oh, that is our salute to spring," one of our Chinese hosts said with great glee, "It's a sparrow."

"Everyone at the table turned green at the thought, knowing they had to eat some of it. Roadrunner just smiled because his was already gone!"

"He learned that lesson in the villages of India, when he traveled with his Dad," Anne told them. "Chew it up and swallow it before you have a chance to find out how repulsive it might be." They all laughed and made faces, but Anne was thinking that eating sparrow was probably the least of Roadrunner's worries right now.

CHAPTER X

Ice Cubes and Baboon Syndrome

February 7, 1972

The limousine stopped in front of Watchdog's house as dawn was breaking and waited for him to appear. The Chief of Staff to the President of the United States [*H. R. Haldeman*] was already in the car, as usual, waiting for his aide so they could prepare for the day ahead while riding to work together. He was a tough task master. He expected perfection from those who were privileged to call the White House their place of business. The only reward for hard work was the continuation of the opportunity to do it. No one should expect anything more than that.

When the limousine pulled up in front of the White House, Watchdog hurried into his office. He had a ton of paper work to review before the conference call convened.

In Peking, Roadrunner gathered his team together. He liked this time in the evening when they would relax and sip after-dinner drinks and compare notes. He was pleased that he had made the extra effort to purchase cordials at the military package store. This small gesture of friendship came to mean a great deal to the Americans, and they all looked forward to this moment of camaraderie.

It was 8:36 in the morning in Washington when Roadrunner's voice was heard coming across the vast distance from Peking.

115

ROADRUNNER: Obviously we are very anxious to receive traffic from you, and we have a considerable amount for you also. Let me go through a couple of points very quickly so you can help us here during the next few days when our aircraft start arriving.

HENKEL: Roadrunner, proceed with the information.

ROADRUNNER: Be advised that I have not and will not ask for an additional steno. [*A tough call, but Roadrunner had decided with all the tension over press changes, he should not make any additional requests.*] We have received tremendous cooperation from the people in our party and I think that we can cover all those areas within our own rank.

HENKEL: I understand, and I will communicate your information to Mike Duval.

ROADRUNNER: It is also imperative that he be aware before he arrives, that it will be necessary for him and the rest of his advance party to put the information that they have to transmit to Peking in long hand. It can be teletyped, it has to be punched anyway, into Peking and from that we will have a fairly good scenario typed for transmittal into Washington.

HENKEL: I understand and again will get this information to Duval today.

ROADRUNNER: That's outstanding. I would appreciate it very much. What is his location?

HENKEL: He is in Hawaii, and will be departing Hawaii tomorrow for Guam.

ROADRUNNER: Relay a message to Duval that he had best take good care of himself before he arrives our location.

HENKEL: Mr. Duval assures me he will be taking good care of himself. What that means I'm not a hundred percent sure. [*Mike was a bachelor with a reputation for enjoying a good time.*]

ROADRUNNER: I copy loud clear. However, relay my concern that he be in good condition to perform his duties in Hangchou.

HENKEL: I assure you that Mike is very much aware of his responsibilities and will act accordingly.

ROADRUNNER: I would like for you to also tell Duval that I am not really sure as to what his job will be. [*Since the Chinese were calling all the shots, this was not a routine job for a Presidential advance man.*]

HENKEL: Roger. Mike and I had a rather lengthy telephone conversation last night my time and in general we discussed this exact subject.

ROADRUNNER: Thank you very much. OK. The next thing we need is in the order of precedence for both the official and the unofficial party, the titles. We have the official party's titles, as well as the unofficial party titles. However, there is a problem with the PRC regarding various members of our party. For example, my title is Director of the Presidential Advance Office, and they don't understand that. If there is any other guidance from Watchdog I would appreciate it. [*In diplomatic jargon, such a title meant absolutely nothing to the Chinese.*]

HENKEL: Watchdog is monitoring. He is with our meeting and he assures me he will be working on that today. [*It was nice to know Watchdog was in the room!*]

ROADRUNNER: It may be the simplest thing to use Staff Assistant to the President for those in the Advance Office. I have also assumed the titles of a number of people I would like to have substantiated from Washington. For example, we are assuming that Holdridge and Lord are assistants to Dr. Kissinger for National Security Affairs.

I need to say one other thing. We had a very, very lengthy meeting this morning with Director of Protocol Han Hsu, and he asked many, many questions which I will get into in a minute. I have already covered a few. If Watchdog is monitoring I will continue with that conversation. I was waiting for him to get on board.

HENKEL: Watchdog will be taking over the conversation right away.

ROADRUNNER: Roger. Then I am prepared to go ahead. Let me ask one other question, Bill. Has the package of Presidential pens, the gold pens we talked about, been put on board one of those two aircraft? [*Ballpoint pens with the Presidential seal and signature to be used as gifts.*]

HENKEL: Those items you speak of will be on the aircraft with Mr. Duval and Mr. Thomas arriving in Shanghai the eleventh. Repeat, the eleventh.

ROADRUNNER: Thank you very much. We have made arrangements with the People's Republic of China that they will provide aircraft on all, repeat all inter-theater travel. [*The Americans would have preferred to have U.S. C-141s move people and equipment while in China.*] So I need to know what equipment will be on board both aircraft arriving the tenth and the eleventh so I might advise the PRC what we are talking about for movement into Peking.

HENKEL: We are working on that figure and will TWX it to you. However, I think there is some misunderstanding here. Is that to convey that the C-141 arriving in Shanghai on the eleventh will in fact be going up to Hangchou also, as manifested now?

ROADRUNNER: That's a roger. The aircraft that arrives on the eleventh will move from Shanghai into Hangchou. The equipment will be off-loaded, the aircraft will return to Shanghai and leave the country. It will not, repeat not, be necessary for either one of the aircraft to move inter-theater as all arrangements for communications and other matters have been settled.

HENKEL: We acknowledge that and understand. Give Watchdog a call then.

ROADRUNNER: Roger, Watchdog, good evening. Be advised that at approximately ten minutes of ten our time this morning, I received a phone call about a meeting between myself, Elbourne, and Schrauth with Director of Protocol Han Hsu. We sat down at 10:30 for approximately an hour and a half.

WATCHDOG: That's very good.

ROADRUNNER: Also be advised that we have been in position the better part of the afternoon to transmit and receive. However, we are just now receiving power to activate our radio. The satellite is not in position. The testing procedure has not been completed by the PRC. [*Roadrunner was convinced that some Chinese functionary was sitting in front of a switch, waiting for orders to flip it and activate their telex. He and Snapshot referred to this waiting as just another form of Chinese torture.*]

WATCHDOG: But I understand everyone is striving to get that accomplished, correct?

ROADRUNNER: That's a roger. We are very hopeful that within the next few hours we will be able to accomplish what we have been hopeful for, for a long time.

WATCHDOG: We are looking forward to that also, Ron.

ROADRUNNER: Also, Director Han Hsu has asked for many things. First of all he is very anxious to receive the protocol list of the 390. He maintains that all his necessary activity revolves around that list, not only for the first banquet, but the cultural show, the gymnastic event, the reciprocal banquet, and any inter-theater travel. I have explained to him that we too are concerned and know that is a major problem, and as soon as our telex is operational we will have that list.

WATCHDOG: We will be TWXing that list to you tomorrow morning, your time. We will not TWX it tonight.

ROADRUNNER: I understand. Have you got anything for me before I go through the list of the things that Mr. Han Hsu asked for?

WATCHDOG: Roger. I only have one thing that I think might be a problem and that is the possibility of a personal assistant with Mrs. Nixon. [*In other words, a hairdresser. This was before First Ladies were able to talk openly about what might be considered a "luxury." Nancy Reagan changed that and a hairdresser became an accepted addition to Presidential entourages.*]

ROADRUNNER: At that level I am not bothered at all about asking for an additional assistant. Be advised that I have cancelled my request for a steno at the third stop. I did not think it wise to ask for it. It was implied by Director Han Hsu this morning that any increase would be a concern to them and I think that we can handle it, and we are prepared to do so.

WATCHDOG: Now why don't you run through your list?

ROADRUNNER: Director Han Hsu asked that we give consideration to any members of our party that can depart Peking after the reciprocal banquet for Hangchou. They are making arrangements for planes. He is extremely concerned about the volume of people and whether Hangchou can handle that. We are working at this end with the personnel, and Snapshot is working with the press corps to determine what people can move that night prior to Searchlight the next morning.

WATCHDOG: OK. We'll give some thought to that. It's a good idea. The other option would be to start moving them out very early, very early in the morning on the twenty-sixth.

ROADRUNNER: I understand that. However, be advised the problem is ground transportation. Repeat, ground transportation. It is approximately thirty minutes from the airport to the hotel. It would mean that we would leave very, very early. I think they are probably correct to move them out after the reciprocal banquet.

WATCHDOG: I understand, Ron. We will get an idea of all the support people that we can move on the twenty-fifth after the banquet.

ROADRUNNER: Good. Thank you. Mr. Han Hsu also said they have prepared to assist us in regard to the reciprocal banquet. I trust that the invitations, the place cards, and the menu cards will be on the aircraft coming in on the tenth or the eleventh.

WATCHDOG: Roadrunner, the invitation will not be there until the fourteenth, but the other stuff will be coming on the eleventh. Did you get into the champagne?

ROADRUNNER: No, sir, that's a negative. I thought I would wait until I received that memorandum coming to me by telex that explains that entire banquet.

WATCHDOG: It's in the material that we are going to TWX to you, so you'll have it all later today.

ROADRUNNER: You should be advised that Dr. Han Hsu indicated that arrangements should be made to bring our own plasma. Did you copy?

WATCHDOG: Roger. We have that. Are you talking about in large quantities or just for the principals?

ROADRUNNER: Just for the principals. Repeat, just for the principals.

WATCHDOG: We will get that message to Dr. Tkach.

ROADRUNNER: Also be advised that in the event of any emergency, they would use ground transportation as opposed to helicopters. [*The Chinese did not have helicopters.*] Director Han Hsu once again reiterated his request that the maximum number of personnel be present at the four events. That is the first banquet, the cultural show, the gymnastics event, and the reciprocal banquet. Quote, he says, "the more the merrier." [*Party time! The Chinese wanted to make sure that none of the support staff were excluded.*]

WATCHDOG: And that means absolutely every one of the Americans. Press and everybody, right?

ROADRUNNER: That's a roger, sir. I am assuming that in all instances the official party will move with Searchlight and Starlight. We are making separate arrangements for everyone else other than the principals and the official party.

WATCHDOG: Yes, I copy you loud and clear on that. I assume you are talking about motorcades and movements to events, and the official party will always move as a unit.

ROADRUNNER: Roger. The rest of the questions that he had were for us here regarding transportation, people staying in hotels, the press list moving to various locations and all the things for the people that are here in the country prior to your arrival. That's all I've got.

WATCHDOG: Hang on one second, Roadrunner. What kind of a report do we have on Colonel Coffey this morning?

ROADRUNNER: He has had a restful day, and it appears that he will be in the hospital for another two days.

WATCHDOG: Let me ask you, how is the rest of the party?

ROADRUNNER: Be advised we have two ground station personnel in the hospital, and there are a few technicians that reported to work today with some minor problems.

WATCHDOG: Roger. But other than that, everybody is OK?

ROADRUNNER: For the most part, everybody has been in very good health.

WATCHDOG: Be advised we're going to announce the names of the press at the briefing this afternoon per schedule.

ROADRUNNER: We had understood that and we had relayed that to the PRC.

WATCHDOG: OK. Let me ask you, besides the meeting that you had this morning with Director Han Hsu and besides the work that you did this afternoon getting all of your materials in order, did anything else happen?

ROADRUNNER: Negative. We met with Director Han Hsu this morning, surveyed the guest house this afternoon, the rest of the time was spent working on the various aspects of the trip. We had a large meeting this evening with the individuals responsible for the personnel in-country now, and then we are making this call.

WATCHDOG: Good. Well, sounds like you had a busy day there.

ROADRUNNER: Be advised that unfortunately we are missing *Patton*, which they are showing upstairs.

WATCHDOG: Well, why don't you go up and watch it and then get a good night's sleep? We do not have anything else from this end at this time. We would like to talk to you tonight, tomorrow morning your time. Is 7:30 your time OK?

ROADRUNNER: That's a roger. But first, are there any other counterparts there? Is Taylor with you or Redman or Ziegler?

WATCHDOG: Well, we've got some of those people. Dick Keiser's here for Taylor. We have General Scowcroft. We also have Al Redman and Bruce Whelihan.

ROADRUNNER: Roger. With your permission, I'd like to put Major Swift on with General Redman, and Livingood will call later. Snapshot is anxious to talk to Whaleboat and will do so later, I assume.

WATCHDOG: OK, Ron. General Redman's on, so put on Swift and I'll talk to you later.

ROADRUNNER: I'll talk to you tomorrow morning. Good night.

SWIFT: Redman, Redman, Swift. (no response) Redman, Redman, Swift.

REDMAN: Swift, Swift, Redman. Go.

SWIFT: Just wanted to amplify what Roadrunner said with regard to our communication here. Now that we have the power, hopefully we can establish contact through the HF radio and the operation with our comm center and also with Intel. In addition, tomorrow I am sure that we will get a single voice channel and one teletype channel through the ground station. Everything has been checked out at that location. The line between the air station and Peking has been checked out. They have a couple of lines punched up in our comm center. However, they have not identified this to us or turned them over for traffic. Again, I am assured that this will happen in the morning.

REDMAN: Swift, Redman. I'd like to have you alert the people at that end, and I will do the same here. We should take the message traffic in anticipation of the comm center coming up and have our people start poking it because I think it's going to take twenty-four to thirty-six hours just to poke and get this traffic out of the way.

SWIFT: Redman, Swift. I presume that's been done at your end, I can assure you that it has been done at this end. They are ready to send it as soon as we get in operation. [*With Abel and Mac sick, everyone pitched in and poked.*]

REDMAN: Swift, Redman. Be advised that much of the information including the protocol list has not even been typed, and when it does hit the comm center it will probably be a couple of hours before it is actually sent.

SWIFT: Redman, Swift. As we are going into our night now, we have twelve hours to receive it prior to our next telephone call.

REDMAN: Swift, that's a Redman . . . (clears throat) Roger. What I would like to know now is when is the earliest you think you'll be up on the High Frequency?

SWIFT: We are standing by now. We are unable to contact our stations in either Guam or Hawaii on our contact frequency. As soon as this call is completed we will get back to Andrews via this means and get on some different frequencies to make contact. The only thing holding us up now is this telephone call and getting back to Andrews.

REDMAN: Is Snapshot available for Whelihan?

SNAPSHOT: Whelihan, Whelihan, Snapshot.

WHELIHAN: What material do you want to talk to Ziegler about? [*Now Whaleboat was having his China calls screened!*]

SNAPSHOT: Well, I'll tell you what I want to talk to you about. Just hold on for a minute. (pause). Number one, in regard to a question from Ron this morning, the PRC will do nothing regarding the release of the press list. In other words, they will let us handle the entire thing and will not do anything at all from this end. [*Who cared in the PRC? They had no exposure to any of the American press personalities.*]

WHELIHAN: Understand. Go ahead.

SNAPSHOT: I would also like Ron and you people there to consider Mr. Han Hsu's request for the majority of the press corps to move from Peking to Hangchou on the day before the President moves. Also from Hangchou to Shanghai the day before the President moves.

WHELIHAN: Understand. That would be after the banquet in Peking, move to Hangchou and move to Shanghai from Hangchou the evening prior to the President's move.

SNAPSHOT: In my opinion, depending on the communications in both places, we could hold an expanded pool here to travel on a separate aircraft from the President and watch the departure.

WHELIHAN: Understand. An expanded pool would be possible and your recommendation is dependent upon communications from Shanghai and Hangchou.

SNAPSHOT: Next point. I would suggest that Cleve Ryan either stay with the pool or come in on the press plane, but not come in on the fourteenth aircraft. [*Ryan was the lighting expert for the networks and still photographers.*]

WHELIHAN: Understand your recommendation that Ryan move with the bulk of the press and not come in on the fourteenth.

SNAPSHOT: He is not needed here.

WHELIHAN: Understand. Continue.

SNAPSHOT: Next point. We need, urgently, Joseph Keating's passport number. Joseph Keating who is taking the place of the technician who came out of the PRC.

WHELIHAN: Understand. That information will be provided in cable to move from here. If you need prior to that, advise. [*They purposely were not giving any information over the phone, hoping to force the PRC to activate the telex.*]

SNAPSHOT: I'd like to have it prior to that, if we could. [*This was a special favor for Mr. Ma, Snapshot's counterpart.*]

WHELIHAN: Understand. Would this evening, in Chapin's call be an appropriate time?

SNAPSHOT: That would work just fine. OK. Next point. The PRC has requested the press corps not use walkie-talkies. This also would go for staff personnel unless there is an emergency. I would advise the wires as such.

WHELIHAN: Understand that press are not to use any portable communications and that there will be some possible curtailment of use of same by staff.

SNAPSHOT: The next point is through a mistake in communication and translation, I do not have approval, from the PRC, to bring in seven days in advance, the support people from ATT, ITT, and RCA.

WHELIHAN: Understand. No approval yet on requests for representatives from three common carriers seven days in advance.

SNAPSHOT: We do not have that approval, however I would have them standing by in case approval should be received.

WHELIHAN: We'll have them standing by in Guam.

SNAPSHOT: Next point. I need an answer from Ron regarding our final position on the toasts. [*What press coverage was going to be allowed.*]

WHELIHAN: Understand, Snapshot. Go ahead.

SNAPSHOT: Roger. Next point. I need the tail numbers and call signs for both press aircraft.

WHELIHAN: Understand. Tail numbers and call signs for press aircraft. Continue.

SNAPSHOT: I also need the names and passport numbers of the crew.

WHELIHAN: Understand. Crew names and passport numbers.

SNAPSHOT: I received, in a meeting I just got out of with my counterpart, certain other answers to questions we had posed. Here we go. On the twenty-eighth of February, the PRC agrees that one

Pan American airplane will stay for a minimum of one hour in Shanghai for filing before departing for the United States.

WHELIHAN: Tim . . . Snapshot, Whelihan. Understand. How much more traffic do you have?

SNAPSHOT: I've got four or five more points.

WHELIHAN: Go ahead.

SNAPSHOT: We have also received approval for the TWA aircraft and a Saturn aircraft to enter three days, three days following the departure in Peking.

WHELIHAN: Understand. Three days following the departure Peking through Shanghai.

SNAPSHOT: Next point. A customs man aboard the press plane into Shanghai has been disapproved, disapproved, therefore we should have customs people meet us in Anchorage when we get there.

WHELIHAN: Understand. Would not approve customs man out of PRC therefore customs necessary in Anchorage.

SNAPSHOT: One more point, and I wish you'd put this to Ziegler exactly the way I'm saying it. Bill Small [*Executive Producer*] has been approved by the PRC to come in seven days in advance, based on Ron Ziegler's request to the PRC. It is my feeling that he is not urgently needed at this time, and I would like your final decision on that.

WHELIHAN: Re-checking Tim. Is that seven days in advance?

SNAPSHOT: That is seven days in advance coming into Peking. It is my feeling that he is not urgently needed and I think you'll catch the nuance of that. [*Small was considered irritating by many and Snapshot was trying to discourage his coming in so far ahead.*]

WHELIHAN: You wouldn't care to be more specific with regard to recommendation?

SNAPSHOT: No, I would not care to be more specific.

WHELIHAN: Understand. If you have no more traffic for me, Taylor is standing by to talk to Livingood.

SNAPSHOT: That is a roger.

LIVINGOOD: This is Livingood. We went to the villa today [*where the Americans will be staying*]. Everything seems in good order there. I have a couple of questions. Number one, do you want a single or shall I put Ready in there with you? If we don't put Ready in there, we can put him in one of the other villas. [*John D. Ready, security.*]

TAYLOR: I'd prefer not to have double accommodations. However, I understand HAK [*Kissinger*] wants Ready in the building. Is it possible to have separate accommodations in the same building?

LIVINGOOD: Negative. But we could put him in a nearby villa which would be just half a block away.

TAYLOR: I'd prefer that if it's impossible to have Ready with HAK.

LIVINGOOD: Will do. Number two, on Starlight's separate movements, do you mind if I send Duncan with her as a second man? [*Secret Service agent Bill Duncan.*]

TAYLOR: I believe that would be all right. Go ahead.

LIVINGOOD: Roger. And the last point I brought up today about the doctor riding in our car, our follow-up, . . . they wouldn't give me an answer on that.

TAYLOR: That's a good request and we'll be waiting to hear the answer on that. We have no answer on the other [*whether an agent can ride in the President's car*]. It's morning here, of course, and we're going for the file that we talked about last night. We'll send you copies of the correspondence just as soon as possible, and we'll be back in touch with you on that one.

LIVINGOOD: Also, be advised Weaver is better today. His temperature has gone down.

TAYLOR: Thank you very much. We will advise all concerned about that. How's Colonel Coffey? I missed the first of this conversation.

LIVINGOOD: He's better today. His temperature has gone down some and they hope that he will be out of the hospital in two or three days.

TAYLOR: I guess Dick told you that I talked to Becky today. She's feeling much better, and she's quite all right. No problem. [*Bill Livingood's wife Becky.*]

LIVINGOOD: Roger. I have nothing further, and will call you tonight your time.

TAYLOR: Roger. We'll be available when you call, hopefully with some answers regarding that other matter. Taylor clear.

LIVINGOOD: That's a roger. Livingood clear.

CROWN: Carnation, Carnation from Crown. Do you have anybody else at this time? If not, we will terminate.

SNAPSHOT: Crown, Crown, this is Snapshot. Is Whelihan still available?

CROWN: I believe he is, wait one. (long wait, several minutes of static) Elbourne, Elbourne, from Crown. Be advised, Whelihan is no longer available to a phone. He will be in his office shortly and we can reconnect at that time, if you wish.

SNAPSHOT: That's a roger. I'd like to reach him.

CROWN: Elbourne, from Crown, roger, sir. At this time I am going to disconnect the conference and just wait until Mr. Whelihan arrives.

SNAPSHOT: Roger, Crown, thank you very much.

CROWN: Roger. Crown out.

Roadrunner sat and watched Snapshot waiting for Whelihan. After several minutes, he said, "Screw it, Tim. Let's go retrieve our ice and have a pop."

They headed for the windowsill. As they were retrieving the tray, the hall attendant entered the room and proudly set a saucer on the table. He was grinning from ear to ear. There were three ice cubes on the saucer. All three of them laughed and shook hands, and Roadrunner and Snapshot proclaimed the presentation a generous and thoughtful gift of friendship. Snapshot put one ice cube in each of three glasses and tried to get the attendant to take one, but he kept smiling and shaking his head back and forth as he left the room.

When he was gone, Roadrunner said, "Boy, those guys don't miss a thing, do they?"

Snapshot said, "I wonder how long it took them to figure out what we were trying to do out there on the windowsill?"

"Well, you notice that they waited until we found success, don't you?" Roadrunner responded. "Do you think they are making these the same way we are?"

They examined the three cubes for clues, but couldn't find any soot particles or terrycloth fibers.

Snapshot said, "I'll bet if we could go exploring in this hotel we'd actually find a refrigerator. I think they made these the old-fashioned way, like our mothers always did, by pouring water into an ice tray and walking very carefully to the refrigerator and spilling some of it before they got it on the little shelf inside the freezer compartment."

"I think you are absolutely, one hundred percent correct," Roadrunner agreed. "Here, you put two cubes in this drink, and when we have the second drink you give one back to me!"

"Sure," Snapshot said absent-mindedly. "Do you want to go on a fridge hunt?"

"Don't even consider it," Roadrunner warned. "That would just make them mad. First of all, they do not want us wandering around this hotel, and secondly, it would look as though we were not grateful for these three very fine cubes."

They sipped in silence. It felt good just to relax. After a while Snapshot said, "I think these are very important ice cubes. They are probably as important as ping pong balls--maybe even more important. We've been sent a signal. They want to do it our way, but within what they consider to be reasonable limits, limits that they are comfortable with."

Snapshot continued, "You know and I know that if we were going to take somebody some ice, we would take a full bucket, or we would buy a whole bag at the corner store. But here, in the PRC, we only get three cubes of ice. It's a wonderful gesture, but it is minuscule compared to what Americans are used to receiving." Then he paused and looked at Roadrunner over the rim of his glass. "That my friend, is a very important message."

Roadrunner fell asleep thinking about the three ice cubes. Suddenly he was awakened by the jangle of the green hotel telephone. He was trying to remember what the three important messages were as he groped to find the phone.

"Mr. Walker, Mr. Walker, please come at once to the third floor sitting room for some very important questions that must receive answers. That is all." With that the call was terminated.

Roadrunner sighed and climbed wearily out of his bed. These frequent middle of the night interruptions were giving him headaches. The questions that needed immediate answers were never earth-shaking; certainly Roadrunner did not think that they required immediate answers. The Chinese usually wanted to clarify something, check the spelling of a name, or verify one of their translations. He knew it was probably another form of their test of his character. He splashed water on his face and dressed hurriedly. In a few minutes he was slurping tea on the third floor and politely answering their questions.

Raodrunner got a little more sleep before he showered and dressed to start the day. At 7:30, he was ready for the conference call, and the telex link was the first thing on his mind. Chinese concerns about security were still dogging the advance party. He raised this with Watchdog immediately.

ROADRUNNER: Good morning, sir. I'm sure you are aware of the situation.
WATCHDOG: I am aware of the situation. I understand that they are working in order to get the problems alleviated so we can start transmitting our documents back and forth.
ROADRUNNER: I'm sure General Redman has informed you, it appears the problem is the eight frequencies they have given us to use. Ahhh . . . just very, very tough guidelines. We are receiving Japan and the Philippines loud and clear but cannot use those facilities.
WATCHDOG: I understand, Ron, and I know that they are working to get the problem squared away.
ROADRUNNER: Yes, sir. Guam is receiving us, however they do not have the capability of transmitting our information on through and Hawaii is too far. Are you copying me?
WATCHDOG: Roger, I copy you loud and clear, Ron, and I understand we are working very hard to alleviate the problem.

ROADRUNNER: You are correct. Our people have been working all night. It just breaks your heart to hear Japan and the Philippines so loud and clear and know that we are that close, but the guidelines are such that we cannot use those facilities. [*In other words, the Polar Bear might listen. PRC guidelines would not let them transmit via Japan and the Philippines because of concern that it would go on to the Soviet Union.*]

WATCHDOG: I understand, and we will keep pushing as hard as possible. I know this is causing you and the People's Republic serious problems because we cannot get the materials to you.

ROADRUNNER: I am trying to work out some way we can remain in Peking. Realizing there is much work to be done I don't think it is possible to move the advance party into Shanghai and Hangchou until we are in a position to answer questions and receive information. The PRC is very anxious to receive information. I'm going to let them know the requirements they have laid on us are very, very tight and causing us trouble. It may be necessary that we make that move at a later date.

WATCHDOG: If you think you've got to make a change, you're in the driver's seat, and you're the one we've got to rely on to make the judgement decision.

ROADRUNNER: I will talk to my counterpart today and establish the ground rules with which we have to operate.

WATCHDOG: Now, when would you leave to go down there, if you went?

ROADRUNNER: If we go we are planning to depart sometime late tomorrow afternoon.

WATCHDOG: Well, we'll have another chance to talk before that. So we'll be able to size up what progress has been made during the day.

ROADRUNNER: I'm really sorry. I wish we had exchanged information in the past twenty-four hours.

WATCHDOG: Yes, and believe me, I'm just as antsy as you are to get it sent back and forth. I know the People's Republic must be rather disturbed too, because this material could be very helpful for them.

ROADRUNNER: That's correct. OK. Be advised I am going to request additional seats on the aircraft moving Searchlight to Hangchou and Shanghai, and also ask for the personal assistant. Also, be advised, we have all of the information punched and ready to be sent. We are ready to send as soon as we have the facility. I hope that by the time you wake up tomorrow morning you have a lot of information.

WATCHDOG: Well, we're going to have disappointments along the way. We're just going to have to cope with them as we move along. I know you understand and I know that you know that I understand and we'll just do the best we can.

ROADRUNNER: Yes, sir.

WATCHDOG: Ron, I do have one major point that I need to raise with you and I need to have you pass it on to Elbourne, OK?

ROADRUNNER: That's a roger. Elbourne. Go.

WATCHDOG: There was a Reuters reporter that filed a story out of there and had an interview with one of the ranking people on our advance team. I have sent you a cable, but I can tell by reading the story that it's one of the television people. The interview makes reference to the fact that he's very pleased you took some liquor in there. Plus, he gets into the schedule and some of the details surrounding the visit. Dr. Kissinger, personally, brought it to my attention, and gave me a few words of advice and asked that I get in touch with you. I assured him that you were not the one that did the interview, and he realized that you weren't, but he has asked and I am asking, both you and Tim, to put the clamps on the network people and everyone there not to release or divulge any information regarding the trip. That will be done by Mr. Ziegler here and by the representatives of the People's Republic at the proper time.

ROADRUNNER: Roger. I am somewhat aware of that story. Apparently Elbourne has talked to Whaleboat regarding that subject. We had a very large meeting in my room of all the principals in our advance party last night and this subject was talked about at great length. Be advised that Siegenthaler and the ranking members are very much aware of the situation. Apparently it was a third-country reporter that was in the vicinity of the transmission center, and it was one of the technicians, the rank and file type individual, that made these comments. Obviously, Siegenthaler was very upset and most apologetic and requested once again that no one, repeat, no one talk to anybody regarding this visit.

WATCHDOG: Well, I know your attitude and I know that you know what the problems are on this end. I did not know that Whaleboat had talked to Snapshot and I'm happy to hear that you're on top of it. You're just going to have to keep riding it all the way through.

ROADRUNNER: I understand. I will, once again, pass on your concern, this morning, to Siegenthaler. And also advise our people once again. I would like you to be advised that the French press had a hand delivered note sent to me last night at the hotel, requesting that I meet with them. I am going to talk to my counterpart this morning, since we have a very good understanding regarding this subject and let him handle it.

Soldiers at the transmission center.

WATCHDOG: That's perfect. I would just continue to do it that way. The same way that Dr. Kissinger handled it on his trip.

ROADRUNNER: Also, the hotel will not allow any reporters in the hotel. We have a badge that they have issued to us and it is for us only. Be advised, they were checking those last night upon entry into the hotel. So everyone in our party had to present these to get into the hotel. The switchboard in the hotel is taking all of those calls and referring them to the appropriate place within the government of the PRC. I think we're pretty closely held here, however the transmission center is another subject.

WATCHDOG: OK. I understand. It sounds like you've got it pretty well under control. I have one other point that gets into the documentary crew area. We need to know the color temperature, I repeat the color temperature for the lamps they are going to use to light for the photo opportunities. [*The documentary crew working on a film for the Committee for the Re-election of the President was another special request that the PRC did not understand and thus another headache for the advance team. It was pure re-election politics and therefore Watchdog's baby.*]

ROADRUNNER: I would like to repeat that. The color temperature of the lamps used for the photo opportunities.

WATCHDOG: Ron, I'm a little out of my league here because I am not sure what they are talking about, but the actual thing is, we need to know the color temperature in kelvin. It's K-E-L-V-I-N. It's evidently a rating chart for color temperature, and once we know that our documentary crew people will know what kind of film to bring.

ROADRUNNER: We have that information. I am familiar with that and I know our people have been working on that subject. I'll get that information and have it for you this evening.

WATCHDOG: That's great.

ROADRUNNER: Also, be advised along that same subject, Mr. Han Hsu made one comment. That was centralization. Repeat, centralization. Realizing that our official photographer, Ollie Atkins, and the documentary crew people are part of the unofficial party. He said centralization could be along the lines with them moving with the press pool. It would help a great deal, in order to coordinate those individuals, have them move properly and not get lost.

WATCHDOG: Yes, yes, I see what you're saying. OK. Fine. Now, I want to stress again with you the point that we made there with Mr. Han Hsu, that we want to maximize the photo opportunities for our official photographers over the press pool photo opportunities.

ROADRUNNER: I have, as I've indicated in the past, relayed this information and was informed that there would be no problems.

WATCHDOG: OK, Ron. I don't have anything else. Let's just keep our fingers crossed we can get these TWX machines working in the next few hours and then we'll be off and rolling.

ROADRUNNER: This is Roadrunner, I'll sign off now.

WATCHDOG: Well, have a very good day and take care of yourself. Tell everyone hello, and everybody here sends their best.

ROADRUNNER: Roger, roger. Roadrunner, out.

Roadrunner hurried out of the room and set out to see which of the Chinese counterparts he could find. Since they seemed to stay up all night, they were probably still asleep. He stopped at the third floor sitting room, but only the hall attendant was there. *"Ni hau,"* Roadrunner said as he waved to him.

At the front desk in the hotel lobby, he considered putting in a call to Mr. Chu's room, but decided to wait a little longer, although it would be fun to see how fast Mr. Chu could get up, dress, and present himself to answer some very important questions. "No, that would be too obvious," Roadrunner decided, and besides, it was not the way he did things.

At 10:30 A.M. he was back on the phone with Washington. It was 9:30 in the evening at home.

CROWN: Roadrunner, this is Crown. We have Henkel on the line. Go ahead, please.

ROADRUNNER: Bill, I have a subject I want to relay to you and I would like you to talk to Watchdog and be prepared to discuss it with me this evening. We are still having problems at our end, but I understand you are receiving our telex and it is not the best but it is readable. Is that correct?

HENKEL: I have not received word of that.

ROADRUNNER: Be advised it is in the process of being sent. However we are not, repeat not, able to receive traffic from your side yet.

HENKEL: I read you. I will check as soon as our call terminates and determine the status of the incoming traffic.

ROADRUNNER: Be advised, you are broken very badly. But, Swift has just confirmed with Redman that they have received and are continuing to receive. Here is my proposal. I am seriously considering asking to hold those additional aircraft due to arrive in the PRC on the tenth and eleventh, in Guam until I am ready for them to come in. Do you copy? [*This was a smoke screen to get the PRC's attention. Roadrunner felt they were not playing ball in completing the communications. To postpone the trip to Shanghai and Hangchou would be viewed as a real setback for the Chinese.*]

HENKEL: I repeat that you are seriously considering the aircraft be held in Guam, repeat, held in Guam until you ask for them to enter the People's Republic.

ROADRUNNER: Here is my reasoning. There is much work to be done here in Peking. Realizing those men will have eleven days prior to Searchlight's arrival, and that's too much time. The majority of decisions for those two stops will be made here. With those personnel in-country it is going to compound my problems. If they are in Guam, there's a possibility that we could bring in those aircraft on or about the fourteenth. Unless things improve at my end during the course of the next twelve hours, we are not going to be in a position to dispatch the team to do the surveys on those two cities because of the amount of work left to be done for the PRC. We cannot be out of touch for three or four days. It is a critical time for all of us.

HENKEL: I totally understand that while you are doing advance surveys in the cities of Hangchou and Shanghai, much would be left unattended which is critical to the overall trip.

ROADRUNNER: And not only from my side but for Elbourne, Swift, Livingood, and the technicians.

HENKEL: I understand your statement is concurred in by Elbourne, Swift, Livingood, plus the technicians.

ROADRUNNER: That's a negative.   I did not say that it was concurred in. I am saying that their problems are just as large as my problems.   It is not wise for us to be gone for three or four days during this very critical time.

HENKEL: I understand. Will convey that message to the appropriate people here.

ROADRUNNER: Be advised that I'll be here at the hotel and can be reached through the satellite.

HENKEL: I think you appreciate that we are working on a request for a listing. We are working very hard and hope to have it to you tomorrow sometime.

ROADRUNNER: What list is that? Of the 390?

HENKEL: That is a roger.

ROADRUNNER: I appreciate that effort. I know how hard you are working. So, I'll look forward to receiving that if we're in a position to receive it.

HENKEL: I think you can understand the amount of input and the balancing and weighing and the decisions made by many, many people, including Welcome, with regard to that document. [*The task of putting the 391 Americans in a protocol order list had thrown the White House a curve that went as high as the Chief of Staff! See Appendix.*]

ROADRUNNER: I understand that. I re-emphasize again, the PRC has requested the document as soon as possible.

HENKEL: I can assure you that document has priority. We are still getting the input, and I am confident that document will be in order by sometime tomorrow afternoon our eastern standard time.

ROADRUNNER: OK, Bill, thank you very much.

This time, Roadrunner had less than an hour before he was back on the suitcase satellite with Washington. He was frustrated. He needed answers. He needed time. He wanted the trip to be over. He had proposed holding up the incoming advance party because he did not need more people to worry about. After the fire yesterday, he realized how quickly an incident could occur and totally screw things up. The more people he had milling around, the greater the chance that something would go awry. He wanted to make sure Henkel had started the ball rolling on his proposal to hold those planes in Guam. He looked at his watch. It was now 10:26 P.M., Eastern Standard Time, in Washington, D.C. He called Watchdog.

ROADRUNNER: Watchdog, Roadrunner. Good evening.

WATCHDOG: Good . . . middle of the day to you, Roadrunner. I'm sorry I missed you earlier, I was on the way home from a meeting.

ROADRUNNER: I understand. Have you talked to Henkel?

WATCHDOG: Yes, I've talked to him, at length, a little while ago. I understand the concept of perhaps delaying our people in Guam until you feel it appropriate and worthwhile for them to enter the country. My feeling on that is to do whatever you feel you need to do. I would not drop the option of your staying in Peking and sending Mike Schrauth down.

ROADRUNNER: The PRC is pushing very heavy for answers. I'm becoming more and more convinced we should hold those two advance parties. In all honesty, we don't need them right now.

WATCHDOG: Well, maybe that's what we'll do.

ROADRUNNER: My present thinking is we hold off the arrival on the tenth and eleventh, giving us three additional days in Peking. Then we have the aircraft begin to arrive on the twelfth and thirteenth, with the aircraft arriving on the fourteenth remaining on schedule.

WATCHDOG: I understand, Ron, I understand. What word do you have on the TWX?

ROADRUNNER: Be advised that Major Swift has just gotten out of a meeting and the satellite, the earth station, is prepared and ready to start receiving traffic. You are presently receiving traffic from us. It is not very good but it is readable. We are sending that through the high frequency radio. As soon as the ground station has been certified by us, they want that in writing, certifying that the earth station is up and ready and operational, before they connect the wires. Somewhere along the line we have wires at our end, the earth station has wires at their end, but there is a problem in between.

WATCHDOG: Well, as soon as you get that approval they can go ahead and start using the big station. Is that the point?

ROADRUNNER: That's a roger. They want it in writing and then they will take it under consideration and be back to us . . . uh . . . they have said, very soon.

WATCHDOG: That's sensational. Maybe we can bust through that way and that would help expedite everything and we can try to stay on schedule. Well, I don't have anything else. Do you?

ROADRUNNER: That's a negative. I wanted to get this flagged so you could be thinking about it. We'll talk to you tomorrow morning, your time. Have a good night's sleep.

WATCHDOG: Be advised that we are at home watching a television show, right this minute, on China, called "An Open Door" that was done by the Associated Press. It's a historical document and very interesting.

ROADRUNNER: I wish I was there to watch it with you. I bet it's very good.

WATCHDOG: There are many specials starting to come on the air. The interest, obviously, is building. We did get our press list announced today and we are very relieved to have that burden off of us.

ROADRUNNER: I can well imagine. Have you had much reaction?

WATCHDOG: Not much reaction so far. Be advised that Bob Haldeman appeared on the TODAY show this morning and he will tomorrow morning and Wednesday. He made some statements in regards to some of the various Senators that have opposed the President's speech [*on Vietnam*] and he was the lead on all three networks. [*In 1972, it was very unusual to see a Chief of Staff on television, although Don Regan and John Sununu changed that.*]

ROADRUNNER: I'm sure he did an outstanding job.

WATCHDOG: He did, and the reaction has been a little overwhelming. He's asked about you a number of times and I've assured him everything's going well.

ROADRUNNER: We're working very hard and doing our very best. We've made an awful lot of very good friends and I hope that helps.

WATCHDOG: I'm sure it will, Ron. Take care. We'll talk to you tomorrow morning and I hope you have a good afternoon.

ROADRUNNER: So do I, sir. Good night, and say "Hi" to Susie for me.

"Well good," he thought to himself. "With the men not coming in from Guam, I can cross that worry off the list for a few more days. Now what else am I worrying about? Oh, yeah! What Watchdog calls the 'health thing'."

Roadrunner was becoming more and more concerned about the health of his men. Col. Coffey's pneumonia was the most upsetting, and the penetrating cold seemed to make it impossible for people to warm up once they got chilled. The other problem that was beginning to get a great deal of attention was the "baboon syndrome." On this subject, Roadrunner decided it was time for action. He took out some paper and drafted a memo.

February 8, 1972
MEMORANDUM FOR: All Members of the American Party
SUBJECT: Health Care Recommendations

The change of climate of this party has been much more severe
than anticipated. Many of you have had colds, coughs, and even
fairly high fevers. We feel that this is primarily due to unnecessary exposure to the deceptively penetrating cold weather in this
area.

We must, therefore, re-emphasize that everyone should be more
concerned with proper clothing for outdoors, particularly hats,
scarves, and warm foot covering. We are grateful to our hosts
for providing us with warm coats and hats. (If you don't have
these items, ask one of the interpreters.) THESE MUST BE
WORN!

We have also noted the first cases of "Baboon Syndrome," the
rash on the buttocks, similar to a poison ivy response. This too,
is due to unnecessary exposure . . . to the lacquered toilet seats.
SIT ON THE PORCELAIN BOWL NOT THE LACQUERED
TOILET SEAT!

Chief Hospital Corpsman Robert Dunn, USN, is available in
Room 606 for any medical problems. 7:30 A.M. to 8:30 A.M.
and 7:30 P.M. to 8:30 P.M. are designated as sick call hours.
                              /s/ Ron Walker

As Roadrunner and Chief Dunn began distributing the memo
under the hotel room doors of the American party, their ever-present
Chinese aides offered help and thus obtained a copy themselves.
Within a day, a huge Chinese delegation of nearly twenty came to
Roadrunner's room and ceremoniously presented him with a new
toilet seat and an apologetic promise that all toilet seats in the
Americans' rooms would soon be replaced.

[*Roadrunner's memo showed up over a year later, on White House
stationery, in* The Washington Monthly's *Memo of the Month, "A
Sampling - some hilarious, some horrifying, all real - from the Culture
of Bureaucracy."   It was included in the chapter "The Bureaucrat Gives
Instructions."*]

CHAPTER XI

BYE-BYE, MISS AMERICAN PIE

FEBRUARY 8, 1972

Although more serious ailments still plagued the military stenographers, Roadrunner was nevertheless able to get his memo typed, copied, and posted in several key locations around the hotel.

It was 9:31 in the evening when he sat down in front of the suitcase satellite to talk to Washington, where it was 8:31 A.M.

WATCHDOG: How does our traffic look?

ROADRUNNER: We have received a good amount of traffic, and are responding to questions where we have answers.

WATCHDOG: How is everyone on the health side?

ROADRUNNER: Be advised that we have one agent that has somewhat of a problem this evening. However, we're hopeful that he'll be in much better shape tomorrow. Both stenographers are still on the mend. There have been a few technicians and earth station people that have had some problems. Colonel Coffey is doing very well today, and we are hopeful he will be able to join us tomorrow and begin familiarizing himself with the information at hand.

WATCHDOG: Can you elaborate on the kinds of problems those people that are not feeling well seem to be having?

ROADRUNNER: It's the same problems as Coffey. It's fever, and the virus. The other one is the symptoms on their bottoms.

WATCHDOG: (To the room: "Dermatology. OK.") Roger, thank you on that. Do you want to run through what your schedule was for today?

ROADRUNNER: We had problems getting the connection for the teletype. Once that was established, the afternoon was spent receiving your communiques.

WATCHDOG: And that material is all readable, is that right?

ROADRUNNER: That's a roger. Everything I have received is up to date. The most recent is the manifest for the aircraft on the tenth and the eleventh, which is very readable.

WATCHDOG: Regarding that, have you any further thoughts on whether we should hold those planes up?

ROADRUNNER: That's a roger. Be advised that I prepared a memorandum to Mr. Chu, explaining the situation, for two reasons. One was to flag the problems that we were having regarding our telex. Secondly, we were going to be in a difficult position to provide information they requested if this facility was not operating within the next few hours. Within the next few hours, it was operational.

WATCHDOG: OK, but the one thing I don't know yet is what you want to do?

ROADRUNNER: It is my advice right now that we hold and go to Shanghai on the twelfth.

WATCHDOG: OK. We will get the word to Duval and the people in Guam.

ROADRUNNER: That is a roger.

WATCHDOG: OK. Ron, the one thing that is very difficult from our end, is the list that you are waiting for, the total protocol list. We will send that as soon as we have it.

ROADRUNNER: That would be very helpful.

WATCHDOG: Are you sending us a list of the press opportunities and where there will be cameras and sound?

ROADRUNNER: That's a roger. Are you in receipt of our traffic that we have sent in the last five or six hours?

WATCHDOG: Negative, I have not looked at any of it yet, Ron. I'm going to do it as soon as we finish talking.

ROADRUNNER: Then I think it advisable that you look at that traffic. We do have the photo opportunities in minute detail.

WATCHDOG: OK.

ROADRUNNER: Be advised we have received approximately two hours of traffic, and were advised by Redman that there was approximately thirty hours.

WATCHDOG: Well, I think that there was a misunderstanding there, we are almost clean from this end.

ROADRUNNER: We were prepared and had everything punched, and it was transmitted as soon as we had our telex circuit open. However, we did not experience the same situation from your end.

WATCHDOG: I understand that. Let me ask, what's the name of the agent that's not feeling well?

ROADRUNNER: Weaver, Weaver. Wait one. . . . Is Taylor with you now, Watchdog? [Secret Service Agent Douglas A. Weaver]

WATCHDOG: Yes he is.

ROADRUNNER: Wait one.

LIVINGOOD: Taylor, this is Livingood. Weaver cancelled for the second day. He is still running a slight temperature, about 99.5 or 6. Hopefully, it will break tomorrow.

WATCHDOG: Bill, is he in the hospital or at the hotel?

ROADRUNNER: Watchdog, this is Roadrunner. He has remained at the hotel, hotel.

WATCHDOG: OK. Did we raise the subject on that personal assistant?

ROADRUNNER: Be advised, I have raised that subject, as well as the extra seat on the PRC aircraft. I have not received an answer.

WATCHDOG: How are you feeling?

ROADRUNNER: Very nicely, thank you.

WATCHDOG: OK. Let's see if we have any other questions here. (static . . . . pause)

WATCHDOG: Swift, Redman would like to know if we have permission to come up on the Hughes satellite?

SWIFT: Redman, the Hughes satellite has been accepted for service by Comsat. We are through from our comm center switchboard to the airport. It is a matter now of coming on into Washington, which I expect will be done momentarily.

REDMAN: That's the same report you gave me about twelve hours ago. Has there been any change?

SWIFT: As I say, we have been accepted by Comsat officially. And the Chinese have officially, approximately four hours ago, told me that the satellite may now be used for traffic. As I say, we have been cut through to the airport and are waiting for the cut from the satellite to your end.

ROADRUNNER: Redman, this is Roadrunner. Be advised that I am convinced that everything at this end that could have been done, has been done, and I would hope that you appreciate that effort. [Redman did not appear to understand that many of the problems were due to the PRC's new exposure to this technology. It took a while to *understand and become comfortable with much of the equipment. It was tediously slow and agonizing for the Americans.*]

REDMAN: Watchdog wants to pass on that we appreciate all the efforts that have been made at your end. [*They wondered why Redman had to make it Watchdog who was appreciative and not himself.*]

ROADRUNNER: I am sure you do, and be advised that there is a considerable effort transpiring at this end and I am hopeful that you appreciate that. [*Roadrunner would not let the General off the hook!*]

REDMAN: That's a roger. I appreciate it.

WATCHDOG: Roadrunner, I appreciate it too, and we know it's been very difficult, but we also know that only with the mutual cooperation could it have been successful.

ROADRUNNER: At this point, do you have anything else for us?

WATCHDOG: Negative. I think I'm going to go read all the traffic and see what we've got. Then we'll be back to you. Let's set that for 6:30 again if that's agreeable. That would be 7:30 tomorrow morning your time.

ROADRUNNER: I appreciate that there is a considerable amount of traffic there. I want you to be advised that we are going to be working this evening late. This is one night we will break curfew to get the information for the PRC. I would like to give this information to Director Han Hsu tomorrow morning. Is there anything else?

WATCHDOG: Hang on one second. Whelihan needs to talk to Elbourne as soon as we're through. Do you read?

ROADRUNNER: That's a roger. Be advised that in these conference calls every evening, we have all the principals present. If there's anything that needs to be raised, that's why they are all here. If others want to conduct their business in a private manner, that is understandable, but we're all gathered together and it would be nice if we all knew what is transpiring.

WATCHDOG: Well, I think we are doing the same thing at this end. Obviously, there's going to be times when it's more productive for the men to talk back and forth separate from these regular sessions.

ROADRUNNER: I understand. It might be wise to advise Whelihan that he can be present at the meetings.

WATCHDOG: He's sitting right here, Ron.

ROADRUNNER: Does he want to talk to Snapshot now? He's sitting right here. [*Roadrunner was getting a bit testy, but he felt that in the interest of time, everyone should be available while these conference calls were in progress.*]

WATCHDOG: He'll talk to him now, but I'm not going to stay for it. If you don't have anything, why don't you and I sign off and let Whelihan and Elbourne talk? [*Snapshot resented the fact that*

Watchdog preparing for a China call.

Watchdog did not hang around and hear what he had to say. Was Watchdog catching the Ziegler-itis now, too?]
ROADRUNNER: Be advised, I'll be available the next few hours regarding the traffic that you have received from our end.
WATCHDOG: We'll be in touch in a few hours.
ROADRUNNER: Break. Whelihan, Whelihan, Snapshot is on.
WHELIHAN: Snapshot, Whelihan. How copy?
SNAPSHOT: Whelihan, this is Snapshot. I don't understand why whenever you talk everybody leaves the room.
WHELIHAN: I think it's probably more productive that way.
SNAPSHOT: Everybody's leaving here also. OK. Go ahead, Bruce.
WHELIHAN: Want to confirm your request for a courier out of Peking. Understand you've requested one for the twenty-fourth. Is that correct?
SNAPSHOT: Did you say a courier out of Peking on the twenty-fourth? I do not understand, don't understand that.
WHELIHAN: In the conversation the other day with Whaleboat, you discussed a courier and times for film, color film, back to the states.

SNAPSHOT: Roger. That is not for the twenty-fourth, we talked approximately and that has not been requested. I do not know how to do that at this point in time because they have no flights out of here. [*There were no commercial airlines, other than those from Communist block countries, flying Peking routes in 1972.*]

WHELIHAN: Understand, then, that you have made no formal request.

SNAPSHOT: That is a roger at this time.

WHELIHAN: Snapshot, what action should we take with regard to signatures on press applications that are not available?

SNAPSHOT: I can't say it over this line, but I would get those signatures. [*Snapshot wanted to say that if the bozos in the press corps would not take time to sign their applications, they should be left behind!*]

WHELIHAN: Understand. Tim, Ron Ziegler concurs with your advice on moving the press corps immediately after the banquet, the day before the President moves.

SNAPSHOT: That is absolutely superb! We totally appreciate that.

WHELIHAN: Roger, Snapshot, but Ron's only concern, which you are aware, is a filing facility. [*A place from which correspondents would "file" their stories back to the states.*]

SNAPSHOT: I am very concerned about the filing facilities. We have asked them what they will be and they cannot give us an answer at this point. [*The advance team had no idea what the accommodations would be. The Chinese kept saying, "Not to worry," But they didn't know how demanding the American press corps could be.*]

WHELIHAN: He is very concerned, though, that when the press move, that they do have adequate facilities if they're ahead of the President.

SNAPSHOT: I would suggest we have adequate time for filing in the press room here, and then depart for Hangchou.

WHELIHAN: Snapshot, did you want the tail numbers of the press aircraft?

SNAPSHOT: Would like that. Would be excellent. Over.

WHELIHAN: Snapshot, Whelihan. I'll pass the numbers now. First aircraft, N as in Nellie, eight, eight, three, P as in Peter. [*After Whelihan passed the aircraft tail numbers, Snapshot gave Whelihan the telephone numbers of the three television networks in New York, so the executive producers in Peking could brief their offices via the satellite.*]

WHELIHAN: Any reason for this station to participate in any of those calls?

SNAPSHOT: That's a negative. We do not want a conference call because it pulls down our transmission too much. We would like to talk to them individually on a unilateral basis, however, the basis of the call is the substitution because of third country parties. The network individuals here feel that is a minor problem at this point. [*Press from countries other than the U.S. and PRC were very interested in the President's visit.*]

WHELIHAN: Understand.

CROWN: This is Crown, can we have transmit, please?

CARNATION: You are in transmit. Go ahead. [*The communications switch was still set for Peking. Now even the operators were getting testy. Tension was building everywhere, because the conditions under which they had to communicate were so difficult.*]

SNAPSHOT: OK. I need a list of the press pool. The fifteen people that will be going to Guam with the President, and arriving in the PRC on the twenty-first.

WHELIHAN: What's your deadline?

SNAPSHOT: A.S.A.P., if you can do it. You've got the list, we don't.

WHELIHAN: Roger, Snapshot. Understand. Go ahead.

SNAPSHOT: OK, Bruce, next point. We have agreed now that the majority of the press corps will travel to Hangchou the night before. Is that correct?

WHELIHAN: That's a roger.

SNAPSHOT: I assume that means that the press corps will also travel to Shanghai the night before, following the banquet in Hangchou.

WHELIHAN: That's a roger, if that is your recommendation.

SNAPSHOT: That would be of great, great help to the PRC and they would appreciate it immensely.

WHELIHAN: Understand, and we are pleased to be able to assist. Again, Whaleboat's concern is having filing facilities up the night before in those respective cities.

SNAPSHOT: That's a roger, Bruce. I would suggest right now to protect ourselves that we arrange that flight so that we can file completely, before we leave.

WHELIHAN: Understand.

SNAPSHOT: Another point, I understand that Cleve Ryan [*lighting expert*] will be coming in with the press plane. Is that correct?

WHELIHAN: That's a roger. Ryan and also Small will be travelling with the bulk of the press contingent.

SNAPSHOT: OK. I was just wondering what you were going to do in Guam, and on the flight from Guam to Shanghai, without a light man aboard.

WHELIHAN: That occurred to me simultaneously, Tim. Would you recommend that Ryan be included in the group arriving Peking the twenty-first?

SNAPSHOT: I think that would be something you would want to figure out there. We have a problem here with baggage and press gear, which will be significant, coming off of those aircraft. Naturally, we would like Ryan with us to handle that gear. [*The White House staff sure spent a lot of time making arrangements for the supposedly independent press!*] However, it seems to me, that should anything occur aboard the Presidential aircraft, that Ryan should be there. I think this would be a decision for Ziegler to make.

WHELIHAN: Roger. Will pose it to him. Do you want to go ahead with your list of items?

SNAPSHOT: That's all I have. We will try to get to the PRC as soon as possible regarding the courier flights out of here on the twenty-fourth for color film.

WHELIHAN: Are you firm in your mind, that is the date we do want to request?

SNAPSHOT: I would think so, Bruce, regarding ample times for deadlines. We could still do it on the twenty-fifth because of the time change, but let's shoot for the twenty-fourth.

WHELIHAN: Anyone there have any more traffic or any need to keep this circuit open?

SNAPSHOT: Let me confirm one thing. Are those two aircraft, that you gave me the tail numbers for Pan Am planes?

WHELIHAN: That is correct, and incidentally, we have not announced, repeat, have not announced who the charter aircraft will be provided by.

SNAPSHOT: Understand. I also need soonest the names of the flight crews on both of those aircraft. They are asking for them right now.

WHELIHAN: Understand that material, names and passport numbers, has been provided and is with, I believe, Jack D'Arcy.

SNAPSHOT: Thank you very much. We will pick up from him, however, it might be sooner by telexing it to us, if you could do that.

WHELIHAN: Will provide back-up by telex.

SNAPSHOT: This is Snapshot out.

WHELIHAN: Whelihan out. Thank you, Crown.

CROWN: Roger. Carnation, Carnation, from Crown. That concludes the call. We have no further traffic at this time.

　　　　　*　　　　　　　　*　　　　　　　　*

Bye—bye, Miss American Pie
Drove my Chevy to the levee but the levee was dry.
Them good ole boys were drinkin' whiskey and rye
Singin' this'll be the day that I die.

Roadrunner and Snapshot lounged on the Chinese couch, their heads resting on the white crochet doilies while they listened to Don McLean sing "American Pie" from a cassette out of Roadrunner's survival suitcase. It had become a regular part of their evening ritual, almost as important as the ice on the window sill.

Snapshot got up and started the tape again. It was his turn.

A long, long time ago
I can still remember
How that music used to make me smile
And I knew if I had my chance
That I could make those people dance
And maybe they'd be happy for a while.

But February made me shiver
With every paper I'd deliver.
Bad news on the doorstep
I couldn't take one more step.

I can't remember if I cried
When I read about his widowed bride,
Something touched me deep inside
The day the music died.

So bye–bye, Miss American Pie . . .

Roadrunner smiled at Snapshot. They knew the Chinese were trying to translate Don McLean's lyrics and make some sense out of them. After all it *was* February and it *was* cold outside and the Chinese *were* waking Roadrunner up at all hours of the night, asking hundreds of questions and wanting him to make copies for them. They were fascinated by the Americans' machine that could make copies in an instant. It must have saved many Chinese desk clerks hours of copying information by hand. They decided that if this trip did nothing else for international trade, it would help Xerox sell copy machines in China.

Did you write the book of love
And do you have faith in God above?
If the bible tells you so.

Now do you believe in rock and roll?
Can music save your mortal soul
And can you teach me how to dance real slow?

Well, I know that you're in love with him
'Cause I saw you dancin' in the gym.
You both kicked off your shoes.
Man, I dig those rythym and blues.

I was a lonely teen-age broncin' buck,
With a pink carnation and a pick-up truck.
But I knew I was out of luck
The day the music died.

I started singin' bye–bye, Miss American Pie . . .

Several members of the group had begun reporting in the evening meetings that their counterparts were asking them the meaning of various slang expressions. "What is a broncin' buck?" Livingood had been asked. "What is rock and roll?" was a question put to Schrauth.

Everyone had laughed and wanted to know how they had responded. It was even funnier when they both admitted they had done a little physical demonstration along with the explanation. "Yeah, I even sang a little bit of 'You ain't nothing but a hound dog,' while I bopped around the commune," Schrauth told them.

Now for ten years we've been on our own,
And moss grows fat on a rollin' stone
But that's not how it used to be

When the jester sang for the king and queen
In a coat he borrowed from James Dean
And a voice that came from you and me.

Oh and while the king was looking down,
The jester stole his thorny crown
The courtroom was adjourned,
No verdict was returned.

And while Lennin read a book on Marx
The quartet practiced in the park
And we sang dirges in the dark
The day the music died.

We were singin' bye–bye, Miss American Pie . . .

"Who was James Dean?" was a question for Swift at the comm center. "Was he a communist?" the Chinese technician asked when Swift said Dean was a movie star.

Helter-skelter in a summer swelter
The birds flew off with a fallout shelter
Eight miles high and fallin' fast,

It landed foul on the grass
The players tried for a forward pass,
With the jester on the sidelines in a cast

Now the half-time air was sweet perfume
While the sergeants played a marching tune
We all got up to dance
But we never got the chance

'Cause the players tried to take the field,
The marching band refused to yield.
Do you recall what was revealed
The day the music died?

We started singin' bye–bye, Miss American Pie . . .

Roadrunner and Snapshot loved to sing along, and tonight they were doing so with great gusto. The telex traffic was moving. Watchdog, sitting on the other side of the world, was finally reading all of the stuff they had been able to send to him. They were no longer stuck on hold; things were beginning to happen.

And there we were all in one place,
A generation lost in space
With no time left to start again.

So come on, Jack be nimble, Jack be quick,
Jack Flash sat on a candlestick
'Cause fire is the devil's only friend

And as I watched him on the stage
My hands were clenched in fists of rage
No angel born in hell
Could break that Satan's spell

And as the flames climbed high into the night
To light the sacrificial rite
I saw Satan laughing with delight
The day the music died.

He was singin' bye–bye, Miss American Pie . . .

I met a girl who sang the blues
And I asked her for some happy news
But she just smiled and turned away.

I went down to the sacred store
Where I heard the music years before
But the man there said the music wouldn't play.

And in the streets the children screamed,
The lovers cried and the poets dreamed.
But not a word was spoken
The church bells all were broken.

And the three men I admire most
The Father, Son, and the Holy Ghost
They caught the last train for the coast
The day the music died.

A young woman interpreter, struggling hard to improve her English, had asked Roadrunner about the Father, Son and Holy Ghost. As he tried to give her a relatively simple description, she interrupted him to ask, "Who is Jesus Christ?" He was really shocked. It was the year of our Lord since Christ was born, 1972. A.D.! Anno Domini! Could this well-educated woman really be asking him such a question? Was she serious, or was he being tested? He prayed he was being tested. That was much easier to deal with than the alternative.

And they were singin' bye–bye, Miss American Pie
Drove my Chevy to the levee but the levee was dry.
Them good ole boys were drinkin' whiskey and rye
Singin' this'll be the day that I die.

They drained their glasses and listened to the rest of the tape. It felt good just to sit and relax. They were both tired. Suddenly there was a knock on the door and instantly Mr. Chu and Mr. Ma walked in. They had several questions that needed answers immediately and they had four documents that would require three copies each, please, and thank you very much.

Roadrunner did not get a very good night's sleep. Mr. Chu came back fifteen minutes later with a few more questions and Watchdog called just as he was falling asleep again.

"Mr. Walker, Mr. Walker," the Chief Warrant Officer was saying over and over. Was it the Chinese again? They usually did not wake the Chief up; he slept like a log. The only thing that woke him up was the smell of fire . . . or the telephone! Roadrunner tried to clear the sleep out of his head once again as he grabbed his pants and shirt and laced up his sand boots. It was thirty-seven minutes past midnight in China and approaching lunch time at the White House.

HENKEL: Roadrunner, this is Henkel. I just got a call from the situation room here, and they informed me that they are in receipt of a cable from a Vacca, V-A-C-C-A, a member of the Peking, repeat Peking television pool and it is addressed to a Mr. Sid Kauffman at CBS in New York. They have requested that we TWX it from Washington to New York as a service. Are you aware of this arrangement?

ROADRUNNER: That is a negative, and I repeat, a negative. I would disregard it.

HENKEL: This is why I called. The concern was that this could get out of hand, and they were interested to know that you were on top of all cables going out.

ROADRUNNER: Wait one. . . . Roger, I'm checking right now, go ahead.

HENKEL: That was my principal reason for this phone call. I will just relate again, that from our operation here, your material is extremely beneficial, and Julie [*Rowe*] is proceeding very, very nicely with updating the schedule.

ROADRUNNER: I'm glad.

WATCHDOG: Roadrunner, Watchdog.

ROADRUNNER: Yes, sir, go ahead.

WATCHDOG: I just received your latest cable that leads off giving room numbers for security documents. Going down quickly to the reciprocal banquet, I think we will bring that fruit peeled, and it will be used in dishes, and not used just as raw fruit on the table. [*The Chinese liked to put a whole tangerine in front of each place setting. The White House was planning to serve a fruit salad.*]

ROADRUNNER: Roger. It sounds great. I would like to mention that to my counterpart. Now, with this information, I will be in a better position to talk in detail about this. I will do that, hopefully, tomorrow morning.

WATCHDOG: Now, regarding the manifest for 26000 [*Air Force One*], we'll get that to you.

ROADRUNNER: Yes, I think it would be a gesture that would be very much appreciated.

WATCHDOG: Regarding the rooming list for Shanghai and Hang-chou, I'm sure that you'll find no problem there, but obviously we will wait until you see it again.

ROADRUNNER: Please, because I am informed from our floor plans the PRC reserves the right for some of those rooms. I think it's necessary that we have a chance to look that over and see which rooms they were talking about.

WATCHDOG: Let me just see what else you have here. You gave me a list for unofficial party with titles. That's fine. I think the titles differ from what we sent, but we can accept yours without any problem.

ROADRUNNER: We are in receipt of both the official and the unofficial titles, and that was very helpful. We will go with yours. I will present that to the PRC tomorrow.

WATCHDOG: Let me ask one question regarding that . . . the arrival sequence and the very first thing that happens in Peking in terms of that introduction. I understand that to be similar to what Ambassador Mosbacher has done before. Is that correct? [*Chief of Protocol, Emil Mosbacher, usually handled the introductions whenever the Nixon's arrived for an official visit.*]

ROADRUNNER: Be advised that Mr. Tong, one of the members of the protocol office that has been most helpful, rode out to the airport with me the other day. It was just after President Bhutto's departure. He had pictures and diagrams and it was extremely helpful to all of us in understanding what the arrival sequence could be. [*Bhutto had over a million people along the streets when he arrived. Musicians and dancers started gathering at 4 A.M. and would march from side streets into position. Roadrunner thought it might be a preview for President Nixon, but no such luck.*]

However, be advised during my conversation with him, he informed me that Director Han Hsu would, in fact, make some introduction, but that he would play it by ear on the ground. He asked if there would be any counterpart for protocol on our side to assist in the introductions. I, as you can well imagine, paused, knowing very well that has been Mosbacher in the past. And I said, yes, that could be Mr. Chapin. Realizing you are on board the plane, I came up with the idea about you getting off at the rear and coming around and receiving the Prime Minister and making the introductions.

WATCHDOG: Well, I'm going to have to ask on that one, I think. I just wanted to get a feel for exactly what you had on your mind, and I think I've read it properly.

ROADRUNNER: The Chinese arrival ceremony is very loose. It is very casual, almost informal. The Prime Minister stands on one side sometimes for honors, and on the other side sometimes for honors. When they make their move after honors, down through the honor guard, the entire Pakistani party followed the Prime Minister and Bhutto. In the pictures I saw, it was not the way we would do an arrival, but then again, this isn't the USA.

WATCHDOG: I read you. I know exactly what you are saying. Over.

ROADRUNNER: Be advised that everyone is exceptionally pleased with the camera position. I wish that I could get you a diagram. [*The FAX wasn't around in 1972.*] The PRC, once we did our survey, took the few suggestions that Snapshot and I made, along with the networks, and reacted immediately and thanked us for those suggestions. With that, I think it will be a very nice arrival. Be advised, I'm not sure there will be anybody there to see it. [*Roadrunner no longer thought crowds would be a part of the arrival ceremony.*]

WATCHDOG: I understand. What's your status there now? Are you getting ready to go to bed?

ROADRUNNER: I've already been in bed, and I plan on going back.

WATCHDOG: (Ha ha) I'm sorry! You said you were going to stay up late. I misread that to think you were going to be up till one, and I apologize for waking you.

ROADRUNNER: No problem at all, except I sat around waiting and decided to go to bed.

WATCHDOG: Good. We're OK here, and we'll keep working through the day. We'll try to have that list out to you tonight.

ROADRUNNER: I understand, and everyone understands. Of course we are very happy that everything is up and working. I just wish in many cases that we had more information for you, but we're progressing nicely.

WATCHDOG: As you can imagine, our problem on this list is trying to interphase all the protocol among the Secret Service, the press corps, the technicians, and everyone else, and so that's our problem.

ROADRUNNER: I can well imagine. That's an exercise in patience as well as intelligence.

WATCHDOG: Well, go to bed, and we'll let you sign off. We don't have anything else. Take care.

ROADRUNNER: Good night, again.

Roadrunner hurried to his room and crawled back into bed. "How many times had he done this tonight," he wondered, "and how many more times before the dawn's early light would herald the beginning of another long day in the People's Republic of China?" He was awake early. After savoring a cup of instant coffee and the now familiar serenade of bicycle bells, he checked on the latest sick call list and the paper traffic from Washington. At 7:40 A.M. he was talking to the White House again, where it was 6:40 in the evening.

ROADRUNNER: Good evening, Watchdog.

WATCHDOG: Good morning to you, Roadrunner. How is everybody today?

ROADRUNNER: Just fine. Be advised, I have Snapshot, Schrauth, and Araiza in the room, and we're ready to receive information.

WATCHDOG: I am going to be departing shortly and Bill Henkel will cover the conversation. I just wanted to check and see how Vern and the rest of the members of the party are, healthwise.

ROADRUNNER: I think everybody is progressing nicely. I just went through the sick call. There are a number of people, but it's the normal things, nothing of an emergency type basis. We are hopeful that Vern will be able to join us from the hospital today to rest here and work with us in-house. If it's not today, I am almost positive it will be tomorrow. Over.

WATCHDOG: Roger, Ron. We have sent a couple of memorandums recently. The main thing is the list of photo opportunities and occasions when cameras will be present. We need to get that from you since Ziegler and I are going to work on that together tomorrow.

ROADRUNNER: As I indicated last night, we are working with Snapshot and he has a very good feel for what opportunities there will be, as is indicated on some of the scenarios. We will do the same for the rest.

WATCHDOG: That's fine. I'm going to turn it over to Henkel. Unless you have any questions related to me, I'm going to be taking off.

ROADRUNNER: Have a nice evening, and we'll talk to you tomorrow morning your time.

WATCHDOG: Have a good day, Roadrunner. This is Chapin off.

ROADRUNNER: Henkel, Roadrunner.

HENKEL: Roadrunner, Henkel. Read you loud and clear. I have a few points to cover with you.

ROADRUNNER: OK, Bill. Let's do it as fast as we can.

HENKEL: I have all four girls working on the master protocol precedence list. We are typing it now, and we will send it to you in the next few hours. However, I must emphasize that this is strictly for your information, as Welcome has not seen it and we will not be able to get it to him until tomorrow morning our time.

ROADRUNNER: Be advised, I would like to be in receipt of that entire list. It would be extremely helpful to me and my counterparts will understand that there is much work left to be done on it, but it is a beginning. ["*Come on! Just get something to us so the Chinese will get off our case," Roadrunner thought.*]

HENKEL: The list will have the name of the individual, a number priority and his affiliation. I want to emphasize Ron, that you and Snapshot, Schrauth, etc., should look at the affiliation, because the total number is correct, however, some of the breakdowns are off by one or two. So I think this will be a very useful document to help us refine our final.

ROADRUNNER: Are they typing that on single pages?

HENKEL: That is a roger. We are typing it in a numerical sequence, one through our agreed to number.

ROADRUNNER: I trust that you are doing that by category within that master list.

HENKEL: It starts with the official party, then with you at the top of the unofficial party, then we have an addition there. Then we go down through Jonathan Howe, then we add the other individuals we mentioned in a separate cable. Then we had some further additions, picked up the balance of the unofficial party and then the press staff. It is in a numerical sequence, one through our final figure.

ROADRUNNER: Let me make a point. We are remiss, at this point, in recognizing various members that, protocol-wise, should fall in position in either the official or the unofficial party. I give you examples: Warren, Elbourne, Redman, etc. Do you copy?

HENKEL: You'll be pleasantly surprised when you see our document.

ROADRUNNER: That's a beautiful! Thank you very much. I'm glad you're on top of it.

HENKEL: We are also breaking down the list, whether they'll be in Peking, Hangchou, or Shanghai. We will note by an X whether they'll be in one location, two, or three. I think this will be very helpful to you.

ROADRUNNER: That sounds great. Thank you. That's good thinking.

HENKEL: Be advised though, that this has pretty well put us behind on other things. I think you can appreciate that this has been a real crash project involving one heck of a lot of people.

ROADRUNNER: Yes, I am very much aware of that. However, if you've almost got it done, then you can start on your other work.

HENKEL: That's a roger.

ROADRUNNER: OK. Next.

HENKEL: With regard to the reciprocal banquet, we will provide you with the following fruit: Florida oranges already sectioned and coming to you in gallon containers, Florida white grapefruit sections, also in gallon containers, and California orange sections in containers. Now the current plan is that these containers will be on the C-141 arriving the fourteenth of February in the People's Republic.

ROADRUNNER: I understand.

HENKEL: Ron Jackson has been working on this project and assures me that their quality will be excellent, their freshness will be maintained and it will not be a major problem to keep them. [*Ron Jackson had been Presidential food service coordinator and Commander of the White House Staff Mess, the most exclusive restaurant in Washington, D.C. since the Johnson administration.*]

ROADRUNNER: Am I to assume, at this end, that this needs refrigeration upon arrival?

HENKEL: Very good question which I will address myself to. I assume that they will need refrigeration when they arrive, but I certainly will cable that information to you immediately.

ROADRUNNER: OK. Go ahead.

HENKEL: We are working on the full manifest for 970 and 26000. The only problem right now is the determination of the press pools.

ROADRUNNER: I understand that. I said last night that both Snapshot and Whelihan are working on that and they may not have it right now. We understand that. However, let's not stop pushing to get those answers.

HENKEL: I can assure you I am a very popular individual around the White House right now.

ROADRUNNER: I can well imagine that you are. However, that's immaterial. It's more important that we get that information as rapidly as possible.

HENKEL: I agree. No, you misunderstood me. We are working on it, and Bruce is cooperating very, very well, and I am confident we'll be able to get that information to you as soon as possible. Going on, we are planning as of now, predicated on your discussions with your counterpart, to have the aircraft arriving in Shanghai, the first C-141 on the twelfth, the next C-141 on the thirteenth to go up to Hangchou, and as scheduled, the two C-141s arriving the fourteenth. Is this still correct for us to be planning on this?

ROADRUNNER: That's a roger. We have had a little bit of a problem from the military side, not having Vern with us. I hope that Bill Gully is staying on top of this as much as possible. If there is anything that we have not provided them, at this end, please let us know. I know that Abel Araiza has been talking to Gully. But just make sure that they've got all the information they need from us.

HENKEL: General Scowcroft has been attending our morning meetings, and I have been working quite closely with the various aides. I don't feel that there is a problem. Just for your information, it looks like the C-141 that includes Mr. Thomas, will stay in Hawaii an extra day because of the limited overnight facilities in Guam.

ROADRUNNER: That's no problem. Just tell those fellows to get some rest and be in good shape. You understand? Please? I cannot emphasize enough, them taking care of themselves and being prepared to dress warmly when they arrive. They will be down south and not have the dramatic weather changes that we've had, but they should still be very cognizant of that fact.

HENKEL: I assure you that I have been conveying that concern of yours to the affected parties. Also, Ron, what is the status of the personal assistant to Mrs. Nixon?

ROADRUNNER: Henkel, be advised, that I will tell you as soon as I have any information. I have not received an answer.

HENKEL: I understand. That's about all I have, Ron, I want to get back to working on our master list so you can be in receipt of it. I will warn you that the poking of it will probably be quite a task.

ROADRUNNER: Yes, Bill, then possibly you'll want to start poking now if you have certain pages done. [*Henkel did not seem to grasp that Roadrunner was not interested in hearing his problems and how hard he was working.*]

HENKEL: Yeah, I'll take a look at that aspect of it. We are trying to keep pretty tight control over the thing. But, I'll see if we can't do that.

ROADRUNNER: It's a pretty sorry situation if we can't keep an in-house control on it. Talk to the duty officer and get it poked and track with someone down there. [*Roadrunner was still in charge of his Advance Office!*]

HENKEL: I understand and we'll work on it.

ROADRUNNER: How are the girls?

HENKEL: They're all doing great. They are really working hard, believe me. We've been involved in a lot of projects and all's going well. The spirit of cooperation is great. I have absolutely no complaints.

ROADRUNNER: I would like to say hello to them, please.

HENKEL: I am in your office right now. I will go get them, can you wait one?

ROADRUNNER: That's a roger. (sound of voices entering the room)

HENKEL: (Give him a call. Say, "Roadrunner, this is Karen.")

REITZ: Roadrunner, Roadrunner, Reitz. [*Karen Ann Dixon Reitz, Advance Office trip coordinator.*]

OPERATOR: Person calling, say again.

ANDREWS: Carnation, Andrews, request you have your teletype operator pull the tape off, pull the tape off.

CARNATION: Andrews, be advised, at this time we have priority traffic up. Do not interfere with this at this time, please. See if you can't locate the party and advise to wait for this call to terminate before they come back again. Please.

ANDREWS: Roger.

ROADRUNNER: Thank you very much (static for three full minutes.) [*Clearly, the operators were not prepared for the women in the White House Advance Office to be talking to the people in China.*]

ROADRUNNER: Henkel, Henkel, this is Roadrunner.

HENKEL: Roadrunner, Henkel. Read you loud and clear. Over.

ROADRUNNER: What are you doing? Henkel?

HENKEL: I've got the girls here. We've been trying to give you a call, and all we've been getting is static. If you'll wait one, Reitz will be giving you a call.

ROADRUNNER: Roger. I've been waiting also. [*Neither Roadrunner nor Henkel seemed to be aware that the signal operators did not approve of what they were attempting to do.*]

REITZ: Roadrunner, Reitz.

ROADRUNNER: Is this Julie? Julie, this is Roadrunner. How are you? [*Julie Rowe, Advance Office trip coordinator.*]

REITZ: Negative. Roadrunner, Reitz.

ROADRUNNER: Who am I talking to?

REITZ: Roadrunner, this is Karen Reitz.

ROADRUNNER: Oh. Hi, Karen. How are you?

REITZ: I'm fine.

ROADRUNNER: OK. That's very good. Let me talk to Marsha. [*Marsha Griswold, Roadrunner's White House secretary.*]

MARSHA: (I don't know what to say.)

KAREN: (Say, "Roadrunner, this is Marsha.")

MARSHA: Roadrunner, this is Marsha.

ROADRUNNER: Hi, Marsha. How are ya? Have you been working hard?

MARSHA: Yes, sir. We're all doing fine. How are you?

ROADRUNNER: Very fine. We're receiving lots of information. Thank you very much. I know it's been an experience for you back there also. We're doing fine, everybody's in good health. You take care of yourself and we'll see you in about three weeks.

MARSHA: Thank you very much.

ROADRUNNER: OK. Let me talk to Julie, please.

HENKEL: Julie just stepped out of the office on an errand and probably won't be back for a few minutes and Nancy is in the press office right now.

ROADRUNNER: Roger. Is Nancy there? [*Nancy Spencer, Press Office staff assistant.*]

HENKEL: Nancy is over at the press office right now and probably won't be back for a few minutes.

ROADRUNNER: All right. Would you please tell her that Snapshot was asking for her, he's here now, and he'll talk to her later. That's all we've got . . . wait one. Snapshot wants to talk to Whelihan. Is he about?

HENKEL: That is a negative. I will try to alert Crown right now, through one of the girls, and have them pick up on this conversation and locate Whelihan.

SNAPSHOT: Crown, Snapshot. Would you see if you can locate Whelihan for me, Whelihan.

CROWN: Snapshot from Crown. Roger, sir, standby. Do you want this portion recorded? Go ahead.

SNAPSHOT: That would be a roger.

CROWN: Roger, sir. Stand by please. (static . . . . long pause)

The conversation was not recorded and Snapshot does not recall if Whelihan came on the line, or if he grew tired of waiting once again, chuckled to himself and said a great big, audible "screw it." He and Roadrunner had a full day ahead of them and they needed to make lots of progress.

CHAPTER XII

A COMMUNIST PLOT

FEBRUARY 9, 1972

"Welcome to the Friendship Store," the diminutive young woman said to Roadrunner as he entered the tastefully appointed shop filled with products made in the People's Republic of China.

"*Shay, shay*," he responded as he bowed slightly, just inside the doorway. All the Chinese counterparts looked very pleased. It was the right way to start the shopping expedition. She had greeted him in English and he had responded in Chinese.

The goods on display were impressive: silk wall hangings, carved jade, cloisonne, cork carvings, and much more of China's most impressive export goods. This was a shop reserved for foreigners. Ordinary Chinese were not allowed inside.

Roadrunner always brought dolls home for his three little girls. His extensive international travels had resulted in quite a remarkable doll collection. They looked forward to receiving these treasures, and they had already talked about what the dolls from China might look like.

"I think mine will be wearing a Mao jacket," Lisa, soon to be eleven, had predicted. Being the oldest, she was very knowledgeable about fashions in the PRC.

159

"I want mine to be a Chinese peasant, wearing a straw hat to shade her from the sun in the rice paddies," Marja, an avid nine-year-old reader, declared.

"I hope mine will be a panda bear," Lynne told her Mom. Since her favorite possession was a slightly disheveled red teddy bear named Teddy, this was a logical choice. Her Mom was slightly surprised that Lynne, only eight, had listened to the talk about the state gifts, but then, the girls never did miss much when it came to events that touched their lives.

Roadrunner chose three dolls, an antique jade heart pendant for his wife, some tapestry wall hangings, cork carvings and some pieces of cloisonne. He had trouble choosing among all the beautiful things, none of which were available in the United States. He hoped the President's trip would change that.

"I would also like to buy some Mao hats, buttons and little red books," Roadrunner told the clerk as she was wrapping up his parcels.

"We do not have those things here," she told him. "Those are for Chinese people to buy."

"On another day, we will go to the Number One Department Store," one of the Chinese counterparts assured him.

"I would like to do that," Roadrunner said.

The Americans, working closely with their Chinese counterparts, continued to try to improve the quality of the satellite transmission. After strictly observing the radio jargon necessary to alert technicians to flip the switches, they were delighted to learn that they didn't have to use such exact language any longer. It was 9:37 that evening when the conference call came in. In Washington, people were starting another day. It was 8:37 in the morning.

ROADRUNNER: Good morning. I'm advised that we need not use our code names, or over and out, and all that stuff, I'm not really sure I can handle it if we don't . . . uh, over. Uh . . . Hi!
WATCHDOG: Ha, ha, ha. We have to change our whole style.
ROADRUNNER: I know it. It sounds like you're right here with us. Great connection. We're in good spirits and everything's fine. How's everybody there?
WATCHDOG: Everything is fine here, Ron. We have this master list and it's in pretty good shape. As Bill pointed out to you, I still need to review it with Haldeman, and I'm going to do that this morning.
ROADRUNNER: OK. We have had some very good exchanges today, but we have not started talking the details we need for our scenarios. So, I don't know where we stand right now.

WATCHDOG: Roger. Your coming in like somebody was turning the volume up and down . . . clipping it . . . or something. When you talk, try to talk in a monotone and at constant volume if you can. (pause) Hello.

ROADRUNNER: Ahhh, yeah, well, we've got a few problems on this end. How does it sound now?

WATCHDOG: Bad.

ROADRUNNER: It does?

WATCHDOG: Yes . . . but that's OK.

ROADRUNNER: You sound great.

WATCHDOG: I just got up! (laughter in room) Roadrunner, let me ask whether it's possible to make that shift the morning of the twenty-second in regard to the First Lady's first event? [*Visit to the hotel kitchen.*]

ROADRUNNER: Yeah. That's done.

WATCHDOG: You've gotta let us know that kind of stuff. ["*Damn!*" *Roadrunner thought. "You know everything we know ten times over. It's the stuff we don't know that's driving us crazy!*"]

ROADRUNNER: Yeah, we did the first day, Dwight.

WATCHDOG: OK.

ROADRUNNER: I told you that the very first day when we sat down and talked to our . . .

WATCHDOG: I don't recall getting word on that.

ROADRUNNER: Well, I'm sorry, but we did.

WATCHDOG: Can you send me a copy, that I can pass on up to her, of the way you see it now, and what you think should be added or deleted and some of the fall backs in case of bad weather and so forth?

ROADRUNNER: Sure can.

WATCHDOG: That will be very helpful if you'll dash that off to us. [*Again Roadrunner was piqued at Watchdog. "Dash it off? Sure! Just dictate it to your White House secretary. What could be simpler?*"] Uh, hang on a minute. Ron, how are we doing in terms of the health thing?

ROADRUNNER: Fine. Coffey has returned this afternoon and he is presently resting. The doctor has told him to stay in his room for the next couple of days. Tomorrow we'll start bringing him up to date on where we stand. Agent Weaver is better this evening and probably, with one more day of rest, he'll be back. Other than that, just normal sick call type events. No major problems.

WATCHDOG: How 'bout the technicians, Ron?

ROADRUNNER: One ground satellite individual who was in the hospital has returned this evening, and there is still one individual in the hospital.

WATCHDOG: OK. Good. Now, be advised, the reason we're asking is we're starting to get some wire stories, and we just want to make sure Ziegler can handle it should the questions come up.

ROADRUNNER: Yeah, I understand that. Mr. Chu raised the Reuters story. They expressed their concern once again that people from our side were talking. We told them we can only guarantee the White House support people, and call upon Siegenthaler to keep reins on the technicians. It's difficult . . .

WATCHDOG: It's probably coming from these conversations.

ROADRUNNER: Well, that's a possibility. I don't necessarily agree with that.

WATCHDOG: Is Swift with you?

ROADRUNNER: Yes, he is. He's right here.

WATCHDOG: It's just damn near impossible to even understand one word that you're saying. The problem is a real fluctuation in the volume. Especially when you go on for a long sentence or a paragraph. It's almost next to impossible to follow you. The best way I can describe it is like the volume being turned up and down very rapidly.

ROADRUNNER: OK. I'm sorry. Does this sound better?

WATCHDOG: Much better. Now I can hear you. What did you do?

ROADRUNNER: Well, we changed telephones. I've got an echo on this one and that's why we're not using it, but if it sounds better on your end, I can stand it.

WATCHDOG: This is fantastic. Now we can hear you loud and clear.

ROADRUNNER: OK. Go ahead.

WATCHDOG: OK. Well, I was just making the point that we were worried about the wire stories getting out of hand.

ROADRUNNER: Yeah . . . I . . . they would have to be almost standing right next to us, unless they've got a tap on one of these wires. That's conceivable, I guess, but I can't believe it. There are too many other ways that they can get a story if they want it, Dwight. They don't have to talk to anybody, they can just stand around the airport. That's on limits for everybody.

There's this guy who has access to every place in town. He can do what he wants, go where he wants, and see what he wants and he doesn't even have to talk to anybody to get a story. We can't live in a vacuum. We're doing that as much as we can now.

WATCHDOG: I'm making the point that anybody in the world can listen to this phone conversation right now.

ROADRUNNER: I'm sorry. [*What other choice was there?*]

WATCHDOG: OK. Did you get any word on that lighting thing for the documentary crew?

ROADRUNNER: I have not.

WATCHDOG: Do you have any word on motorcades?

ROADRUNNER: No, I do not.

WATCHDOG: Oooooookay. (pause) Now, in regard to the UPI and the AP boxes that are going to be coming in on one of the C-141s, we're going to have to make arrangements, as you know, for those to be transported up to Peking from Shanghai.

ROADRUNNER: Yeah, I am aware of that, as are the Chinese and right now they are planning on doing that on PRC aircraft.

WATCHDOG: Great. Perfect. OK, I thought that was the case. When do you get back to Peking from Hangchou?

ROADRUNNER: OK. You obviously have not seen my wire. Let me just reiterate once again the schedule that we have come up with. [*Roadrunner couldn't help wondering why they couldn't take a few minutes to read their cable traffic before these phone calls?*] I'd also like for you to be advised that the PRC was extremely grateful, in that they need the time here in Peking as much as we do. In our conversation this morning, they most graciously thanked us for considering that and being on top it and changing the schedule.

The schedule now is that there will be thirteen of us departing Peking on the evening of the eleventh of February at 5 P.M. We will fly to Shanghai and survey the guest house that evening. The next morning, receive the first aircraft arriving at 10 A.M. from Guam. We will continue the survey during the course of that day, allowing Elbourne with D'Arcy, Livingood with Jenkins, and Swift with Bruff, to meet with their counterparts. Mike and I will be there also, to survey and discuss the situation as it stands now. We will overnight the night of the twelfth. On the morning of the thirteenth receive the aircraft coming in from Guam. We will travel on PRC aircraft.

Now, the question is, if the aircraft that departs Shanghai will go to Hangchou and depart for Peking or return through Shanghai? This is a PRC decision. We have four people, plus baggage that must join the PRC in Shanghai that do not need to go to Hangchou. So we're working on it, and the PRC is agreeable.

WATCHDOG: OK, that's good. So, by the night of the fourteenth, you will be back in Peking, which is the point where we have to go through the final rundown in the schedule. Is that right?

ROADRUNNER: That's a roger. As I pointed out to my counterpart this morning, we were attempting to put together a detailed schedule and they must realize our party is departing Washington on the seventeenth. So we need as much information as we can get from their side. For example, who is going to meet the President in

Shanghai? What will the greeting committee be like when he arrives in Peking? The motorcade assignments to the various events? We have given them questions, but have received nothing back. [*Roadrunner was becoming convinced that the Chinese were so inexperienced in dealing with delegations such as the American advance team that some logistical subjects that were being raised had never occurred to them before. The long delays were therefore a result of the Chinese needing to learn enough about a new subject to be able to give a complete, intelligent answer.*]

WATCHDOG: OK. I understand and sympathize with your problem. Let me see now. Ron, we are going to send a list of everyone that would be on the PRC aircraft with the President.

ROADRUNNER: The only names I'm missing would be the interpreter, and the three press. Swift will be the individual that rides representing the White House Communications Agency. And those are the only four names I'm missing. Be advised, I got approval for the personal assistant [*Mrs. Nixon's hairdresser*], as I'm sure you are aware.

WATCHDOG: Yes, sir. I'm not surprised, are you?

ROADRUNNER: Not at all. The only reason I'm not surprised is because we haven't asked for anybody else. But I just know they were aware of us possibly asking for another steno, for a doctor, and other things. I'm convinced of it.

WATCHDOG: Right, but I think we're in good shape.

ROADRUNNER: Yeah. I think we're in good shape here. Everybody's gotta be conditioned, though. It could be a dog and pony show, but I am convinced that once our party arrives, the PRC, if they have to, will have an advance person for every member. We have had various interpreters rotating through us. They are bringing in people from all over this country that speak English and are moving them through us. I've had at least four different interpreters. They're bringing them in and getting them accustomed to us, our mannerisms and our customs.

WATCHDOG: Right. That's very good. I think it is very kind of them to make this gesture in order to see that operationally it goes smooth.

ROADRUNNER: I agree. OK. I'd just like to raise one point. I had to call Bill Gully about 3 A.M. his time, because the PRC had received a phone call from Guam saying they were making radio checks to clear our C-141 in tomorrow. I assured the PRC that the C-141 was not coming in tomorrow. It couldn't have been an hour and a half later that the PRC received another call from Shanghai. It appears to me that we've got an overanxious radio operator in Guam that's trying to do his thing with China China China China.

If we could get that turned off, there would be great appreciation on my part.
WATCHDOG: Done. We've done it.
ROADRUNNER: Thank you.
WATCHDOG: We just talked to them a few moments ago, and re-confirmed the current plan.
ROADRUNNER: Great. Thank you. One question on the personal assistant. How does Miss DeSantis spell her name?
WATCHDOG: It's Mrs.
ROADRUNNER: Right.
WATCHDOG: And it's Rita.
ROADRUNNER: Rita.
WATCHDOG: Then it's capitol D-E capitol F-A-N-T-I-S.
ROADRUNNER: F as in fox trot?
WATCHDOG: Right.
ROADRUNNER: OK. I assume that she does not have a passport. She has an alien card number, and that is what you have sent us. Is that a roger?
WATCHDOG: That's right. She is what's classified as a permanent resident alien.
ROADRUNNER: OK. I hope they understand that. [*He was wondering how he was going to explain "permanent resident alien" to the Chinese.*]
WATCHDOG: I do, too. I sent that to you in a cable, didn't I?
ROADRUNNER: Yes, we got it. I felt relatively confident that she did not have a passport, but I didn't know whether she did from another country. I understand now.
WATCHDOG: OK, well, can you give us a rundown on what you did today, other than talk to Gully and some of the rest of us on the phone?
ROADRUNNER: Ah, yeah. Be very happy to. We had quite a bit of traffic to read this morning. About 8:40 we got a call that Mr. Chu would like to see me. Mr. Chu, Mr. Ma, and Mr. Wong had a meeting with Mr. Schrauth, Mr. Elbourne, Mr. Manning, and myself. We spent about two and a half hours going through manifests, aircraft schedules, passport numbers, all kinds of nitty gritty activity. We then came back and worked for about two hours on putting the information together. We went back with the revised official and unofficial parties to include Mrs. DeFantis. At that point we sat down and watched *The Graduate*. At about four o'clock the PRC called upon me again for about an hour and then we went shopping. And here we are.
WATCHDOG: Did you host anybody for *The Graduate*? Did any government representative . . .?

ROADRUNNER: Well, we did have a representative from the PRC walk into the room, and it just happened to be one of those moments that I wished he hadn't walked in . . . (laughter erupts in Washington) [*Mrs. Robinson had been undressing!*] . . . and so I got up and stood in front of him and Livingood stood in front of the lens . . . (laughter in Washington and Peking) . . . so, other than that, we invited no more of our friends. [*Muffled sounds of people trying to gain control of themselves lasted several seconds. Watchdog did not want it to appear that they were laughing at the Chinese.*]
WATCHDOG: OK. Well . . . everything's OK here. It's a typical cold, damp, dreary, Washington day. (A mock sympathetic "Awwwww" from Peking.)
ROADRUNNER: You ought to see this place! (shrieks of laughter)
WATCHDOG: Hang on a minute. [*Again, it is very obvious that the group needed time to recover and did not want to sound insulting to the PRC.*]
WATCHDOG: OK. Just a minute. (To the people in the room: "Do we have anything else here?") By morning your time, Ron, we will have to you the full manifest for the Spirit of '76 and 970.
ROADRUNNER: That's outstanding. We are receiving the 391 Americans list. It'll probably take a few hours, but it is coming in now.
WATCHDOG: Yeah, we're gonna have changes on it, we'll do it at the end, won't be many, be rather insignificant.
ROADRUNNER: Yes, they understand that. All they need is something to start with. They'll prepare name cards, I'm convinced, for every American on that list. And then once we come in with the list of who will attend the various functions, they will just simply pull these out of a master file.
WATCHDOG: OK. Uh, hang on a minute. Now, Bruce Whelihan is asking if we have to make a change in the press pool, would this be understood and acceptable?
ROADRUNNER: No. In the press pool, Elbourne is saying a loud negative.
WATCHDOG: OK. So we should come in with what we are going to hold with.
ROADRUNNER: That's correct. I don't think they are big on those changes, as you can well imagine, but I think Timmie has such a good relationship with Mr. Ma that he understands.
WATCHDOG: OK. Good.
ROADRUNNER: I think you read me. [*"We just can't be making changes," Roadrunner wanted to remind them. "It absolutely throws the Chinese into a tail spin."*]
WATCHDOG: I do.

ROADRUNNER: It's very difficult for them to understand why we are not better organized. [*Roadrunner felt better that he had finally said it!*]

WATCHDOG: Well, we're moving X number of people, and I repeat X number. I don't want to talk the numbers, over there, and there's changing circumstances here all the time. People get the flu, sick, can't go, get other assignments, and so forth. That's part of our problem. (To someone in the room: "Yeah!") [*Watchdog was frustrated, too. Ziegler and the press expected too much flexibility and Roadrunner and the Chinese wouldn't allow any. Where was a happy medium?*] Hang on a minute . . . Ron?

ROADRUNNER: Yes.

WATCHDOG: When will Vern be back with you and be able to sit in the meetings? And also to communicate with General Scowcroft?

ROADRUNNER: I would think tomorrow. I talked to him this evening and he wants to start going through some of the paper work tomorrow. We do not plan on taking Vern with us, he will be in charge here during my absence. I plan on spending time with him tomorrow and by day after tomorrow he'll start getting back in to the groove of things.

WATCHDOG: OK. That's fine. It's good to know who's been designated to lead there in your absence, so if anything happens we'll look to Vern, and we'll look to him to notify us of any unforseen situations.

ROADRUNNER: Yes sir. Be advised, I'm convinced there will be very little happening in Peking, because our counterparts are all going with us to Shanghai and Hangchou. Then we come back and their spring festival is the fifteenth, which is comparable to our Christmas. So that is why we are anxious to get back and allow these people to have their Christmas eve at home.

WATCHDOG: OK, Ron, well thank you very much. This communication is just fantastic, I tell you it sounds like you are right across the street at 1701. It's loud and clear and very good. [*1701 Pennsylvania Avenue was the national headquarters of the Committee for the Re-election of the President, whose acronym, "CRP," was pronounced with varying degrees of affection as "CREEP."*]

ROADRUNNER: Yeah, it's nice to have it, for a change.

WATCHDOG: OK. Are you getting the news summaries okay?

ROADRUNNER: We got one news summary this afternoon and it was outstanding. Jeez, it's like a whole new world.

WATCHDOG: OK. We'll keep getting that stuff to you.

ROADRUNNER: Yeah, it's great. I can't tell you, we're all very, very excited. It's just been two glorious days for us, when the telex went up and our phones started to work.

WATCHDOG: Fine.

ROADRUNNER: OK, give everybody my best. Timmie is standing by. He'd like to talk to Whelihan, and Swift has a message for Redman. Wait one.

SWIFT: I just want to let you know, that teletype is in now.

WATCHDOG: Thanks a lot, Fred. OK. Hang on.

SNAPSHOT: Hello?

WHELIHAN: Tim?

SNAPSHOT: Yeah. Hi, Bruce.

WHELIHAN: How are ya?

SNAPSHOT: When you and I get on, everybody leaves the room.

WHELIHAN: Same as always.

SNAPSHOT: That's right. We're the ones that get the crap when it's all over, but nobody cares in the beginning. OK, a couple of things. Number one, I would certainly like to be informed before we start loading AP and UPI boxes on airplanes. The PRC didn't understand that, can't understand what we need, because, as I indicated, they are planning on doing all of the transmission of photos. I told them this was back-up photo gear and chemicals and what have you for their own dark rooms, which they finally bought, but it hit me a little sideways. I would just appreciate being notified, because they don't understand what this equipment is for. As I have indicated, they are going to be doing the transmission of all photos. Not AP & UPI. It is a matter of principle with them. They will do it.

WHELIHAN: That's a roger, Tim. I understand that. As it's set now, that gear is gonna go in to Shanghai, and not into Peking. The techs are to go into Peking on the fourteenth. Is there any point in our changing equipment to the flight of the fourteenth out of Guam?

SNAPSHOT: No, let's get it into Shanghai. I will know better . . . just a second. (To someone in the room: "Well, Mr. Walker is not here. You've got Mr. Walker?") Bruce, Chapin wants to talk to Walker, so we're off.

WATCHDOG: Oh no, no, no, no. Go ahead and finish this.

WHELIHAN: Tim? Tim?

SNAPSHOT: Go ahead, let Dwight go. I have a lot for Bruce. Go ahead, Dwight.

WATCHDOG: Roadrunner?

ROADRUNNER: Yes, Dwight.

WATCHDOG: Two things. It would seem to me that on one of those C-141s that's headed back toward Guam, and back to Andrews, or Hawaii, that we could get a drawing of the arrival ceremony for Peking. Do you think that would be worth our having so that we can review that with the principals?

ROADRUNNER: Yes, sir, I have sent all this information to you, diagrams for everything, Dwight, including camera positions and movement of cameras and movement of principals. For everything we've done, every survey we've made. I'm not sure we can get it to Andrews but you will have those diagrams in Hawaii when you arrive. They'll just hold it for you, and if by chance we miss in Hawaii, they'll definitely have it there for you in Guam.

WATCHDOG: OK. You're way ahead of me again, as usual, but I checked the traffic here this morning. I think maybe the shut down while they worked on the new satellite held us up. [*Roadrunner was sending traffic overnight and all during the day. Somehow it was not getting out of the White House Situation Room.*]

ROADRUNNER: You haven't gotten anything from me, huh? [*No wonder he hasn't read anything! Roadrunner realized.*]

WATCHDOG: No, checked first thing this morning, in fact I've been coming in early to see if there's any traffic before these calls. So, I'll go over there right now and try to find out what's happening. Now the other thing that would be helpful is a list of eight or ten suggestions for party members, just little things that we should point out to them in the outset of the schedule. For example, everybody should always be on time, for everything, in fact be a few minutes early. Things like that. If you could put a list together, I think it would be helpful for us.

ROADRUNNER: Yes, that is a very good idea. I'll sit down with the people here and come up with nuances that will be helpful to you in preparing your cover sheet. [*Guidance on how one is to behave while in the People's Republic of China.*]

WATCHDOG: OK, you are right on target, and that is precisely what I need. Well, have a good evening. Bruce still needs to talk to Tim. OK?

ROADRUNNER: OK. Wait one. I just talked to Carl Prince about that kelvin reading. They don't have a kelvin meter here, but he said the lighting in that room is perfect, and they shouldn't have to worry about a kelvin reading. [*Carl Prince was one of the engineers.*]

WATCHDOG: OK, but see, we're worried about when they're not lighting it because we hope to have official photo opportunities separate from the press corps.

ROADRUNNER: Then maybe I will have to ask the PRC, which I have not done so far.

SNAPSHOT: I have.

ROADRUNNER: Oh, Timmie has got the answer. Here he is.

. . . but Washington was gone. Only silence came in via the satellite. The operator said the satellite was down. It was a scary, lonely feeling at first to have Washington just be gone like that. They sat for a few minutes and looked at each other. They were all there, in Peking, alone. They smiled and tried to cheer each other up, then headed off to their own rooms.

Snapshot followed Roadrunner into his sitting room. "It's a real, honest to goodness Communist plot that's running in two directions," Roadrunner said with a laugh. "The satellite is down and the weather has warmed up just enough outside that our ice won't freeze. Can you believe it? That combination is enough to piss off the Good Humor man."

"Yeah, and I'm not the Good Humor man, so I gotta get on a big iron bird and fly this trap," Snapshot said seriously. He really wanted to leave.

Roadrunner again tried to reassure his friend. "I know you really want to go, Tim, and I understand all the reasons why you do, but I am really worried about what will happen here in your absence," Roadrunner told him. "Mr. Ma trusts and depends on you, and if you are out of pocket, who knows what will get screwed up. It just makes me nervous to lose the edge you have gained on all the press stuff. It ain't my bag, Timmie, and you know that. You do it like nobody else can."

"Thanks, I know you mean that and I do thank you, but it sure would be great to get away for a few days and brief the incoming heavies and then come back here with an improved mental outlook. I could probably make *really* wonderful things happen if I could have an attitude overhaul with some good old-fashioned R and R!"

"I hear you," Roadrunner said sympathetically, "but can't you just go and scream into your pillow for a few more days?"

Snapshot had to laugh. He was surprised that Roadrunner knew he screamed in his pillow. "Do you do that, too?"

"I've been screaming in my pillow for years. Ever since I was a little kid and we'd fly those old transatlantic Pan Am planes that had bunks. We'd go from Texas to India, via Europe. Those flights were so damned long, I just knew I couldn't be still one minute longer, but the blasted plane just droned on and on. It was pitch black outside and I was bored stiff. So, I started screaming in my pillow. It's great for those kind of endless moments in life." He started to tell Snapshot that yelling dirty words while swimming underwater helped relieve stress, too, but he realized that would make him think more about Hawaii, since they had no chance of going swimming in China in the wintertime.

Roadrunner looked up at the heater vent like he saw something other than just the heater vent. "In fact, I think I'll go scream in my pillow very soon," he said in a louder than normal voice, "but before

I go do that, we'd like some ice, please! Two saucers' full would be just outstanding. *Shay shay.* Oh, yeah . . . and two cold bottles of *pijou*, please. Thanks, guys." Pijou was Chinese beer and they'd actually grown rather fond of it.

Snapshot looked at Roadrunner and laughed again. "You are great. A cold beer sounds really good. Good idea!"

Roadrunner switched on the tape recorder. They sat down and rested their heads on the doilies. The Mike Curb Congregation was singing.

> *It was a good time. It was the best time.*
> *It was a party, just to be near you.*
> *It was a good time. It was the best time.*

"Listen, Snapshot. What would I do if you weren't here?" Roadrunner asked.

"Do you think they will really bring us beer and ice, just because you asked the heater vent?"

Just then the hall attendant came into the room with a bamboo tray. He set a bowl of ice cubes on the table and two brown bottles of *Great Wall* beer. Roadrunner and Snapshot jumped up and bowed and thanked him, and they all bowed and laughed and grinned at each other. Roadrunner and Snapshot picked up the bottles, clinked them together and raised them toward the hall attendant. "To your health and long life," Roadrunner told him.

"Yeah, and here's to no warm Hawaiian anythings and more pillow screamings," Snapshot said in a very sad voice.

"*Shay, shay,*" Roadrunner said, and he was looking at Snapshot when he said it.

They smiled and sipped their bottles of Chinese beer. They leaned their heads back and joined Mike Curb's group as they sang:

> *A man's gotta live by the code of the west,*
> *Where the good guys beat the bad guys*
> *When they're put to the test.*
> *Since there has to be a villain for the good guys to be killin',*
> *It's the reason I'm a bad guy, it's the code of the west.*
>
> *I'm Dengis McGee, Dirty Dengis McGee.*
> *Rotten to the core, plain mean and ornery.*
> *I've lived a life of sin and let me tell you Gunga Din,*
> *I'm a better man than, I'm a better man than,*
> *Well I can't think of anyone I'm a better man than.*

When the song ended, Roadrunner said, "You see, we've really got no choice. We really do gotta live by the code of the west. We've gotta be polite and mannerly on the outside, but by God we're gonna be rotten to the core, plain mean and ornery on the inside and we're gonna make this mother happen."

Roadrunner got a fairly good night's sleep. The Chinese only woke him up three times. The last time they wanted a translation for "railroad job" because they could not find it in their English phrase book. Roadrunner, momentarily speechless, listened while they explained Livingood's description of Henry Kissinger's characteristic maneuvering to ride in the car with the President as a railroad job. Roadrunner told the Chinese that Livingood was indeed the technical expert and that they should check the accuracy of the translation with him. When he got back in bed, he wondered if they were calling Livingood; it struck him funny, and he had a hard time falling asleep again.

He was starting to cough and still felt pretty tired the next morning as he waited for the conference call. It came in at 7:40. It was 6:40 in the evening in Washington.

OPERATOR: Gentleman, At this time, Mr. Chapin will not be in conference and per your request, this telephone conversation is recorded by the audio visual branch of the White House Communications Agency. Please go ahead with your conference.
HENKEL: Ron?
ROADRUNNER: Yeah.
HENKEL: OK. I'm sending some stuff to you.
ROADRUNNER: Great. Yeah, the thing we need to know is who gets off in what cities and what equipment gets off in what cities? [*Roadrunner was really being hounded by the Chinese on this point. He came to realize it was because they didn't have sophisticated equipment and therefore didn't understand what it would be used for.*]
HENKEL: Well, I've got you the personnel, but I'll have to get you what equipment. It is my understanding that most of that equipment is mobile, though, if you look at the manifest.
ROADRUNNER: That doesn't make any difference. Bill, they want to know exactly what pieces of equipment are getting off. If we can get them what it is, that's outstanding. If we can't, then we should tell them at least the number of boxes, the poundage, and the cube. [*This was the terminology the Chinese were using, but it was probably to save face and not wanting to come right out and say, "What is this and what do you intend to do with it?"*]
HENKEL: You'll get it. I'll start asking that question.

ROADRUNNER: Great.

HENKEL: I want to discuss . . .

ROADRUNNER: I am also in receipt of a cable from Chapin. It says regarding all communications we should continue the formal diplomatic attitude at all times. We will do so. [*A reminder to conduct business only and not kid around or engage in small talk.*]

HENKEL: Yeah, I . . .

ROADRUNNER: The next thing is that Elbourne has, in fact, discussed with his counterparts the possibility of a courier flight going out of here on the twenty-fourth. Predicated on the cable that I received from Chapin this morning regarding a courier flight into China with items of importance for the President [*documents to be signed, legislative reports, etc.*], I do not anticipate any problems on that at all, but I will make that request as soon as I have my next meeting.

HENKEL: OK, Ron, but you are saying . . .

ROADRUNNER: We might even approach it from the standpoint of it being the same flight coming in, being the courier flight out for film for Ollie and LIFE magazine and everybody else.

HENKEL: OK. That courier flight out has been agreed on. Did you say . . . ?

ROADRUNNER: Wait one. Why are you saying it's been agreed on?

HENKEL: Well, no. Didn't you tell me that your counterparts there had agreed to it?

ROADRUNNER: No, I did not.

HENKEL: Oh, I thought . . . I misunderstood what Elbourne had told you.

ROADRUNNER: No, I did not. It had been approached. The subject is in the mill.

HENKEL: OK, Ron. I just want to specify that, that's all. I'm sorry. OK. Let's . . .

ROADRUNNER: Yes, let me say it again. The PRC has been approached on the possibility of a courier flight taking film out of here on the twenty-fourth. We have not, repeat not received an answer. I will now substantiate that request and give it some clout with the information regarding Searchlight. (pause) Henkel?

HENKEL: Yes, I'm listening, Ron. I'm just trying to take notes.

ROADRUNNER: OK. (clears throat) Be advised, I have not talked to my counterpart about a twenty-fourth flight. I will do so as soon as possible.

HENKEL: OK.

ROADRUNNER: To this point it did not affect the President, and it was primarily on Elbourne's side. It very obviously affects the

President now. Now, in regard to Elbourne coming out of the country and briefing the press in Hawaii and Guam. Elbourne and I have discussed this problem . . . or not a problem . . . have discussed this possibility. My personal feelings are that things are going very well now. Elbourne has a very fine relationship with his counterpart. I think it's necessary for us to wait a while and see how Elbourne feels about it and make a decision a little later. I don't think we're in a position to make that decision now. And Elbourne agrees with me.

HENKEL: Fine. Got it, Ron. Now . . .

ROADRUNNER: There's no doubt in my mind that Bob Manning could cover in Elbourne's absence if the PRC will accept that. [*Manning was sitting there and Roadrunner felt he needed to say that.*]

HENKEL: OK. I certainly understand that. Ron, have you heard anything from your counterparts about the acceptability of the draft release that is going to be released on the fourteenth?

ROADRUNNER: That is a negative.

HENKEL: OK.

ROADRUNNER: You know I appreciate your asking these questions, and I know you have to. But be advised from my end, as soon as I receive any answers regarding any of these what I consider to be very critical questions, I will call you no matter what time of day it is.

HENKEL: That's perfectly fair. I understand, Ron. And, I think you just said it a second ago. You understand the position I'm in, too.

ROADRUNNER: Absolutely. I understand that. I just want you to be clear that no matter what time of day it is, my time or your time, as soon as I receive those answers, I will immediately get on the horn and let you know.

HENKEL: Great. On the master precedence list. Haldeman . . .

ROADRUNNER: I have it in front of me now.

HENKEL: Yeah. Haldeman reviewed it, and there's only four changes in the whole thing and then it is approved.

ROADRUNNER: OK. I'm with you. Just a moment.

HENKEL: OK, sir. When we come down the list to Wilson Livingood.

ROADRUNNER: Wait a minute . . . Yes?

HENKEL: OK. After Bill Livingood should come William Duncan, Bill Duncan.

ROADRUNNER: Wait a minute. OK. Did we leave Duncan off the original list?

HENKEL: No, sir. He was on a lower order.

ROADRUNNER: OK, fine.

HENKEL: Following Bill Duncan should be William Hudson, Bill Hudson.

ROADRUNNER: All right, after Duncan should be Hudson.

HENKEL: Right.

ROADRUNNER: All righty.

HENKEL: Then comes General Redman. So, Duncan and Hudson, we're slipping them in higher up.

ROADRUNNER: All right, fine.

HENKEL: OK. Then after Vern Coffey which was number twenty-nine, should come Major John V. Brennan. Then he's followed by Timmie, OK?

ROADRUNNER: Yes.

HENKEL: Then after number forty-five, should come Rita DeFantis. Affiliation, unofficial party.

ROADRUNNER: I understand.

HENKEL: Then Diane Sawyer. They are the only changes and then Rita is a plus. That makes our list 390 when it should be 391.

ROADRUNNER: Well, I think you've missed a guy named Keating. And that's the Joseph Keating who is a . . .

HENKEL: Yeah, I know just who he is. He's coming in, he's a replacement for the technician.

ROADRUNNER: That's right, and that's who's not on the list.

HENKEL: Do we have the other technician that Keating replaces? Have you noticed if he is on our list?

ROADRUNNER: Mark Richards? He is not on list.

HENKEL: Oh, well, we're in sync, partner.

ROADRUNNER: He is not on the list, and so we should put Joseph Keating . . . oh, I take that back, Joseph Keating is on it, number eighty-eight, so we are missing someone else.

HENKEL: OK. I thought that sounded too simple.

ROADRUNNER: We'll start checking here, from this end, wait one. (Roadrunner says to Elbourne, "Do we want Siegenthaler and Small to come after all the press corps? Tim? It's what they've done. They've put them into alphabetical order, all the press corps. OK, well we'll have to correct that.") OK, well let us work on this thing, Bill. I haven't had it in my hands very long. We'll see if we can come up with who the missing person is.

HENKEL: OK. And as I say, hopefully, by breaking it down by stop, it will be helpful to you too.

ROADRUNNER: Yes, very much so.

HENKEL: Now, we got our list out against our comeback copy in trying to make sure they got the X's in the right spot. I would say it is probably ninety-nine percent accurate, but that's not good enough. We are still working on it.

ROADRUNNER: OK. I understand that. It looks like they've done a very nice job, and please tell them that. When did Welcome approve this list?

HENKEL: This afternoon, sir. Our time. I'd say about 12:30 our time.

ROADRUNNER: Yeah. OK, 12:30 P.M. on the ninth, huh?

HENKEL: Yeah, and that's incorporating, of course, these minor changes that I've just mentioned, and you can assure Timmie that Ziegler was very much a part of it.

ROADRUNNER: I understand that. OK, where did you have Brennan before?

HENKEL: On a strictly military protocol with the other Majors, and that was number 164. This was a request of General Scowcroft.

ROADRUNNER: I think Elbourne ought to be right underneath Tkach. That's my first opinion.

HENKEL: Should be underneath Tkach, and ahead of Schrauth?

ROADRUNNER: That's correct.

HENKEL: He has approved this to go to you. I think that there is flexibility for your input. Do you understand?

ROADRUNNER: I understand. (cough) OK. Why would Diane Sawyer come before Jack D'Arcy?

HENKEL: This is the list that Ziegler gave us.

ROADRUNNER: Uh, huh. (Roadrunner to Snapshot, "Did you see this? First the unofficial party, then it goes to the press staff, Rita DeFantis goes in there, Diane Sawyer, Jack D'Arcy, Zook, Manning, Gerrard, Dale.)

HENKEL: By title Diane Sawyer is Assistant to the Press Secretary. She's got a high . . . you know . . . she's not just a secretary. [*And she went on to become one of the highest paid women in television!*]

ROADRUNNER: OK. I understand. Maybe that's the reason. (To Snapshot, "She's got a title that's higher than D'Arcy's.") OK. [*Roadrunner was trying to keep D'Arcy's status as high as possible since he was there on the ground working with the PRC.*] You got anything else for me?

HENKEL: OK. Number one. Watchdog wants to give you a call at noon your time today, which would be 11 P.M. our time tonight. Are you going to be out doing a survey or something?

ROADRUNNER: No, I have no schedule this morning, but it's not nine o'clock yet. (chuckle) I don't receive my phone calls for my daily schedule till between 8:30 and 9:00.

HENKEL: OK. The plan is that tomorrow after our conference call, Watchdog, Steve Bull, myself, Chuck Maguire, and Julie Rowe are going to closet ourselves and try to piece a schedule together, so State can start printing it. I've alerted our office that tomorrow may be a late night so we can get this put together and cabled to you. So before you leave Peking, you'll have what we're thinking about putting in the schedule. Does that hit you OK? [*Chuck Maguire worked for John Thomas at the State Department.*]

ROADRUNNER: That hits me fine. I'll try to get as much of this input as I can to you during the course of this evening so you'll have additional information to work with tomorrow.

HENKEL: Great. Our intention is to cable to you what Maguire will start working on.

ROADRUNNER: OK. How is everything going with Maguire?

HENKEL: Well, he's been attending every meeting, but he will really start getting active tomorrow. That's when we're really going to start attacking the schedule. Up until now, a lot of the stuff has been logistical, military, White House in-house stuff.

ROADRUNNER: How about John Thomas? What's his attitude been like?

HENKEL: Pretty good. I briefed him today in Hawaii.

ROADRUNNER: Have you talked to Duval?

HENKEL: Yeah, he's chompin' a little.

ROADRUNNER: Chompin' at who?

HENKEL: No, not chompin', he's anxious to get there. He's receiving his cables in Guam. He sounded in good shape. As a matter of fact, I had to cut him off when your call came in.

ROADRUNNER: We're going to call him this morning. I want to have Schrauth brief him and bring him up to date on the situation here.

HENKEL: I think he's just anxious to get going and is looking forward to participating. I think he's really taken good care of himself, and is deadly serious and wants to do a good job.

ROADRUNNER: OK, great.

HENKEL: I think he was disappointed that there was a delay. Other than that, I think he's all right.

ROADRUNNER: Well, it's the smartest thing we could have done. I'm convinced of that now.

HENKEL: Yeah, well I agree with you one hundred percent. And, Foust and I talked for about forty-five minutes through the Hawaii schedule. On top of China, we got this South Lawn departure ceremony. Then, I've got an in-towner tomorrow night. I tell you, I've been a busy little boy. [*An 'in-towner' was a Washington, D.C. event the President was attending. With so many of the advance men away, Henkel was filling a lot of voids.*]

ROADRUNNER: Yeah, I'm sure you have, Bill. How is Foust doing?

HENKEL: Sounds great. Jon sounds confident, is well up on top of everything. I think he went into this thing with as good a leg up as anyone could on an advance. And that's . . .

ROADRUNNER: Is Clower in Guam? [*Dewey Clower was another full time White House advance man.*]

HENKEL: Yes, sir. I've also talked to him. Our primary problem is that none of these things have been announced. So, in terms of crowd raising they haven't been able to do a thing, and the political officials haven't been approached yet. Dewey was going to do some surveys. I asked him to get rooming assignments and stuff like that back to me.

ROADRUNNER: Is (cough) the President staying on the Marine base in Hawaii?

HENKEL: He's staying at the General's residence at Kanahowi.

ROADRUNNER: Is he staying at the Admiral's residence in Guam?

HENKEL: That has not been approved. It is the recommendation and that's the way it is on the schedule, but there's just a shadow of a doubt. Part of it was waiting for Dewey to get there. I would say it is ninety-nine percent sure that he'll be staying at the Admiral's residence.

ROADRUNNER: Has Dewey locked in the hotel rooms in Guam at the Cliff Hotel?

HENKEL: He was going to do two things this morning. He was going to look at the Admiral's quarters and then he was going over to the Cliff Hotel.

ROADRUNNER: Roger, I understand. (cough) Where is Dwight this morning?

HENKEL: Tonight? Right now, he is at Welcome's, for dinner.

ROADRUNNER: I see. (pause). OK.

HENKEL: OK, Ron, let's see, the in-towner the other night went well.

ROADRUNNER: Are we using our new trainees, Bill? [*Roadrunner was in the process of identifying volunteer advance men for the '72 campaign and was anxious to find out who his strongest ones would be.*]

HENKEL: Yes, sir.

ROADRUNNER: How are they working out?

HENKEL: Good. Good. We've got some good men.

ROADRUNNER: Oh, that's outstanding.

HENKEL: And, you are aware Phil Martyr and Bill Moeller are going into Guam. Sandy Abbey and Dave Bottoms are on their way to Hawaii on the same C-141. So, they will be there to give an assist. You've got good teams there, and I have instilled in Dewey and Jon, your words, that it's critical that these stops be restful and that things go well. They certainly understand.

ROADRUNNER: I'm sure they do. I'm sure they do.

HENKEL: Ha, ha, ha, ha. Hey, we're sending you a picture in tomorrow's packet from a Muskie stop in Florida. He had two people there for an outdoor rally and a speech at noon. One kid's on a bicycle. [*Senator Ed Muskie's Presidential campaign.*]

ROADRUNNER: You are kidding.

HENKEL: No, we're sending you the picture. You won't believe it.

ROADRUNNER: Oh, that's outstanding.

HENKEL: Yeah, it's great.

ROADRUNNER: Are there any newspapers, and magazines and stuff coming in on these planes?

HENKEL: Yes, sir. John Thomas has a suitcase with him, with magazines galore plus all the news summaries up until last Monday.

ROADRUNNER: Oh, that's great.

HENKEL: I've got that biography photo album, and I think we did a nice job on it. It might be very suitable for your use, but you also said there may be another use for it. [*Roadrunner wanted to share the photographs from his first trip with his Chinese counterparts, and the CIA was very anxious to have the Americans identify high ranking Chinese officials when they returned to Washington.*]

ROADRUNNER: Yes.

HENKEL: Now, Ron, I had to take the liberty of selection, so blame no one else.

ROADRUNNER: That's fine, Bill. That's fine. I trust you. The thing we have there is an awful lot of pictures with our friends.

HENKEL: That's all I've picked, pictures where we have part of our American party with their Chinese counterparts.

ROADRUNNER: That's outstanding. OK, that's great.

HENKEL: OK, anything else you can think of, because all that stuff has to go out tomorrow night.

ROADRUNNER: I'll tell you someone could throw in a couple of six packs of 7-Up. Maybe John could stick that in one of his cases.

HENKEL: Well, John's already left. WHCA will bring this in, to your attention.

ROADRUNNER: Well, why don't you have Ron Jackson maybe wrap a case of 7-Up and put that on a plane for us.

HENKEL: OK, Ron's in Hawaii, but I'll take care of it.

ROADRUNNER: OK. That's about the only thing at this point. We still have no ice. We can put stuff outside our windows if it gets cold. I had an ice tray, and made ice for a while. It was so damn cold, but then it warmed up and my ice won't freeze.

HENKEL: Ha, ha, ha, ha, ha.

The Americans with their Chinese counterparts.

ROADRUNNER: So, I'm sitting here holding an ice tray with no ice.
HENKEL: Ha, ha, ha. I talked to Anne yesterday. She sounds in great health and good spirits.
ROADRUNNER: I appreciate that very much. OK. Bill, are you all going to get out of there soon?
HENKEL: Yeah, well I am, because I promised. This will be the earliest in a long while, because I know tomorrow's gonna be late.
ROADRUNNER: OK. Why don't you get a good night's sleep, and give my best to your family and tell the girls we appreciate their effort very much and we're with them.
HENKEL: OK. Well, we're with you guys and we always think about you, and, go to it, pal.
ROADRUNNER: Believe me, we've got some stories to tell.
HENKEL: Ha, I can't wait. Ha, ha, ha.
ROADRUNNER: Yeah. Believe me!
HENKEL: OK, Ron, have a good day.
ROADRUNNER: OK, partner. Thanks very much, Bill.
HENKEL: Bye, now.

Roadrunner stood up and stretched. He was sore from sitting and talking on the damn telephone for such long stretches of time.

"These calls are going to get longer and longer as the time gets shorter and shorter. You know that, don't you?" he said to everyone in the room.

"Yeah, lucky us," Schrauth responded.

"Hey Swift," Livingood said. "Do you think the leaks are coming from people listening in on these conversations?"

"I doubt it," Swift responded.

Snapshot laughed. "Hell, if Roadrunner can order two beers and some ice by talking at the heater vent, anything is possible."

All the men got a big kick out of the story about the two beers from last night. They laughed and came up with some great ideas for lunch.

"Hey Timmie, tell the vent we'd like cheeseburgers, medium rare with french fries," Manning suggested.

"Pepperoni pizza with extra cheese," Schrauth said. "Anything would be better than Chinese food at this point."

"I like Chinese food," Livingood told them.

Everyone laughed. It was true. Livingood was always the last one to leave the table. He also appeared to be the only one among them who was gaining weight. He had started to complain about his pants feeling tight around the waist. They had been kidding him about licking the dumpling bowl after every meal, and many of the Americans were grateful that they could unload some of their least favorite delicacies on Bill.

"He even likes that dish they fix with the chicken lips in it," Snapshot reminded everyone.

"Hey Livingood, why don't you order a thousand-year-old egg omelette tomorrow," Schrauth suggested.

Swift added, "Maybe they'll even put sea slugs in it if you are a really good boy."

Everyone moaned and grimaced at the very thought of such a concoction. They were all dying for an ice cold 7-Up, bubbling in a huge glass filled with ice.

CHAPTER XIII

A GYMNASIUM WITH WAITERS

FEBRUARY 10, 1972

Roadrunner and the Chinese were always cordial to one another, but the cordiality never amounted to anything concrete. They exchanged many pleasantries, but little information. He decided that the Chinese probably attended classes to learn how to talk constantly and yet say nothing at all. That had to be the reason they did not want the White House to announce anything; it was not the Chinese way. Chinese reporters never asked questions, and the citizens certainly never did. Roadrunner worried that his counterparts would just keep smiling and stalling and that he would never be able to tell the White House anything. If he tried to pinpoint a room for a meeting, he would be told they could not specify a room because that room might be occupied that day. They could not decide on a day to go to the Great Wall because it might snow. The Chinese always had reasons, but Roadrunner needed some answers. He knew the President would fare well once he arrived in China, but he worried about being able to brief the First Lady adequately.

Roadrunner was especially fond of Mrs. Nixon. He had watched her endure many agonizingly long days with very little time to herself, and he had never heard her complain. She always had a smile on her face and kind words for everyone around her. He had never seen her lose her composure. Occasionally she would cast a quick glance in Roadrunner's direction when she wanted to be excused, and he would interrupt and tell her that she needed to come with him. The people around her never had a clue that she was the one who wanted to leave. He admired this remarkable woman and wanted her China experience to be memorable and rewarding.

Even though Roadrunner did not have much information for Watchdog, he was looking forward to telling him about the evening's surprise from the Chinese. He still could not believe they had done it in such a short time. It was 9:44 when the conference call began. In Washington, it was 8:44 in the morning.

OPERATOR: Mr. Chapin is on the circuit now, Peking.

WATCHDOG: Roadrunner?

ROADRUNNER: Yes, Dwight, can you hear me?

WATCHDOG: Yes, how are you all?

ROADRUNNER: Just fine. We have Colonel Gibbons, Schrauth, Elbourne, Swift, Livingood, and Colonel Coffey with us this evening, and Bob Manning.

WATCHDOG: Well, Vern, nice to have you around.

COFFEY: Thank you, Dwight. It's nice to be around.

WATCHDOG: Ha, ha, ha. I bet it is. We have General Scowcroft and General Redman, Steve Bull, Whelihan, Julie Rowe, Bill Henkel, and Chuck Maguire. Bob Taylor is not here with us yet. He probably will come in, he's always late.

Let me start with a couple of things. First the courier we've talked about before, Ron. This would be the courier in case of an emergency. We also have the question of the courier regarding film. Now, we have a problem here as to who the carrier is going to be. Does Tim want to use TWA, or who does he want to use? We're not prepared to use military aircraft.

SNAPSHOT: We assumed it would be military aircraft. We've got those aircraft standing by in Guam. I don't know that the pool people, who need to get film out, LIFE and the other black and white pooler, have the dollars to pay for a commercial aircraft from Washington to Peking and return. I think it's a little much to ask. It would probably be $102,000 to get the film back.

WATCHDOG: Well, that's what it is going to cost the taxpayers, Tim. I think you better be thinking of a commercial schedule out of Guam. I know that Ollie has said all he needed was to get it outside the country and he'd have it couriered back. So, our problem is to get somebody to make a run in from Guam and back to Guam.

SNAPSHOT: Yeah, that's right, and I would think that would be military, Dwight. It would be a lot easier for a military aircraft to come in than it would be for a commercial aircraft. It would only have to be from Guam to Peking and back to Guam, and it would go commercial from there on. Still, that's an awful lot of money just to get the film out. Maybe Ron Ziegler has other information, but I'm questioning whether those news magazines are going to want to spend that kind of money to do it.

WATCHDOG: We have a difference of feeling here. We tend to think we cannot use military craft for a mission that is solely a press function, and that is what this is.

SNAPSHOT: Well, then I would leave it up to the news magazines to see if they want to do it or not.

WATCHDOG: OK. Bruce will talk to Ron about it and we'll come back to it later. Roadrunner?

ROADRUNNER: Yes.

WATCHDOG: I got the information from you on what can be released. It would seem to me the most productive thing is for you to tell me what we should say. In other words, instead of my drafting something and sending it back, just tell me by cable exactly what we can say. We do have a problem because of *TV GUIDE*. I would not be surprised to see a lot of this stuff start leaking. [TV GUIDE *had a very early deadline for programming information.*]

ROADRUNNER: Well, then if that's the case, I think we are in trouble. The Chinese don't want to mention any names, any places, any times, any dates. It's as simple as that. That includes the Great Hall of the People and the guest house.

WATCHDOG: You mean . . . I don't understand why we can't say the President is staying at a guest house. Explain the logic on that to me.

ROADRUNNER: OK. I'll explain the logic to you as I understand it. Mr. Chu said he "was extremely concerned" and that he felt "there was too much information." Where we said, "The President will arrive and the Prime Minister will meet him," he said, "meets with our Chinese leaders" is all we can say. They told me they don't want to say anything else about the first day.

The next paragraph about banquets the first evening . . . "No, you should simply say there will be a banquet and reciprocal banquet. Don't give any evenings." I asked him about the guest house and the Great Hall of the People and he asked me not to discuss places.

WATCHDOG: Ron?

ROADRUNNER: I've pushed as hard as I can push. I've asked every day.

WATCHDOG: Ron, drop it. Just drop it.

ROADRUNNER: All right.

WATCHDOG: It's going to cause Ziegler some serious problems, but nothing that we can't handle. I think that it should be clearly understood there, that we have *not*, I repeat, have *not* released anything. We have been extremely careful about holding all of the information. That's why I sent you the cable to get their approval. A lot of people are guessing over here. They are guessing based on information that the technicians came back with from the last trip. Some of the guessing is wrong and some of it is right. We can't do much about the guessing.

ROADRUNNER: I understand perfectly. I pointed this out to Mr. Chu this afternoon. I also told him magazines go to press and Mr. Ziegler would like to give some information. Now, the thing is, they are not going to be locked into a day for anything. Without having days, and not being able to mention places, what kind of a release have you got?

WATCHDOG: Well, we've got to do some thinking. I've just sent you a cable that is very important, and that you should read certain things into. You'll see that there may be an opportunity for things to be said publicly today. We're just going to have to deal with it here and it's our problem.

ROADRUNNER: Is it going to affect us?

WATCHDOG: No, I don't really think so. I think using words like "flexibility" and "not knowing until immediately ahead of time" and "being different from other foreign travel" and so forth, could serve to be very helpful for us and the People's Republic . . . especially in terms of conditioning people.

ROADRUNNER: I understand what you are saying. I understand. [*The President was personally going to comment on the trip, using certain key words that the Chinese would appreciate.*]

WATCHDOG: OK.

ROADRUNNER: I'll wait for that. (cough, cough)

WATCHDOG: It's on its way. [*True to Watchdog's word, Searchlight told a news conference that afternoon in the Oval Office, "With regard to agenda, both governments have decided that we will not make any announcements on agenda items prior to the meetings. . . . With regard to the itinerary itself, the itinerary, generally as you know, has been announced for three cities. With regard to what we do in each city, it is being kept flexible, and no final decisions have been made and none will be announced at this time."*] Now, a couple of things in your recent cables. Recommending the Peking Hotel event, and I would argue that we should do something like the children's event we visited on our last trip. I think it would be better for the first morning.

SNAPSHOT: Dwight, could I say a word on that?

WATCHDOG: Yeah.

SNAPSHOT: I think people are going to be concentrating on the banquet the evening before. They'll be talking about the food. The sense from here is that it might be good for Mrs. Nixon to go to that food preparation facility, because it would be good follow-up. People would be very interested and it would be fresh in their minds from the evening before. This kitchen is just fantastic, and you can see everything being prepared in great detail with 115 cooks doing it. It just seems to me to be excellent follow-up.

WATCHDOG: OK. Thank you. We'll look at it that way. Ron, do we have any problem with using the Sierra around there for staff? [Sierra was the radio frequency for staff to communicate with each other.]

ROADRUNNER: Yes, we certainly do have a problem. We have a major problem. (cough) I'd like to ask Major Swift to speak to that.

WATCHDOG: OK. Al's here. [Al Redman.]

SWIFT: The Chinese have made quite a point about the security involved with the radio net. Transmission from our radios during any movement of the leaders would pinpoint the location of their leader. They have made quite a thing out of this and have asked us to be sure our transmissions are kept to a bare minimum.

REDMAN: Swift, this is Redman.

ROADRUNNER: They've asked us to use it on an emergency basis only. Everyone, including Livingood's people.

LIVINGOOD: That's affirmative Dwight, they have. They asked us to keep it to a bare minimum for security reasons for their principal.

WATCHDOG: OK, Bill. Be advised, Bob's here now. Go ahead, Al.

REDMAN: Swift, this is Redman. I would like you to establish procedures for the use of the small radios and get the concurrence of the PRC. I would like to suggest that these are not associated with the movements of the Presidential party. The procedures would deal with monitoring only. We would execute radio silence and receive when we had a movement or had radios in the vicinity of the heads of state.

SWIFT: Well, this is precisely what we plan to do. In fact, they have asked us to provide them with a plan for operation. We've still got to formulate this operational plan, and I've referred it here to both Livingood and Mr. Walker. It's just one of those things we haven't come to grips with yet because it's a pretty damn difficult thing to work out. I don't think there is any problem when it does not involve a movement of the leaders. They have tied this to the pinpointing of the location of their leaders during movement. They've got a point. I don't understand it. I've asked Livingood to explain it to me and I don't know as he's got an explanation for it, either.

ROADRUNNER: Well, my evaluation is that they are talking about some kind of a system that can zero in on that frequency, which, yes, it can be done. I guess it could be done from the atmosphere as well as . . . [*Roadrunner decided that he had said enough. Today we know the Chinese were exactly right. Radio signals can be used as targets!*] But, be that as it may, it's a problem. We have been told to keep it to a minimum and use it on an emergency basis only during motorcades.

WATCHDOG: OK.   Well, let's go the route that Al Redman suggested and see what kind of a procedures agreement we can get. Then we will notify our people prior to departure. The press staff, White House staff, official party, and everyone is to know exactly what we can do.

SNAPSHOT: Dwight, there's one more point on this. This is how it initially came to my attention. The networks also use small radios to line up microwave equipment and talk to their cameramen. The Chinese have also asked them not to use their radios.

WATCHDOG: OK. One thing we can do is limit the people who carry radios. Perhaps, for example, we take off Haldeman, Chapin, people like that and limit it to a few men who are there now, because we'll be in touch with you all the time.

ROADRUNNER: I understand, but what we would like to do is come up with this recommendation and see how it flies. If it comes down to a point where I have to talk to Mr. Chu, I'm perfectly willing to do so.

WATCHDOG: Very good. Now, be advised, we are really starting to come up against a crunch on the number of pounds of material we are trying to put on these aircraft. We cannot accept any more requests to bring over any kind of equipment.

As you know, Ron, we put a limit of two bags on everybody coming over. We are restricting purchases to what can be carried back in their individual suitcases. Any exceptions will have to be approved by General Scowcroft and me working with the aides after we get there. All the men buying stuff over there are going to have to get it on aircraft other than the Spirit of '76 and 970. You've got to make it clear to everybody that this is a very serious problem for all of us. Across the board.

ROADRUNNER: Yes, sir, I think everybody understands that.

WATCHDOG: (To the room: "Why don't we have a copy of that baggage memo?")

SNAPSHOT: Hey Dwight, if you send it here, we've got a Xerox and we could get you several copies and zing them back to you. (laughter in both places)

ROADRUNNER: I have a little sidelight on that. We have, I think, opened up Pandora's box with our Xerox. We started giving the PRC a copy of everything.   Now they want three to eight copies of everything. We are working hand in hand, and they are helping us Xerox them.

WATCHDOG: Perfect.

ROADRUNNER: I have one other story to tell. About 8:30 tonight, we got invited next door to the opening of some facilities. There was a basketball court, ping pong facilities, pool facilities, and a bowling alley. They had built it for us!

The first day we were here, we talked about athletic facilities. I told them people would like to get out and get some exercise. I asked if we could go to a gymnasium to play basketball and ping pong. I didn't hear anything more, and tonight we found out they have built a facility for us, right next door! [*This was quite an amazing gesture of hospitality and friendship. The Chinese were very proud of this surprise for their guests, and rightly so.*] I am not kidding you. It's open from nine in the morning until twelve midnight and it's taken them a week to build it. [*In the evening they even had waiters serving beer!*]

WATCHDOG: That's sensational. That was very, very nice.

ROADRUNNER: You can rest assured that we are very, very pleased and I'm sure the men will enjoy it very much.

WATCHDOG: Right. OK. We don't have anything else here, Ron. We've got to move on to working on these schedules.

ROADRUNNER: Wait, I want Swift to fill you in on the rates.

WATCHDOG: Go ahead.

SWIFT: OK, what it amounts to is using the tariffs worked out during our last visit. We all had a hand in it. The PRC would have lost approximately $90,000 on this whole communications thing. However, now that we can estimate a little more accurately, it looks like they're going to lose about $156,000. After many, many hours of discussion, it really comes down to the fact that although they were willing to lose 90 thou, they are completely unwilling to lose 156 thou.

In an effort to work this out, we have proposed that the broadcasters ante up a minimum amount of dollars. I am quite certain this is not going to sit well with our broadcaster friends, and I'm looking to Tim to soften the blow. I really see no other way out. The People's Republic has made it clear that they knew nothing about television rates and leased circuit rates. They looked to us for advice, and we proposed a tariff, which they accepted. Now they realize, as we do, that they are going to lose their shirts. Frankly, they are a little bit unhappy about it. I suppose we could force it down their throats, but I just don't think we should.

REDMAN: Swift, this is Redman here. There are a couple of things I would like your reaction to. Number one is their extremely low rate for message traffic. I don't think anyone expected a half a cent a word. Number two, when we signed that agreement, we had no idea that some of the revenue was going to be skimmed off by the RCA terminal in Shanghai.

SWIFT: Right. It's in fact twenty-one yuan, which is ten cents a word, of which they would collect half. That's where the half came from. Instead of them collecting a half-cent a word, they will collect five cents a word. This amounts to some $50,000 additional for them. These figures do not take into account any skimming as far as the RCA terminal is concerned. They asked me if I had heard how this RCA business was coming? I assured them I would ask. So if you have anything I might tell them, I would appreciate it.

REDMAN: I think we must acknowledge any TV from Shanghai is going to skim revenue off the WUI [Western Union International] facility, so this is a factor we did not work out when we worked out that schedule. One other thing, Swift, if you are going to derive $50,000 more than you estimated initially, it would appear we're getting fairly close to the original figure of around $90,000 loss.

SNAPSHOT: No, that's really wrong. What has happened here, Al, is the networks had guaranteed a minimum of twenty-two hours of television. We doubled that to forty-four hours. The networks wanted more and it came up to forty-seven hours. Remember the lid situation that we talked about, Al?

REDMAN: That's a roger.

SNAPSHOT: So the computations were based on a lid of forty-seven hours. The message rate for telegrams is going to be ten cents a word and the telephone rate will be $14 for the first three minutes and $4.50 for each additional minute. I think they will come through OK on that one, but where we are stuck is on the TV side.

WHELIHAN: Tim, is the business about the cost and the networks going to embroil Ron in any controversy here?

SNAPSHOT: Yes, it is going to embroil Ron in a controversy.

WHELIHAN: Tim, do your hosts understand the unique position of the wires and that they serve all the others that are accompanying the President?

SNAPSHOT: I think they understand the wires better than you and I understand the wires.

REDMAN: Fred, have you made provisions so we can continue these conversations when you go south?

SWIFT: Again, today they assured me that when we get to Shanghai, there will be an instrument which we can use to reach a switchboard here in Peking.

REDMAN: One other thing, Fred. I want to make sure that with this restriction on radios, you have enough pageboys over there, because if we have to reduce the amount of traffic, pageboys might be the answer. If a pageboy goes off, the fellow can get to a telephone and not use the radio. Do you feel you have adequate pageboys over there to do this?

SWIFT: That's a negative. If you could arrange ten additional pageboys, we would appreciate it. This will be part of our plan that we will receive a page and go to a line to answer.

REDMAN: Swift, Redman, that's a roger. And if I can't find a way to transport them, I'll carry them on the plane with me.

SWIFT: That will be plenty of time. You'll be in here a day in advance, that's very adequate. Yes, sir.

REDMAN: I have nothing further. Do you have anything for me?

SWIFT: I would ask that you tell RCA, especially being the bagman for this (chuckle) telex business, of the change from a half-cent to five cents per word that they are going to owe to the People's Republic.

REDMAN: That's a roger, Swift. You and Tim need to be aware we still have a problem on the rate. The half-cent a word. John Thomas has already departed and RCA has already made their deposit to him, so it appears John Thomas is going to have to make up the difference and bill these people after the trip is over.

SNAPSHOT: That's a roger.

ROADRUNNER: Believe me, that ain't the only problem John Thomas is going to have. (laughter in Peking)

SNAPSHOT: However, I think it would be worthwhile to get to RCA and have them deposit more money into that account.

REDMAN: What do you estimate the total to be for RCA so I can speak to this thing intelligently?

SNAPSHOT: I'm not sure, Al. I would say $35,000 more. Give them a $50,000 total. I am basing this on a million words, which is a real horseback ride on my part.

REDMAN: I think RCA deposited ten. You say they should deposit forty more under those conditions?

SNAPSHOT: I would think at least that, yes.

REDMAN: That's a roger, Tim.

ROADRUNNER: (cough, cough, cough)

LIVINGOOD: Is Taylor there?

REDMAN: That's a negative, Bill. Taylor departed. (laughter in Peking)

LIVINGOOD: Thank you . . . that was a long wait.

SNAPSHOT: Livingood's going to bed now.

WATCHDOG: Roadrunner?

ROADRUNNER: Yes, sir?

WATCHDOG: Did that cable come in yet?

ROADRUNNER: Yes, I've got it in front of me.

WATCHDOG: Do you understand what I'm saying?   [*That the President would be talking about the trip and would be saying what the Chinese did not want Ziegler to say.*]

ROADRUNNER: I understand what you are saying.   I hope the Chinese do.   (cough, cough, cough)

WATCHDOG: OK.   I just talked with Buchanan.   I assure you that I don't think we'll have any problems at all.   [*Patrick J. Buchanan was then a Presidential speech writer.*]

ROADRUNNER: What kind of information would that be, Dwight?

WATCHDOG: He will mention riding in their vehicle.   He will mention that all standard precautions have been taken, and just get into some of the questions that are being asked.   You can not believe the pressure for information here, and we have got to say something. We can not just act like not a damn thing's happening.   We've got to indicate that everything's being done according to procedure and no one should worry.   [*Members of the press were asking lots of questions about the security arrangements for the trip and specifically about the precautions being taken for the safety of the President.   As it happened, the President did not go into all the detail Watchdog had hoped he would.   Searchlight was not the kind of President who did exactly what his staff told him to do.   He did, however, use the key word Watchdog had passed along, "flexible," and when Roadrunner learned about it, he was pleased the commander-in-chief had backed him up.*]

ROADRUNNER: OK.   I understand.

WATCHDOG: It's tough.   I know it's tough.   And I know exactly what you are warning me about, OK?

ROADRUNNER: Yes. I . . . I . . . uh . . . What I'm going to do now is ask for a little guidance on how I should play this.   Should I approach my counterparts or . . .?

WATCHDOG: Don't do anything until I come back to you.   OK?

ROADRUNNER: Roger.   OK.   (cough, cough, cough)   I don't know that I've been very successful in relaying to my counterparts the urgency of what you are saying to me.   What they are asking of us and our government at this point, is that the President and his whole party, all the Americans, all 391 of them, come to China in a vacuum and have everything just happen as it happens and not worry about it.

SNAPSHOT: They've seen it done that way in the past.

ROADRUNNER: As hard as I have tried to tell them, and Tim has tried to tell them, they have not bent one inch.

WATCHDOG: Let me just make one point, because I think it's fundamental to the whole thing.   The only thing we need to know is this . . . is the schedule . . . the very, very confidential schedule we gave to Han Hsu, the schedule that they plan on using for the

President? That's the most basic thing that we need to know, and I think the answer is yes. It is the basis upon which the President is preparing for this trip. It is the way he feels it is going to happen. If that is not the case, then they need to tell us confidentially so we can let the President know. That is the basic element. Do you agree.

ROADRUNNER: Yes, I agree. I agree wholeheartedly. (cough)

SNAPSHOT: We all agree.

WATCHDOG: I'm sure they understand this. I know that Mr. Han Hsu understands this. He told me when he read it over that it was fine. He had one change and that was the name of the committee in Shanghai. He inserted the word revolution, Municipal Revolution Committee. That was the only change he made in the whole document.

ROADRUNNER: I remember the incident. I remember. (cough, cough)

SNAPSHOT: Dwight?

WATCHDOG: Yes, Timmie.

SNAPSHOT: I think what they are concerned about is that the press, and therefore the world, because of the sophisticated communications equipment we have, will find out about this before it all happens. Therefore, I am suggesting that we do a daily subschedule on the evening before. This is the kind of safeguard that I think they would understand and be able to live with.

WATCHDOG: Well, Tim, let's just take a situation. Say that the People's Republic decided that on Wednesday morning the President was going to go to the Wall. Now, are you implying that we would not tell the networks about this until Tuesday night?

SNAPSHOT: That's correct. Tuesday night we would put out a press schedule. We would do a press schedule by event and I could switch events day by day. I can pull one event out and if it doesn't happen then I could switch events.

WATCHDOG: OK. Bruce is going to have to talk to Ron and they are going to have to get back to you.

SNAPSHOT: I'd like to talk to Ron myself about this. I feel pretty strongly. I feel this is a major hangup in our negotiations.

ROADRUNNER: Let me make one point, quickly. I was taken aback this afternoon by their inability to understand that our schedule would be kept in-house.

WATCHDOG: OK, fine. We'll let Tim and Ron talk. Let me ask a couple of other things. In looking at my movies of the Wall last night, it becomes very obvious what's going to happen if the entire press corps and unofficial party and other strap hangers go marching up that thing all in one group.

SNAPSHOT: Negative.   Negative.

WATCHDOG: We're gonna have to have pre-positioning of the press and a very limited number moving with the President and talk to the PRC about who they want to have along. Perhaps, we just take the top three or four people in each party and let them walk along. Then, we hold the others back twenty-five yards or something.

SNAPSHOT: Roger. (cough, cough). It should be the President, Mrs. Nixon, Secretary of State, and Dr. Kissinger. Period. There are going to be more members of the PRC, because they're going to have interpreters, guides, and you're going to have officials. I think that will number anywhere from eight to fifteen. In my mind that's OK.

WATCHDOG: Right. Let me make a suggestion.

ROADRUNNER: Timmie wants to say something about the press. (cough, cough, cough)

WATCHDOG: May I make a suggestion?

ROADRUNNER: Yes.

WATCHDOG: As Searchlight gets out of his car, I would send the people up the Wall in waves. The first people I would send would be the official and unofficial party, then the press pool, and then the President and his group. So we get the other people moving up ahead which gives you a clear shot back. We move them way up ahead, past the point where the President will stop and turn around and go back down. Then they follow him back down. We could move the press ahead of him on the way back down or something. That really gets the official and unofficial party out of the way. It gets rid of people like Haldeman who want to be taking movies, and gets them on up the Wall so they can take their damn movies. [*Watchdog already had his movies from his trip in October, and Haldeman was famous for his obsessive home movie-making.*]

SNAPSHOT: Dwight, we've got a whole different plan here and we've gone over it many, many, many times. From a press point of view, we are totally covered in advance. We do not need a press pool on the Wall in front of him. That would destroy everything we are trying to do. We've got a press pool operation on the first turret . . . it's not really a turret, it's that flat area . . .

WATCHDOG: I remember it.

SNAPSHOT: OK. There are some press there, on the right hand side. There's also a live television camera there to catch the arrival and his walking up. There is a second turret also with a live television camera. AP and UPI are up on top of that first turret and catch him walking up the Wall. He walks underneath the first turret, up to the second turret, an easy walk. AP, UPI are going to get their pictures. Everybody is going to make beautiful pictures. The press will be pre-positioned forty-five minutes before the President arrives.

Watchdog already had movies from his October trip.

They will get to romp around the wall a bit and then take their positions. Everybody can see everything from on top of the turrets. To me it's an excellent way to do it.

ROADRUNNER: Dwight, he can walk up about fifty yards past the second turret to where that great big steep part of the Wall begins, and it would just be a fantastic shot. You've got that dragon effect of the Wall and the President and Mrs. Nixon and their hosts.

SNAPSHOT: Beautiful. The live cameras are absolutely ecstatic about this. [*The photo that was seen around the world did indeed show the Wall snaking up behind the group that paused to pose, but it was a much larger group than was originally planned. It included, along with numerous Chinese, the President and Mrs. Nixon, Secretary Rogers, Haldeman, John Scali, Ziegler, Buchanan, Watchdog, Redman, Taylor, Coffey, Roadrunner and at least nine other unidentified Americans.*]

Swift, Redman & Schrauth pose for camera angles.

WATCHDOG: Listen now, we don't want an Apollo 13 thing here. We want to put this whole thing indoors. [*A joking reference to the arrival in Hawaii of the Apollo 13 crew for a meeting with the President. Roadrunner had worked hard to arrange a magnificent photo opportunity in which Diamondhead loomed in the background.*]

ROADRUNNER: (pause) OK. We'll build a top over the turret. Ha, ha, ha. You had me for a minute. I gotcha now!

SNAPSHOT: Dwight, we're not doing a production. We're just walking up . . .

WATCHDOG: I'm only kidding. I'm only kidding.

SNAPSHOT: He's walking up with a party of official Chinese rather than having press guys running all around him and all over the damn place.

WATCHDOG: I understand. Boy, I'm with you on that.

SNAPSHOT: Also, the networks want to ship video tape after ten minutes. They want to move that out of there immediately. We'll have a car standing by for the networks to get their video tape back first. Then the film, AP and UPI film, processors will go next. I think it is the ideal way to do it.

WATCHDOG: I'm with you. You guys know more about what you are doing that we do.

SNAPSHOT: We've thought about it a lot, Dwight, because it's important.

WATCHDOG: Yes it is. Now, Ron, you mentioned that's only one of the many problems Thomas is going to have, or some famous quote like that a few minutes ago. Would you elaborate on what else you've got in mind?

ROADRUNNER: Well, with John Thomas designated as the accounts and finance individual, the things they are going to be asking of him are unbelievable. They want to cut deals and they are talking thousands and thousands and thousands of dollars, and it's coming in from all these different aspects represented here, and they're going to want to deal with Thomas. Fortunately he's got some outstanding pros that are presently in-country and will be coming in seven days ahead. He's going to have to rely on these people. The problem he is going to have is pulling this whole thing together with those various carriers.

MAGUIRE: Ron, Maguire. You realize how important it is to get an answer to some of these options? [*Chuck Maguire was John Thomas' representative from the State Department.*]

ROADRUNNER: Believe me, Chuck, I am very much aware of that.

WATCHDOG: (chuckles) Well, we don't have anything else here.

SNAPSHOT: Dwight, Dwight?

WATCHDOG: Yeah.

SNAPSHOT: Maybe you can shake this out. I'm been trying for a long time. I need an answer on the toasts. I need it pretty quick. [*Snapshot needed to know whether the press coverage would be live or taped.*]

WATCHDOG: Right. Ron and I will have that for you when you wake up.

SNAPSHOT: Thank you.

WHELIHAN: Tim, one thing Whaleboat wanted me to mention to you is the procedures over filing. He is very concerned that the media, particularly the wires, are going to complain of some sort of procedural censorship. You need to get assurances there from your counterpart that this is not going to be the case. They will file promptly and immediately on phone calls and telex.

WATCHDOG: Got that?

SNAPSHOT: Roger. I understand that completely. This is one thing I was concerned about and the PRC understood I was concerned. Once the press sees the press center, and where the copy will be filed, they will understand. There is more telex equipment there than you have ever seen. When I asked for a comeback copy of what was

filed, they said we don't have to look over their shoulder. They will
file it the way we want it filed. It is a matter of principle. They
don't want an American standing over their shoulder to tell them how
to do it. They will do it their way, accurately and timely.

WHELIHAN: I understand. But, we do not have an opportunity to
prepare, or condition so to speak, the attitudes of the press in this
country with regard to these dealings. There is a concern here about
the equipment and the procedures.

WATCHDOG: I know what you are saying, Tim. It sure as hell is
a point of principle. I know they are going to file it exactly as
written and so does Ziegler and so does Whelihan.

WHELIHAN: That's correct.

WATCHDOG: You can't believe the damn number of questions they
are coming up with, like will we be able to get to the machines fast
enough and are we going to have to wait long periods of time to give
a copy to somebody. We'll assure them that's being done as
expeditiously as it possibly can. Right? Right?

SNAPSHOT: It'll be done, Dwight, as expeditiously as it can within
the realm of principle within the PRC.

WATCHDOG: OK. I understand.

ROADRUNNER: I have one thing to cover with you, Dwight, real
quickly.

WATCHDOG: Go ahead.

ROADRUNNER: The technicians have asked that I assist in acquiring
a telephone for members of their group to contact their families. I
sensed a morale problem from the second Reuters story about
technicians being ill in-country. They are worrying that their families
are worrying about whether it is them or not. Many of these people
have not had any communications with their families in almost two
weeks now. I would like to go ahead and do this, but I recall a
conversation we had with Woodcutter about people having to be very
cautious about calling home and divulging information and having it
end up in the newspapers. I would like your permission to talk to
Siegenthaler and lay some ground rules and then come up with a
circuit for them.

WATCHDOG: OK. Do it. Let him know there is a standard
recording thing going on. [*The recording was usually halted when a
personal call began, although the men did not know it at the time.*]

ROADRUNNER: All righty. Thank you.

WATCHDOG: Just make sure you and Tim talk to Siegenthaler.

ROADRUNNER: You can rest assured of that. Siegenthaler has
done one hell of a job.

WATCHDOG: He's a sensational guy.

ROADRUNNER: He's held to every ground rule that was laid, and when he's had problems, he's come straight to us. He's had very good control of those men and for that we are very grateful.

SNAPSHOT: I wish someone would get to those network representatives over there and say something. He's been magnificent.

WATCHDOG: OK. We'll mention this to Ron and he may want to make a couple of calls.

ROADRUNNER: Thank you. That's all I've got. Schrauth would like to talk to Henkel. Have a nice day.

WATCHDOG: Same to you. Good evening and thanks for everything, men.

SCHRAUTH: What we want to do is . . .

HENKEL: Yeah, Mike?

SCHRAUTH: We need to marry up people and equipment, specifically the AP and UPI gear with the people that are coming in on the fourteenth, and John Thomas and his gear. We want to move that all to the fourteenth. Do you understand?

HENKEL: Schrauth, let me get this straight. You have people and gear scheduled for arrivals on the twelfth, thirteenth and fourteenth. You are proposing that in Guam, this stuff be off-loaded and then put on the aircraft arriving the fourteenth?

SCHRAUTH: That's a roge. You've got a people plane, lots of gear and equipment to service S'76 and 970, the two mobile vans, and all the AP and UPI gear. It can all be consolidated and come in on those two airplanes on the fourteenth.

HENKEL: So the people come in as scheduled, but the equipment is re-organized so it can come in and be brought up to Peking on our own aircraft?

SCHRAUTH: That's right. We don't want the gear to be off-loaded and sitting around waiting to come up here. OK?

HENKEL: I totally understand, and I can assure you there will be a howl. I'm sure they will do their best, we all will, to accomplish this, but I'm sure you appreciate there may be some problems involved.

SCHRAUTH: I know there will be! I appreciate it wholeheartedly, my friend. OK.

WATCHDOG: Hey, Mike? Has Ron left?

SCHRAUTH: Yeah, he's across the way with Siegenthaler.

WATCHDOG: OK. Let him know after he's done with that meeting, and in private, that whatever is said by Searchlight regarding the visit, I'll make sure we get on the wire so you will have it.

SCHRAUTH: OK, fine. This is Schrauth out.

HENKEL: Good night, Mike.

SCHRAUTH: Night.

Schrauth grinned at the men still in the room. It had been another long session. Everyone stood to stretch. It felt good to shake the kinks out, especially for someone as tall as Mike Schrauth. He went looking for Roadrunner and Snapshot.

"Hey, Timmie," he said as he walked into the Roadrunner's sitting room. "It sure sounds like those press prima donnas are starting to throw their weight around back home."

"Yeah, does it ever."

"Do you think the White House can buy time by saying the same things in a few more different ways?"

"Hell, no. You aren't going to fool anybody for one minute. But if we're lucky, they'll be smart enough to keep their questions to themselves for just a little bit longer. There should be a feeling of excitement and anticipation building around this trip," Snapshot told him.

"You mean a history-in-the-making feeling?" Roadrunner wanted to know.

"Well, why not? It sure as hell is historic. It's exciting. The American press corps is not in control. It is not their party. They are invited guests of the Chinese. If they, individually, want to be jerks, they can be replaced by countless other reporters, correspondents, or talking heads. Just think about how many newsies, all over the United States, would love to be making this trip. I would like to think that they, the chosen few, might start realizing that. But then, I'm probably dreaming again; I've been here too long. I'm thinking idealistically, like the Chinese. Do you think I'm becoming a Communist? Get me outta here. Get me to a pub. I need to be surrounded by real people. I'm starting to get really scared." Tim covered his head with his hands.

Schrauth looked intently at Snapshot for a moment. "I know what you mean," he said, with a faint hint of astonishment in his voice. "I'm starting to feel it, too. We sit in those meetings and I swear to you, sometimes I know what they are going to say before they say it. They are totally predictable. I know exactly how they will react as soon as the question is presented to them."

"Tim! Mike! You know what?" Roadrunner asked. "You are absolutely, one hundred percent correct. This can work to our advantage. Now listen a minute. Watchdog wants the Chinese to release more of the schedule details, but they are dead set against releasing details of any kind; a classic Catch-22. So let me come at you with some questions, and you two put on your Chinese thinking caps and come up with the answers. OK?"

"Fire away," Schrauth said.

"But first," Snapshot insisted quietly, "have a tangerine. Have a cup of tea. Enjoy a piece of candy. Did you have a pleasant day? Were you able to pause and enjoy the singing of a bird? Was there a rainbow after the rain? Did the fragrance of a beautiful flower come your way? Did the smile of a child grace your day? Did you see the butterfly in the garden? Did the turtle safely cross the road?"

Snapshot paused, and looked intently at Schrauth. Then he turned to Roadrunner, "When we have talked about these things, we can discuss other, less important matters. Now what did you want to ask me?"

Roadrunner, Snapshot, and Schrauth threw American questions and Chinese answers back and forth until the green hotel phone rang. It was Bob Siegenthaler. He suggested they have a little get together and bring everyone up to date. His men were asking a lot of questions and rumors were flying. He suggested it was time they got the straight scoop from Roadrunner directly.

It was a good session. Roadrunner could not believe some of the rumors that were circulating among the press: "The Chinese are not giving us answers because Chairman Mao had a stroke and his people do not know what to do next." . . . "Mao is dead." . . . "Ho Chi Minh is demanding that the Chinese snub the American President." Roadrunner could only imagine what would happen if some of these rumors found there way to the front page of the Washington *Post*.

The next morning the conference call convened at 7:40. As the operator reminded everyone about the recording, Glen Campbell could be heard singing *Wichita Lineman* in the background. It was a strange serenade from so far away. It was 6:40 in the evening, Washington time.

WATCHDOG: Good morning, Roadrunner.
ROADRUNNER: Good evening, Watchdog.
HENKEL: Hi, Ron.
ROADRUNNER: Hi, Bill. Did you all have a pleasant day?
WATCHDOG: Yes, did you have a pleasant rest?
ROADRUNNER: Yes, we met with the technicians until about, oh, I guess . . . one o'clock our time.
WATCHDOG: You sound tired.
ROADRUNNER: We just needed to let them know what was going on.
WATCHDOG: Yeah.
ROADRUNNER: We still did not get into the subject of asking them for additional money. They are going to shit in their pants when they hear that! Whoa! Wooooh! It's going to be a real problem.

WATCHDOG: Who's going to do that?

ROADRUNNER: We're going to do it tonight in Shanghai. We kind of set them up for it last night, and I'm sure they know something is coming. We let them use our phone last night to call and they all sat in the same room listening to each other. It was an unbelievable scene. They all listened to what the others said.

WATCHDOG: You mean, because they won't let anybody talk to anybody separately, right?

ROADRUNNER: Yeah. (Ha, ha).

WATCHDOG: OK. I've just sent you a transcript of the President's press conference.

ROADRUNNER: It's already happened?

WATCHDOG: Yes.

ROADRUNNER: Huh, OK (cough, cough, cough, cough).

WATCHDOG: Did you get word to your counterpart?

ROADRUNNER: Yes.

WATCHDOG: OK. Well, then . . . they knew it before it happened?

ROADRUNNER: Yes.

WATCHDOG: OK. Good. *Muy importante.*

ROADRUNNER: Yes.

WATCHDOG: I am sending you a TWX of the President's excerpts from his news conference on China.

ROADRUNNER: Was it on many subjects, Dwight?

WATCHDOG: No, it was on his schedule, which he said would have to be very flexible and would be different from almost any trip he had ever taken, and he used the word "flexible."

ROADRUNNER: Great.

WATCHDOG: That Mrs. Nixon would have a much more public schedule than he would. And we would not know the lengths of the meetings, that his trip was not for sightseeing although he hoped to be able to do some of that, but it was going to be very substantively oriented. I think it is exactly what the government would approve of our saying. I would let them have a copy, after you've read it.

ROADRUNNER: Yes, I will do that. (cough, cough) Excuse me, what time our time did he do that, Dwight?

WATCHDOG: He did it at 5:00 in the morning your time.

ROADRUNNER: OK, very good. (cough, cough)

WATCHDOG: It was four o'clock here, an in-office press conference.

ROADRUNNER: Ahhh. OK. (cough, cough, cough) Excuse me.

WATCHDOG: He called the press in instead of Ron's 4:00 briefing. What's all this coughing and crap? Are you sick?

ROADRUNNER: No, I've got a little cough.

WATCHDOG: Yeah, well then, don't stay up so late.

ROADRUNNER: We didn't get off the phone here with you until almost quarter to twelve.

WATCHDOG: Yeah, that's right.

ROADRUNNER: But it was very productive.   And, you wouldn't believe . . . I couldn't see one foot outside my window this morning.

WATCHDOG: Why, you mean it's so foggy?

ROADRUNNER: Well it's the crap in the air and everything. It's a wonder we're not all going to have lung cancer.

WATCHDOG: Shhhhhhh. OK. [As always, Watchdog was concerned with offending the Chinese.]

ROADRUNNER: (cough, cough) Excuse me.

WATCHDOG: What time do you leave now?

ROADRUNNER: Five P.M. our time. This is what I am hopeful will transpire. We'll leave here around 3:30, go to the airport, and have a chance to look at the departure from Peking. We haven't discussed the departure. I would like to do that. We depart at five. I expect to be in the hotel sometime around 8:00 or 8:15.

WATCHDOG: Well, hell, maybe you can call us in the morning.

ROADRUNNER: OK. We will attempt to call as soon as we arrive at the hotel.

WATCHDOG: OK. Listen, the Mrs. Nixon stuff looked good. I sent it over to her this afternoon. One thing we don't know is would she have any live TV, like at the commune?

SCHRAUTH: Not planned for right now.

ROADRUNNER: No, it's not . . . no live.

WATCHDOG: That probably could be accomplished, couldn't it?

ROADRUNNER: They aren't thinking about it at all.

SCHRAUTH: That morning there is a meeting [on the President's schedule] which would not be live so, in other words, their cameras should be available.

WATCHDOG: That's what I mean. The same thing would hold true for the Peking kitchen and the hotel.

ROADRUNNER: The hotel would be very difficult to do.

WATCHDOG: OK. How 'bout . . . let's see, the commune, that's about it, isn't it?

SCHRAUTH: Yeah, well, for instance, the Temple of Heaven, that would be a possibility.

WATCHDOG: That would be beautiful. That's such a pretty place, didn't you think?

SCHRAUTH: Mmmm, hmmmm.

ROADRUNNER: The day we went there, it was absolutely gorgeous.

WATCHDOG: Oh, I'm telling you, I remember that. That's sensational. Well, we really don't have anything else here. We spent a lot of time on the schedule, about three or four hours after we hung up this morning and it's going on tape at State. Dewey's getting his stuff in tomorrow, and I guess Foust will be getting his stuff in tomorrow. So it's starting to come together and it will all fall apart in another day or so . . .

ROADRUNNER: Ha, I know it!

WATCHDOG: . . . but it is starting to piece together.

ROADRUNNER: Well, we haven't guessed at stuff. We've given you facts, and I think that's the best way to go. As we get additional facts hopefully we will be able to plug them in. If we can't do it in Washington, maybe somewhere along the way. I know those two guys in both Guam and Hawaii are probably going to have to make some arrangements to help you.

HENKEL: I volunteer to go to Hawaii.

WATCHDOG: I think we may have to plan like a daily newspaper, a little deal that says schedule changes and items for tomorrow or whatever and just run it off on a mimeograph. Use it as a . . . .

ROADRUNNER: (cough, cough) I agree with you.

HENKEL: John Thomas is bringing in printing capability, isn't that correct?

ROADRUNNER: Yes, he is.

HENKEL: Just for that purpose.

WATCHDOG: We've got a whole bunch of equipment now that my brilliant documentary crew has come up with a damn ton of equipment.

HENKEL: No, no, it's five hundred pounds short of a ton.

WATCHDOG: Five hundred pounds short of a ton! (laugh)

ROADRUNNER: Are you kidding? [*He was not kidding.*]

WATCHDOG: That may be my newest problem.

ROADRUNNER: Oh, my God.

WATCHDOG: So . . .

ROADRUNNER: Let me ask you a question. We asked for a breakdown of what their responsibilities are based on getting them to split up for Elbourne's pools and everything.

WATCHDOG: Well, they've been meeting all day today, and they will meet with me tomorrow morning to come up with assignments by name for each event. I've done the photo opportunities, situations at the compound, Mrs. Nixon's stuff and everything else. I'm breaking the crews down by who's going where. I can TWX you all that tomorrow.

ROADRUNNER: OK. That will be great. (cough, cough)

HENKEL: Ron, I got those photographs for you today.

ROADRUNNER: I think that's outstanding.

HENKEL: There are a couple of pictures you may want to give out and autograph.

WATCHDOG: Oh my God.

ROADRUNNER: Thank you. (laugh) That would be a first.

HENKEL: Yeah. It may sound corny, but you may want to leave them with a picture. Wherever I could get you talking with people, I sent that. [*Henkel meant their Chinese counterparts.*]

ROADRUNNER: They'll appreciate that very much. I just know they will. It's something we can do and not have to worry about being acceptable. [*There was a problem giving gifts to individuals. In a Communist society, gifts were for "all the people." The Americans hoped that photographs of them working together would be acceptable gifts.*]

HENKEL: Yeah, and you got my thing about the film, right?

ROADRUNNER: Yes. (cough, cough) We may be able to buy the film in Guam, that's no problem. The problem is that people have run out here. The technicians are willing to pay for it. . . . and the PRC has asked.

HENKEL: I'll get Dewey working on it right now, out of Guam.

WATCHDOG: Have Thomas buy it. Have Thomas buy it in Guam.

ROADRUNNER: Yeah.

WATCHDOG: Have Thomas take it out of his funds. We'll take care of it.

ROADRUNNER: I would like to get some of that to the PRC. To our friends. They just don't have colored film. And Kitchell says they'll be able to process it in the studio.

WATCHDOG: Hey Ron? Ron?

ROADRUNNER: Yes?

WATCHDOG: Hang on a minute. I think maybe we can give you Rather's comments on China. Just a minute.

DAN RATHER FROM CBS-TV NEWS: The President said he would leave for China on February seventeenth, going by way of Hawaii and Guam. He repeated that there would be no new taxes this year, that he does plan to submit a program later to do away with . . .

WATCHDOG: Did you hear that?

ROADRUNNER: Yes.

WATCHDOG: In other words, it was just that little of a deal here so you can tell he didn't say much.

ROADRUNNER: Right. I understand. OK, as soon as I get the transcript, I'll make it available to Mr. Chu and go from there.

WATCHDOG: OK. Ron? Ron?

ROADRUNNER: Yes?

WATCHDOG: Hang on just a minute. Somebody wants to say hello.

ROADRUNNER: Yes.

HAIG: Ron? General Haig.

ROADRUNNER: Oh, General. How are you, sir?

HAIG: Just fine. We're following your work very closely. Think you're doing a great job.

ROADRUNNER: Oh, thank you, sir. I think everybody is. We couldn't have asked for ninety-nine better men. They've all conducted themselves beautifully. I think they have represented our country very well.

HAIG: Good. Well, we're following everything and I think your hosts are following the same very hospitable treatment that they gave us when we were there earlier.

ROADRUNNER: Yes, sir. That is correct.

HAIG: Fine. OK.

ROADRUNNER: It's sure nice to talk to you. Wish we were going to see you. They've often asked about you and have often said that they wish you were returning, too. But as you said, you must stay home when the President and Dr. Kissinger are gone. They understand.

HAIG: Right. [*So! The General was used to being in charge in the absence of the President, as we learned moments after President Reagan was shot in 1981.*]

ROADRUNNER: They send their best to you.

HAIG: OK, fine. Give my best to everybody.

WATCHDOG: Ron?

ROADRUNNER: Yes.

WATCHDOG: OK. Let me see . . . Do you know what we're bringing as gifts? Do you remember what we wanted to do in Hangchou?

ROADRUNNER: Uhhhhhhhhh. No.

WATCHDOG: We mentioned planting something in Hangchou. Does that help? [*The President was bringing giant redwood trees from California.*]

ROADRUNNER: Yes.

WATCHDOG: Now we're moving off on that and bringing a couple. One and a back-up and maybe even two back-ups. It's got everybody over here in hysterics. But it should be nice, and it's something you ought to talk to them about at some juncture. [*The logistics of transporting giant redwood trees to China was causing some difficulty. Discussions ranged from whether they should sit in the head or with the press, some of whom were stiff as trees anyway.*]

ROADRUNNER: OK.

WATCHDOG: I'm looking here to see if there's anything else. Have you been having your meals down there in that dining room?

ROADRUNNER: Well, on occasions, to make an appearance. We've been eating in the room, when we've been eating. We haven't been eating a great deal. But they've done a very nice job downstairs and the meals have been excellent, but if you ate all three meals you'd weigh a hundred pounds more than you did when you came in here. (cough, cough) [*The Chinese really tested them at banquets. They wanted to see how the Americans would react to sea slugs and sparrow, and other things that are not usually considered edible at home.*]

WATCHDOG: I see. But the general pattern is for people to be eating down there once or twice a day, huh?

ROADRUNNER: (cough, cough) Yes. Well, the technicians eat at the airport, at noon.

WATCHDOG: Yes.

ROADRUNNER: Which is one of the problems, because they eat at the airport restaurant.

WATCHDOG: Yes.

ROADRUNNER: That gives them their open game. [*Ability to talk to third-country reporters*]

WATCHDOG: I see.

ROADRUNNER: If you understand what I mean.

WATCHDOG: Oh, I know. I think we've hit that pretty hard. The problem is, and I say it again, I think that our discussions are monitored. I believe that a lot of this stuff is starting to seep out. It's not us here, and we want to make that clear. It's not. I think another key point is the fact that on our trips, Dr. Kissinger in October and General Haig in January, our patterns are so much the same. You know, where we visited, where the meetings were held, the Great Hall of the People, the Forbidden City, the Great Wall, the government guest house. If you piece it all together, it doesn't take too much intelligence to figure out what the hell is happening.

ROADRUNNER: Yes, I understand.

WATCHDOG: You know, the welcoming banquet, it kind of makes sense that it's the first night, the reciprocal banquet, it kind of makes sense it's the last night. And . . . that's what's happening to us over here. If you follow me.

ROADRUNNER: Yes, I do.

WATCHDOG: I know it's a problem. I know they're concerned and I understand the reasons and I know they want to keep the lid on it and therefore, we'll honor their request and keep it as confidential as possible.

ROADRUNNER: Right, sir.

WATCHDOG: The President makes that very clear in his remarks today.

ROADRUNNER: OK.

WATCHDOG: He's going to Florida in about an hour. He's going to work down there this weekend, which is great. He is looking forward to this trip very much and is deeply interested and involved in its preparation as is Mrs. Nixon. They are, I would say, very excited about it.

ROADRUNNER: I'm glad he's going. That will be a great help to him, I'm sure.

WATCHDOG: That's right. Uh. OK, now we don't have any indication yet, obviously, of any of the Chinese ladies that would be with Mrs. Nixon. Is that right?

ROADRUNNER: Not one, not one piece of information.

WATCHDOG: OK. Well, it sure would be helpful, obviously, from her standpoint.

SCHRAUTH: Dwight, after the conversations last night I talked to Connie, and passed that same information on. We've been trying to get the information, but . . . [*Connie Stewart, Mrs. Nixon's Chief of Staff, was not particularly popular among the President's aides, although it was obvious that Schrauth was unaware of the situation.*]

WATCHDOG: Well, let's don't ever do that again, OK? Let's just cut that, zilch on that, absolutely nothing . . . all of it's to be handled via Rose Woods. OK? [*Obviously, Watchdog felt strongly about this subject.*]

SCHRAUTH: OK.

WATCHDOG: That can cause us ungodly problems at this end. That's why we prepared a lengthy report from you to Mrs. Nixon directly that's not passing through the channel that you just mentioned.

SCHRAUTH: OK, I understand perfectly.

WATCHDOG: OK. Ron? Have you got anything else there?

ROADRUNNER: No sir, we're clean at this end. (cough, cough) Have a nice evening. We'll look forward to talking to you from Shanghai this evening.

HENKEL: Have a safe flight.

WATCHDOG: Yeah, and good luck. I'll be at home, if you need me tonight, for any reason.

ROADRUNNER: OK, sir. Don't be alarmed if we don't get through to you. We'll be fine.

WATCHDOG: How is Vern doing now?

ROADRUNNER: He didn't look very good last night during that conference call. He's still in his pajamas and robe. I sent my counterpart a note expressing our deep appreciation for the kindness and assistance they gave Vern in his speedy recovery and indicated he would be remaining and would be responsible and could answer any questions and had my full confidence while I was gone.

WATCHDOG: OK, now who's Vern's back-up?

ROADRUNNER: Tom Benedict of the Secret Service and Colonel Hank Gibbons of the White House Communications Agency.

WATCHDOG: You might have a little talk with them. You know just in case Vern . . . he could have a relapse of some kind.
ROADRUNNER: Yes, I understand. All right, I will do that.
WATCHDOG: OK, Ron. Well, you have a good day and as I said, we'll be at home and you can get in touch with us.
ROADRUNNER: OK. Very good. We'll look forward to talking with you this evening.
WATCHDOG: Take care.

Watchdog had a sinking feeling when he said goodbye to Roadrunner, but he took a deep breath and assured himself that the men would be perfectly safe flying through the freezing, wintry skies of the People's Republic of China. Somehow, though, he could not shake the feeling and he thought about it all evening and as he was trying to fall asleep.

Watchdog was freezing. It was as cold on the CAAC airplane [Civil Air Administration of China] *as it was outside. "Don't the Chinese have heat on their passenger planes?" he wondered. "Perhaps not. After all they do wear quilted jackets and trousers in the winter time. But, if they have airplane phones, they ought to have heat, for heaven's sake." Watchdog listened as the phone on the plane rang, but nobody else seemed to hear it. "Why wasn't anybody answering it?" he wondered.*

Then Watchdog woke up. He was not on a Chinese airplane; he was at home. The bedroom window on Baltimore Avenue was wide open and the cold wind had made the whole room feel like a deep freeze. The telephone was still ringing.

Watchdog looked at his bedside clock. It wasn't *that* late, only 11:25 P.M. He blinked and forced himself to concentrate. That meant it was twenty-five minutes past noon in China. Roadrunner had not yet left Peking. Watchdog grabbed the phone and listened impatiently to the recording spiel.

OPERATOR: Gentlemen, per your request, this telephone conversation is being recorded by the audio visual branch of the White House Communications Agency. Please go ahead with your conversation.
ROADRUNNER: Dwight?
WATCHDOG: Ron?
ROADRUNNER: Dwight?
WATCHDOG: Yeah.
ROADRUNNER: Are you awake?
WATCHDOG: Yeah.
ROADRUNNER: I'm sorry, we just came out of what I consider to be a very, very fine meeting. I have Tim with me.

WATCHDOG: OK, go ahead.

ROADRUNNER: We met with our counterparts about 10:30. I took a copy of the President's remarks with me. It was an excellent presentation on the President's part, it was just outstanding.

WATCHDOG: It was perfect for you, right?

ROADRUNNER: Absolutely, you just don't have any idea.

WATCHDOG: I think I know.

ROADRUNNER: I know you do. I had it Xeroxed and took copies down and invited Mr. Chu and Mr. Ma, Timmie's counterpart. I handed them the President's remarks and they read it while we waited in the room.

They were pleased. And then I went into a very long explanation of what was transpiring in America, the concern and the enthusiasm and the interest that was building all across the country. Not only the press, but the American people themselves, about what the President was going to be doing, what Mrs. Nixon was going to be doing, what their schedules were going to be. I said we have held the line on everything, but it's fast coming to the point that we are going to have speculation. And the speculation is what will cause problems, not only for our government, but for their government. As a result we feel it is extremely important to set ground rules, as the President has just done today, on what our two governments have agreed on.

I then stated that we are getting pressure in Washington for the most minute details, which to their government may not appear very important, but to the American people it is very important. Security arrangements, communications arrangements, press arrangements, where is the President staying, what kind of aircraft is he riding on? And then I explained that a good reporter can write his own story from things that have been talked about by Dr. Kissinger and by Mr. Ziegler.

Timmie and I said the time has come to set the ground rules and lay the proper foundation for the right information and the correct information to be coming out of the White House, not out of some reporter when he doesn't have the facts. The speculation is what will kill us.

They understood and they were shaking their heads. "Yes, we understand, and although we don't have those kinds of problems in our country, we understand that you are having those kind of problems."

So, it was an outstanding meeting.

WATCHDOG: Great.

ROADRUNNER: I said it is conceivable that unless the White House gives information out, someone may leak it. So then it comes from a source other than the official source that we have agreed to. So they have said, OK, fine, we understand, go back and draft up another release. That's what we're doing.

WATCHDOG: You're going to write it?

ROADRUNNER: Yes, sir. I've just dictated it. I've taken many of the points in your original release, but I've toned down activities.

WATCHDOG: OK.

ROADRUNNER: I've gone through Hangchou and Shanghai, and it's being typed now. Timmie can interject any comments that he has on the press side, and I am assured by Mr. Chu that they will give it their highest priority.

WATCHDOG: Then once you get it approved there, you'll send it, right? Or maybe just send me a TWX if it's late at night.

ROADRUNNER: Yes sir, I will if there are no major changes. I don't think there will be, I think they are going to buy it, Dwight.

WATCHDOG: Good. Well, that's great. I gave the wording to Buchanan, and I knew that we were on target.

ROADRUNNER: Absolutely, it was perfect. Here, Timmie wants to talk to you.

SNAPSHOT: Dwight?

WATCHDOG: Timmie, go ahead.

SNAPSHOT: This was an excellent meeting. They understand our point about speculation and how one story will lead to another story and another story and another story. If we don't say the President will be staying at the Peking guest house, reporters are likely to say nobody knows where he is staying. And it will start building. We said we've got to say certain points that will lead to a logical news flow from the White House. That will keep news coming from the White House. They've got something to write that's concrete. They understood that completely and totally, and that's when they asked us to please do another draft.

WATCHDOG: Right.

SNAPSHOT: I think we're on the right track.

WATCHDOG: That's great, that's great. I felt it was perfect. I knew the words like flexibility, and . . .

SNAPSHOT: Yes, it was just absolutely outstanding.

WATCHDOG: Good.

SNAPSHOT: Couldn't be better.

WATCHDOG: Good.

SNAPSHOT: Then we went into the possibility of Mrs. Nixon meeting with the press before she leaves to tell them about her preparations. This is the color side, of course, which they all laughed at. We've been talking about color every time we turn around. They understand completely.

WATCHDOG: OK. Thank you, Tim.

ROADRUNNER: OK. That's all I've got, and I'm sorry to have bothered you this late.

WATCHDOG: No, no, that's OK. Let me ask you something. How's Vern?

ROADRUNNER: Vern looks (pause) like he got hit up side the head with a mallet or something.

WATCHDOG: Why?

ROADRUNNER: Well, his eyes are all dark and sunken back into his head and his coloring is still not too swift. He says that we can call him "The Pajama Kid," he hasn't been out of pajamas in over a week. The doctor spent about an hour and a half with him this morning, they are taking very good care of him. He just can't do too much too fast.

WATCHDOG: OK. Well, I talked to Anne a little while ago. She's fine and she's going to a party tomorrow night at the Whitakers. [John C. Whitaker was Secretary to the Cabinet]

ROADRUNNER: Is she going to go? I'm sure glad.

WATCHDOG: And evidently the Semples and the Kaplows are going to be there so she wanted some press advice. I gave her some PR advice and I am going to send her the bill shortly. [Robert Semple, New York Times and Herbert Kaplow, ABC News]

ROADRUNNER: Ha, ha, ha. Well, hopefully they don't know I'm over here.

WATCHDOG: The hell they don't! Everybody in the country knows. You've been getting a lot of press. I don't know what we are going to do about you once you get your clippings, we're going to have a problem.

ROADRUNNER: I don't believe that for a minute. My passion for anonymity is overwhelming.

WATCHDOG: Ha, ha, ha.

ROADRUNNER: Ha, ha, ha. OK, Dwight, again I'm sorry to bother you, and say "Hi" to Susie for me.

WATCHDOG: I'm glad it worked out and I appreciate your calling. I think that's sensational, and I know that the People's Republic has got to understand, at the highest levels we are on track on this.

ROADRUNNER: Well, the most beautiful thing about it was the President.

WATCHDOG: Well, he talked to us about it and he knew exactly what he was supposed to say and he did it.

ROADRUNNER: Well it certainly set the foundation for exactly what we wanted and boy, that was a hell of a way of going about doing it. He's a very perceptive man.

WATCHDOG: OK. I'll talk to you tomorrow.

ROADRUNNER: Right. Look forward to it. Bye, bye.
WATCHDOG: Bye, bye.

Roadrunner was elated! His President had reached around the world and had flipped the right switch in the People's Republic of China. The Chinese drew confidence from his words and were now ready to follow the suggestions of the American advance party.

"Wow! The Old Man is something else, isn't he?" Roadrunner said to Snapshot and Schrauth. "Isn't it amazing that he himself is the one that finally makes the difference and gets their attention?"

"He knew exactly what needed to be said," Snapshot agreed.

"You know, with all we have to deal with, and as much as we bitch about the cold and the food and the tangerines and the tea, we are really in the middle of an incredible happening. We are making history," Roadrunner reminded them.

"You are so right," Schrauth said. "Would you have ever thought, when we were Army lieutenants stationed on Okinawa, that someday we would be the President's men in the People's Republic of China?"

Roadrunner thought back to those days in the early 1960s. John Fitzgerald Kennedy was President and members of the armed services were "advisors" in Southeast Asia. Nobody was allowed to say they were being sent to Vietnam. Instead, they were going to be spending some time "off island" and would be receiving their mail addressed to an APO number in Karat, Thailand.

"God, no," he said, "and remember all those really scary guys they called DACs, Department of Army civilians, and how they kept talking about all the Communist activity that went on behind the bamboo curtain? They must have all been spies."

Snapshot looked at them both, "That's where you two met, wasn't it?"

"Yeah," Roadrunner answered first. "I was the only Army second lieutenant on the entire island, and it was a pretty exciting day when Anne and I were assigned to sponsor the arrival of Lieutenants Schrauth and Ryan and their families. We became great friends, and we all had children born there. Then, it was just accepted that there were eight hundred million people in China that we didn't talk to."

"Not any more," Snapshot said. "The President had a vision. He started working on this China initiative before he was ever elected President. He knew this was the right thing to do."

"He sure did," Roadrunner agreed. "He was quietly working on his China plan during his trip around the world in the summer of 1969. That was one hell of a summer. Neil Armstrong walked on the moon, the Manson murders took place in California, Teddy

Kennedy drove off the one-lane bridge in Chappaquidick, I was the advance man in New Delhi, and my pal Dick Howard was advancing Lahore, Pakistan. Only we met on that trip, so I didn't know he was my pal yet. The President sent word that he wanted to meet, one-on-one, with Pakistan's President, Yahya Khan. He insisted that there be no aides present. I remember Howard laughing about how mad people were over the request. Kissinger's people were beside themselves and of course, the State Department and Embassy folks were completely bonkers. It was that meeting that made it possible for the President to open the so-called Yahya Channel in 1970.

"And he made it happen, because here we are," Roadrunner continued. "We've had our ups and downs since we got here, but this is the best! I feel like the Chinese finally realize the importance of doing it this way. Sometimes it just seems like they agree to do something because we ask them. Tonight is different. It's understanding! And that understanding has finally led to some progress."

"Progress is right," Snapshot whooped. "We're going to Shanghai, and hopefully, we're not going to be shanghaied anymore!"

"Ha! That's very clever," Schrauth laughed. "We'll have to remember you said that."

Snapshot got serious. "I really like Shanghai; it's so different from Peking. It looks and feels more like a European City."

"It really does," Schrauth agreed. "It was once called the most sinful city in the world. Now it's stuffy and old, but it's got a feel of what it must have been like long ago. It has a cosmopolitan sense that you certainly don't get here in Peking."

"I definitely liked the Shanghai food much better," Snapshot said. "Remember that great sauce they always had on the table? It helped lots of things taste better. It even camouflaged the liver." Snapshot made a face and wrinkled his nose.

"I like liver," Roadrunner said.

"Ugh! Not me! Gawd, thinking about that sauce makes me think of salsa. You know what I want? A taco. Doesn't that sound delicious?" Snapshot said, his mouth watering.

"I'd prefer a Big Mac," Schrauth told them.

"If I could choose right this minute, I'd like to go sit out on a warm, sunlit patch of green grass and dig into some fried chicken, with a bowl of my mother's potato salad to go with it," Roadrunner said.

"Not me. A taco and some enchiladas. A couple of cheese ones and a couple of the chicken sour cream kind, and a big bunch of refried beans!" Snapshot insisted.

Schrauth stood up. "This is torture, you fools. Why are we doing this to ourselves? We need to get ready to get on the airplane.

Do you think we'll be flying first class? Do you think Chinese airplane food will be better than stateside airline food?"

"No way, Jose." Snapshot laughed.

"Oh, I don't know about that. A tangerine sure tastes better than a piece of plastic chicken, covered with some mystery sauce that makes the whole airplane smell awful," Roadrunner declared.

Snapshot jumped up from his chair, "Great, let's go pack. I can't wait to have another tangerine!"

CHAPTER XIV

THE STRANGEST IMAGINABLE SORT OF PEOPLE

FEBRUARY 11, 1972

The CAAC airplane was filled to capacity, and the Chinese passengers did not try to conceal their intense interest in the strange group of foreigners. While boarding, they would stop dead in the aisle and stare. Only shoving and shouting from behind would get them moving again. The Americans had not had much opportunity to mingle with local citizens, and they smiled and tried to use their very limited language capability to say a few words of greeting. This brought more surprise to the face of the person being addressed, and then either laughter or fright.

"Jeez, are we *that* scary looking?" Schrauth wanted to know.

"Only you, Mike. They probably think you are a giant. No, now that I watch them closely, I realize they think you're some kind of weird mutation," Snapshot kidded him.

"Don't laugh," Roadrunner said. "One of the books I read recently was *Moment In Peking*, a novel written in 1939 by Lin Yutang. The author described foreigners as 'the strangest imaginable sort of people.' They did everything upside down. Their writing went

The strangest imaginable people on a site survey.

from left to right, instead of right to left, and horizontally in 'crab walk' fashion instead of top to bottom. They put their personal names before their family names. Their women had large feet, a foot long, talked in a loud voice, had curly hair and blue eyes and went about arm in arm with men when walking.' Now doesn't that sound like a perfect description of Anne Walker?"

At least they did not have to worry about whether they were flying first class. There was no first class. Nor did they need to worry about liking the food. There was no food.

A stewardess, dressed just like every other woman they had seen in China, walked down the aisle handing out paper bags. They contained candy, a fan, a metal 'CAAC' pin, cigarettes, and a packet of tea. Another stewardess followed a short distance behind her with a metal kettle of hot water. That was it.

"Can you believe we don't even get a damn tangerine?" Snapshot whispered to Roadrunner when the stewardesses were out of earshot.

"I hope the fan doesn't predict what the on-board temperature is going to be during this flight," Roadrunner told him.

Unfortunately, it did! It got unbearably hot, but they all changed seats so they could spend time with their counterparts.

By late evening they had reached the hotel in Shanghai. They were on the phone to Washington at 11:10; it was mid-morning at the White House.

ROADRUNNER: We checked into the hotel about an hour ago. Major Swift was told that all we had to do was step into the office that was set up for us, and pick up the phone, and we would have Peking. Unbelievable. [*The Americans never had a clue this would happen, and it was a welcome surprise.*]

WATCHDOG: That's great. Well, they've done an outstanding job again and please let them know how much we appreciate being in touch with you and how important it is to us.

ROADRUNNER: Yes, I will, most assuredly. Our counterparts have been concerned about our rest and our working so hard, and have graciously given us the evening free, and I think most of us will go to bed after this call. (cough, cough) [*The Chinese were tired, too, and they had a big holiday to celebrate when they got home.*]

WATCHDOG: Well, I can tell by listening to your voice that you should go to sleep and try to shake off that cold.

ROADRUNNER: OK. Chief Dunn is taking very good care of me.

WATCHDOG: OK, Ron. Why don't you recap what you did in Peking prior to departure, and then we can come to the questions.

ROADRUNNER: Yes. After I talked to you, we sat down and wrote a release. I drafted it and Timmie inserted comments. Then we sent it directly in to the PRC. (cough, cough) Have you received yours?

WATCHDOG: Yes, I received it. Has the PRC approved that yet?

ROADRUNNER: No, sir. They have not. I did not raise the question on the plane. I talked to my counterpart the whole way. He didn't raise it either, so hopefully we'll have an answer tomorrow morning. [*Roadrunner was beginning to understand that no answer was the answer. He felt they would have known almost immediately if the Chinese had any problem with what they had written.*]

WATCHDOG: Let us know. We're shooting for Monday on that.

ROADRUNNER: They know. As is stated at the top of that release, it was for the fourteenth of February. They have assured us an answer soon. So I am hopeful that we'll have a decision on that by tomorrow. I know Mr. Chu is talking to (cough) Peking constantly.

WATCHDOG: OK, that's good. That's fine. Go ahead.

ROADRUNNER: After that we worked on the 391 list, gave that to them, gave them the cable on all of the scenarios you had prepared. We have no comments to make. I think an excellent job was done. We have no corrections.

WATCHDOG: Well, quit doing this! I don't want to have Bill and Julie get big heads until we're done with this job.

ROADRUNNER: Yeah, I don't want that either, because I have to come back some day, (cough, cough) I hope. (laughter)

WATCHDOG: Henkel's already got your office.

ROADRUNNER: I understand that.

WATCHDOG: Listen. Will you be done with Shanghai during the day tomorrow?

ROADRUNNER: Roger, we depart the guest house here at 8:30 for the airport. Hopefully, survey the airport for both the arrival and departure, meet the C-141 at 10:00 A.M., return to survey the guest house, have lunch, and then be at the Children's Palace at two o'clock. The networks are now contemplating live television of Mrs. Nixon's visit to the Children's palace. [*Established in 1960, the Palace was a favorite place for the Chinese to take foreign visitors. One hundred carefully selected, well-behaved school children with good grades performed musicals and plays.*]

This is the first time we've heard this. Timmie did not know about live TV either. After the Children's Palace we will go to the Shanghai Industrial Exhibit and then survey the Banquet Hall and the hall for the cultural show. Then they are hosting a banquet tomorrow night.

WATCHDOG: Roadrunner, I'm confused as to why they would want live television at the Children's Palace if it's in the afternoon and would be 2:00 A.M. Eastern Standard time.

ROADRUNNER: We picked it up in a casual conversation while we were relaying the schedule for tomorrow. We were talking about the amount of time we would spend there and the pool people indicated they needed more time because they were considering live coverage. We will pursue it and get back to you. (cough, cough, cough)

WATCHDOG: Yeah, It seems to me that there's a lot more logic in doing the Evergreen Commune [*near Peking*] live.

SNAPSHOT: Dwight, this is Tim. I talked to them about the Commune. They don't have any interest in doing that live.

WATCHDOG: Ooookay! (pause) What are they going to put on the air that night?

SNAPSHOT: I didn't ask them what they were going to put on the air that night, but they didn't have an interest. They thought it would be better covered by film. They'll probably put it on the air with film. I really don't know, Dwight.

WATCHDOG: OK. Roadrunner, are you on the line?

ROADRUNNER: Yes, Dwight. Be advised you're a little high-pitched and broken, but we are able to comprehend you.

WATCHDOG: Roger, the high-pitched thing and the cracking is just my state of mind. [*Watchdog did sound harassed.*] Umm, I know that we have press coverage for the first meeting. Do the Chinese plan on taking official photographs for the record, of all the other meetings? We would recommend this. In other words, I think we ought to document every meeting.

ROADRUNNER: Sir, I understand exactly what you're saying. I have not talked past the first meeting on official coverage. Please be advised that on the plane to Shanghai this evening, Mr. Chu told me that we will have many, many answers to questions upon our return to Peking. I am hopeful to cover all these details at that time. I realize that is going to be late for a detailed schedule to be on board S'76 when you depart, but it looks like it's the best we are going to be able to do.

As far as documenting, I personally have been assured that it can be worked out. However, be advised that Elbourne has been informed our documentary crew is going to be considered press corps. The PRC does not have what we call official photographers They are all governmental press photographers. This may become a problem once we start discussing it, but at this point, I have been assured our photographers will be able to move with their photographers at all locations.

WATCHDOG: Well, we have a point of principle arising here, and I would encourage you to be very strong on this particular item.

ROADRUNNER: Yes, sir, I have told them our official photographers are documenting the official White House records primarily for the Archives. An historical record. (cough, cough, cough)

WATCHDOG: OK. That's perfect. Ron, did you submit this protocol list to the PRC yet? The complete list with everybody's name in protocol order?

ROADRUNNER: Yes, we have given them six copies, repeat six copies, that we Xeroxed, and they were very pleased and surprised that we could come up with it that rapidly. We have doublechecked the spelling. So I think it was in real good shape. Since you've gotten our copy back have you got any comments?

WATCHDOG: Yeah, hang on a minute. Is Timmie there? Well, I know Timmie's there. On sixty to sixty-four you made changes and added the producers at the top of the list. Was that on purpose?

ROADRUNNER: I'm sorry. Sixty to sixty-four was Andres, Manning, Sheehan, and Small?

WATCHDOG: That's a change, isn't it?

ROADRUNNER: Yes, we did change that. Elbourne felt that the vice presidents of companies should be ranked above (cough, cough) the other press-type people.

WATCHDOG: Whelihan says absolutely not. They should be ranked like we originally had them. (click, clank, click).
WATCHDOG: Hello?
SNAPSHOT: Bruce, I don't understand that. However, I suppose we can go back and make a change. It's going to be very difficult. What's your reasoning?
WHELIHAN: It's not my reasoning. It's Ziegler's. I addressed this problem with him earlier, Tim, on these high-powered guys going over there. He said he wanted them ranked alphabetically with the rest of the producers, directors, etc., and in with the correspondents. You will note that we did not give any precedence to the wires.
SNAPSHOT: I didn't hear you at all. You're going to have to get right next to the speaker.
WATCHDOG: Hang on.
WHELIHAN: Can you hear me all right? (no answer) Tim, you copy?
SNAPSHOT: We didn't copy you at all. Not even a little. You have to get right next to the speaker. [*Snapshot didn't want to copy. He didn't want to hear this.*]
WHELIHAN: You copy now?
SNAPSHOT: Yes, now we copy.
WHELIHAN: You will note we didn't give any priorities at all to the wires or correspondents, or anybody else. All the producers, correspondents, reporters are to be ranked together and alphabetically. (pause) OK?
SNAPSHOT: Yes, I copy you on that. I don't understand it, but I copy.
WHELIHAN: OK. And it would be easier on these things if you would let us know about this change when it was anticipated.
WATCHDOG: Exactly.
SNAPSHOT: We had a deadline to get it out and you were sleeping at 4:00 this afternoon our time.
WATCHDOG: Let's make a point on this because it's important. We're available twenty-four hours a day. On these lists, if we're going to start changing protocol order, we've got to check back and forth, because we've gone to a lot of trouble as you all know just to get the damn thing put together right.
SNAPSHOT: We've tried the same thing.
WATCHDOG: OK. I wouldn't say anything until we've made sure we don't have any further changes.
ROADRUNNER: Roger, I understand. OK. Dwight, these are the only changes we have made and that was due to their being vice presidents of their respective organizations. (cough, cough)
WATCHDOG: OK. Hey, Ron, how was Vern when you left?

ROADRUNNER: Coffey is monitoring this call, Chapin. Be advised that he, Colonel Gibbons and Tom Benedict are sitting in Peking monitoring this call. Vern, would you answer that please?

COFFEY: Yeah, Dwight, I'm doing real fine. I'm still confined to my pajamas and my room. I am scheduled to get two more shots tomorrow, and hopefully after that they are going to tell me I can put my clothes on and return to normal. As far as I am concerned, I am in good shape and I'm ready to go.

WATCHDOG: OK, well, don't push it, and we're glad to hear you are better. Did you have any acupuncture?

COFFEY: Listen, I had the next thing to it and I am having a hell of a time sitting on what I am sitting on right now. Believe me. (laughter)

WATCHDOG: OK. Good, Vern. Ron, do you have anything more for us?

ROADRUNNER: No, sir, I think we're all pretty tired and I am sure you all are, too. I think we are going to try to get a good night's sleep.

WATCHDOG: Hang on a minute. Redman wants to ask Swift something.

REDMAN: Swift, Redman, did you have an opportunity to discuss this ham radio thing?

SWIFT: That's a negative. I have not and I do not intend to unless you particularly want me too. I personally think it inappropriate. We have a ham with us who brought his gear and I have made it very, very plain to them that we'd slit his throat if he even unpacked it.

REDMAN: That's a roger. I understand. But we've had requests we need to answer. I think we know the answer and it shouldn't be pursued, but there are other people who want to bring equipment in and I'd rather slit their throats before they go than to do it over there.

WATCHDOG: Slit it now, Al! Hang on a minute, Fred. (inaudible discussion in Washington) Fred, what we would like to do is just say that we had a request and we asked through you people and the answer we got back was no. So we get this thing solved right now.

ROADRUNNER: The answer that I have received regarding ham radios is a negative. (cough)

WATCHDOG: OK. Done. That settles it right there, and tell that guy over there not to take anything out.

ROADRUNNER: Let me just say one last thing about this precedence list. The only people that have copies are the PRC. I realize, and I know you do, that it is unprecedented to do something like this. I am making one copy available to the office in Peking, one copy to

Schrauth, and I am going to hand (cough, cough) deliver one copy to Duval.

This information, at this end, will not be disseminated to anyone else. I am resting assured that it's the same at that end. We are going to control this thing. If there are any changes that you want us to make, we can do it and we'll get it to the PRC. They know that we crashed very hard to get it to them and I think they were appreciative, and I think if we make any changes they will understand. If it's going to cause that much problem then we'll make the changes.

WATCHDOG: OK, the most important thing that you were saying there is that we do not want that list disseminated to anyone in our party under any conditions. It should not be posted anywhere. It should not be printed anywhere. The PRC can use it for seating or whatever, but they should not hand it out. Is that understood?

ROADRUNNER: Absolutely, and that is the agreement that each of us in this room have, and we have the tightest of controls on that document. I can guarantee you that.

WATCHDOG: (To the room: "We do too don't we?") Yeah, we do too here. We have not given it out and we will not give it out. OK. Just a minute. (To the room: "Anybody else here have anything?") OK, Ron. We don't have anything else here, unless you have something, why don't you get some rest?

ROADRUNNER: Yes, sir. Everybody here sends their best to everyone there. Do you desire to talk to us tomorrow morning?

WATCHDOG: Well, hang on a minute. It seems to me you ought to sleep in late and then go do your surveys, and we'll talk tomorrow night your time. Is that OK?

ROADRUNNER: Thank you very much. I think we'll all appreciate that. Let's shoot for 10:00, realizing that we have that banquet. We will initiate the call as soon as we (cough, cough) are able.

WATCHDOG: OK. That's perfect. Take care of yourselves and get some sleep.

ROADRUNNER: OK, Dwight. Thank you very much. Wait one for Major Swift.

SIGNAL: Roger.

SWIFT: Signal, Swift here. I just wanted to advise you this phone is located in an area where we will not be able to monitor or receive any incoming calls tonight. So, as far as we're concerned here in Shanghai, we are going to be unavailable, and we will check in with you in the morning when we are again able to monitor this phone. Do you understand?

SIGNAL: Roger, Major Swift. Understand.

SWIFT: I want you in Washington to know that you cannot call us here in Shanghai until we check in with you in approximately eight to ten hours.
SIGNAL: Roger, sir. No problem there because we have to go through Peking and they'll be kept to your availability and location.
SWIFT: Roger.

Ah, how wonderful—eight to ten whole hours with no phone calls! Roadrunner thought this might mean he could get a good night's sleep. In Peking, the Chinese had not stopped their habit of calling him several times during the night to get answers to their many questions. He felt it was just one more part of the testing process they were using on him, but he hoped it might be different in Shanghai. If not, it was certain that the Chinese who had made the trip with them were just as tired as the Americans. Besides that, his throat was killing him, his head ached, his chest felt like a huge boulder was sitting on it, his arms and legs were like lead, his ears were ringing, and he couldn't stop coughing. "Other than that," he assured himself, "I feel fine." He wished he had some Vicks Formula 44 to *gombay*. All he needed was some sleep.

The next day was a busy one. As they left the hotel, Roadrunner stopped to look out at the "the bund," the name for this part of the west bank of the Whangpoo River. The name Shanghai meant "on the sea" and the huge port city had been the business center of the country before the revolution. The western-style skyline was still very impressive. It was not only China's largest city, it was one of the largest cities in the world. Once, it had been clearly divided between the poor, crowded, native section and the wealthy, spacious, foreign part of town. This morning, Roadrunner got the impression that the people hurrying through the streets appeared better dressed and might have a higher standard of living than the people in Peking.

The Children's Palace proved to be very interesting. It was set up as a joint venture between the Chinese Communist Party and the People's Government for extracurricular activities: dance, chorus, traditional music, and handicrafts. Another section, ("Geared more to the boy students?" Roadrunner wondered) focused on radio assembly, and airplane and ship construction. Every afternoon, from 3:15 to 5:30, carefully selected area school children gathered for training classes and cultural activities. Roadrunner and the other Americans watched a recitation group sing and dance in praise of Chairman Mao, complete with militaristic hand motions, clenched fists, and set jaws. Roadrunner knew the child in the front row had seen him smile and wink, but he gave no outward indication of the gesture. The small boy continued to stomp his feet and sing with fierce determination. When the performance was over, Roadrunner again tried to make friends with the youngster, but never succeeded in piercing the invisible barrier between them. He could not help thinking about the comparison to American kids when they perform in school plays. The seriousness of such tiny children saddened him.

The President's schedule would also include a visit to the Shanghai Industrial Exhibition. During the actual visit, both the President and the Premier took off their coats. The President told Chou En-lai, "My heart is warm, just like yours." This obviously meant a great deal to the Chinese, because today, a photograph of Nixon and Chou in shirtsleeves is prominently displayed in the Exhibition Hall, and most guides relate the story to their visitors.

Now, ten days before the President arrived, the Americans surveyed the huge building that was typical of the Stalinist style emulated so often during the years of Chinese-Russian friendship. All the new products of Shanghai industry were on display: television sets, radios, textiles, dental equipment, watches, cameras, clocks and even Chinese cars. Roadrunner's favorite was the typewriter, with its stack of extra boxes to hold the most commonly used keys for this language of forty thousand characters. Mr. Chu told him that Shanghai was one of the largest industrial cities in Asia, with more than one hundred industrial complexes that included electrical equipment, ship building, iron and steel, textiles, printing and publishing, fertilizers, and chemicals. "Wouldn't it be wonderful if the President's visit here resulted in renewed trade between the two countries," Roadrunner thought to himself.

They made a stop at the "Number One Department Store" on Nanking Road, the largest store in China. It gave the small group of Americans a chance to see how the local people shopped and the goods and services that were available to them. Mr. Chu told them that the store had 10,000 shoppers daily and offered 27,000 products for sale.

"They sure like to spout statistics," Snapshot whispered to Roadrunner as they watched a group of shoppers recoil at the sight of the Americans.

"The strangest imaginable sort of people," Roadrunner whispered back, as he nodded toward the shoppers.

"*Ni hau,*" the Americans said as they smiled and moved through the crowd. They were creating a sensation and being studied from top to bottom. Roadrunner attempted to speak to several of the clerks and soon realized that, unlike the Friendship stores that were exclusively for foreign shoppers, none of the clerks here spoke English. "Perhaps it's because they didn't know we were coming," he reasoned.

He noticed that no attempt had been made to highlight the abundant domestic products available. The lighting was very poor and the escalators were not running, yet the shelves and counters were very well-stocked. Their Chinese counterparts were very gracious and helped Roadrunner purchase some Mao buttons, hats, and little red books containing the Chairman's words of wisdom. He was fascinated with the music department, always his favorite shop at home, and selected several long-playing records.

They surveyed the theatre where the cultural exhibition was going to be held. Chinese acrobats are famous the world over, and the Americans enjoyed watching them rehearse. Their precision was fantastic, and the supporting acts—bird callers, clowns, trained animals, and mimes—were equally talented.

As they returned to the hotel, Roadrunner could not help but marvel at being in the largest city in the world. Here he was, too damn tired to even go out and take a walk. Of course, he was not sure how the Chinese would view such an excursion if he tried, and he really did not want to tempt fate. He settled instead for a hot shower before the banquet.

CHAPTER XV

750 POUNDS LOOKING FOR A FORKLIFT

FEBRUARY 12, 1972

It was ten o'clock in the evening when Roadrunner walked into the room where preparations were being made for the conference call with Washington. He looked at his watch and calculated the time difference. It was nine A.M. at home. His three little girls would already be at school. Roadrunner had to smile as he listened to Grant Jurgensen, the White House Communications Agency operator, describing the banquet they had just attended.

SHANGHAI OPERATOR: . . . yes, we did *gombay*, but they let us get away with the wine rather than the mao-tai. [*During the trip, Dan Rather of CBS described the mao-tai drink as "liquid razor blades."*]
PEKING OPERATOR: Chickens!
SHANGHAI OPERATOR: Yeah, chicken, pheasant, fish . . .
PEKING OPERATOR: No, I mean you're the chicken for not gombaying the mao-tai.
SHANGHAI OPERATOR: No, uh, uh! I did it once, that was enough.
PEKING OPERATOR: Yeah, that was the way I felt, too.
SIGNAL: Hello, Jergie. How do you hear me? Go ahead.
SHANGHAI OPERATOR: Yeah, you're sounding great right now.

SIGNAL: Roger, Jerg, is Ron Walker available at your location now?
SHANGHAI OPERATOR: Roger, he's available at this location and says to go ahead and set up the conference call.
ROADRUNNER: Yes, this is Shanghai, go.
SIGNAL: Mr. Walker, Mr. Chapin asks to hold the conference call for about four minutes. Is that all right with you, sir?
ROADRUNNER: That's a roger. I got a big choice, don't I?
SIGNAL: Ha, ha. That seems to be the definite roge on that question.
ROADRUNNER: How about us saying that we'll be on a delay for three minutes after he comes on?
SIGNAL: Ha, ha. Uhhh, I think I'll just get out of the middle of that one, Mr. Walker, and let you handle it.
ROADRUNNER: That's a roger. I don't blame you. We'll be available at his convenience.
SIGNAL: Roger. (long wait)
SIGNAL: Go ahead, Mr. Chapin. Your conference is convened.
WATCHDOG: Roadrunner?
ROADRUNNER: Dwight, Dwight. This is Walker.
WATCHDOG: Yeah, Ron. Go ahead.
ROADRUNNER: Well . . . how are you this morning?
WATCHDOG: Well . . . I'm fine, how are you tonight?
ROADRUNNER: We're fine. Be advised our first wave into Shanghai is all in good shape. They have experienced their first day in China and a very, very nice banquet hosted by the Shanghai Municipal Revolutionary Committee. In the room with me are Jack D'Arcy on his first evening, Bob Manning, Bill Livingood, Mike Schrauth.
WATCHDOG: Where's Swift?
ROADRUNNER: Be advised that Elbourne and Swift are talking to the networks and should be joining us shortly.
WATCHDOG: OK, Ron. Good. We have General Scowcroft, General Redman, no one from the Secret Service, Henkel, Julie Rowe, Chuck Maguire, Whelihan, and myself . . . and Steve Bull. What do you have?
ROADRUNNER: Everyone arriving from Guam is tired, and most people have retired, and tomorrow will be a better day. Mike Schrauth has a couple of things to cover with you. [Roadrunner's throat hurt so badly he didn't want to talk unless it was absolutely necessary. He just wanted to crawl into bed and get some sleep.]
SCHRAUTH: Dwight, after we talked last we did the surveys of all the events. We started with the arrival into Shanghai on the twenty-first. We went through all the movements for the President and Mrs.

Nixon and we are now putting that into scenario form for you. Then we went through the guest house.

WATCHDOG: OK, Mike, that's sensational. When do you think you'll TWX that to us?

SCHRAUTH: Well, we have no steno capabilities here in Shanghai, so I have written some of the scenarios and will give those to Roadrunner to take to Peking. He can have them punched and sent on to you. The rest I will write in longhand and get them to Roadrunner on one of the aircraft going to Peking on the fourteenth.

WATCHDOG: OK. Good. That will be fine as far as we're concerned.

SCHRAUTH: Let me just point out one problem that has come up here in Shanghai today. I think our number of people on Sunday the twenty-seventh is far and above what we had initially calculated. I am meeting tomorrow with my counterpart and we will go through rooming assignments. If we have any problems I'll be getting back to Roadrunner and he can get to you.

WATCHDOG: Well, I would like to see a plane on the twenty-seventh that would hit Peking and pick up equipment and a bunch of people, go into Hangchou after we've left and pick up those people and fly right on out of the country. And not haul them over to Shanghai. Let's just start moving things out.

SCHRAUTH: Well, to be real honest, there has not been a hell of a lot of thought given to departures of the party here and I think what we've got to do is start thinking about that, and come up with a departure plan. Most of the thinking has been either to depart the day the President departs or have a sweep the day after.

WATCHDOG: Well, I think we better get everybody trying to figure out exactly how everybody moves out of there, because that's very vital, obviously. Will you get in touch with Vern and make sure we're working on a plan?

SCHRAUTH: Sure will.

WATCHDOG: Mike, how long is that Children's Palace thing going to take?

SCHRAUTH: I would estimate about an hour and fifteen minutes. It's only a five-minute motorcade from the guest house to the Children's Palace.

WATCHDOG: What's the President going to do that afternoon?

SCHRAUTH: We don't know, but . . . we just don't know.

WATCHDOG: If he's not in meetings do you think it's a possibility he would go to that bird's-eye view? [*The roof of an apartment building that has a spectacular panoramic view of Shanghai.*] You might want to bring that up. I think we'd want to have members of our party go there if possible. It's such a sensational thing to see.

Han Hsu and the bird's-eye view of Shanghai.

SCHRAUTH: I agree.

WATCHDOG: OK. Anything else?

SCHRAUTH: An enjoyable evening this evening. Roadrunner gave one of his better toasts again. He's an expert in that field. It's just adding to our prestige around the country, and it went very well.

WATCHDOG: That's sensational. Very good. Is he there? Roadrunner?

ROADRUNNER: Yes, sir.

WATCHDOG: You're not trying to run for office over there, are you?

ROADRUNNER: No, sir, I am not. I'd rather take a whipping than have to do these things, but we're getting through it OK.

WATCHDOG: OK, I'm sure you are.

ROADRUNNER: I'd like to make a few comments regarding Shanghai.

WATCHDOG: OK.

ROADRUNNER: It is my reaction that what we have thought about all along is going to transpire. However, I sensed one additional thing today. On the morning of the twenty-eighth it is highly conceivable that there will be a gathering of people, just prior to

Mr. Ma atop the Shanghai apartment building.

departing. I'm sure that goes with your thinking as far as a communique is concerned. Do you understand what I am saying?

WATCHDOG: Hang on a minute. (To the people in the room: "I don't think I did. Mao. . . Yeah, Mao.") Roadrunner? [*Roadrunner is suggesting that the Prime Minister and the Chairman might be there, in Shanghai, to bid farewell to President Nixon.*]

ROADRUNNER: Yes, sir.

WATCHDOG: Do you feel that any substantive release of details covering the visit are definitely being thought of for Shanghai?

ROADRUNNER: That's a definite YES. [*The Shanghai Communique was signed at the conclusion of the visit.*]

WATCHDOG: OK. That's . . . . Thank you very much.

ROADRUNNER: But be advised that's only a gut reaction from my conversations on the sidelines. [*"But you might want to alert Searchlight and Wisdom," Roadrunner thought.*]

WATCHDOG: OK. Well, that's very good to know, and I need to talk to Dr. Kissinger and I will do so.

ROADRUNNER: At least two different things have slipped that have indicated that to me. Also, the thing that is concerning me more than anything else after our surveys today is it was colder than the hinges, if you know what I mean.

WATCHDOG: OK. Do you mean you are worried about making sure our people dress warmly?

ROADRUNNER: Yes, sir, and I am also very concerned about Starlight. I just cannot tell you how cold it was today. They must dress warmly, they must have good foot covering. Also, be advised there is a totally different attitude in Shanghai, and I am expecting the same attitude in Hangchou, compared to Peking. I think you will pick up on what I mean. [*The Chinese were much more relaxed in Shanghai than they had been in Peking.*]

WATCHDOG: Roger, I do. OK. That's interesting.

ROADRUNNER: Roger, be advised . . . this is our schedule for tomorrow morning. We depart the guest house at 8:30, for Hangchou. We will do the survey of the airport at Hangchou. We will meet the airplane from Guam with Duval, John Thomas and party, and proceed to the guest house. We'll do a survey of the guest house and the walk through the park. I'm trying to cut out the boat ride and do the survey of the hotel itself. Then there is another banquet tomorrow night. (cough, cough) And we depart at 9:00 the next morning to arrive in Peking before lunch. [*Roadrunner was really feeling sick, and he was afraid the boat ride would completely do him in.*]

WATCHDOG: OK, good. I don't think that we need to talk with you tomorrow morning. We will want to talk to you tomorrow night your time.

ROADRUNNER: That's outstanding, because we'll be up early. Our baggage call is 7:15. We'll have the same facilities, I am sure, tomorrow night in Hangchou, and realizing it will be Sunday your time, I apologize for that. Maybe we can talk again at 10:00 A.M. your time. Is that convenient? (cough, cough)

WATCHDOG: Yes, Ron, that's OK, and Henkel and I will take that call at our individual residences. No problem. Do you have anything else, Ron?

ROADRUNNER: That's a negative. I sure as hell wish Coffey was on this line because he had a meeting with the PRC in Peking, and I'd just like to know what's going on. I'm sure you would, too.

COFFEY: Dwight, I am on the line, can you hear me?

WATCHDOG: Yeah, go ahead. What's happened, Vern?

COFFEY: We came in late. I heard the last part.

ROADRUNNER: If you could give us a brief of what transpired at your meeting?

WATCHDOG: Ron, go ahead, say what you were going to say. Roadrunner? What were you saying when Vern came on?

ROADRUNNER: I was saying I sure wish we had Vern Coffey on the line. Vern's on, so if Vern will tell us what has happened, we will both know.

WATCHDOG: OK. Go ahead, Vern.

COFFEY: Well, I had a meeting with the people from protocol again today, and they discussed the same points that they discussed late last night, and accordingly I have revised the proposed release to incorporate their changes. They are not anything major, it's really to tone down our release so it deals in generalities.

As an example, we indicated the President was going to arrive at 9:00 A.M. and spend approximately forty-five minutes on the ground, and then arrive in Peking at 11:30. They have asked that we reword it: That the President will depart Guam the morning of February twenty-first arriving in Shanghai at approximately 9:00 A.M. After a short rest in Shanghai, the President will fly to Peking, arriving later the same day. The President and Mrs. Nixon will be greeted by government leaders and officials of the People's Republic of China.

So the general change they made to that paragraph was taking out the forty-five minute rest in Shanghai and the arrival at 11:30. They were very insistent that for security reasons no specific times should be in the release. For that reason I went ahead and changed that paragraph.

The other paragraph involved the President being accompanied by Prime Minister Chou En-lai. That has been changed to reflect that the President and Mrs. Nixon will be accompanied by Chinese government leaders.

Another was that they did not want to indicate the name of the guest house in Hangchou. Accordingly I changed the paragraph to say that while in Hangchou the President and Mrs. Nixon will stay at the guest house on West Lake . . . and that's all that we've said.

They were very insistent that we take out the word morning on both the twenty-sixth and twenty-seventh, and just say on the twenty-seventh the President and Mrs. Nixon accompanied by Chinese government leaders will fly to Shanghai from Hangchou. Again, any reference to Prime Minister Chou En-lai has been deleted.

The final change was that in Shanghai they did not want to name the guest house, so that just says that while in Shanghai, the President and Mrs. Nixon will stay at the guest house along with members of the official party.

Those are all of the changes and do not really change the overall thrust of the proposed release. So if you have no objections, I'll send it back to Mr. Chu for their consideration again. Do you have any questions on that, Ron?

ROADRUNNER: I just have one comment. I will have almost twenty-four hours before Ziegler needs this for his briefing, and that will give me time in Peking to discuss this once again before Ziegler goes on stage. Do you copy?

WATCHDOG: You have time to do that, Ron?

ROADRUNNER: Yes, sir. Because I feel strongly about a couple of these points. I think we might be able to pull out a couple of rabbits to assist Whaleboat (cough, cough) in making a proper presentation.

WATCHDOG: Have you got that, Vern?

COFFEY: I will give it back to them with the changes so they can see we have incorporated them and I'll tell them to hold it until you return, Ron, and you can have whatever final discussion you want with them before it is turned back to us for release.

WATCHDOG: So, we're in good shape. Thank you very much. Anything else there, Vern?

COFFEY: We had one other member of the party admitted to the hospital last night. He is a television camera man, his name is Groom, and his diagnosis is pneumonia. [*Peter Groom was a video tape recorder with NBC*] It appears he is going to be in the hospital for some time. I have discussed this with Kitchell. [*James Kitchell was NBC Vice Chairman*]

If Groom does not get out of the hospital in time, Kitchell will take someone from the Olympics in Sapporo and have him come in with the press bird on the twentieth of February which would be plenty of time. Other than that we've had no other significant happenings here while Ron's been away. [*The 1972 Winter Olympics were held in Sapporo, Japan.*]

WATCHDOG: OK. Hang on a minute. Roadrunner?

ROADRUNNER: Yes, sir?

WATCHDOG: Tomorrow night, your time, will you have Elbourne call Whelihan? [*They were beginning to call Whelihan "Roadblock." Not only was he a big man physically, he seemed to be the one who was shielding the press secretary.*]

ROADRUNNER: That's a roger. I will do so. Be advised, Manning is in the room and Timmie is still out with Swift in that meeting with the networks. I plan on joining that as soon as this conference call is over. I am sure it's relatively interesting.

WATCHDOG: Oooooooooookay. We don't have anything here, do you have anything else?

ROADRUNNER: That's a negative.

COFFEY: Dwight, I need to talk to Bill Henkel if he is there. If I could talk to him after this conference call I would appreciate it.

WATCHDOG: OK. How are you feeling, Vern?

COFFEY: I'm feeling great. I'm ready to get back into action and I plan on putting my clothes on tomorrow. They haven't told me I could do it but I plan on doing it. I supposedly received my last shot today, and I'm now taking medicine orally. They tell me that I can go ahead and start operating. I do not plan to do a lot of outside work, but I think I will be able to do more than what I have been doing.

WATCHDOG: Great. Roadrunner?

ROADRUNNER: Yes, sir?

WATCHDOG: OK, Roadrunner. Tell Timmie that Rawlins is carrying the press applications in. [*LTC Robert W. Rawlins, Air Force One advance*]

ROADRUNNER: Roger, I understand. (cough, cough) Are they complete?

WATCHDOG: Yes. Tim has a cable on that so he knows what the situation is.

ROADRUNNER: OK. That's all we've got. Nice talking to you. Have a nice day and we'll talk to you tomorrow evening from Hangchou.

WATCHDOG: OK. Have a good night's rest and good luck with that meeting with the networks and thanks for calling. We'll talk to you tomorrow. Vern, thank you and we're out . . . oh wait, Vern, you want to talk to Bill?

COFFEY: Yeah. I do need to talk some schedule things with him.

WATCHDOG: Here he is. I'll put him on.

COFFEY: OK. Bill, are you there?

HENKEL: Yeah, Vern.

COFFEY: Yeah, I just wanted to check a couple of things with you. One is, on the message we got from you today, do I understand that the medallions have been scrapped completely, that they are not going to be a part of the program? [*Medallions cased in lucite, commemorating the visit, were originally to have been a gift at the joint banquet.*]

HENKEL: (To the room: "Is that true? Medallions out?") Yeah, the medallions are out. Period. How deep have we gone on that? Are they expecting them?

COFFEY: No. No. I just wanted to be sure I interpreted the message correctly.

HENKEL: That's absolutely correct, Vern. We are unable to bring them in. We apologize but we'll have to explain to you later what developed on that situation. [*The medallions did not get ordered.*]

ROADRUNNER: OK, Henkel. That's one mark against you there. We'll (cough, cough, cough) have to cover it for you.

HENKEL: OK, I'll take the blame for it, but I'll let it start flowing here. (laughter)

COFFEY: OK, Bill. On the schedule we need to show 970 departing after 26000 from Guam and Shanghai. Somehow it appears in the schedule that 970 is in front of 26000. It's our reserve aircraft, and if 26000 should have any problems, the President is going to be stranded if that plane has left thirty minutes ahead. Do you follow what I mean?

HENKEL: Yes, I follow what you mean, but this is a monstrous problem because there are very, very critical people on board 970 that have to be ahead of S'76. General Scowcroft is right here . . .

COFFEY: They're all secretaries and people like that, Bill, it looks to me, and do you try to pre-position people with your back-up aircraft and then your whole show is gone in China because you've got to recall a plane which is thirty minutes in front of you? That means, turn it around, bring it back, unload it, get people on board and try to make up time. If you have people who need to come to Peking in front of 26000 maybe our solution is to ask the Chinese to provide a plane. I don't believe that we can accept the loss of a reserve aircraft and take a chance on stranding the President. We've done this all around the world for three years now, keeping a reserve plane on the ground until we get the President airborne. And now, one of the most important things we've got, we're going to blow it by trying to position some people in front of the President.

ROADRUNNER: Let me comment on that. Bill, are you listening?

HENKEL: Yes, Ron. We've got the problem with the documentary crew. [*The main objective was to have our documentary crew film the President's arrival in the People's Republic of China.*]

ROADRUNNER: In the latter part of December . . . and from that point on the schedule has shown exactly what we are talking about now. This is one hell of a time to bring this up when I know I have talked about it with you. I talked about it when General Scowcroft was present. General Scowcroft has read those schedules, the Secret Service has been present and it's a little hard to understand why thirteen or fourteen days before the President arrives, we've got a problem. I have been informed that we can and we have taken our back-up planes up before and if there is a problem the aircraft can return. Yeah, I know it's taking a gamble, and I don't know whether it's worth that gamble, but I think it's worth considering whether we should start changing all our procedures at this point. We've made arrangements. The PRC is expecting those arrangements, and it's a little tough to go back now. Over.

COFFEY: OK, Ron. Let me say this. Several points, number one, yes, the business of having the reserve plane taking off in front was discussed by me with you and that was all it was. It was a discussion. In your schedules, you never did show an actual departure time for 970. I have a copy of one here right now which just merely says 970 departs, without a time. More importantly though, the guy who has to make this fly is Albertazzie, and we've never been able to give him a schedule because you've held everything fairly tight and close. [*Colonel Ralph Albertazzie was the pilot of Air Force One, which was renamed the Spirit of '76 by President Nixon.*]

But, nevertheless, thirteen or fourteen days notwithstanding, I maintain that you're taking a hell of a risk and a hell of a gamble. Now, if you want to play that kind of game we most certainly can take a look at it and see what we can come up with. [*Roadrunner and Watchdog did not view this as playing a "game." This was a historic arrival and they felt it needed to be appropriately documented by American photographers.*]

But, nevertheless, I want to go on record right now as saying that I do not recommend that 970 precede 26000 by any appreciable distance, either from Guam or from Shanghai. Now, Albertazzie has not been consulted on this and I think we ought to bring him as well as General Scowcroft and the people who actually have to make this thing work and see what their opinion is. But, I feel very certain that Albertazzie will also take the approach that you are taking away his only capability of getting the President there on time by trying to use the aircraft for the purpose of positioning people. Don't forget, the primary purpose of that aircraft is a reserve or a back-up. It is not to move people around as a taxi service.

WATCHDOG: Vern, Vern, Dwight.

ROADRUNNER: I understand that and always have. I realize how things have progressed in your absence. That's unfortunate. (cough, cough) I think it is extremely worthwhile for you to bring this to General Scowcroft's attention . . . again. He should be aware of it and possibly should have raised this question sooner than having you come out of the hospital and raise it. We want to do what is right. We want to do what is best for us and for the PRC. However, we should do it rapidly and make the decision and make it quickly. Unfortunately, it wasn't figured out in your absence and for that I apologize, but now let's get on with it.

WATCHDOG: Hey, Vern. Vern and Ron, this is Dwight.

COFFEY: OK, Dwight.

WATCHDOG: Well, let me just say, we're going to have to sit here and work on it. In October we talked about this. It's not a new or recent decision at all. We have always talked about 970 going into Shanghai and Peking ahead. You just used the words "they should not be a distance too appreciably ahead of the Spirit of '76" and I agree.

The idea was for them to take off in Shanghai and circle and be where they could land if need be, and if they don't need to land then they split and go right on into Peking. We have got people staged on there for very important reasons and I will hold that we not change it unless it's just absolutely mandatory. In other words, I think they need to go on ahead and if it takes twenty-five to thirty minutes to land the plane and put Searchlight on in an emergency, then we will be late getting into Peking.

COFFEY: OK, Dwight, rather than take up everyone's time with this, let me talk with General Scowcroft and Colonel Albertazzie and we'll come back to you with a plan. I think we've all said enough on it tonight.

WATCHDOG: OK. Uhhhhh, Roadrunner, let me ask you something. Are you still there?

ROADRUNNER: Yes, sir, I'm right here.

WATCHDOG: Do you agree with me on that?

ROADRUNNER: I absolutely agree. I know we've talked about it on any number of occasions, and we're at this point now, and I think we ought to stick with it unless there is some monumental reason we can't do it. I agree with you. If something happens, then we blew it.

WATCHDOG: Ron, is it possible to cut our time in half, in other words instead of thirty minutes ahead make it fifteen minutes?

ROADRUNNER: Yes, sir. Absolutely. Absolutely.

WATCHDOG: OK. I think Albertazzie ought to know that we can do that.

COFFEY: OK, well, as I said before we can make it work. Just bear in mind, you all may have been discussing this but it has been in a vacuum among yourselves. We can make it work as long as everyone understands the risks. I am simply speaking to you as a professional and that's my job. Now, if you want to go against it, then we'll come up with a plan and make it work. And I'm happy. At least I've advised you of the problem. So, let me talk with Albertazzie and General Scowcroft, we'll work up something, and I'll get back to you on it. [*It appears Coffey wanted the record to show that the military had expressed their concerns and that the political types would make the final decision.*]

ROADRUNNER: Roger. On another subject, be advised we have put everybody from State, except the interpreters, in one villa. We have a small room that can be used as a State Department office. Room 107 will be the Advance Office (cough) in that villa and when Collins and Araiza move to their rooms to overnight, they will take all the classified material and documents with them.

WATCHDOG: Roadrunner, this is Watchdog. Let me go to that a minute, if I can. Let's don't have two or three offices working in each one of these places.

ROADRUNNER: Well, that's fine. On every other trip the State Department always wanted to control their own material. If they want to combine it, that's fine with me.

WATCHDOG: We're not giving them that choice. They will control their own material. It's their office too, and Platt's their man. [*Nicholas Platt, Department of State*] I think we just set up one office in that villa, make that the secure room, and then at night it can be moved into Platt's room. Just do it that way.

ROADRUNNER: That's fine. Be advised that we have one problem with room 107. That room is on a corner of the villa, and the heat is not working properly. We've been informed that it's too cold for anybody to sleep in. It is cold because it is on that north end of the villa. So we plan on using that as the Advance Office for notification procedures. The office, Room 107, will be a contact point for the PRC to call and have them notify everyone. I am sure you know what I am talking about.

WATCHDOG: I know what you're talking about, but I sure don't agree. I think we're setting up too damn many offices. You set up one office in each villa, and the office should be that room across from Platt's room. I don't care if a room is cold. They can get more blankets and somebody can sleep in there. That's no problem.

ROADRUNNER: Well, it is a problem, Dwight. It's a problem for the PRC. They don't want any of our people housed in that room.

WATCHDOG: OK, well then, just don't turn it into an office.

ROADRUNNER: I repeat, we cannot afford to have Collins and Araiza covering the State Department. They've got their secretary and I need to have my own operation covered.

WATCHDOG: That's fine. You've got your own operation over in the President's villa. [*Roadrunner's room!*]

ROADRUNNER: I do, but I don't plan on having the entire operation working out of my room, to include Abel and Collins and Schrauth.

WATCHDOG: OK. Well, I'm not going to argue about it. The main thing is Collins and Araiza do not have to form the notification procedures in the Secretary of State's villa. That can be very well handled by John Thomas. (pause)

ROADRUNNER: OK. I won't argue that.

WATCHDOG: I mean, I am just worried about us setting up so damn many offices that we've got more people running offices than doing the work.

ROADRUNNER: Roger. I understand what you're saying. Be advised that we are attempting to do this thing right and we'll give it some more thought and see what we can come up with.

WATCHDOG: OK, obviously, you know more about it than I do and you know how best it's going to work when we get there. I'm not trying to second guess you, but I do want to be careful not to set up too many offices. There is no reason why all of the people in the Secretary of State's villa cannot be notified through the Secretary of State's office across from Platt's room. Now, if you need to have Araiza and Collins in another room typing, that's fine, but we ought to keep that off bounds for the general public.

ROADRUNNER: John Thomas is going to bring in his whole dog and pony show, and there is going to be very little room for anybody else, and it's going to be a State Department operation. I understand that. I've experienced it in the past. I want to make damn sure that everybody is plugged in to what is going to transpire, and we've got everything covered. I'd like to wait and talk to John and figure out the best way to handle that villa. We do have a housing problem, we don't have any place else to put Schrauth, Abel, and Collins, along with Scowcroft and the other people.

HENKEL: OK. Ron, this is Bill again. We are going to put document and briefcase security in 201-A . . . per Watchdog.

ROADRUNNER: That's fine. Go ahead and do it. Beautiful. If that's all Platt's got to do that's fine. He can move those bags himself. That's what we planned for Collins and Araiza to do, but if the State Department can handle it, let Thomas and Platt handle it.

HENKEL: That's exactly right, Ron. Then Collins and Araiza are available for other functions and duties.

ROADRUNNER: Fine. Thank you.

HENKEL: OK, Ron. If you don't have anything more, have a good night's sleep and we look forward to talking with you tomorrow after the banquet.

ROADRUNNER: OK. Thank you very much. We'll look forward to talking to you tomorrow night also.

SNAPSHOT: Is Whelihan there?

ROADRUNNER: Be advised that Swift and Elbourne have just joined our entourage, and if Bruce is still there Timmie would like to talk to him.

WATCHDOG: Roadrunner?

ROADRUNNER: Yes, sir.

WATCHDOG: Ask Timmie to give us just a little report. Did it go OK?

ROADRUNNER: Wait one.

WATCHDOG: (To the people in the room: "We have got to get moving if we're doing that schedule tonight.")

WASHINGTON VOICE: (. . . it's been going for an hour and a half.) [*Reference to the length of this phone call.*]

SNAPSHOT: OK. Yes. We had a very, very good meeting. We covered many, many points. Among them were the three executive producers that arrived today, and were being typical executive producers. We wanted to make sure that the pool and the pool technicians maintain the decorum that they've maintained throughout the trip. We got into quite a discussion on that and Siegenthaler said he would work with the pool producers to orient them to Chinese customs and habits.

WATCHDOG: OK, Tim, I understand. To be honest, all I'm really interested in is whether you got your dollar problem taken care of.

SNAPSHOT: That's a roger. We got an agreement in principal with the pool on the dollar problem. They understand completely. They feel they will use the time, but with some exceptions. The exceptions are the Shanghai Station, because we are not sure it will work, based on the evaluation from the Chinese at this point in time. There are some other considerations involved with it, but I would rather telex that to you.

WATCHDOG: OK, Tim. Thank you. Bruce wants to talk to you, and I am going to have you transferred over to him. OK?

SNAPSHOT: OK, all in all it was a very, very good, successful meeting and we had an excellent meeting of the minds.

WATCHDOG: Very good, Tim. Great. Roadrunner?

ROADRUNNER: Yes, sir?

WATCHDOG: We're going to sign off here. Have a good trip to Hangchou. We're going to keep grinding on this schedule and thank you so much for everything.

ROADRUNNER: All right, sir. Thank you also, and everybody there. We'll talk to you tomorrow night.

WATCHDOG: Wait now. Signal is going to transfer this call to Whelihan, so Signal, please perform your duty.

SIGNAL: Thank you, sir, we will do it now.

GIBBONS: (from Peking) Hey, Swift.

SIGNAL: One moment, China.

SWIFT: Yeah, Hank, what do you want?

GIBBONS: Have you got communications set up for Hangchou tomorrow?

SWIFT: Hell, yes. You're darn right. It's all set and ready to go.

ROADRUNNER: Hank, everybody was asking for you. (laughter in Shanghai)

GIBBONS: Yes, what were they asking?

ROADRUNNER: Well, your health, and if you had a pleasant rest, and if you enjoyed your dinner this evening?

SNAPSHOT: And had a good tangerine? [*The Chinese were always offering tangerines at meetings, perceived as both a stalling tactic and a genuine gesture of hospitality. They would then ask if the tangerines were good.*]

ROADRUNNER: ("Snapshot!") Disregard that last comment. Hank, everybody here is fine, how is everybody there?

GIBBONS: Real fine.

ROADRUNNER: Is Vern still with you?

COFFEY: Yep. The pajama kid is still here.

ROADRUNNER: OK, sir. Just a minute, Timmie wants to talk to you.

SIGNAL: This is Signal, sir, we have Mr. Whelihan coming to the phone now, sir, for Mr. Elbourne.

SNAPSHOT: This is Tim. I need to talk to Vern.

COFFEY: OK. They just cut in to tell us that Whelihan was coming, so, do you want to talk now or wait till you get through talking to Bruce?

SNAPSHOT: I want to talk to you now. [*"Let Whelihan wait,"* *Snapshot thought impatiently.*]

COFFEY: OK. The chemicals. I told them to put them on the same plane with John Thomas' equipment so that we would have only one plane with the equipment that needs to be transloaded and brought to Peking. And my question to you was, do you want to change that?

SNAPSHOT: That's exactly a roger. We must change it, and I'll tell you why we must change it. I have found that there is a 750-pound package from AP on that airplane that takes a forklift to lift and there is no way that you are going to get that package on an Ileutian 18 aircraft. It must come in on the C-141 coming into Peking.

COFFEY: OK, Timmie, the way I set it up was that all of the chemicals and John Thomas' equipment would go to Shanghai. It would be off-loaded and stored for twenty-four hours and then put on the C-141 and come to Peking. I made no arrangements for it to be put on the IL-18.

Mr. Chu with a bowl full of tangerines.

ROADRUNNER: Excuse me, Vern, we've made those arrangements this evening based on what Larzelere communicated earlier. [*Commander Larzelere was the first and, to date, only U.S. Coast Guard aide to the President*]

COFFEY: Well, Ron, what I don't understand is why you guys are talking to somebody else, rather than talking to me. I'm the one who's making the arrangements and Larzelere has been told, by me, eight times that the equipment would go on the plane with Thomas.

Secondly, Larzelere does not know how much room is on Rawlins' plane because the plane is in Hawaii. I'm the only one who knows that. I don't understand why you are taking someone else's word on something without giving me the benefit of getting involved. I'm at a loss now to tell you what the hell to do. The only thing I can do now is try to call Larzelere, but I don't know how he could be making plans when he doesn't know anything about the plane. It's in Hawaii.

ROADRUNNER: OK, this is the next point in that problem. The PRC does not want the aircraft for Hangchou to spend any more that fifteen minutes on the ground in Shanghai. They want fifteen minutes to process the passports and then move directly into Hangchou. This proposes monumental problems for us if we have a large unloading process.

COFFEY: No, it doesn't. Because another solution is to just leave John Thomas' equipment and the chemicals on the plane and let it go to Hangchou. If they have a forklift that can handle a 750-pound load, we are still in business because we will have Rawlins pick it up in Hangchou rather than in Shanghai. So now, can you find out whether they have a forklift in Hangchou? That would solve the problem.

ROADRUNNER: Roger. I will attempt to do so, and be advised that is a very, very good solution.

COFFEY: Well, that's affirmative. I will rely on you to tie down the forklift. What I will do is call your Commander Larzelere who is doing all this and tell him all he has to do is get it on the plane, and we'll decide where it comes off. Then we'll tell WHCA, not to let it come off until it gets to Hangchou.

ROADRUNNER: Roger, I understand. I have to make one comment. He is your Commander Larzelere and not ours. I was getting pressure from the PRC for the breakdown. I gave them what I (cough, cough, cough) thought would include the chemicals. The only thing I kept off the manifest was that 750-pound dude that had to come off by forklift . . .

SNAPSHOT: (Ha, ha, ha)

ROADRUNNER: . . . and if that thing is coming in on that aircraft it's going to be a big surprise to an awful lot of people.

COFFEY: OK, well let me go back and review the bidding now. (ha, ha) Do you or don't you, you and Timmie, want me to change the loading arrangements I've made? The chemicals and John Thomas' equipment are on a plane. Instead of having it come off at Shanghai now, have it continue on to Hangchou and have Rawlins' plane pick it up there. Do you want to make a change on that or is that a go?

ROADRUNNER: No, that's OK. Be advised when everybody starts talking about forklifts, the Chinese don't have those like you and I have them in various locations. So that's the problem and that's what we're confronted with. I can see Timmie and me out there trying to push that dude off on our backs.

COFFEY: OK, I understand. The point is well taken. How about letting me ask you to do this, then? Because maybe we have made a decision here and still don't have the loop closed. Could you find out whether there is in fact a forklift in Hangchou that can handle a 750-pound load because we still have time to make a decision as to where the equipment is off-loaded.

ROADRUNNER: OK, Vern, we'll find out if they have a forklift in Hangchou.
COFFEY: Now let me give you another option. I think the plane has to come back to Shanghai to drop off the radio operator and navigator. If that's the case, it could go back to Shanghai the second time and be unloaded then when there is no urgency for the plane to clear. Do you roger on that?
SNAPSHOT: That's a good idea. I understand that.
COFFEY: However, I'd sure appreciate it if you would let me know where it is going to be done so I can keep Rawlins informed as well as Larzelere. (pause)
SNAPSHOT: Is this the end? (laughter in Shanghai and Washington)
WHELIHAN: Timmie?
SNAPSHOT: Yeah, just a second now. Bruce, just a second, let me continue with Vern. Vern, there's one more solution.
WHELIHAN: Ha, ha, ha, ha,
SNAPSHOT: Cogitate on this for a minute. We could take a pair of steps off and put that 750-pound load in its place. The 750-pound box would end up in Peking and the pair of steps would end up in Hangchou and we could just roll it on.
COFFEY: OK, Timmie, let me give you another idea. Why don't you get seventy-five bottles and pour chemicals in them and that would give you seventy-five bottles that weigh ten pounds each and they can be carried off one by one by you and Walker. (laughter) OK, that's all I've got, Timmie. Why don't you and Bruce go ahead (ha, ha) and carry on your traffic.
SNAPSHOT: Vern, thank you very much. You understand the problem now.
WHELIHAN: You need a chopstick lift truck, right?
SNAPSHOT: Roger. Go ahead, Bruce.
WHELIHAN: Gotta question or two. Number one, hours of daylight?
SNAPSHOT: Seven . . . teen.
WHELIHAN: Starting when?
SNAPSHOT: It starts at 7 A.M. . . . wait a second, we've got a disagreement here. Negative. Negative, Bruce. It's eleven hours of daylight starting at 7 A.M. to 6 P.M. [*This varied greatly, however, since all of China was on "Peking time."*]
WHELIHAN: Do you think we can get some more on that 141?
SNAPSHOT: No more hours of daylight. (laughter)
WHELIHAN: That's too bad. Number two. In the press rooms. The common carrier representatives. What is their function to be?
SNAPSHOT: Their function is: RCA will handle the billing charges for the telegraph. ITT will handle the billing charges for the

television. AT&T will handle the billing charges for the telephone. And that is all.

WHELIHAN: So really their just serving an accounting function. They'll just be there tallying up the slips as the calls go in.

SNAPSHOT: That's exactly correct. And no other function, and if they try to perform any other function, I'll hit them on the side of the head with a board.

WHELIHAN: OK, Timmie, we've pretty much locked up the press schedule into Peking, and I'm going to send you a copy. Take a quick look and come back with comments and we'll go to print with the damn thing.

SNAPSHOT: OK. That's a roger. Walker, the Roadrunner suggests that . . . excuse me, I just blew a code, I understand. [*As if they hadn't blown codes before!*] He's a little upset right now because we've got an awful lot of typing to do on precedence lists.

WHELIHAN: Tim, you wouldn't have had all that typing to do if you'd taken it the way we had it the first time.

SNAPSHOT: Yeah, but it was wrong the first time.

WHELIHAN: It's a moot point now, with Ziegler's decision having been made. Let's get it in the way he wants it.

SNAPSHOT: Well, that's exactly the way were gonna do it, but I think it's absolutely wrong and I'll maintain that.

WHELIHAN: OK. Tim, be advised, we forgot to indicate that Sarahito, or whatever his name is, has a Japanese issue passport.

SNAPSHOT: That's a roger. I wondered about that at the time, but because it matched our passport numbers, I thought that he had achieved . . . greatness (ha, ha, ha) in the meantime.

WHELIHAN: That's a negative. That's his phone number in Tokyo. OK. I'll talk to you all tomorrow morning, our time, after Walker's conference call with whatchamacallit, Dwight.

ROADRUNNER: He sends regards to you too, Bruce.

SNAPSHOT: (Ha, ha, ha, ha.) Uh, Bruce, thank you very much. We'll look forward to talking to you at some point in time. OK. We're out.

WHELIHAN: See ya later. Goodbye.

Bruce Whelihan hung up the phone and smiled at the crisp, wintry day outside the White House windows. They had a few major problems to solve in Shanghai, but the men were certainly sounding more relaxed. It was good to hear Snapshot laugh again. He chuckled to himself at the thought of a 750-pound load looking for a fork lift. "Did they even have lift trucks in the People's Republic of China?" He thought the chances were remote. "After all, these were the folks who built the Great Wall without them." He figured they would have lots of help unloading the airplanes, and most of it would be of the two-legged variety.

In Shanghai the mood was indeed more relaxed. The Chinese counterparts seemed to have left their aloofness and some of their formality back in Peking. They almost seemed like different people. They were more open and less cautious, and they seemed more anxious to help. They even seemed . . . happy. Roadrunner had not quite figured out the reason for the dramatic change, but he certainly was not complaining.

"Hey Snapshot," he said, "my throat hurts like hell. I wonder if some scotch would help? Let's see what kind of an ice order we get in Shanghai. Hopefully, this cosmopolitan city with its reputation as a former international financial center will have some leftover remnants of catering to the ghosts of visitors past."

"I'm ready," Snapshot assured him.

CHAPTER XVI

ANCIENT CHINESE HERBAL MEDICINE

FEBRUARY 13, 1972

"There is a famous saying in China," Mr. Chu told Roadrunner, "Above is heaven, below there is Hangchou. In English it is pronounced 'hong JOE,' just like our Premier's name."

Mr. Chu was stalling, and Roadrunner could not help but feel sorry for the circumstances that were causing the delay in Hangchou. The group of Americans coming in to join Roadrunner had been delayed in Shanghai, and he finally insisted on doing the survey without them.

The city was famous for the scenic beauty of West Lake, but Roadrunner had been dreading the boat ride. He had tried to cancel it but could not get the Chinese to agree. He just knew that a boat ride in February was not the smartest thing for him to do right now. His cough was deep, and he was worried that more exposure to the cold would do him in.

Mr. Chu told him, "West Lake owed its beauty to the wisdom and talent of many centuries of working people. However, in old China, the beautiful lake was uncared for and carved up by the reactionary ruling classes and it became full of silt. After Liberation, the party and the People's Government, demonstrating that beautiful places should serve production and the working people, renovated the

251

entire area. Between 1954 and 1958, the lake was thoroughly dredged, something that had not been done for three hundred years. The picturesque West Lake is now a favorite resort for both the working people at home and for foreign visitors."

Somehow Roadrunner made it through the day, and the second wave of the American advance party finally arrived in Hangchou. Roadrunner was glad to see Michael Raoul-Duval, one of the five full-time staff members in the White House Advance Office. Mike was a fun loving bachelor whose warmth and friendliness made everyone like him instantly. It was great to see all of the other men, too, and everyone felt a little frustrated at the few short minutes they could spend together before the banquet began.

After the banquet they had a countdown meeting to brief the new arrivals. Roadrunner knew he desperately needed to get some sleep and adjourned the meeting as soon as he could. The group lingered for a few minutes, but by then everyone was almost too tired to enjoy the reunion. It was actually hard to tell which group was more exhausted, those who had been traveling for so many hours or those who had been in China for almost two weeks.

Mr. Chu, Snapshot, Schrauth and another man were huddled in the hall. Roadrunner tried to go around them as he headed to his room to crawl into bed.

"Wait one," Schrauth said to him. "This is Dr. Yey from the Hangchou Hotel clinic. I told him you have been coughing and not feeling very well."

"I am most honored to meet you, Mr. Walker," Dr. Yey said as they shook hands. "I am medical doctor, trained at famous teaching hospital in Shanghai. I am not a barefoot doctor."

When the whole group of Americans looked down at his feet, Dr. Yey laughed and said, "No, the name has nothing to do with shoes. It is Chinese name for what you call paramedics. They treat simple illnesses and help in emergencies. I am fully trained doctor and have something here that might make you feel better."

Roadrunner was touched at this kind offer of assistance, until he caught the look on Snapshot's face, the look that people get when they smell something really foul and sickening.

"What kind of something to make me feel better?" Roadrunner wanted to know.

"It is ancient Chinese herbal medicine. It will help you to feel very much better. For generations, Chinese people have found this to be often times soothing for wracking-of-whole-body coughing."

"Hmmm," Roadrunner said, before he started to cough again. "Let me see what it is."

American flag flying over the guest house in Hangchou.

Dr. Yey had a small envelope in his hand, with Chinese characters written on it. He opened it and took out a pinch of the potion. He told Roadrunner that it was to be mixed with hot water.

Roadrunner agreed, and the entourage followed him down the hall to his room. They went over to the desk and watched as the Chinese doctor measured some of the contents of the envelope into a tea cup and poured scalding hot water over it. The stuff in the cup began to grow. Some of it looked like sponges and hollow places appeared as it expanded. The dark brown things puffed up and began to grow hair. The greenish-orange particles wiggled and looked like swimming amoebas. Snapshot turned ash white, gagged, ran into Roadrunner's bathroom and threw up with resounding gusto.

Roadrunner, holding firm to his training in the rural villages of India, closed his eyes and swallowed the contents of the tea cup. He knew by the look on Mr. Chu's face that he had passed another Chinese test of character. He would feel a greater reward, though, if it would just make him feel better.

CHAPTER XVII

No Room For Valentines

February 14, 1972

Roadrunner had slept like a log after his dose of chinese herbal medicine, but he still was not in top form. One good night's sleep simply did not compensate for all the others lost to interruptions. He did think he was physically a little better, however, and his spirits were certainly improved. Many lingering questions had been answered during his time in Shanghai and Hangchou. The attitude there was definitely more relaxed, but now that they were back in Peking it was time to turn those friendly discussions and conversational agreements into lines of type on the President's schedule.

At 9:30 in the evening they were talking to Washington, where it was 8:30 in the morning . . . on Valentine's Day.

WATCHDOG: How was Hangchou?
ROADRUNNER: The weather wasn't very nice. The damn airplanes broke down. We stood there, three and a half hours at the airport. It was not a very good stop. I think our hosts, however, responded remarkably well. They used their aircraft to bring the personnel and their baggage up from Shanghai, and as a result we were able to, at least, visit with them for a few hours last night. However, we had to

do our survey without them and that was, as you can well imagine, a problem.

WATCHDOG: OK. What's the health report there in Peking?

ROADRUNNER: We're in good shape, but Vern's gone back to the hospital.

WATCHDOG: Vern has?

ROADRUNNER: Yes, he has a temperature of 101. We didn't know until we got back. We set up meetings for Vern on aircraft coming in and out, the flow chart of personnel, and everything else. Then I find out that Vern had a temperature, and it was rather shocking because he appeared in pretty good health when we got back this afternoon.

WATCHDOG: OK. Is Duval off and tracking down Hangchou?

ROADRUNNER: Yes, sir. They got to the hotel last night about 7:00. We had a banquet at 7:30. Then we had a meeting with the personnel that would remain in Hangchou. Be advised they we're approaching their twenty-third hour of being awake and we're pretty damn tired. So we tried to cover it as rapidly as possible. This morning we met about the survey we had done yesterday in their absence. Unfortunately, their not being able to be with us was a problem.

WATCHDOG: OK. Where do we stand schedule-wise in regards to Shanghai and Hangchou?

ROADRUNNER: I am prepared to write scenarios. However, I would like to hold off for another twelve hours to give them an opportunity to come in with their input.

WATCHDOG: OK, Ron. We have pretty well polished up the Peking schedule here. But what we need tomorrow morning will be Hangchou and Shanghai as best you have it. I think we've got time to wait for Mike . . . both Mikes . . . to send their stuff. Can't they TWX that to you and then just pass it on over the satellite?

ROADRUNNER: Yes, sir, we sure can, but right now we don't have any communications with those two cities.

OPERATOR: Excuse me, gentlemen. I am going to place Shanghai in the conference with Mike Schrauth, Major Bruff and Dick Keiser. [*Major Reginald W. Bruff of WHCA and Richard E. Keiser of the Secret Service*]

WATCHDOG: You can eat those words now, Roadrunner!

OPERATOR: Shanghai in conference.

ROADRUNNER: Roger, I just ate 'em. Schrauth, this is Walker, are you plugged into this dude?

SCHRAUTH: Roge.

ROADRUNNER: Well, welcome.

WATCHDOG: (ha, ha) Mike, this is Dwight. When will you have your schedule to Roadrunner?

SCHRAUTH: Our schedules for Shanghai are now in the comm center here. We understand that our lines should be clear for transmission this evening so tomorrow morning Peking should have all of the scenarios. Do you copy?

WATCHDOG: Roger, I copy. Do you copy, Roadrunner?

ROADRUNNER: That's a roger. I copy loud and clear. Thank you, Mike.

WATCHDOG: So, Ron, that may mean that the only one that you would have to worry about doing would be Hangchou, right?

ROADRUNNER: Yeah, I'm convinced that Duval is not going to be up. They had too many problems while we were there and they just got their equipment late this afternoon and there is just no way. I'll write those scenarios.

WATCHDOG: OK. We'll gamble on being able to get Schrauth's, and you'll do Hangchou. That's perfect. Roadrunner, do you know whether the military people, General Scowcroft, Major Brennan, and Coffey can wear their uniforms?

ROADRUNNER: I'll find out just as soon as I have an opportunity to talk with my counterpart. Be advised, tomorrow's a holiday. I had about a two hour meeting this evening and that may be it for the next twenty-four hours.

WATCHDOG: OK. I understand your problem. Roadrunner, can you tell me if we have approval for the documentary crew people to come in with the press corps, two of them?

ROADRUNNER: Yes, sir, that's a roger. That's an absolute roger.

WATCHDOG: Beautiful. Thank you. This is a question for Livingood. I need to know the names of the two agents that will be riding on the Prime Minister's aircraft and the two agents that will ride on the Spirit of '76.

ROADRUNNER: The two agents on the PRC aircraft are Taylor and Zboril.

WATCHDOG: Roger. Taylor and Zboril on the Prime Minister's.

ROADRUNNER: Roger. On 26000 it will be Hal Thomas and the shift from 8 A.M. to 8 P.M.

WATCHDOG: You mean the whole shift?

LIVINGOOD: It'll be Hal Thomas' shift which is a total of six agents.

WATCHDOG: OK, a total of six. OK. Now, Roadrunner?

ROADRUNNER: Yes, Dwight. Go ahead.

WATCHDOG: At the top of the gift memo where all this garbage is that Redman's people put on it . . . [*The transmittal information, date, time, operator, etc.*]

ROADRUNNER: All I have is a clean copy. Wait one.

WATCHDOG: Wait. Do you . . . is it dated?

ROADRUNNER: Wait one, I said. [*Sounded like he was talking through clenched teeth*]

WATCHDOG: OK.

ROADRUNNER: Please, wait one.

WATCHDOG: I will. [*But Watchdog could not be quiet and wait a minute.*] Schrauth, Watchdog. (To the room: "That's exactly what I am going to do.") Schrauth, Watchdog.

ROADRUNNER: Ahhhhhh, Dwight, I don't think Mike's on right now. We've had problems with interference from our end, if you have not been copying it, and I think Shanghai might be off right now.

WATCHDOG: OK, Ron, that protocol memo that we talked about regarding the gifts? Hangchou?

ROADRUNNER: Yes, sir, I know exactly what you're talking about. I would like to tell you who's present with us this evening. It's Livingood, Swift, we are very honored to have John Thomas with us for the first time, Bob Rollins, Abel Araiza is with us, and Hank Gibbons. Timmie is meeting with his counterpart about his possible departure tomorrow. [*State gifts were confidential, and Roadrunner wanted to make sure Washington knew who was listening.*]

WATCHDOG: Roger. Well, we've got with us this morning Ray Zook, Maguire, Henkel, Scowcroft, Whelihan, Redman, Bull, Brennan, Julie, and myself. Ah, I have always been against Tim leaving the country, just so you know. How do you feel?

ROADRUNNER: Well, I have mixed emotions. I'm not keen on Elbourne leaving from the standpoint of the arrangements and the relationship that he has developed with Mr. Ma. However, he is very keen on the idea that Ziegler needs him. He also feels it is extremely important to prepare the press coming into this country. From that standpoint, I think there is a great deal of preparation that is going to be needed.

WATCHDOG: To what degree are there outstanding points to be resolved in the movement of the press corps and the logistics that Tim would be working on?

ROADRUNNER: There are still minute details that need to be worked out, as far as movements are concerned. We're not sure we are going to have the vehicles to move pools around, to include the documentary crew. That kind of detail may not happen until the sisteenth, seventeenth, and possibly the eighteenth, at this point.

WATCHDOG: Ron, listening to you right now is so clear, you're coming through just perfect. I cannot comprehend why we could not put Timmie on a conference call into a press center in Hawaii, and have him do the damn thing over a speaker phone. To waste all that time for him to fly back and be in Hawaii, to psychologically condition the press, and not be able to say any more than he would say over the air, seems ridiculous. I sure as hell don't need him to brief me. You're very good at communicating the stuff to me. I would argue strongly that he should remain there and that he should not saddle you and the rest of the support people with the problem of trying to work out the press logistics.

ROADRUNNER: I understand what you're saying and read you very loud and clear, in regard to that opinion. It's a situation that Timmie and I have discussed at great length. He feels that it's extremely important not only to the press corps, but to Ziegler. I think that we should let Timmie and Ziegler talk before I commit myself on that answer.

WATCHDOG: OK. But what I want to know from you is what your gut feeling is. I am going to get together with Ron and let him know how I feel, and I would like to know how you come out on this. What do you say? He should or he shouldn't? Yes or no?

ROADRUNNER: No.

WATCHDOG: OK. Thank you.

ROADRUNNER: That's a gut call. [*Snapshot desperately wanted a few days out of the PRC. He was going stir crazy, and besides, he would have been a big shot in Hawaii, the expert, the guy every reporter needed to talk with.*]

WATCHDOG: I know it is, Ron, and so's mine, but there comes a time and a place.

ROADRUNNER: Well, Manning has done a very fine job, but Manning is not Elbourne.

WATCHDOG: OK. (pause) OK. We've got something written up in the schedule. You look at it when it gets in there, we indicate who from the official/unofficial party can go on down to Hangchou the night of the twenty-fifth.

ROADRUNNER: Wait one. (pause) OK, please go ahead and give me that list.

WATCHDOG: OK. Hang on a minute. (paper shuffling) OK, here are the ones we came up with. Jenkins, Holdridge, Thomas, but that's a call that you can make.

ROADRUNNER: Yes, sir.

WATCHDOG: Interpreter by the name of . . . (To the room: "How do you pronounce this?") . . . Mehlert.

ROADRUNNER: Mehlert, right.

WATCHDOG: And (To the room: "How do you pronounce this?") Kovenock.

ROADRUNNER: Kovenock, right.

WATCHDOG: Hartigan.
ROADRUNNER: Right.
WATCHDOG: And Gold.
ROADRUNNER: Right.
WATCHDOG: That's it.
ROADRUNNER: Roger.
WATCHDOG: Now, we didn't get into the support people.
ROADRUNNER: (Sounding like he's tickled) No, that's OK. We will cover that end here. [*Roadrunner had been ready for a much longer list of names.*] So what you are telling me is that all the Secretary of State's people, to include Maggie and Nick, need to remain behind to accompany the Secretary of State on an aircraft that next morning? [*Maggie C. Runkle and Nicholas Platt of the Department of State*]
WATCHDOG: Well, we don't know what's going to happen that night or the next morning. In other words, we cannot eliminate staff unless we know precisely what's happening, and in order to be flexible we've got to keep our options open in case there is work to be done.
ROADRUNNER: Yes, sir, I understand.
WATCHDOG: OK.
ROADRUNNER: Be advised we have TWXed back to you the precedence list with the changes that were suggested by Whelihan. We have a few problems as far as the PRC is concerned, because our numbers have increased by forty-two people. We have a problem in Shanghai because they can not accommodate that number of people. Schrauth is very much aware of that problem.

Be advised he has an extremely fine relationship with his counterpart in Shanghai as does Duval in Hangchou. It's very different in those two cities than it has been here. They are very anxious to accommodate. Many more answers were acquired out of those two cities than we have previously been accustomed to.
WATCHDOG: That's fantastic. That's great, Ron. I'm glad to know that we have that relationship. In Shanghai, that banquet room was not quite as large, and maybe some people could eat at the hotel or the guest house and then come to the cultural show.
ROADRUNNER: Yes, sir, that's a good idea. Right now it looks like we are going have two hundred people available to go to the banquet in Shanghai. And we're approaching about 263 for the banquet here in Peking. That's based on input from the counterparts here, and the encouragement we have received from the PRC. To quote Director Han Hsu, "The more the merrier."
WATCHDOG: I understand. Is Tim still in that meeting?
ROADRUNNER: Yes, sir, he's not here yet.

WATCHDOG: Ziegler is here with us now, so I'd have Tim call Ron on that.

ROADRUNNER: Let me relay my conversations with my counterpart during this swing through Shanghai and Hangchou.

WATCHDOG: Ron. Ron?

ROADRUNNER: Yes? Yes, I'm listening.

WATCHDOG: Ron, can you stop one minute? Ziegler's got two questions he wants to ask, because then he has to leave. So let me put him on here with you. [*The press secretary was evidently too busy to wait his turn.*]

ROADRUNNER: Please.

WHALEBOAT: Ron? What is your thinking about Elbourne coming out? (pause) Ron, can you hear me? [*No greetings or exchange of pleasantries.*]

ROADRUNNER: Yes, Zee, I hear you loud and clear. How are you? Over. (laughter)

WHALEBOAT: (surprised) Well, I'm just fine, Ron.

ROADRUNNER: Uhhhh, I think Tim feels that it's extremely vital that he be available, not only to you, but to the members of our illustrious press corps, to prepare them properly for their entry into the People's Republic of China. He's gone to great lengths to explain this to his counterpart, as well as explain it to me, and I have attempted to explain it to my counterpart. It has been sold. He says that Mr. Ma feels that it is a good idea. The only comment I've had from my counterpart is, "Yes, we agree that Mr. Elbourne can leave the country." [*Roadrunner did not think the Chinese really cared one way or the other.*]

WHALEBOAT: When would he leave?

ROADRUNNER: We are holding an aircraft on the ground right now, a C-141, for his departure sometime tomorrow. They will go to Guam and from Guam catch a commercial flight into Hawaii.

WHALEBOAT: Well, we'll think about that, Ron. Let me ask you another question.

WATCHDOG: (To Ziegler: "Have Timmie call you.")

WHALEBOAT: Yeah, have Tim call me after the meeting, but let me ask you another question. What problem do you think it would pose, and I'm not suggesting this yet, but something has come up that leads me to ask this question. What problem do you think it would pose, to substitute four names on that list? The press list of eighty-seven?

ROADRUNNER: Well, Ron, all I can say to you is . . . that if it's necessary, we'll attempt in every effort that we've got to sell it, but it's going to be tough. [*It was a very touchy point to raise with the Chinese.*]

WATCHDOG: Hey, Ron, hang on a minute. (Muffled discussion in Washington) [*It was obvious that Watchdog had placed his hand over the telephone.*]

WHALEBOAT: (To the room, at the end of discussion: "That's what I want to find out . . . if the networks think it's all covered, they are going to pull the rug out.") [*He probably meant if it looked "too staged."*]

WATCHDOG: Roadrunner, we understand what your problem is on that. He just wanted to get a gut reaction.

ROADRUNNER: My gut reaction is that we better back off of that, but if it is vitally necessary we'll do the best we can.

WATCHDOG: OK, well we won't have anything on that until morning, your time. In other words we'll work on it today.

ROADRUNNER: May I ask one question on that? So I can start mentally preparing myself? Is that an addition of four people, or is it . . .

WATCHDOG: Oh no, no, it's strictly a substitution based upon some new information that Ron has here. In other words, just a change of a name here and there. Four to five name changes.

ROADRUNNER: Yes, sir, I understand. OK, I think we could probably get away with that. But be advised, they have prepared the press floors of this hotel with every individual's name on their doors. I am pointing out the detail they have gone into with information we have given them to this point.

WATCHDOG: OK, Ron, we understand. OK, now, go ahead with your report. Thank you.

ROADRUNNER: OK. This is not in any order of priority or anything. I'd like just to go through these notes so that you have a feel of what we got into this evening. Mr. Chu called me at 5:15 for a meeting at 6:00. I was told that there are occasions that principals exchange gifts. Person to person. As far as giving gifts to members of the PRC, I was told that it would be appropriate to label those by name, and present them to the Office of Protocol and they will guarantee their presentation.

I did not raise the gift you were referring to the other day. I would like guidance on how I approach that. I'm not sure they will be able to translate it into Chinese. [*Mao had told Kissinger that they wanted musk oxen from Alaska. Roadrunner tried to explain them to the Chinese, but they could not translate the information. Roadrunner was not sure that Chou En-lai understood what they were getting.*]

WATCHDOG: OK. I'll send you a note on that tonight.

ROADRUNNER: Please, I would appreciate it very much. On the first day that the President arrives, on the twenty-first, the PRC most graciously are waiving all diplomatic requirements for 970 and 26000, as far as passports and visas are concerned.

WATCHDOG: Oh, that's very kind and generous. We appreciate that very much.

ROADRUNNER: I will relay that. The crew however, must have their passports, and it will be necessary for someone on board both 26000 and 970 to give the passports to the People's Republic of China. I would like the names of who will be responsible for that so counterparts will be able to meet them in Shanghai.

WATCHDOG: Hang on a minute. (To the room: "OK, who should we assign? Maguire on 970. No, that's not it. Just read a couple of names off. No, no, Brennan will be working. On what?") On 26000 we'll designate Oldenburg. [*SP7 Herbert G. Oldenburg*]

ROADRUNNER: Roger, that's a good suggestion. On 970 who do you suggest?

WATCHDOG: Well, we're working on it. (To the room: "Ought to have a military, support type person, if we can. We have it for Air Force One. Who is it?")

ROADRUNNER: How about Platt?

WATCHDOG: Done. Platt.

ROADRUNNER: Platt. Roger.

WATCHDOG: Next?

ROADRUNNER: Roger. I was asked what kind of meal Searchlight and Starlight would like upon arriving at the guest house. I was given a choice of Chinese food or Western food, and I said they would like very much to have their first meal be Chinese food.

WATCHDOG: Roger!   OK, Ron, that's fine.

ROADRUNNER: Thank you. The PRC is most anxious to know what kinds of food they enjoy and would like to have. Colonel Coffey is scheduled, predicated on his condition, to do a survey of the guest house on the sixteenth, the day after tomorrow. Realizing tomorrow is a holiday, I have tried not to tie up any of our friends.

Anyway the menus during the five-day period will be laid out in detail prior to the President's arrival. Vern is going to work on that, but they have made a suggestion which I think might be worthy of consideration. Knowing very well the President is not a heavy eater, nor is Mrs. Nixon, provide a portion of Chinese meal and a portion of Western meal. So at this point that is how we are going to proceed. I have also made it very clear they do not want to be wasting food.

WATCHDOG: OK, Ron. I think that's been handled very well. I agree that the portion break-down is a good idea, and the idea of keeping the meals fairly light is important. As you know for lunch, the President, and it's been written about many times, will have a scoop of cottage cheese and a glass of milk. He just does not eat a lot of food and never has. In fact, I can recall that their Prime Minister is not a big eater either, so it's very similar, and we will advise both the President and Mrs. Nixon as to what has been worked out.

ROADRUNNER: OK, sir. Thank you. They wanted to know what the President's desirable temperature of the villa was. I told them twenty degrees centigrade or seventy degrees fahrenheit. Also . . .

WATCHDOG: That's true, seventy degrees is true.

ROADRUNNER: Roger, that's what I said. Also they would like for us to put on our notice . . . I don't know how they know, but they know we are putting out an information sheet that tells them how to get along in China. And they would like us to say they can put shoes outside their door and they will be shined. I've raised the point now and you can do what you want to with it. They also approved Elbourne, if it is decided that he will go. They have approved for us to enter the guest house as of tomorrow.

WATCHDOG: Good.

ROADRUNNER: However, I do not feel that it is necessary for us to get into that villa until approximately the nineteenth. We can move the comm center in a matter of a few hours, and it's better to be together in the hotel at this point. [*Roadrunner felt he had more control in the hotel. When the move was made, some people would stay in the hotel, and others would be spread out in several different buildings on the grounds of the guest house.*]

WATCHDOG: OK.

ROADRUNNER: Next . . . the banquet. They want the numbers of people that will be attending the banquet. That includes Hangchou and Shanghai. The next thing we talked about was the Chinese opera. Be advised, it is my gut reaction, and I hope you will know what I am saying, they are attempting to perform something out of the ordinary, and relatively new. [*Roadrunner still thought it would be "The Red Detachment of Women." When the Chinese realized the Americans liked to watch movies, they made a screen version of it available for them to watch!*]

WATCHDOG: Got it.

ROADRUNNER: Motorcades. I have encouraged shortening the motorcades and using buses for members other than the official party. I think they have finally bought this. I have also finally convinced my counterpart that it is not necessary to move the entire party. So I think we're having people pre-positioned. Are you copying me?

WATCHDOG: Yes. I would think that on movements where the President, the Secretary and Dr. Kissinger go, we would take the Secretary of State over and have him go in the Presidential motorcade. [*Kissinger would have preferred accompanying the President without the Secretary of State; that's exactly what happened when the President went to visit Mao.*]

ROADRUNNER: Yes, sir. They are agreeable to that. The Secretary of State in all movements in Peking will be a part of the Presidential motorcade.

WATCHDOG: Good. OK.

ROADRUNNER: There are principals that will move with the President in every instance. I think we can pre-position all the other people, so that you only have a small party actually moving with the President.

WATCHDOG: That's good. You're right. Go ahead.

ROADRUNNER: We are going to have buses in various motorcades, the Great Wall, the Forbidden City, I am convinced of that. They think it's a good idea. [*In the end, there were no buses. It may have been a good idea, but the Chinese did not use them.*] I also have a gut reaction that everybody in Shanghai is going to receive cards that will be their security cards for clearance. It will have their motorcade assignment and their room number and where they are housed. It happened to us. I can't see any change on that.

WATCHDOG: Fine. We have in our schedule that "past procedure has been to have motorcade assignments given to people on a card which will be distributed between Shanghai and Peking."

ROADRUNNER: Roger. But, this evening we went into minute detail on how we handle our motorcades. Mr. Chu was extremely interested and they took minute notes on, for example, follow-up cars, press cars, communication car, and all those points we have been trying to talk about and haven't been able to.

WATCHDOG: Right. Do you think there will be such an animal as a control car?

ROADRUNNER: Well, believe me, I talked about it at great length. Right now I think there is a good possibility. They talked about me and Livingood in a car similar to what we call a pilot car. Moving ahead to precede the motorcade, or to move ahead to the next location, so the things we have been talking about for two weeks may be happening. Unless that's the way they do it normally. Which very possibly might be.

WATCHDOG: OK. Good, Ron. Go ahead.

ROADRUNNER: On the departure, we are putting together a flow chart on getting people out of country, and the Chinese are beginning to focus on that also. [*Roadrunner thought it was great fun to plan how they were going to get out of town!*] I plan on bringing Duval in from Hangchou with us to ride the last aircraft out.

WATCHDOG: OK, right. We can talk about this when I get on the ground, but just for your planning, you will find yourself manifested with Schrauth on 970 out of country, and not on a press plane. We got word on some document, that you were manifested on the press plane and we'd like to have you on 970. [*Advance men liked to ride the press plane home after a big trip because it was much more fun. However, the White House did not want Roadrunner available to the press until he had been de-briefed by the CIA.*]

ROADRUNNER: OK. That's all. I've got some points regarding Hangchou and Shanghai, but I can put those into scenario form.

WATCHDOG: OK. Well, I guess I should give you a kiss. It's Valentine's Day.

ROADRUNNER: I know that.

WATCHDOG: Listen. We . . . You're family had a box that was to come to you, a Valentine's box that we had a problem with . . . and . . . it's not going to make it. So you'll just have to get it later. But anyway, everybody sends their love. [*The "box" was an envelope of Valentines that Roadrunner's three little girls had made for him. Word came back from Bill Gully that there was "no room on the plane; it was full."*]

ROADRUNNER: Well, thank you very much. Pass mine back to them please.

WATCHDOG: OK. Uh . . . hang on a minute. Roadrunner, Did you get my documentary crew memo?

ROADRUNNER: Yes, sir. And we've got some problems.

WATCHDOG: OK. Well, no problems, just opportunities.

ROADRUNNER: We have any number of opportunities, but we may have some problems. We have been informed by Director Han Hsu that it must be centralization. His word, and he is hopeful that crew will be controlled through the press operation.

WATCHDOG: OK. Ron, when we arrive at the guest house and go into the sitting room, the President would be there with the Prime Minister. We would like to have our official photographers and their photographers, but not the press corps.

ROADRUNNER: Yes, sir. I have put this in writing. I have also indicated it is extremely important. I have no reason to doubt that what I have been told is going to transpire. However, Elbourne is getting different input from his counterpart. It's kind of a . . .

WATCHDOG: Tell Tim he should not discuss documentary crews with them at all. All those questions should be referred to you. If Mr. Ma has a question regarding the documentary crew, do not treat it as a press question. [*The documentary crew's job was to get campaign footage for the fall election.*]

ROADRUNNER: Yes, sir, I understand, but I don't believe it's Elbourne raising the questions. I believe it's his counterpart. Over.

WATCHDOG: OK. The other thing would be that in situations like I just described at the guest house, those pictures would be exclusive pictures, official pictures for the White House. Then also on their side, official pictures for them to maintain, but not releasable through the New China News Agency. In other words we would reach an agreement there that they would be official pictures for historic purposes. [*The PRC did not understand the difference. Cameras were press!*]

ROADRUNNER: Yes, sir. I understand what you are saying.

WATCHDOG: Ron, should we put anything in this schedule on currency?

ROADRUNNER: Uhhhh. I would say yes. I would think that it would be extremely worthwhile to get a currency breakdown on Chinese *yuan*.

WATCHDOG: Why don't we just put a note in that currency information will be available upon arrival and they should contact John Thomas.

ROADRUNNER: That's a roger. We'll handle that.

WATCHDOG: OK. How about a note on shopping? What should we say? Do you have any indication yet?

ROADRUNNER: Yes. They will make provisions for everyone to go shopping. They also have asked when not everyone is going to the various locations, should we make other arrangements? I said no, it was not necessary for any other tours to be arranged or make any specific arrangements for people not moving with the President.

WATCHDOG: OK. Hang on a minute, Ron. (To the room: "Does anybody here have anything?")

ROADRUNNER: Roger. I would just like to re-emphasize once again, that if this weather continues, it is colder than the hinges of hell. I hope that everybody understands they must be dressed warmly, because there are many people on our trip here now that are experiencing difficulties because they had not dressed properly.

WATCHDOG: Right. OK, Ron. Put in that Kovovich, or whatever that guy's . . . Kovenock . . . will make all movements with Mrs. Nixon.

ROADRUNNER: Kovenock, the interpreter, will be accompanying Mrs. Nixon.

WATCHDOG: We'll rename him Smith before we get there!

ROADRUNNER: Roger. I think that would be most appropriate. It's relatively difficult for us also.

WATCHDOG: OK. Ummm. Hang on. (To the room: "Anything else?") (long pause)

WATCHDOG: Hello?

ROADRUNNER: Well Fred had something, but we're not going to recognize him.

WATCHDOG: Ha, ha, ha.

ROADRUNNER: Roger. Major Swift has something. I assume it's for . . . (To Swift, "Do you want to talk to General Scowcroft?") (laughter) Oh no, he wants to talk to General Redman, excuse me. [*Swift may have liked to talk to General Scowcroft, but military protocol dictated that he talk to Redman.*] (sounds of microphone shuffling)

WATCHDOG: Roadrunner?

ROADRUNNER: (from far away) Yes, sir.

WATCHDOG: Sounds like he's dead.

SOMEONE: Go ahead, Fred, talk. [*Swift was embarrassed at this point.*]

WATCHDOG: Roadrunner?

ROADRUNNER: (sounds of his moving and bumping into something) Yes, Dwight. That's all I've got. Fred's got something for General Redman. Thank you very much. We'll look forward to talking with you tomorrow.

WATCHDOG: Whoa, whoa, whoa, whoa! I've got something more for you.

ROADRUNNER: Oh, I'm sorry.

SWIFT: (To Roadrunner, "Tell him I'll call later.")

ROADRUNNER: Swift will call Redman separately. Let's disregard that last transmission.

WATCHDOG: OK. Just a minute now. On Saturday, the twenty-sixth, that's Saturday the twenty-sixth, at one in the morning, we are going to put in a baggage call for equipment and footlockers, and you'll find that in our schedule. But we're trying to figure out how we can help you get some of that equipment out of there ahead of time. [*Baggage call meant that luggage was to be placed outside the hotel room door by the specified time for transport to the aircraft.*]

ROADRUNNER: Roger, I understand.

WATCHDOG: Then we would do the personal baggage at 7:00 A.M.

ROADRUNNER: OK.

WATCHDOG: OK. We don't have anything else, so I guess we'll sign off here. Have a good night's sleep, take care, and all is fine here. The President's back from Florida.

ROADRUNNER: OK. Thank you very much. We all send our best to everyone there. Everybody is looking forward to a week from today with great anticipation of an extremely fine trip.

WATCHDOG: Well, a week from right now we'll be at the banquet.

ROADRUNNER: That's a roger, I hope we make it.

WATCHDOG: We will. Talk to you later.

ROADRUNNER: Roger. That's Roadrunner out.
WATCHDOG: Out. (click . . . click . . . click . . . dial tone)

Finally! Roadrunner was exhausted. He needed to get some more sleep. His throat was worse than ever and talking on the phone for hours, going over the same things again and again, was making it worse. "And Snapshot still wanted to go to Hawaii!" Roadrunner thought to himself. "It just was not right." "Snapshot has no business doing that. Sure, everyone would like to be able to leave and go live it up for a couple of days in beautiful, warm, sunny Hawaii, see some of their pals and flirt with the stewardesses on the press plane. Everyone had worked very hard and under the same difficult conditions. If Zee wanted the press briefed, Watchdog was right, let them do it over a speaker phone." Roadrunner really did not think that the press secretary cared if Elbourne was in Hawaii. If he did, he would have directed flat out that he be there. Instead, he wanted to know what Roadrunner thought about it.

Roadrunner thought about it again. It would be great fun for Snapshot, but it would not be in the best interest of the trip to have him gone for the last critical days of preparation, and it definitely would send the wrong signal to the rest of the Americans.

"That's it," he thought as he climbed into bed. "Snapshot stays here." As the responsible person in charge of preparations, he knew it was the right decision, but in his heart he felt, "Oh dear, poor Timmie."

The next morning, Snapshot took the news with a shrug, just like Roadrunner knew he would. He was a professional, serious about his job, and he understood Roadrunner's decision. He managed to hide his disappointment from everyone as they gathered for the conference call. It was 8:40 A.M. in China, and 7:40 P.M. at home.

ROADRUNNER: Now, wait a minute, just so you know, they're talking about twenty-two official/unofficial types on the boat ride in Hangchou. And limiting it to three members of the press corps on board that boat. They will have, for your planning purposes, an additional boat if necessary, for other members of our party that don't ride on the President's boat. I'm maintaining that we ought to leave everybody else home.
HENKEL: Amen. Don't forget, you'll need one WHCA guy on there too, while he's on that boat, right?
ROADRUNNER: Yeah, well we're working on that. I need to have you find out for me, exactly who needs to go on that boat?
HENKEL: OK.

ROADRUNNER: On the President's boat. For example: Does Assistant Secretary Green need to go on that boat? Does Jenkins need to go on that boat? Does Holdridge need to go on that boat? Does Lord? Does Rose Mary Woods? Does Buchanan? Does Howe?

HENKEL: I . . . I . . .

ROADRUNNER: For example, I can see taking off Holdridge and Lord, possibly Buchanan. But Chapin may think they'll never have a chance like this again in a lifetime. We've got additional boats we can put them on. It doesn't necessarily have to be on the President's boat, is what I'm saying. [*President Nixon always wanted fewer Americans and more Chinese surrounding him to provide a better photo opportunity.*]

HENKEL: Ron, I will do anything you want, but why don't you send us what you think is reasonable and when I get it, I will explain the philosophy, and hopefully they will just approve your list as the go list.

ROADRUNNER: Do you mean to tell me that for the first time since I've been advancing, that what I'm recommending is flying?

HENKEL: I think so, partner.

ROADRUNNER: I'm just kidding.

HENKEL: No, really, there's been no resistance here, believe me.

ROADRUNNER: Give me a gut feel of the attitude of people as far as the preparation and everything is going.

HENKEL: OK. I think, no bullshit, I think people are extremely proud of the job you're doing. I think everyone has a lot of confidence in what you've been doing, and I think Dwight has been articulating the difficulties you've had, the patience you've exhibited. We've been giving a lot of material, to a very, very limited few, HAK [*Henry Kissinger*], HRH [*H. R. Haldeman*], etc. And there has been very little that they've tried to change. And I would say that Dwight's been given a tremendous amount of latitude in this whole situation too.

ROADRUNNER: Uh, huh.

HENKEL: So I would say, very, very frankly, it's your show and Dwight's show, and the others are basically accepting what comes to them.

ROADRUNNER: Uh huh. Well good. I'm glad to hear that.

HENKEL: One other thing. You might want to check with John Thomas, because I think this is critical. (To someone in the room: "Remember that suitcase for Ron Walker? OK, it got on the plane. Yeah, the aluminum one. Yes. Yeah.") Chuck Maguire saw that suitcase of yours get on the plane.

ROADRUNNER: Well, we haven't been able to find the suitcase. So, it's either got to be in Hangchou or in Shanghai.

HENKEL: We've got an awful lot of material in there that's very, very important. Gee, I mean, if they haven't found it, we'll have to figure out a system real fast to get that stuff to you.

ROADRUNNER: I understand that. I'll talk to Duval and try and determine the status of it.

MAGUIRE: OK, Ron, Chuck Maguire, how are you?

ROADRUNNER: Hi, Chuck.

MAGUIRE: How is everybody? How's my leader?

ROADRUNNER: He's fine. Just a minute. (microphone shuffle)

THOMAS: Hello.

MAGUIRE: Hello, Coach.

THOMAS: Hi, Chuck. How are you?

MAGUIRE: Very fine, sir. Very fine. Did you see that aluminum suitcase go on the plane, or did you know it was on there?

THOMAS: No, sir.

MAGUIRE: OK. It was aluminum, had Ron Walker all over it, I saw it. But, I wasn't at the airport.

THOMAS: You've only got one problem, Chuck.

MAGUIRE: Yes, sir.

THOMAS: We've been loaded and off-loaded about seventy-eight times. I think probably it's down in Hangchou.

MAGUIRE: OK. John? As soon as Dwight clears this schedule, we want a distribution list.

THOMAS: What?

MAGUIRE: It's NODIS, in the department. Then it's sent over here and transmitted immediately, to you folks. [*NODIS is State Department shorthand for "No Distribution."*] We were gonna send you Guam, and also Hono. [*Honolulu schedule*] All right?

THOMAS: That's fine with me, yeah. Sure.

MAGUIRE: OK. We just don't want to plug up your circuit, if at some point we're plugging it up, if you'd tell us to stop on this end, we'll stop. What we're trying to do is send you the whole book, as we did it.

THOMAS: Yeah, sure. Yeah. Incidently, where are the cigarettes? Do you know? For the dinner.

MAGUIRE: Did you ask me to do that?

THOMAS: You told me that, Dwight told you to get together with Gully. To get cigarettes and matches. Right? For the dinner. [*Cigarettes and matches with the Presidential seal were to be on the tables at the reciprocal banquet.*]

MAGUIRE: I'll find out about it. I thought Ron Jackson was doing that. And was going to include it with the dessert stuff, but I'll check on it tomorrow.

THOMAS: Well, we . . . we've got the matches. That may be the answer, but, as of last night we didn't know where the cigarettes were.

MAGUIRE: OK. We'll find out. Oh! Come on! Mrs. DeFantis is now Mrs. DeSantis. Jeez.

THOMAS: Oh, pardon me!

MAGUIRE: Ha, ha, pardon me!

THOMAS: All righty. It's still spelled D-E, isn't it?

MAGUIRE: That's correct, sir.

THOMAS: And then a capital F-A-N-T-I-S?

MAGUIRE: Negative. Capital S, as in Sam. DeSantis.

THOMAS: Well how come Immigration, and Dwight Chapin, and everybody's got it . . .

MAGUIRE: I can't explain that. Mrs. DeSantis, DeFantis, whatever, called Nell Yates and said her name really is De-San-TIS. With an S. (To Henkel: "How come Immigration had this with an F?") We'll find out, I don't know.

THOMAS: Jeeeeeese!

MAGUIRE: . . . and on the yachtsman's area, it's a go with the four, four legs. [*Chief of Protocol Buzz Mosbacher was called the yachtsman because he skippered the America's Cup race. The four, four legs referred to the two pair of musk oxen.*]

THOMAS: Yeah, all right.

MAGUIRE: And they come in afterwards. I'll give you the information on that, and the guys that grow . . . will be on 970. [*Giant redwood trees for Hangchou. Everyone was still being vague about the State gifts lest they be overheard.*]

THOMAS: They will?

MAGUIRE: That's a roger. They need someplace to go be stored, where they're going to be healthy, until they get to Hangchou. Dwight's also agreed, that the guy that's in charge of the big pen here, where they keep all those four-legged things, should also go along with them. [*Director of the National Zoo in Washington*]

THOMAS: Well, I should think so.

MAGUIRE: And . . . we found out today, from our Canadian friends, that we're going to get something that's very rare. [*Giant pandas*] We will be the second place in the world that has one. OK? Little fuzzy feller.

THOMAS: Uh, huh, Mmm, mmm.

MAGUIRE: So don't you agree that's more reason why he ought to go?

THOMAS: Absolutely.

MAGUIRE: OK. Dwight's supposed to give me a memo, and . . . your yachtsman friend can't see straight. [*The memo was to state that the Director of the Zoo would be going to China, and that the Chief of Protocol would not.*]

THOMAS: Why?

MAGUIRE: Oh! Lord! Can't even talk to the man. He is so furious.

THOMAS: Why?

MAGUIRE: Why? Ha, ha, ha. Because . . . he . . . ain't . . . GOING! He wrote the most ridiculous memo I ever read in my life.

THOMAS: About what?

MAGUIRE: About things, in general. He did it as a joke, but I'm afraid S.S. [*the Secretary of State*] didn't read it as a joke. They read it seriously, and it sort of back-fired on him. But then, I made it clear to everybody, that's not my business.

THOMAS: All right. Are you sending us a cable on the gifts?

MAGUIRE: Yes, we are. As soon as everything is approved, locked, agreed upon and done, bought, in hand, eye-balled and wrapped. OK?

THOMAS: Yeah. Sure.

MAGUIRE: OK. Do I owe you anything?

THOMAS: No, at this point, I owe you information on the money situation, and I just don't have it, that's all.

MAGUIRE: OK. Whelihan is now going to pick up on signal. Signal? Signal?

SIGNAL: Hello, Peking?

THOMAS: Hello.

SIGNAL: Mr. Whelihan is on the line.

THOMAS: Bruce?

WHELIHAN: Roadrunner?

THOMAS: Just a moment please. (phone drops)

WHELIHAN: Who's this?

SNAPSHOT: Hellooo?

WHELIHAN: Timmie!

SNAPSHOT: Hi, Bruce.

WHELIHAN: How are you?

ELBOURNE: Super fine. Tell me about this UPI wire story from here fed by Lyon.

WHELIHAN: Fred Lyons? Let me grab a copy. Hold on a second.

SNAPSHOT: (To the room: "I'm going to put it on speaker so you can hear it. He's gonna read it.") (long pause)

WHELIHAN: You there?

SNAPSHOT: Yeah, we're here. Could you read the story, Bruce? Ron Walker and John Thomas are in the room, we're on a speaker phone.

WHELIHAN: OK. It's filed out of Peking. But, probably, actually came out of New York.

It says, "A small second advance group of photography technicians and U.S. government aides arrived in Peking Monday to make arrangements for news coverage of President Nixon's week long visit beginning February 21. UPI news pictures general manager Fred W. (Bill) Lyon said it was 'a clear, clear day' marred only by some smog when the party of about twenty Americans arrived in Peking. The first advance group of about eighty electronic and broadcast technicians working to establish satellite communications with the United States for the President's visit arrived in Peking February 1. The Americans are housed in a ten-story, British-style hotel in downtown Peking and take their meals in the hotel dining room. Lyon said when the second advance group arrived there was 'considerable smog in the air apparently caused by industrial fumes as there are virtually no automobiles on the streets and very few motor buses. Practically all transportation for civilians seems to be either by electric bus or bicycle. The roads are lined with trees, the bases of which have been painted white.' He said the White House has arranged for American movies to be shown in the room of the hotel's tenth floor every night 'because night life in Peking is at a minimum.' The Americans can leave the hotel if they have a Chinese escort and a specific destination." That's the end of the story.

SNAPSHOT: Uh, Bruce? Could we get Ron Ziegler on?

WHELIHAN: He's not here, he's over at this dinner.

SNAPSHOT: (sigh) What do you suppose Ron wants us to do about that here? I'm definitely going to talk with Mr. Lyon, but what do you want us to do, move him out?

WHELIHAN: No, he realizes all you can do is talk to him, Tim, and just raise again that these guys are not to be filing stories, or filing copy, or anything else out of there. That's the principle objection. But, of course the tone of the story is not in keeping with the fine accommodations provided by our hosts.

SNAPSHOT: Well, this is just . . . I don't even believe that one. He obviously did not make the call over our lines, he must have done it commercially. [*He did indeed. The PRC must have known what he was doing and could very easily have cut him off.*]

WHELIHAN: Well, I think you see the point. He's a new arrival, just got over there and hasn't seen what's been going on, or worked with these people at all, it's just irresponsible on his part, Ron feels.

SNAPSHOT: Well, I would have assumed that when he got here, he was familiar with the guidelines. Everybody else on his aircraft were, and are, and . . . I don't understand it.

WHELIHAN: Well, there's nothing you can do about moving him out of there. It just shouldn't happen again. That's Ron's only feeling.

SNAPSHOT: Well, we've got a major problem here, I'm sure. We're gonna have a major problem as soon as they see it. It's gonna be a big one.

ROADRUNNER: (To Tim: "We should show it to them.") [*Roadrunner felt it was important to show the article to the Chinese before someone else did.*]

SNAPSHOT: We need a copy, immediately, Bruce. You can telex one, so we can give it to them here, and try to explain it.

WHELIHAN: Shall do.

SNAPSHOT: Great. OK. Do you have any questions this morning?

WHELIHAN: I do, for you, yes, if you've got a second. Uh. You got my thing on the courier, I guess.

SNAPSHOT: What thing on the courier?

WHELIHAN: Well, Ron met this afternoon with the magazines about getting stuff out. And I've sent you a TWX, which I don't have a copy of because it's not come back yet from the sit room. We want to request a courier out on the twenty-third. It would be one of the Pan Am planes sitting in Guam, that will come in, the magazines will pay for it. It has to be in Guam by about four o'clock, Guam time, on the afternoon of the twenty-third. And he says make whatever arrangements you feel are necessary, in accord with the desires of our hosts, so we can get some film out.

SNAPSHOT: That's a roger. As you are aware, that request is pending before them, for either on the twenty-third or the twenty-fourth, we weren't sure, so, I'm safe there. They haven't come back with an answer.

WHELIHAN: All right, the magazines have, you know, their deadline problems, and *Newsweek* is the only one that can make it if they come out on the twenty-fourth.

SNAPSHOT: I understand. Now you want that airplane to come into Peking.

WHELIHAN: Into Peking, or if the PRC would like, we would be pleased to have an assist on a courier coming down on a PRC aircraft from Peking to Shanghai, that morning, or the night before.

SNAPSHOT: OK. That's a roger. I understand. We'll bring this up with them.

WHELIHAN: Tim, a couple of other things. Number one, are travelers checks gonna be negotiable over there, or will they have to have cash?

SNAPSHOT: Travelers checks are negotiable.

WHELIHAN: This will be at the normal cashier's window at the hotel, or will there be a special facility?

SNAPSHOT: Yes, there is a special facility at the hotel where you can change money.

WHELIHAN: OK. Tim, do you have a schedule for the dining room at the hotel? Breakfast, lunch and dinner? The hours that they'll be serving?

SNAPSHOT: Yeah, just a second, I can give you exactly. OK, Bruce, breakfast is 7:30 to 9.

WHELIHAN: Mmm, hmmm.

SNAPSHOT: Lunch is 12 to 1:30.

WHELIHAN: Mmm, hmmm.

SNAPSHOT: Dinner is 7 to 8:30.

WHELIHAN: OK, now Tim, can anybody order anything in their rooms? Meals are paid for, so does that mean they have to go to the dining room?

SNAPSHOT: Negative. They can order in their rooms, however, I would discourage it as much as possible.

WHELIHAN: Will they be billed additionally, other than what has already been paid?

SNAPSHOT: No. There's only going to be one flat service charge for everything, and no additional charges.

WHELIHAN: OK. Understand. Next item, you can turn off the request for substitution of writers or broadcasters. Ron said just forget about it.

SNAPSHOT: Thank goodness. [*This was a giant relief to Roadrunner and Snapshot because they were convinced that the PRC would remain firm on their point of principle about changing members of the American party.*]

WHELIHAN: OK. Curious with regards names of party that will be meeting Searchlight when he arrives in Shanghai. When do you anticipate we'll have those names of PRC officials?

SNAPSHOT: I think Ron Walker says right now that we probably won't have it, period.

WHELIHAN: OK. Can you give me a rundown on TV possibilities out of Shanghai?

SNAPSHOT: We're still in a cloudy area regarding TV out of Shanghai. However, I think that we're planning, right now, and the networks are planning, to use courier flights back to Peking for any film or video tape transmission from Shanghai in Hangchou.

WHELIHAN: Now, what difficulties do the networks face, and do we face with regard to telephone communications when this satellite goes up, assuming it goes up? I mean, is it a simple thing for the networks to plug in, or are they going to be up in the air until the twenty-fourth or fifth and wondering if it's gonna work?

SNAPSHOT: I think we're going to be up in the air on the twenty-fourth or fifth, to see if it's gonna work. We've made the request, Bruce, and we're just stuck with that, right now.

WHELIHAN: OK. Tim, the Hangchou Hotel, where is the press room in the hotel?

SNAPSHOT: It's the theater adjacent to the hotel. Uh, oh, hold on a minute . . . our friends have just called us regarding a story that's come out on the wires. Stick with me. [*The Lyons story*]

WHELIHAN: I'm with you. (long pause)

SNAPSHOT: Well, they're aware of the story. They're aware he called last night. We still want to give them a copy, so if you'd send it to us, we'd appreciate it.

Snapshot threw a little temper tantrum when the conference call was over. He was furious about the Lyons story. "That bastard knew exactly what he was doing," he said. "He just scooped everybody else. Why do you think the Chinese didn't stop him?"

"I'm not sure they really understood what he was doing," Roadrunner suggested. "Remember that we asked permission for these guys to talk to their families, and I don't think they scrutinize those men like they do us."

"So, now I'm supposed to have a 'come to Jesus' meeting with him," Snapshot said. "It is my least favorite thing in the world to do. I hate it when I have to discipline my kids. It even breaks my heart when I have to chew out Potus for misbehaving." The Elbourne family basset hound was named Potus, the bureaucratic acronym in government documents for President of the United States.

"I can understand about Potus," Roadrunner sympathized. "That dog always looks sad. Even when you are giving her a cookie she looks like someone just shot her mother. Now Scoshi Walker is another story. When he gets in trouble, he just gives you that 'up yours' look and keeps right on chewing or digging or whatever."

"She's a great old dog," Snapshot said, wistfully. "I miss Potus. Now when you think of it that way, it's not so bad that I'm not going to Hawaii, because Potus would not have been there anyway."

Roadrunner laughed. "You are a piece of work, Snapshot. Thanks for saying that. Now let's go talk to this Lyons character."

CHAPTER XVIII

DATELINE: PEKING

FEBRUARY 15, 1972

Snapshot knew in his heart that he could forgive a hungry reporter's overwhelming, professional urge to jump the fence and scoop all his colleagues. Filing the first story in over twenty years datelined Peking was, after all, exciting stuff. "But Mr. Fred W. Lyon, Jr. was a wire photographer, for God's sake," Snapshot thought angrily. "He should have been concentrating on the photograph destined to be seen around the world." Snapshot became more and more convinced that Lyon must have been acting on orders from a superior. Someone, somewhere, had made the decision to ignore the ground rules established by the White House and the People's Republic of China, and it fell to Snapshot to deal with the problem.

It was 9:30 that evening when he joined the others for the conference call. He had kicked the brass spittoon by the elevator, hoping to relieve some of his tension. It hadn't helped. The throbbing pain in his foot just made him more uptight. He looked at his watch. It was 8:30 in the morning at the White House.

ROADRUNNER: Be advised Schrauth is on from Shanghai. We are still experiencing difficulties from Hangchou and Duval is at a banquet and should be joining us shortly.

DUVAL: Roadrunner?

ROADRUNNER: Wait one. Hangchou, are you on this line?

DUVAL: That's a roger.

ROADRUNNER: OK. Be advised, all three stops are on the air, Watchdog.

WATCHDOG: OK. That's great. How's Vern?

ROADRUNNER: He's sitting right here. He's been resting today and doing some work. I think he feels good this evening. Just a moment, I'll ask him. Yes, he feels fine. (laughter)

WATCHDOG: Is his fever gone?

ROADRUNNER: It's gone this evening, but he had it this morning.

WATCHDOG: OK. Why don't we talk to Duval and find out how we are going to get the schedule from him. I think maybe he's going to have to do it by voice to you.

ROADRUNNER: Yes, OK. Mike go ahead.

DUVAL: (fading in and out) Ron, with the problems we've experienced, this line is the best we've ever had. I think we're better off holding until we have telex capability.

WATCHDOG: I couldn't hear him, Ron.

ROADRUNNER: Roger, they are experiencing difficulties with the equipment in Hangchou. I don't think we'll have telex and we're prepared to do it by voice. He has relayed the room assignments for the hotel.

WATCHDOG: (sigh) Are you going to try to get the schedule from him? And forward that to us?

ROADRUNNER: Yes, sir. Do you have a copy of the scenario I sent for Hangchou?

WATCHDOG: Ron, all we have is Shanghai. We do not have anything on Hangchou or the departure from Peking.

ROADRUNNER: I sent those at least six to eight hours ago.

WATCHDOG: OK, we're checking on that. Why don't you run through what happened there today.

ROADRUNNER: Roger. We stayed in the hotel. The first thing we attacked was the Lyon problem. I called Mr. Chu and told him I would give him a copy once it arrived in Peking. I did so, along with a copy of Mr. Ziegler's briefing. I assured Mr. Chu that Mr. Elbourne and I would take immediate action. We in turn did so. I think it's important that you understand exactly what transpired. So I would like to put Elbourne on first and then I'll tell you what I talked to Lyon about.

SNAPSHOT: Are you with me there?

WATCHDOG: Yeah, go ahead, Timmie.

SNAPSHOT: OK. I immediately asked Mr. Lyon to come to my room. Not having the text at that time, I also brought in Mr. Achatz [*Associated Press photo technician*] because they are both photo technicians. Mr. Lyon [*United Press International photo technician*] told me that he did not know the ground rules and he did not file the story. I knew he filed the story because of the way it was written. I just caught him. I started out trying to be very nice, and then came down about as hard as I could. In fact, as hard as I have come down on anybody in my life. And he walked out visibly upset. Ron can take it from there, but I talked with him for a good thirty minutes. I had a lot of ammunition because I had the details from the briefing they got in Guam. In fact, I had the notes from that briefing and the guidelines were specifically pointed out four different times. So, he just filed the first UPI story, slug lined . . . Peking! Here's Walker.

ROADRUNNER: OK. I talked to Mr. Lyon at great length. I think his attitude is a problem. I did not threaten him with removal, that was never mentioned. Then Mr. Chu called on me this afternoon and the conversation started off with that subject. I assured him that Mr. Elbourne and I had taken corrective measures, and the advisory members of the press corps were extremely concerned, as were the technicians and every member of our party. He told me we had prepared them quite well for this kind of situation, that our press corps is different than theirs. I think he understands that as long as the PRC and the White House are tracking together, that's all they can ask. They understand we are attempting to guarantee that. I feel my relationship has not been hampered, and I feel certain that Elbourne's has not also.

WATCHDOG: OK. Well, if Lyon causes any more problems maybe we will just have to have him removed.

ROADRUNNER: I indicated to Mr. Chu that if he caused additional embarrassment to either of our governments, I would have to ask their assistance in removing him.

WATCHDOG: OK. Was there anything else?

ROADRUNNER: Yes, I will continue. Their guests in the receiving line for the first banquet and the reciprocal banquets will be approximately one hundred people. If you look at our precedence list, the one hundred people runs right smack dab into the press corps. That obviously causes problems. I think it's to our benefit to come up with one hundred people that could be represented in that receiving line. A hundred fifty, I sensed, was too many.

WATCHDOG: Can we handle that by eliminating some of the people from our unofficial party?

ROADRUNNER: Yes, absolutely.

WATCHDOG: Well I'm going to have to spend time on that one. That's a nice little ball you threw this way.

ROADRUNNER: Well, I'm sorry. I tried on many occasions to get numbers. I only received it this evening.

WATCHDOG: Don't be sorry. We'll handle it. I think we'll put in the newspaper/magazine correspondents and commentators and take out all the technical type people.

ROADRUNNER: All right, sir. Be advised, I raised the conversation with Mr. Han Hsu, that the more the merrier. They had even encouraged the cameramen, that once the banquet begins they go to their seats, and when the lights come on for coverage, move to their pool situation. I informed them that this could be extremely disrupting.

WATCHDOG: If you take out the people that would be working, what number would you end up with?

ROADRUNNER: Probably somewhere in the vicinity of 100 and 125.

WATCHDOG: So actually, we are only talking about trying to cut out, maybe twenty to twenty-five people.

ROADRUNNER: Yes sir, I think if we went to the number of 125, they'd be agreeable to that.

WATCHDOG: Well, right now, we don't have a problem

ROADRUNNER: No, I don't think we have a problem. It's just that my concern is, and Elbourne's concern is, we don't want to misrepresent anyone in the press corps, or get in a bind along those lines.

WATCHDOG: OK. Well, but I think maybe we've got a solution here.

ROADRUNNER: Yes, sir, I'm with you.

WATCHDOG: OK. Tim's going to have to get a list from the networks of everybody that would be working, plus we take off the cameramen and documentary crew, and Ollie Atkins, who will be working. And we can take out the agents that are working. I think we'll end up right down there around 120.

ROADRUNNER: OK, why don't you let us work on that with those ground rules in mind.

WATCHDOG: Yeah. Send us a copy of what you end up with, but hit us before you give it to the Chinese. OK?

ROADRUNNER: That's absolutely correct. Just a minute.

SNAPSHOT: Dwight, this is Tim, it wouldn't be out of the ordinary to not have any of the press corps in that receiving line. (silence) Did you copy me at all?

WATCHDOG: Yeah, I'm thinking about it.

SNAPSHOT: Yeah, so am I.

WATCHDOG: In other words we would end up with a receiving line of sixty.

SNAPSHOT: Roger. And that would speed things up. I don't think the wires and pool would cover the receiving line anyway. It is not out of the ordinary for the press not to be in a receiving line in our country, but it would be up to all of you there.

WATCHDOG: Roadrunner?

ROADRUNNER: Yes, Dwight.

WATCHDOG: What else do you have?

ROADRUNNER: OK, the next thing that we talked about was the menu. Do you have a copy of the menu they submitted to us?

WATCHDOG: Yes.

ROADRUNNER: You have the menu, but you do not have the departure ceremony from Peking, or the scenario from Hangchou?

WATCHDOG: Correct.

ROADRUNNER: Well, I sent those before I sent the menu.

WATCHDOG: Well, we just didn't get it, Ron.

ROADRUNNER: Be advised, I am informed that our comm center was clean at 7:00 our time, which would have been 4 A.M. your time. Possibly Henkel could check with both the comm center and the situation room to see if they have it.

WATCHDOG: Julie is checking right now. [*Roadrunner was really getting frustrated that they could never seem to find things.*] Have you been through the schedule yet?

ROADRUNNER: Yes, sir, I've been through the schedule.

WATCHDOG: What's the verdict?

ROADRUNNER: Very good.

WATCHDOG: Any changes?

ROADRUNNER: No. But on the timing at the Great Wall and Ming tombs, I'd like to flag a problem.

WATCHDOG: Lunch?

ROADRUNNER: I anticipate . . .

WATCHDOG: Lunch?

ROADRUNNER: I'm sorry?

WATCHDOG: Lunch?

ROADRUNNER: Possibly.

WATCHDOG: Well, I'd like to resolve this right now. Because we're gonna go to final print here in a few minutes.

ROADRUNNER: Ooooookay. Give me a moment, please.

WATCHDOG: Swift, are you there?

SWIFT: Yes, sir, I'm here.

WATCHDOG: Can you check the time those pieces of traffic were sent to us? We've just checked the comm center and the situation room and we don't have anything pending. Whatever that means.

SWIFT: OK. Will do.

WATCHDOG: Thank you.

ROADRUNNER: OK, we ought to figure on about twenty minutes at the Great Wall.

WATCHDOG: Thirty. I would say thirty, Ron.

ROADRUNNER: Yes, sir.

WATCHDOG: Ten thirty?

ROADRUNNER: Wait one. (To the room: "I have forty-five minutes.") (cough, cough) Yeah, Livingood is verifying forty-five minutes. Last Sunday, it took us forty-five minutes, so we're better off leaving forty-five minutes driving time. Let's make it 11:15 we arrive at the Ming Tombs.

WATCHDOG: OK.

ROADRUNNER: And then you walk to the entrance of the underground palace.

WATCHDOG: I recall. Yes. How long in there?

ROADRUNNER: We can do it in forty-five minutes, very graciously and very easily. We will go down the four flights of stairs, go into the area where the Emperor and the Empress were buried. Look at that. Check the walls. Check the doors. Come back out. We can get out of there in thirty minutes.

WATCHDOG: OK. Now, let's please take it slow. Let's go back to where we have arrived at the entrance to the underground palace. My question was, how long do we have to spend in that little sitting room?

ROADRUNNER: Fifteen minutes. Wait one. Elbourne is pointing out that sitting room is for the press to get pre-positioned inside the underground palace.

WATCHDOG: Just a minute. (To the room: "Bruce, we are not going to hold the President up while the press are pre-positioned.") Uh, Ron?

ROADRUNNER: Yes, sir.

WATCHDOG: Whelihan is asking if we have enough time to move all the press from the Wall to the Underground Palace? If it means splitting the press corps, and pre-positioning people, I'm for doing that. We are not going to hold the President up for an hour and a half while we get the goddamn press in position.

ROADRUNNER: Yes, sir, I have a suggestion on that. We've got fifteen minutes in the holding room, plus another ten minutes while he moves into the museum. So we are talking about almost twenty-five minutes to pre-position those pools. I think that's enough time to work with. Elbourne's shaking his head, no.

WATCHDOG: So is Whelihan. But they're just gonna have to come up with something. It just may be that everybody can't go to the Wall. (pause) You got Chinooks there? [Watchdog was kidding. Chinook is a type of helicopter.]

ROADRUNNER: No, but maybe Vern could work on that and get us some. Oh!

WATCHDOG: (Ha, ha) OK. So to be safe let's say 12:20 they board the motorcade.

ROADRUNNER: OK.

WATCHDOG: And, so around 1:20 they arrive at the guest house.

ROADRUNNER: That's correct.

WATCHDOG: OK. Good. Well, we picked up forty minutes there.

ROADRUNNER: Uh . . . there's a couple of hookers we best be prepared for. Mr. Chu took me from the museum to the stone pagoda. There's a spectacular view of the other Ming Tombs. It is conceivable they will want to take the President and Mrs. Nixon, if it's a nice day, to see the other Ming Tombs in the distance and the mountains, etc. We might be smart to allow for that.

WATCHDOG: Oookay. Sooo . . . I'd like to know what other things you have found in the schedule.

ROADRUNNER: Roger, wait one.

PEKING OPERATOR: That message you are looking for is number twenty-five. It was a teletype message, and it was processed from the comm center in Washington to the sit room at 2020 our time, which was 0720 your time.

WATCHDOG: Morning or last night? [*Watchdog had obviously never served in the military.*]

PEKING OPERATOR: This morning.

WATCHDOG: Thank you. We'll try to find it.

ROADRUNNER: OK. If you haven't found it within the next hour, let me know and we'll do it again. [*Roadrunner wanted to get on with it.*]

WATCHDOG: Redman says it's here.

ROADRUNNER: OK. Thank you, Al.

WATCHDOG: Well, no, he just means he thinks it's here. (laughter) OK. Anything else on the schedule, Ron?

ROADRUNNER: Roger. On the arrival in Peking.

WATCHDOG: Right.

ROADRUNNER: Monday, February 21, 1972.

WATCHDOG: OK.

ROADRUNNER: About halfway down that page, that one note spooks me. (pause)

WATCHDOG: Well, I think that we've got to say that to our people, don't you?

ROADRUNNER: Uhhh, I just have one comment. Is that going to be in their books?

WATCHDOG: Yeah, unless you want it out. Woodcutter [*Kissinger*] is convinced that will happen.

ROADRUNNER: Then leave it in. I hope Woodcutter's right, because we don't have that feeling.

WATCHDOG: I'll bet I have been asked that three hundred times and I've just said that we don't have any indication.

ROADRUNNER: (Roadrunner reads the note to people in the room: "There is a possibility motorcade may stop. All Americans should remain in their cars unless invited out by PRC.") [*This would have been an opportunity for the President to get out and greet the crowd along the motorcade route. As it turned out, there were no crowds in the streets because the Chinese government had not announced the President's arrival time.*]

WATCHDOG: Taylor is saying, that should that transpire, obviously men from the follow-up car would go on foot. [*The Secret Service agents would get out with the President.*]

ROADRUNNER: Well, we know exactly what you meant in regard to everybody else getting out of their cars unless invited to. We understand that.

WATCHDOG: Right. OK. Taylor just wanted to make sure that was understood.

ROADRUNNER: Livingood says he doesn't pay any attention to our notes.

WATCHDOG: Or us to his!

LIVINGOOD: Ha, ha, ha. *Touche!* (laughter)

WATCHDOG: Anything else, Ron?

ROADRUNNER: I raised again Mr. Ziegler's concern that the official White House photographers will move with the pools, but they are not pool people. I have been assured that they understand that. Timmie is still convinced since the PRC does not have official photographers, only government photographers, that is going to cause us some problems. So we'll have to get a feel from our documentary crew when they get in.

WATCHDOG: OK. Be advised, we now have Hangchou and Peking. [*He offered no explanation of where those draft schedules had been hiding.*]

ROADRUNNER: Outstanding. I hope it helps.

WATCHDOG: Thanks.

ROADRUNNER: We are presently setting up facilities to notify people. My feeling is the times in the schedule should stay the same.

WATCHDOG: That's fine. Now, I think we need to give some thought to exactly how we are going to disseminate information, so we don't put out thirty different pieces of paper a day. Maybe we just put out one fact sheet every evening for the following day, but we can figure that out.

ROADRUNNER: Roger. We've given a considerable amount of thought to that and we're in total agreement with you. It should be one fact sheet controlled from one central point.

WATCHDOG: You ought to cover that with your counterpart, because they should know we will do that and they need not worry about it.

ROADRUNNER: Be advised they don't worry about it. All they're looking for is one contact and they expect it to transpire.

WATCHDOG: The key is centralization.

ROADRUNNER: That's correct, sir.

WATCHDOG: OK. Anything else in the schedule? (static)

ROADRUNNER: That's a negative. I have no other comments in regard to the schedule. (static)

WATCHDOG: OK. Schrauth, can you hear me?

SCHRAUTH: (static) Barely, there is a lot of noise on the line, go ahead.

WATCHDOG: I think the noise is Hangchou. Can we cut Hangchou off and tell Duval goodnight? (pause, click) Schrauth, can you hear me now?

SCHRAUTH: That's a roger.

WATCHDOG: How are you doing down there?

SCHRAUTH: We're doing fine. We have all had meetings with our counterparts. This afternoon we attended a gymnastic event. And we will, each day during the holiday, attend a function. Tomorrow evening we go to a ballet. The following evening we go to an acrobatic event. During the day we will be meeting and carrying on our business. Our biggest problem is space. We can put up just under two hundred people in the guest house hotel, so that means we then have air crews and technicians that we're going to have to find space for.

WATCHDOG: OK. Schrauth, on that arrival in Shanghai, we do not know if there will be live television, is that right?

SCHRAUTH: That is correct, I don't have that answer.

SNAPSHOT: Dwight, this is Tim. There will be no live television from Shanghai at anytime. To the United States of America. General Redman is quite aware of this and he can explain it all to you.

WATCHDOG: OK. I did not know that. We'll talk to Redman here. Schrauth?

SCHRAUTH: Yeah.

WATCHDOG: Are there any sneakers that you want me to look at while we're on the phone?

SCHRAUTH: No, I don't think so. In concurrence with Roadrunner's remarks about pre-positioning, the PRC here is in complete agreement on pre-positioning anybody who could be pre-positioned in any of the activities here. Everybody will either not go or they will be pre-positioned.

WATCHDOG: OK. Good. We'll pre-position everybody there that's going.

ROADRUNNER: We've already done it.

WATCHDOG: Roadrunner?

ROADRUNNER: Yes, Dwight.

WATCHDOG: Ron, our cut-off for schedule information to put in the book would be 5:00 your time tomorrow evening.

ROADRUNNER: Roger. I understand.

WATCHDOG: OK. Schrauth, do you have anything else?

SCHRAUTH: Yes, I have one more thing. We do not have our high frequency radio up. There seems to be a misunderstanding as to the agreement. I think it all revolves around the fact the President is going to Peking on the twenty-first and he's not coming here until the twenty-seventh, and our hosts are reluctant to let us put it up at this time.

ROADRUNNER: Roger. Let me zero in tomorrow morning. I'll raise it with my counterpart and I'm sure we can get it resolved very rapidly.

SCHRAUTH: OK.

ROADRUNNER: I also indicated the same thing to Duval. I am assured the problem in Hangchou is simply the capability for those facilities. Let's just wait till tomorrow morning and see how you make out. [*The Chinese were simply overwhelmed at this point.*]

SCHRAUTH: OK.

ROADRUNNER: I also need to talk to you in regard to the courier. The PRC this evening agreed to the courier for Searchlight. If it is necessary, it should be the same tail number, same call signs, same crew members that have previously entered this country. I assured them it would be one of the aircraft that had come in the country before.

WATCHDOG: Thank you. I understand.

ROADRUNNER: All right, the next subject, the press courier. They have approved it in principle, for the twenty-third. It would be one of the Pan American airplanes, again staged on Guam, same call signs, same crew, etc. However, in order to get this approved, they may want this material on board their aircraft to Shanghai, and our aircraft could come from Guam, receive the material and leave Shanghai. They were not keen on having airplanes outside our agreed upon number in country at that time. I think that they will allow us to do that with our aircraft on the twenty-third, but I flag it for your attention and your awareness.

WATCHDOG: OK. Fine. I don't think we can do it with just the plane going to Shanghai unless we had a courier on the flight that the PRC would run from Peking to Shanghai.

ROADRUNNER: I understand that. However, the effort is to get the film out. Otherwise we may not get anything out of here. [*The PRC just did not understand the importance of the movement of this film.*]

WATCHDOG: OK. Ron will agree to that.

ROADRUNNER: Wait one. OK. There's one other thing. They did make the comment that it might be possible to combine that effort on a military aircraft if there is a need for anything to come in for Searchlight. They have agreed to that.

WATCHDOG: OK. Well that, of course, is something we won't know until it happens, and we would only do that based upon a special need for the President. If, by coincidence, it was the same time, that would be fine. Otherwise we would want to go the press plane route.

SNAPSHOT: That's a roger. Dwight, this is Tim.

WATCHDOG: Yeah, Timmie.

SNAPSHOT: I've asked about seven times now. I need a decision on the toasts. Maybe you can help find out how we want to cover them. The PRC has proposed that the toasts on all banquets be capable of feeding live.

WATCHDOG: You don't have an answer on that yet?

SNAPSHOT: Negative!

WATCHDOG: Yeah, I'll ask Ron. I thought it was yes, but I'll have to find out.

SNAPSHOT: Every time I've asked he's been in with the President talking to him about it. (laughter)

WATCHDOG: He doesn't have anything else to do here.

SNAPSHOT: Understand. Neither have we! That's all. I bring it up because you might be able to help expedite.

WATCHDOG: OK.

ROADRUNNER: I'd like to compliment everyone there on the schedule. It's outstanding. Everyone here agrees. We know how much work went into it there.

WATCHDOG: Well, needless to say we appreciate everything, too. Redman needs to talk to Swift, but I think we can sign off. I'll talk to you same time your time tomorrow morning. OK?

ROADRUNNER: Yes, sir. And I'll be available for a few hours if you have any questions about the scenarios you've just received and have not had a chance to go over.

WATCHDOG: OK. Take care.

ROADRUNNER: Roger. Roger. Break. Swift's on.

SWIFT: General?

REDMAN: One thing you might have your people do there is a testing ahead of time. When we have time on the circuit, just run a telecon through to Hawaii. There's no reason why it shouldn't work, but I'd feel better if we ran a few tests.

SWIFT: Yes sir. We run them to Guam all the time so I'm sure they'll work to Hawaii.

REDMAN: That's a roger. Here's one for Walker. Bill Henkel just handed this to me. He needs the background info on Mrs. Nixon's activities in all locations. What they need is a descriptive write up of her activities.

SWIFT: Fine. I'll pass that on.

REDMAN: OK. Swift, do you have anything further for me?

SWIFT: We met with the carriers today, and that went quite well. Except one of our friends brought up the fact that his corporation owed the PRC a certain amount of dollars, and they'd been trying for twenty years to figure out how to pay it and where should they send it? And then one of the other corporations piped up and said, "We owe money, too." About that time I cut them off and said I didn't really think that was what we were here to discuss.

REDMAN: Well, that's absolutely right and I can probably name the people that brought it up, too. OK. I have nothing further here, unless you do. [*RCA was one corporation that had owed the PRC money since before the 1949 revolution.*]

SWIFT: All right, sir, I have nothing further. Would you put Mr. Taylor on?

LIVINGOOD: Hello?

TAYLOR: Livingood, this is Taylor, you read me all right?

LIVINGOOD: Yeah, Bob. Just let me check here. Shanghai, are you still on?

SCHRAUTH: That's a rog.

LIVINGOOD: Oh. OK. Ha, ha, just wanted to check. Uhhhhh. Mmmmmm. Uhhh. Well . . . I'll go ahead. Two things, Bob: number one, the I.D. that was sent. [*Livingood obviously did not want to talk in front of Schrauth, and have the other cities worry.*]

TAYLOR: Yes, go ahead.

LIVINGOOD: Well, they didn't give Hartwig any for his stop, Hangchou, and they didn't give Kaiser any for Shanghai. They have none and I have it all here. We'll mail it if we have to.

TAYLOR: OK, Bill. I've made a note of it.

LIVINGOOD: Sir, the other problem is, he only sent me a hundred. It's not enough. One hundred of the blue ones? The staff ones?

TAYLOR: Yeah.

LIVINGOOD: So, out of that one hundred, I have to give thirty-five to Hangchou and use fifty-five here in Peking. Which is a total of ninety. That gives me ten extra here. Shanghai needs thirty-six. So could you get thirty-six more blue pins, and have Pontius give them to Jenkins when he arrives in Shanghai the day before the visit? [*United States Secret Service agents Ron Pontius and Gary Jenkins*]

TAYLOR: Roger, Bill, thirty-six more blue ones for Shanghai.

LIVINGOOD: For Jenkins in Shanghai . . . Jenkins are you on the line? Jenkins?

JENKINS: Yes, go ahead.

LIVINGOOD: You'll have to meet Pontius's press plane, then, and get them from him.

JENKINS: Fine. I've asked for about ten extra Bill. Might need them on an overnight.

LIVINGOOD: We don't have extra, Gary. We only had a total of about ten extra for the whole trip.

JENKINS: Roger.

TAYLOR: I don't know why we'd need more than that, Gary; we're not adding any people anywhere.

JENKINS: OK. I'll take what I can get.

TAYLOR: We'll see if we can send forty, then, to Jenkins, by way of Pontius, OK?

LIVINGOOD: Yes, sir. If possible. If there's any problem, just let me know.

TAYLOR: OK.

LIVINGOOD: When you issue them at your end, you will need them for everybody on both aircraft, including the crews.

TAYLOR: Roger, Bill. When can we expect instructions to agents for Peking? Can we get that before we leave Washington?

ROADRUNNER: (Ooooh)

LIVINGOOD: Uhhh. Be advised I am going to include the instructions and the itinerary for the first stop at Jenkins' location.

TAYLOR: That's a roger. That will be very good. We know your problems so whenever you can.

LIVINGOOD: We're just waiting for answers.

TAYLOR: That's a roger.

LIVINGOOD: Be advised, it's going to be extremely lengthy because of the six days. It's already twenty-five typewritten pages.

TAYLOR: That's a roger. I understand, Bill, and that's good. The more we can get, the better.

LIVINGOOD: OK. Last thing, on the PRC aircraft, I have you and Zboril with Searchlight. Would you want to change that and put Hudson on there, or just keep Zboril on there? [*The President was going to be traveling on a PRC airplane. Livingood was asking about Secret Service agents Chuck Zboril and Bill Hudson.*]

TAYLOR: Uuuh, I believe it is up to you, Bill. I don't know the whole story. If you see a need, make whatever switch you want, up to and including my position, if you need to travel on that plane.

LIVINGOOD: No, not me. I meant Hudson, since he's with Starlight.

TAYLOR: I understand. Whichever you feel would be best. And again, if you need to be on that airplane, that's all right with me.

LIVINGOOD: No, I don't. Uhhh. Last thing. There is a possibility we might get a control car. Slight possibility. If so, I'd put myself there. That would make us a little bit short on the halfback. [*Halfback is the Secret Service follow-up car.*]

TAYLOR: That's a roger. But, I don't anticipate a problem with that.

LIVINGOOD: There's two solutions. I can throw somebody else in with halfback. Or, I could put Mr. Boggs up in the pilot car with Mr. Walker. [*Lilburn E. "Pat" Boggs, Secret Service Deputy Director*]

TAYLOR: Roger. I think probably you would rather be up there yourself, wouldn't you?

LIVINGOOD: Yes, sir. I think so.

TAYLOR: I think that would be the best, and put Mr. Boggs wherever you think best. If they do have a front car, I think it would be better if you were in it.

LIVINGOOD: OK. Can we put Mr. Boggs in halfback some of the time?

TAYLOR: That would be all right. He'll want to make all the stops, so that's the most convenient way. He's made no requirements on us. That'll be fine.

LIVINGOOD: OK. We'll take care of it. That's all I have. As yet, we've heard no answers. I sent my counterpart a memo instead of seeing him, because of this holiday. I did not think he'd want to come in on a holiday. I didn't want to impose upon him.

TAYLOR: That's a roger. Is that holiday completed there now?

LIVINGOOD: No, sir, it lasts three days, two more days to go. But I think we'll hear. I hope we'll hear.

TAYLOR: Well, we can't do much at this point. We'll just wait until we hear from them. I don't think I have anything else for you. It's late there now, but we'll be available here during our day all day.

LIVINGOOD: OK, Bob. Thank you very much.

MAGUIRE: Is John Thomas there?

LIVINGOOD: Yes, John Thomas is here. Wait one.

MAGUIRE: Roger, thank you.

THOMAS: Hello.

MAGUIRE: Evening, John, Chuck. Do you have anything for me, sir?

THOMAS: Chuck, I have a meeting tomorrow morning, and I will try to be in touch with you, regardless of the hour at your location.

MAGUIRE: Ah, ha! I'm with you. I'll feel much better when we know item number one.

THOMAS: I would, too. I'll pass it to you regardless of the time.

MAGUIRE: What do you suggest? Since it takes them two days to proceed with the bulky one. [*Cash*]

THOMAS: Yeah, right.

MAGUIRE: Do you want me to go ahead and ask them to get it ready? Just in case that's what you are going to ask for?

THOMAS: Chuck, I hate to impose on them to draw that much together. However, it is better to have it and return it, if we don't move that way.

MAGUIRE: OK. Roger. I agree. Uuuhh. If we don't get item one, should I be prepared to have a temporary piece of paper? [*Check*]

THOMAS: Negative. Negative. I talked to Paul Benson today. He is prepared to contact his people, after this meeting we've just been in, and tell them we don't have it. So you're telling me you do not have what you need from Paul Benson? [*Paul Benson of AT&T with an authorization for a wire transfer of funds*]

MAGUIRE: That's absolutely affirmative.

THOMAS: So at the moment, of the three, one needs to be bumped and the others we still need to get. [*The State Department was using three sources for trip money.*]

MAGUIRE: That's a roger. We have approximately fifty percent, if my addition serves me correctly.

THOMAS: Very good. Very good. All right Chuck, I'll call you as soon as I know.

MAGUIRE: You don't want to do any office business tonight, do you?

THOMAS: Got a problem?

MAGUIRE: Not a big one, no. Wanted to pass on to you where we go with the cuts. [*Budget cuts for their State Department office*]

THOMAS: Oh, is that up again?

MAGUIRE: It's up and over and done, your figure is ten percent.

THOMAS: Well, it only took them six months to decide that.

MAGUIRE: Let's hope it takes them another sixteen months to implement it. Ha!

THOMAS: Couldn't agree more. OK, Chuck, anything else?

MAGUIRE: Negative. I do have some things to go over, but we can do that after you get some sleep and I get finished with the schedule. Have a good night's sleep, John.

THOMAS: All right, is Bill Henkel available? Ron would like to talk with him.

MAGUIRE: OK. Bill Henkel's on. Roadrunner, go ahead. Thomas good night. Maguire out.

HENKEL: Yeah, Ron?

ROADRUNNER: Hey, Bill? How are you?

HENKEL: Oh, I'm great.

ROADRUNNER: OK, fine. On the gift thing, I'd like to know what's going on.

HENKEL: OK, Ron. I can be very, very frank with you. I can talk to you about where it is right now and how it got there, but I am not sure what is coming over. Other than the principal gifts, we are replacing the medallion with a lucite block. A very, very pretty and significant memento.

ROADRUNNER: I'm sure it is. I'm only aware of it after John Thomas' arrival.

HENKEL: Uh, roger, Ron. We only went with it a day ago and I apologize. I think Chuck probably talked with Thomas when he was in Guam and the final decision was not made until thirty-six hours ago.

ROADRUNNER: Roger. I request again, a copy of the gift proposals. And I would like to have as much information as you've got on what the gift situation is at this point. The reason is the PRC knows, but we don't.

HENKEL: OK, Ron, my priority right now is this schedule. Then as soon as I'm through, Maguire and I and Dwight Chapin will try to put you up to the exact level where we are right now.

ROADRUNNER: OK. Thank you very much. Snapshot wants to talk to Whelihan.

HENKEL: Righto!

ROADRUNNER: Break. Signal?

SIGNAL: Signal. Flashing?

ROADRUNNER: Signal, this is Ron Walker. Would you please get Bruce Whelihan for Tim Elbourne, please?

SIGNAL: Surely, sir. Just a moment.

ROADRUNNER: Thank you. (ring, ring)

RECEPTIONIST: Office of the Press Secretary.

SNAPSHOT: Hi, can you get me Bruce, please?

RECEPTIONIST: Yes, one moment. (long pause)

WHELIHAN: Hello.

SNAPSHOT: Hi, Bruce. I'll try to make this quick if I can.

WHELIHAN: Let me grab my pad here. I've got some stuff on it somewhere. (papers rustling) Go ahead, Timmie.

SNAPSHOT: OK, Bruce. We're going to need, as soon as we can, the press staff list for various aircraft.

WHELIHAN: All right. Go with what Manning has from Zook unless you hear from me.

SNAPSHOT: (exasperated) He doesn't have anything from Zook that has the press staff list on it. I need that and also the passport numbers of all the press staff.

WHELIHAN: OK.

SNAPSHOT: It's really critical.

WHELIHAN: Understand.

SNAPSHOT: And it can't be "use his list unless we use our list." It's gotta be right the first time.

WHELIHAN: Understand. Will do.

SNAPSHOT: OK. I'm sorry, but I just knew that you would answer if you had a decision on those toasts. This is getting critical now.

WHELIHAN: I thought Ron had come to you on that, Tim, because he sent me out of the room and I thought he had given it to you. That was days . . . two days ago.

SNAPSHOT: Well, maybe he wanted to, but I never got it.

WHELIHAN: Understand . . . You'll have that today.

SNAPSHOT: OK, that's great. Is two hours before arrival for television transmission acceptable to Ron?

WHELIHAN: He said he is going to talk to the networks. Their understanding is they'll be able to feed an hour before, for half an hour. Then the final half hour they'll be able to feed just pictures. That I got from Small. Uhhh, but I'll have to double-check with Ron. He does know that's where it stands now.

SNAPSHOT: OK. I asked them exactly how long we could go full transmission in advance. And they said, "Oh, we're not sure, what would you like?" And I said, "Well, anything within two hours would be great," and they said, "OK. Two hours." So two is now the number.

WHELIHAN: OK.

SNAPSHOT: You also understand it's a psychological problem, in as much as the writing press people will be able to file as soon as they get into the hotel on the twentieth.

WHELIHAN: Understand. Yes.

SNAPSHOT: OK. (pause) The networks have asked for an additional shuttle flight, not a courier flight, on the twenty-sixth and twenty-seventh from Shanghai and Hangchou to Peking. I'm not so sure I should ask for that. On one flight they want twenty-four people and on another flight they want eight people.

WHELIHAN: (eating something) The reason you use the word shuttle instead of courier is because you'll be carrying a number of people rather than one with a container.

SNAPSHOT: Yeah, that's right. This flight goes at a different time from the couriers they've proposed. This is an additional flight on both days to move people back and forth. Let me tell you my gut reaction, this is going to throw these people quite heavily. They are spread thin during this period. I just think it's a heavy request to make.

WHELIHAN: Understand. Let me take it up with the chief.

SNAPSHOT: Roger. What I have proposed is they leave one anchor here in Peking and let him handle it all, with a courier. (pause) They don't buy that, incidentally.

WHELIHAN: Would they be able to file to the transmission center from Shanghai and Hangchou, could they get a voice circuit so they could feed to him?

SNAPSHOT: Don't know that yet.

WHELIHAN: What else you got?

SNAPSHOT: Well, would you relay to Ron, I had a long talk with Mr. Lyon, and . . . you would have been proud of that.

WHELIHAN: Yes, Tim. The point that I made to Ron, was that it's just totally irresponsible journalism.

SNAPSHOT: Well, the problem is, he ain't no journalist.

WHELIHAN: Well, yeah, but the decision I think was made elsewhere with . . . regard to moving that story with that dateline.

SNAPSHOT: I'm sure it was. But, he's a technician. Unbelievable. OK. Thank you very much, Bruce.

WHELIHAN: Two other points. Can we?

SNAPSHOT: Yep.

WHELIHAN: Ron is wondering whether there will be interpreters available in the filing facility?

SNAPSHOT: The filing facility will be manned twenty-four hours a day with interpreters and full facilities for easy flow of information, access, everything. No problem.

WHELIHAN: I understand. Ron is also concerned that the wires have a copy boy. To take copy from the wires for transmission. Is there somebody that can be assigned, specifically to them, that would have a bilingual capability, and assist in arranging for transmission and attend to their needs of that nature?

SNAPSHOT: I can ask them. I will ask the Chinese if they can have somebody like a copy boy, but . . .

WHELIHAN: Will the drivers of the two pool cars be bilingual?

SNAPSHOT: I haven't asked, Bruce. I'll ask. I doubt it.

WHELIHAN: OK. Tim, have you heard any more regarding pictures from the airport? UPI, AP?

SNAPSHOT: Yes. It looks like it's going to be a negative, the way it's sounding. They have a major problem in doing it.

WHELIHAN: I understand completely. Uhhh, clarification, Tim, on the documentary crews not being included in pools. Because you'll note in that memorandum from Chapin regarding the documentary crew, he's moving those guys around quite a bit, and I'm terribly concerned in determining the travel pools, where those guys are going to go.

SNAPSHOT: That's right. Ron seems to think they're going to have a car of their own, but I don't think we have that car in the motorcade yet. We are going to have to work on that.

WHELIHAN: OK. Timmie, I understand, I think (ha, ha), but any further clarification you provide will be most welcome here, believe me.

SNAPSHOT: If you understand, you're beautiful. I'm not quite clear.

WHELIHAN: Well, I understand that it's not quite clear, is about all I understand right now, but if we can resolve this further let's do it with all dispatch. The only other thing, a message to Walker passed earlier by Redman with regard to details on Mrs. Nixon's events. It's essential. We have nothing for Mrs. Nixon. You can imagine the pressure here for some details on events she might participate in. She'll be active in sightseeing where the President perhaps may not be. (pause) How garbled was that?

SNAPSHOT: We know what you are talking about, Bruce. You want the color.

WHELIHAN: Exactly.

SNAPSHOT: OK. How long can you hold on that, Bruce?

WHELIHAN: (sigh) Well, we want to lock stuff up as best we can in the next twenty-four to thirty-six hours.

SNAPSHOT: That's why I was suggesting we put this schedule together in Honolulu.

WHELIHAN: Tim, that's understood, but Whaleboat wants to be able to provide some background. As much as he can. For example, yesterday, he gave some indication of the President's sightseeing events. This has not been done for Mrs. Nixon. We hope to be able to do so prior to departure from Hawaii.

SNAPSHOT: OK. I understand. We'll work on that right away, Bruce.

WHELIHAN: That's about all at this point. I'll try to get you a decision on those toasts.

SNAPSHOT: Yeah. I sure need that. Immediately. That's really urgent. Ron Walker wants to talk to you for a minute.

WHELIHAN: OK.

ROADRUNNER: Bruce, how are you?

WHELIHAN: Yes, sir. Very well.

ROADRUNNER: Bruce, be advised we put together what we consider to be a fairly good document for Mrs. Nixon, and have sent that to Washington. Watchdog and Henkel should have copies of that. Do you have that presently in hand?

WHELIHAN: That's a negative. All I have, with regard to Starlight, is in the staff schedule that was sent to you overnight last night.

ROADRUNNER: Well, we have sent a summary on what we propose she do on a daily basis. We are still waiting for decisions from our hosts and am hopeful we can get you an answer during the course of our twelve working hours tomorrow.

WHELIHAN: OK. There is much more emphasis on her activities than we would have anticipated, and right now we're a little short on information, from a press color standpoint.

ROADRUNNER: Believe me, we're very much aware of it. Right now we're going to have eight options for her. Dwight has that.

WHELIHAN: Thank you, sir. Give my best to all there, you are doing a great job.

SNAPSHOT: OK, Bruce, there's one more thing. I've got a feeling the Chinese are going to start asking about pools for Mrs. Nixon. You know, she likes press around her, and likes to talk to them, so we don't use the same measures that we use for the President. I got a feeling, however, that they're going to start asking for pools. [*They wanted as much press as possible to be able to sightsee with Mrs. Nixon. The coverage would show a warm and gracious First Lady and highlight places and people in the PRC.*]

WHELIHAN: I understand and I appreciate being made aware of that.

SNAPSHOT: Oh, Roger. One other request before I get off your ear. I may have to start calling you at night, because questions come up during the day. I hate to do that to you, but if you could take home whatever you're working from, I'd sure appreciate it.

WHELIHAN: Tim, I've been doing that already, anticipating this, and (chuckle) naturally I didn't want to encourage it, but I am prepared. My hours are already long, so by all means knock me out of the rack in the middle of the night. That's no problem at all, we've gotta get the job done. And I'm the one. Now I'll go to Guam to take care of the pool for Whaleboat. If I can time it so my point of exhaustion is when everybody leaves Guam, we'll be in good shape. So I got a long way to go before I'm worn out.

SNAPSHOT: OK, babe!

WHELIHAN: See you later.

SNAPSHOT: Thank you very much, Bruce. We sure do appreciate the hand. I'll tell you!

Good lord, how late was it? Roadrunner had wondered if the conference call would ever end. "Let's order a bucket of *bing* and have a nightcap," Roadrunner suggested to the group.

"I'm really impressed with your language capability," Livingood told him when he recognized *bing* as the Chinese word for ice.

"Yeah, but I still haven't figured out how to order Scotch," Roadrunner said with a chuckle.

"That's because they don't have any," Snapshot teased him. "If the Chinese made Scotch, you would have figured out how to order it by now."

"I bought a bottle of Chinese whiskey in Shanghai," Livingood told them. "Why don't we try it?"

"They make a pretty good pijou. Maybe their whiskey won't be so bad," Snapshot said hopefully.

They agreed to meet in Roadrunner's sitting room, and everyone started to arrive just as the hall attendant was leaving. He had placed five saucers, each with three ice cubes, on the table.

"I ordered a bucket of *bing*, not five saucers with three cubes on each one," Roadrunner yelled at the heater vent when the attendant had left. "I would have ordered fifteen, but I didn't think there would be room on the table."

"Doesn't the kitchen have a big mixing bowl you could use?" Snapshot asked the same heater vent.

Livingood showed them his bottle of whiskey with Chinese characters all over the label. "See, it says whisky in English right here, and down here in tiny letters it says Bottled by China National Cereals, Oils and Foodstuffs Import and Export Corp., Tsingtao, China."

"Ugh! I don't think I want any if it's going to taste like oil and cereal," Snapshot said, wrinkling up his nose.

"I wonder what all the Chinese writing says?" Livingood said as he unscrewed the lid and passed the bottle under everyone's nose.

"It smells like bourbon," Snapshot said.

"Very raw bourbon," Roadrunner added. "They should have named it Early Times or Southern Comfort."

"Maybe they did. We don't know what they call it," Livingood said as he poured some of the brown liquid in everyone's glass.

Snapshot took the bottle from Livingood and pretended to study the label. "The name is "Weeping Willow Beside Babbling Brook Whiskey," he told them. And peering closer, he read, "Chinese

Acupuncture General warns continued consumption may cause weeping and babbling."

"What the hell," Roadrunner laughed as he raised his glass. "That's about the only problem we don't have right now!"

"To the President," said the Americans as they tasted the Chinese whiskey.

*   *   *

"Hey Livingood," Roadrunner said the next morning. "Your Chinese whiskey was just what I needed. I slept like a rock until Bob Siegenthaler woke me up."

"What's up with Siegenthaler?" Livingood asked.

"I guess they had a pretty bad scene in the hotel. A bunch of the technicians got drunk and had a fight. Poor Bob, he was really upset about it."

"Well, damn it, I don't blame him. Those guys ought to know how to behave," Livingood agreed.

"It's just plain stupid," Roadrunner said. "We look so coarse and uncivilized to our hosts. It's also very embarrassing. They are probably telling each other privately that this is the way they expected Americans to behave. Listen, I don't remember coughing once last night. Do you think we can get some more of that stuff?"

It was 7:40 A.M. when Livingood and Roadrunner sat down beside the suitcase satellite. Jergie was already talking to Washington, where it was 6:40 in the evening.

PEKING OPERATOR: Are you going to put Mr. Chapin on?
SIGNAL: No, I'm going to get Mr. Walker on the line first.
PEKING OPERATOR: That's just fine. He said just a minute while he got his notes together.
SIGNAL: OK, no problem. I think it will be better this way. Chapin probably doesn't wanna . . .
PEKING OPERATOR: Doesn't wanna what?
SIGNAL: Be sitting on the line. (Roadrunner smiled at Jergie.)
PEKING OPERATOR: Right. (long wait) (sigh) (long wait)
PEKING OPERATOR: Signal?
SIGNAL: Yes.
PEKING OPERATOR: Mr. Walker's on the line.
SIGNAL: Mr. Walker?
ROADRUNNER: Yes.
SIGNAL: One moment for Mr. Chapin, please sir.
ROADRUNNER: Thank you.

OPERATOR: Gentlemen, per your request this telephone conversation is recorded by the audio visual branch of the White House Communications Agency. Go ahead please.

WATCHDOG: (singing) Good Mooooooorninggggggg.

ROADRUNNER: Hi, Dwight.

WATCHDOG: (chuckle) You awake?

ROADRUNNER: Yes.

WATCHDOG: How are you?

ROADRUNNER: I'm fine, thank you. Everything is just . . . just fine.

WATCHDOG: Well . . . gooooood!

ROADRUNNER: How are you? Have you had a nice day?

WATCHDOG: We've had a wild day today. Trying to get this goddamned stuff untangled. But we're coming along. We're just weak on Hangchou and Shanghai, and you had warned us, so we understand. And . . . I think we're in good shape in Peking. Bill's on the line, too.

HENKEL: Hi, Ron.

ROADRUNNER: Hi, Bill.

WATCHDOG: What did you have for breakfast, cream of wheat? [*The traditional Chinese breakfast was Congee, a gruel that resembles our Cream of Wheat in appearance, but it usually had fish parts and vegetables in it.*]

ROADRUNNER: No. And I haven't gained any weight, but Livingood has gained about eleven pounds.

HENKEL & WATCHDOG: You're kidding!

WATCHDOG: Eleven pounds?

ROADRUNNER: Well, he has really gained weight, I'm not kidding. So has Elbourne, but nothing like Livingood.

WATCHDOG: Hang on a minute, I'll be right back.

HENKEL: Boy! What a horse of a day today's been.

ROADRUNNER: Huh?

HENKEL: What a day this has been, trying to get this thing to bed.

ROADRUNNER: Well, you did get those scenarios and stuff?

HENKEL: Yeah, you gave us a real good outline and we had to put people with it. Motorcades, manifests and stuff like that. I think it looks all right. Peking looks great, and there will probably be changes made along the road, on Hangchou and Shanghai.

WATCHDOG: ("Bill, ah . . .")

ROADRUNNER: Go ahead.

WATCHDOG: ("Bill, one minor thing, Ziegler wants to ride from the Kahala Hilton back to the base on the chopper. Should we call over and tell Chuck that now?") [*Chuck Larsen was the President's Naval Aide*]

HENKEL: ("Didn't he plan to be on that?")
WATCHDOG: ("No, doesn't show on here.")
ROADRUNNER: Sigh.
WATCHDOG: Ron, I'm sorry. We have two other stops besides yours. Ha, ha, ha.
ROADRUNNER: Yes, sir, I've very much aware of that.
WATCHDOG: Now we've got a third. We've got Alaska.
ROADRUNNER: Oh, really?
HENKEL: Yes.
WATCHDOG: Not only that, we're overnighting.
ROADRUNNER: Ohhhhhhhhh! You're kidding?
WATCHDOG: Not only that . . . so are you!   Ha, ha, ha, ha.
ROADRUNNER: Ha, ha, Ha, Ha, HAA, HAAA, HAAAAAA! HAAAAAAA!   OHHHH! Great! Well, that's really nice! [*The thought of American food, an American hotel, ice, leaving China, and heading for home was welcome indeed!*]
WATCHDOG: That's confidential.
ROADRUNNER: Yes, I understand. Whoa!
WATCHDOG: Um, well, I've got a couple of questions. It will only take me a minute.
ROADRUNNER: Please.
WATCHDOG: Someone read, perhaps in the papers here, that some of the ladies in China would wear long dresses to the banquet. [*What an absolutely ridiculous rumor! They wore nothing but Mao jackets and pants. They had not seen one woman in a skirt since they had been in the PRC. In fact, the "fashion triangle," the collar and first two buttons on a blouse, was the only indication that women individually chose what they wore.*]
ROADRUNNER: Oh, my God!
WATCHDOG: Now, Mrs. Nixon was not planning on bringing long dresses, based upon information from us. But, we need to double-check that quick. Like I need to know tomorrow morning. I think something's wrong, but I want you to check.
ROADRUNNER: Yes, I will. You betcha.
WATCHDOG: OK, then, Mitchell resigned today. [*Attorney General John Mitchell*]
ROADRUNNER: He did?
WATCHDOG: To head the campaign.   And Kleindienst was nominated by the President. [*Richard Kleindienst, to become Attorney General*]
ROADRUNNER: Oh, that's great.
WATCHDOG: Ron, on the secure briefcases, like Dr. Kissinger's, when the Spirit of '76 lands, will there be some special care taken to transport those into the guest house?

ROADRUNNER: That is correct. They can leave them on board and we will transport them directly to the guest house and make dissemination there.

WATCHDOG: OK. Well, you're tracking on it. That's fine. That's just exactly how it should be handled. And no one should have to leave the plane carrying something. OK. Good. Has this introduction thing at the Peking airport come back up again?

ROADRUNNER: No, it has not. I put that in writing, Dwight, and have heard nothing else.

WATCHDOG: OK. You're keeping a list of that stuff you haven't gotten answers to?

ROADRUNNER: You betcha!

WATCHDOG: OK. Good. Because by the time I get to Guam I'll be going out of my mind trying to . . .

ROADRUNNER: Yes, I understand that. Right now I understand from Mr. Chu, that the President and Mrs. Nixon will be escorted out of the Spirit of '76, down the ramp, side by side. They will reach the bottom of the steps, the President will be introduced to the Prime Minister by either Director Han Hsu or one of the cabinet officers that will be on board S '76.

WATCHDOG: Yes, I know what you're saying.

ROADRUNNER: Director Han Hsu will move behind, and someone will do the same thing for Mrs. Nixon. Then there will not be personal introductions of everyone coming down. There will be one person standing there that will say, this is the Secretary of State, this is Dr. Kissinger.

WATCHDOG: In Chinese or English?

ROADRUNNER: They'll be saying it in English.

WATCHDOG: There will be a Chinese person saying it?

ROADRUNNER: That is correct.

WATCHDOG: Perfect. OK.

ROADRUNNER: I agree. I talked to Mr. Chu and Mr. Tong. We are hopeful we can talk ceremony at the airport, but I am hopeful that we can just leave it in their hands and make it a very clean, nice ceremony. [*Roadrunner meant short and simple.*] I've got until 5:00 this afternoon to get any information to you before the final print, right?

WATCHDOG: Ha, ha. Yeah. Well, they are saying we can't make any changes now, but I think we can talk them into a few. Maguire's done a fantastic job, I must admit, but he's ha, ha, ha . . . getting to the end of his rope.

ROADRUNNER: Really?

WATCHDOG: No, he just wants to get it done right. You can't knock a guy for that.

ROADRUNNER: No. No, no, you sure can't. What I am doing at this end, is giving them copies. I've just given them tons of this stuff and they've never talked to me about it.

WATCHDOG: Well, I'm going buggy over here trying to weed it out. You put it in over there and then it keeps popping up here.

ROADRUNNER: Yes.

WATCHDOG: But that's OK. I guess we'll just have to suffer. It's just one of those many sacrifices we're making for you over here.

ROADRUNNER: Ha, ha, ha.

WATCHDOG: Did you have any fireworks, or anything for the Chinese holiday?

ROADRUNNER: Yeah, not as much as I suspected. I learned yesterday they stayed here. I never expected to see any of our counterparts, but they stayed here. They worked.

WATCHDOG: Really?

ROADRUNNER: The spring festival is celebrated more in the countryside and families are together. I guess the city does participate, but not so much. We're going for Peking duck tonight, in Peking's oldest restaurant!

WATCHDOG: Oh! Well you know the brother of the owner is the cook at the Peking duck restaurant here, The Empress. [*The Empress Restaurant on Connecticut Avenue, near the Washington Hilton Hotel.*]

ROADRUNNER: Oh, is that right? His name was Fong, wasn't it?

WATCHDOG: Do you think we could get out and go over to that?

ROADRUNNER: Oh, sure! No doubt in my mind.

WATCHDOG: Really? God, I'd like to do that one night.

ROADRUNNER: Well, they feel we have been working so hard with no time for relaxation, so we going in groups with counterparts. Last night the technicians went.

WATCHDOG: Oh! That's very nice!

ROADRUNNER: There will be twenty-six of us, security, and Timmie's people, and the protocol side people.

WATCHDOG: Good. Good.

ROADRUNNER: I have one incident I have to report. Late last night, after the technicians went to this big banquet and I guess they just Mao-taied up the ying yang, they got back and some of them were upstairs playing pool. Three of them got into an argument.

WATCHDOG: Oh . . . (sigh)

ROADRUNNER: And so two of them tried to take one of the guys out. Apparently he was really drunk and causing a scene. They got him on the elevator. Then a guy he had been giving a rough time hauls toward the elevator. They get on the elevator and then they have a fight. With one of the Chinese girls operating the elevator. I have not seen the guy. Siegenthaler came down very late last night and woke me up and told me that I may be hearing about it. It was all in-house. Siegenthaler guarantees me that he has talked to the people and Joe Di Giovanna [*engineer*] has. Siegenthaler said shortly after that, there must have been twenty-five blue coats on the floor, and around the poolroom and everything else. No one was involved as far as the PRC was concerned. The girl in the elevator, I guess, was really shook. But it's taken care of now and I have no intention, unless it's mentioned to me, of bringing the subject up.

WATCHDOG: Those goddamned guys. That just really upsets me. When you have hosts that are being as generous and as gracious as the Chinese have been, it's just very humiliating to this country to have people over there representing us in that fashion. (sigh) Well! I hope you have a good time tonight. That's just too bad. Siegenthaler probably feels worse than anybody.

ROADRUNNER: I'm telling you he does. I've never met a man that I have as much respect for as I have Bob, coming into this and the job he's done. He's had one hell of a job to do also.

WATCHDOG: Yeah.

ROADRUNNER: So, let me give you a couple of other things. The uniforms, the three Aide de Camps to the President will have no problem wearing their uniforms. That's Scowcroft, Coffey, and Brennan. We got our staff pins. Outstanding, aren't they?

WATCHDOG: Yeah!

ROADRUNNER: Just outstanding!

WATCHDOG: I think they're going to keep one for you to have. Ha, ha, ha.

ROADRUNNER: I hope they do, ha, ha. (pause)

HENKEL: Ron, Dwight's talking to Ron Ziegler. On the reciprocal banquet memo you sent to us?

ROADRUNNER: Yes.

HENKEL: But, you didn't say down at the bottom, "no substitutions." No, I'm kidding. [*That's what official White House invitations always said.*]

ROADRUNNER: Ha, I know what you're saying. One other thing. John Thomas brought a box of American flag lapel pins? Are you with me?

HENKEL: Yes.

ROADRUNNER: OK. Everyone on the ground, here, is wearing an American flag in his lapel.

HENKEL: OK. We'll pick up on it. OK. The documentary film crew equipment will be coming in on the press plane. That's 1,750 pounds of equipment. It will have our White House blue strip luggage tags. I just wanted to alert you, that not everything coming off the press plane will be going to the hotel. There will be this pretty big lump of equipment that belongs to the documentary film crew that will have to get to Villa 6.

ROADRUNNER: Right. I'll alert Bob Manning to it here.

HENKEL: Yes. What's getting on in Washington are fourteen cases, and they'll be adding equipment in Hawaii. I can tell you 1,750, that's the gross weight. It will be about nine cubes, total, when they put it all together.

ROADRUNNER: (cough, cough) Boy, you're really picking up on that stuff fast aren't you?

HENKEL: Shit. I got a slide rule. I can tell you about how much you can put in the belly of an aircraft. Not quite, but . . .

ROADRUNNER: Well, maybe one of the documentary film crew could tell me approximately what the cases weigh.

HENKEL: I believe I can give you that right now. The maximum for one will be a 130 pounds.

ROADRUNNER: Great. That's what I wanted. So, it's a two-man operation.

HENKEL: Yeah.

ROADRUNNER: Thank you.

WATCHDOG: Ron?

ROADRUNNER: Yes, sir.

WATCHDOG: I met with this documentary crew today, again, and they're virtually going to film every damn thing that happens. But, talking with them, I came across something that I've come across other places, and that's a need to try to get people to put things into proper perspective.

ROADRUNNER: Yes.

WATCHDOG: In terms of movements, attitudes, and how they should act. It's not like jumping off a plane in Paris and being able to go anywhere you want. And, uh, I think that as key people such as the documentary crew arrive there, a few well chosen words by you may be something you're going to have to try to get across to them.

ROADRUNNER: I understand that. I understand it very well. I think a good idea would be to meet the two press birds and Mr. Hartigan and Mr. Gold. I'll make a point of sitting down with them and having a cup of tea. (cough, cough)

WATCHDOG: OK. Well, I know you are going to be so busy, but, I'll tell you another thing I'm concerned about, besides your coughing, is the press corps.

ROADRUNNER: Yes.

WATCHDOG: And what they have to go through to get in there, in terms of the long flight from Hawaii. All the way through to Shanghai and the time change and their enjoyment on the way . . .

as you can imagine. I think it's extremely important that whatever is planned for that evening is kept to a minimum.

ROADRUNNER: Yes, sir, I understand. I would not be surprised if someone from the Ministry of Information had something planned for the press corps the first evening.

WATCHDOG: Yeah, I understand that. I understand the hospitality and the need to show them around and so forth, but perhaps somebody would want to talk to Mr. Ma or Mr. Han Hsu, or your Mr. Chu or whoever, about keeping it so they get to bed fairly early. The last thing that the People's Republic of China wants is a lot of the press getting sick, after a day or two.

ROADRUNNER: Right.

WATCHDOG: And you know as well as I do that the minute people start losing sleep they lose their resistance and then bang.

ROADRUNNER: That's correct. That's correct. Both Tim and I are extremely concerned. I'm sure that Ron and everybody will do a great job with the press corps en route, but a good example is the three producers that came blowing in here expecting to have this and that and shuttle flights and down to this and over there and look at this. They have not seen one thing. They have not even seen the press center. They have not seen anything. And only last evening were they beginning to realize the things we told them when they arrived. Now they know. Now they understand, and I think we've got three more ambassadors within the press corps operation. Siegenthaler feels the press corps is going to have to talk to their people as they arrive. And there is a genuine effort among everyone here to guarantee those people have the right frame of mind as soon as they get into this country. So, I'm sure it will be done from your end, but I think you will also be relieved to know that there are a number of people here who will be assisting in that effort also.

WATCHDOG: OK. I understand.

HENKEL: One minor thing, Ron. I checked with General Redman about the availability of the little IBM dictating units. He assured me they have the battery operated IBM executive units, but you may want to check . . .

ROADRUNNER: I've already checked. That's affirmative. They will have them.

HENKEL: Great.

WATCHDOG: I had a fairly long talk with the President today and he asked a number of questions. Wanted to know how it was going, and so forth, and I said fine, and that everything was proceeding smoothly and that we were coming along in good shape. He's busy preparing. He's gone to Camp David tonight and is going to work up

there tonight and tomorrow, and then will be back down here
tomorrow afternoon. And then we leave!
ROADRUNNER: I know it, it's right on top of you.
WATCHDOG: Can you believe how fast it's gone?
ROADRUNNER: It really has gone. [*Roadrunner chose not to repeat
"fast."*]
WATCHDOG: Has it gone fast over there?
ROADRUNNER: There have been some days that have been very,
very long. But for the most part, it's hard to believe that we've been
here in excess of two weeks.
WATCHDOG: Yeah, I know it. Listen, what do you think they are
going to have at the first banquet? Is it what I think?
ROADRUNNER: Yes. [*Peking duck is what Watchdog hoped they
would have, but Roadrunner thought it would be more like Goldfish in
Champagne, Eel Surprise, or some other typically outrageous thing the
Chinese delighted in serving.*]
WATCHDOG: OK. Good. Great!
ROADRUNNER: I am not aware of what entertainment they will
have, if any, and I am not aware of what entertainment we will have,
if any. [*As it turned out, Chinese musicians played "Home on the
Range" and other such selections.*]
ROADRUNNER: Uh, I have a humorous sidelight. Remember the
recommendation that Duval and Steve came up with about in-country
personnel putting together something? Well, I want to tell you right
now, we've got a pretty swinging group here. I guess they've been
having some pretty wild jam sessions. I haven't been able to attend
any of them, but they've really been having fun. Those technicians
have done a very, very fine job. They have made many friends, and
there has been an exchange of gifts, pool producer pins with the two
flags. They also brought in some books. They are very amazed at
the ability and knowledge of the PRC. They just did not have the
practical experience, but they certainly have the technical knowledge.
[*For each piece of equipment the Americans brought in, the Chinese
requested copies of the operating manuals, which they translated into
Chinese for their technicians to study.*]
WATCHDOG: Right.
ROADRUNNER: So I think it's been a good two-way street, because
maybe the technicians on our side had forgotten the theory and
they've had to go back to a manual on numerous occasions to catch
up with their counterparts.
WATCHDOG: One thing I am going to want to talk about. When
we will have time to hold a meeting? It seems to me that we ought
to group with our top people and get a lock on where we stand as of
that moment.

ROADRUNNER: Yes, sir.

WATCHDOG: And so I will take your signal on that. The other thing is . . .

ROADRUNNER: (cough, cough) We will be prepared. To change the subject quickly. On the Mrs. Nixon stuff that Bruce wants, we did a summary page, after we did all the surveys here, of Mrs. Nixon and a possible suggested schedule for her.

WATCHDOG: We have that. That's not what he's talking about. He's talking about background information on like, on the . . .

HENKEL: Kitchen.

WATCHDOG: Peking kitchen.

ROADRUNNER: Yes.

WATCHDOG: Or on the Temple of Heavenly Peace.

ROADRUNNER: Uh, huh.

WATCHDOG: Just like we have for Searchlight. Hang on a minute. I'll be right back to you.

ROADRUNNER: Right. Bill, what have you got, sir?

HENKEL: Nothing! Really. My principle thing, the schedule, is behind me. Tomorrow will be checking, rechecking, and double-checking to make sure things happen. With all the aides gone, Brennan has been down in Florida and today he's in Camp David. It's been tough at times. We get used to an aide for a lot of support and now we've picked up those functions.

WATCHDOG: Ummm, Ron?

ROADRUNNER: Yes.

WATCHDOG: Zee just raved with me. I went off the line there for a minute. We have pressure here for details, or an idea of how things may fall together. Do you think that we could get permission for him to do that on background in Hawaii?

ROADRUNNER: (cough) I don't know. I have talked to Mr. Chu and tried to explain what a backgrounder is. They just don't understood what we classify as a backgrounder, but we have laid that groundwork. I will pursue that today. [A "backgrounder" is information provided to help reporters understand the subject matter better, but not for publication.]

WATCHDOG: OK. Good. If you get the chance.

HENKEL: Ron? If we are going to start putting together a piece of paper for Mrs. Nixon for each of her events, do you have anything you can TWX to us? Would there be anything on the concept of the commune? I think that will be the one thing that he will want. Are there any specifics that you have been able to develop?

ROADRUNNER: Yes. I'll get them to you.

WATCHDOG: OK. Good. Yes. That would be very helpful, Ron. Uh, how is Abel doing? Araiza?

ROADRUNNER: They are fine. They have been fighting it ever since they got in and they have good days and they have bad. They've done an awful lot of work in the last couple of days. You know, they're typing for everybody. Livingood's long, lengthy security reports, they've been helping the technicians type reports for the Chinese, and of course all of Timmie's stuff. It's been an awful lot of work for two guys. I've been breaking them off around seven and letting them take a couple of hours before the conference calls, and they've been working after that. But once you get something over here it's tougher than hell to shake it.

WATCHDOG: Well, that's right. Yeah. Now, why don't we let you do some work today?

ROADRUNNER: I will attempt to do so.

WATCHDOG: Ha, ha, ha, Take care.

ROADRUNNER: OK. Nice talking to you.

WATCHDOG: Everybody's fine here. Have you talked to Anne lately?

ROADRUNNER: No, I haven't.

WATCHDOG: Why don't we try to transfer you now?

ROADRUNNER: OK. That would be outstanding.

WATCHDOG: OK. Hang on, I'll . . .

ROADRUNNER: Just a minute. Bill? You're working on that gift memorandum, that's the big thing. Is China starting to build?

HENKEL: Yes, sir. It was the cover story in *Newsweek*, big section. And *Time* magazine accused Clifford Irving of fraud and he admitted it [*a bogus interview with Howard Hughes*], and that story bumped the President's trip to China off the cover, but there is a special supplement section to it. Very, very extensive. Eight, ten pages. Many, many color pictures and photos, et cetera. And it's building.

ROADRUNNER: Oooookay.

HENKEL: The operator is ready to pick up on you, Ron. So we'll be talking to you tonight your time.

ROADRUNNER: Take care. Bye, bye.

HENKEL: Bye.

Roadrunner was connected to his home in suburban Washington and had a nice conversation with his wife and three little girls. The girls were excited about the President's trip, but much more excited about counting the days until their daddy would come home.

After the call, Roadrunner sat down and drafted several pages describing the concept of a Chinese commune for Henkel. He began to read over the notes he had taken on his tour of the commune that Mrs. Nixon would visit. The Chinese guides had provided an excruciatingly detailed account of life at the commune, more than Mrs.

Snapshot at the Chinese commune.

Nixon or any member of the American party would want to know. He read the conclusion of his report:

PERSONAL THOUGHTS: It is inevitable to compare the children with the old people as the representatives of ancient China and the China since liberation. How come the children are so puppet-like and lacking in spontaneity? What does it take to extinguish the twinkle in a tiny tot's eyes? The obedient children are told what to do by the Motherland and they do not question her wisdom in planning their lives. National pride is their only motivator. By comparison, the old people knew life before communism and it was cruel and hard. The peasants had been mistreated and exploited. Now they have freedoms. Not the freedom of choice that is every American's birthright,

but freedom from . . . freedom from starvation, freedom from
sickness, freedom from the cold, and freedom from cruelties.
For these they are everlastingly grateful for the wise and
glorious leadership of Chairman Mao. How can we fault their
exuberance, gratitude, and devotion? We never had our homes
looted by officials or had to try and walk on tiny, bound feet.

Roadrunner finished reading and sat pensively looking around
his room. After a few minutes, he tore up his paper. It wasn't his
place to pass judgement on the Chinese commune. After another
hour of work, he sent a sanitized and considerably shorter version of
the concept of a commune to the White House.

CHAPTER XIX

YOU LOST GENERAL REDMAN?

FEBRUARY 16, 1972

The food at the famous Peking Duck Restaurant was delicious, but the duck was a long time in coming. The Americans and their counterparts were served course after course of vegetables and fish and dumplings and things that were beyond the Americans' ability to identify. Between courses, they toasted each other and the spirit of cooperation and friendship that had developed. The duck itself was the highlight of the evening. Tender shreds of duck, young green onions, delicious plum sauce and feathery, light pancakes to hold it all together. It was Roadrunner's favorite Chinese dish and he savored the delightful combination of tastes.

It was common knowledge that southpaw Snapshot was not exactly an expert with chopsticks. His colleagues, pretending to adopt the Chinese custom of adding delicacies to an honored guest's plate, bombarded him with extra helpings of the slipperiest morsels on the table. Sea slugs, mushrooms, and small noodles were especially entertaining when Snapshot tried to tackle them. Tonight, however, one of the Chinese gentlemen at the table had solved the riddle of Snapshot's difficulties with chopsticks, "You are using the wrong hand," he said. "Put your chopsticks in your right hand and you will have no more trouble!"

313

It was 9:32 P.M. in China when the Americans, full of Peking Duck, got ready to talk to Washington, where it was 8:32 A.M.

OPERATOR: Hangchou is now in conference.
ROADRUNNER: Hi, Mike. Duval?
DUVAL: Hi, Ron. How are you?
SIGNAL: Mr. Chapin is on the circuit now, gentlemen. Go ahead, it is being recorded for you.
ROADRUNNER: Roger. Duval, it's nice to hear your voice and not have it broken and cracking.
DUVAL: Roger, Ron. It's good to hear your voice in any form.
ROADRUNNER: Watchdog, this is Roadrunner.
WATCHDOG: I was just listening to the love conference.
ROADRUNNER: Yes, sir, there's a mutual admiration society among all the people in the People's Republic of China. (laughter)
WATCHDOG: Good evening, how are you?
ROADRUNNER: Just fine, thank you. We have just returned from the famous Peking Duck Restaurant. It is over a hundred years old, and we partook of great duck. It was outstanding. (laughter) [*The restaurant appeared to have been opened just for the Americans.*] Director Han Hsu sends his very, very best to you. He asked that I relay his best regards and he's looking forward to seeing you when you arrive in Peking.
WATCHDOG: OK. Good. Who all is on the line, Ron?
ROADRUNNER: Well, we have Hangchou. Be advised Shanghai had been invited to an opera. They are hopeful of joining shortly. We have Elbourne, Thomas, Gibbons, and Colonel Coffey.
WATCHDOG: OK, well, we have Bill Duncan, Maguire, Henkel, Whelihan, Scowcroft, Redman, Zook, Bull, Julie, and myself. Why don't we get a report from Duval on the situation there and then go to the individuals there with you. Mike, can you hear me?
DUVAL: Ron, tell me what Watchdog wants. I didn't copy that.
WATCHDOG: OK, Ron, I can hear Mike very clearly.
ROADRUNNER: Watchdog would like to get a status and what your day was like.
DUVAL: We had an extremely busy and productive day. First of all, everybody continues to be in excellent health. Our counterparts met, telex is in, and the switchboard is up and ready to plug in. We have no problems on the communications front, except for the quality of the voice line and I think that's purely a technical thing. Jack D'Arcy, Denny Shaw, and I had productive meetings with counterparts. By tomorrow we will have seen every event for Searchlight. Cooperation is excellent. I'm pleased with the development thus far.
WATCHDOG: That's outstanding, Mike. That's great.

DUVAL: Dwight, for your information, we are showing a movie downstairs. All Chinese counterparts are at the movie with our people.

WATCHDOG: OK. What are you watching tonight?

DUVAL: It's a biggie . . . *20,000 Leagues Under the Sea*. (laughter)

WATCHDOG: Good. That's great. We're going to move on to Walker. Are you going to stay on the line?

DUVAL: If we don't develop trouble and have to be dropped again, we'd like to.

WATCHDOG: Roadrunner, why don't you take it from there?

ROADRUNNER: I'd like to turn it over to Vern. He had what I consider to be the most important meeting today.

COFFEY: We were asking whether the American party would be covered in case of an accident on a PRC aircraft. The PRC assured us they were being doubly, triply cautious. Particularly with our President. However, in the event of an accident, they would handle it by the usual Warsaw Convention which deals with liabilities for international carriers. Another point, we can use our C-141 aircraft to move the mobile vans.

WATCHDOG: Good.

COFFEY: OK. The next point, also very vital, is the PRC has confirmed we may have a plane take off after the Premier and the President and land prior to the Premier's plane, both in Shanghai and Hangchou. On this plane will be the press pool Timmie was concerned about and security people. I won't go into technical details, but I am satisfied it is a safe way of doing it.

WATCHDOG: OK. We understand there are two PRC aircraft in the movement. The Prime Minister's and the President's, but it is PRC aircraft.

COFFEY: That's correct. In both cases, the Spirit of '76 will take off first, and in both cases it will land after the Premier's plane.

WATCHDOG: That's just ideal and couldn't be better. Thank you.

COFFEY: OK. They agreed to move 970 at Shanghai terminal for refueling so it would not interfere with Spirit of '76's arrival and coverage taking place with the President.

WATCHDOG: Perfect.

COFFEY: One other point, a courier flight for the press. They wanted to combine this with the one to bring documents for the President. We explained they were two separate requests. The one involving the President was a contingency, with no idea of when it might be used. It might not ever be used. But the request by the press was a hard, firm request for a mission to be flown on the twenty-third. After great discussions, by both myself and Ron, it was dropped and we'll come back to it. We do not have approval for

Pan Am on the twenty-third to take film out. We do have an agreement in principle for a military aircraft from Guam to bring documents for the President.

WATCHDOG: Well, good. We appreciate the government's gesture and we would only use it in an emergency. We will give them ample notification and get it cleared with them . . . as we should.

COFFEY: Right. Roadrunner made all those points. That's all I have, Dwight. Unless someone has some questions, I'll turn it back to Roadrunner.

WATCHDOG: I want to get a reading on getting that film out. What are our chances of having that plane go to Peking and pick up that film?

ROADRUNNER: OK. I sensed concern by the Director of the CAAC in having that Pan Am airplane come in. They are going to have a courier every day from here to Shanghai. I think the clipper aircraft will be allowed to come to Shanghai and the CAAC material off-loaded, escorted, moved to that Pan Am plane and moved back into Guam. It is my gut reaction it will probably go that way.

REDMAN: (To Watchdog: "What about the courier?")

WATCHDOG: (To Redman: "It's something they have.") Ron, the PRC has a daily courier to Shanghai just during the visit, is that it?

ROADRUNNER: That's correct.

WATCHDOG: Good. Thank you. Have we given you the names of the press on the PRC aircraft?

ROADRUNNER: That's a negative.

WATCHDOG: (To Whelihan: "Why can't we get that, Bruce?") I'm putting a little needle in here . . . go ahead.

ROADRUNNER: Thank you. I appreciate that. It would be very helpful. Believe me, I understand the problems the press corps has, but it's putting a great burden on the PRC and me because of what events people will go to. I know it's difficult. We also need the names of the two press people who will ride on 26000 from Peking to Hangchou.

WATCHDOG: We'll give you that when we get the three for the PM's plane.

ROADRUNNER: OK. I don't mean to complain, but there is a great deal of pressure being applied because they have much work to be done. Please. At your earliest convenience.

WATCHDOG: We are really tired of you guys complaining from over there. (laughter)

ROADRUNNER: Ooookay. (laughter)

WATCHDOG: Ron, any word on that long dress?

ROADRUNNER: Yes. I had a very lengthy discussion with my counterpart this afternoon trying to explain long dresses and short dresses . . . when they wear pants. (laughter) I think the ground rules now are exactly the ground rules established all along. I hope to hell I'm right because if I'm not I'm going to be looking for a new job. I'll explain it as it was explained to me, so maybe you'll understand it, ahhh, to the degree that I did. They wear black and that's formal. The shades of color indicate formality or informality, and it will be relatively informal because they don't necessarily have formal dinners. That's exactly the way it was told to me.

WATCHDOG: Are you telling me the President should wear a dark suit to the welcoming banquet?

ROADRUNNER: I would say yes, but I don't think Mrs. Nixon should wear a long dress.

WATCHDOG: Should she wear a dark dress?

ROADRUNNER: Yes.

WATCHDOG: I don't think she will. I think she'll wear a very colorful dress. [*She wore red with black braid trim.*]

ROADRUNNER: Well, she's the First Lady and I've made that very clear. I asked about other heads of state who brought wives, if they've worn long dress and they said, "No." It's always informal.

WATCHDOG: OK. Thank you.

ROADRUNNER: OK. (sigh) Wait one. I have asked once again for the names of the delegation who will meet Searchlight and Starlight in Shanghai. I am told that we will have a meeting tomorrow morning where we will go over many, many details. The scenarios are approved and they are using our times. With the exception of weather conditions, it will transpire that way. So that should be good news.

WATCHDOG: That's fantastic. Sensational.

ROADRUNNER: OK. The next thing is . . . wait one.

WATCHDOG: Ron? Did you get the cigarettes?

ROADRUNNER: Yes, we have the cigarettes. I have a point I'd like to make. There are no Marlboros. The Marlboros are the ones that have the American flag and the Presidential seal. The theme generating here is the American flag. I just think that would be very nice. We also have the matches. I am going to give those to the PRC and they will be put with the champagne and the fruit. Except not in the refrigerator. (laughter)

WATCHDOG: Good thinking!

ROADRUNNER: Thank you. (laughter) I raised "on background," and got absolutely zero. I will bring that up again tomorrow when we talk motorcades. We will talk banquet placing of individuals to include security. On motorcades we will talk communication cars and security and personnel. So needless to say we are looking forward to that meeting tomorrow morning.

WATCHDOG: That's great. That's going to be a very helpful session, and I can imagine that you *are* looking forward to it.

ROADRUNNER: I requested the White House Communications Agency be allowed to use a Red Flag vehicle. Their communications equipment is large, and if Searchlight needs the phone he would be speaking in a car worthy of that conversation, and it would not stand out like a sore thumb in the motorcade. [*Red Flag is the name of the top of the line Chinese-made car.*]

WATCHDOG: OK.

ROADRUNNER: I have received information that Miss Chang, whom you are familiar with, will be Mrs. Nixon's interpreter.

WATCHDOG: Oh! Sensational. That's great.

ROADRUNNER: I knew you'd feel that way. If someone could relay that information to her and that we are very pleased that Miss Chang will be with her.

WATCHDOG: Oh, that's just outstanding. Thank Mr. Han Hsu very much.

ROADRUNNER: Roger. OK, I have a list of who should accompany Searchlight to the Great Wall. It is a very small list, and I have requested an additional trip for members of our party who will not be accompanying the President to the Great Wall. I would like to send you that list and have you give consideration to it.

WATCHDOG: Well, hang on just a minute. Let me just read what we've got here. ("We don't have page numbers yet? Oh!") Hang on a minute. ("To the Wall, To the Wall, To the Wall . . .")

ROADRUNNER: Roger. Duval, are you still monitoring this conversation?

DUVAL: Ron, you were very badly broken. Rather than have you say it again, could you put the essence of that into a message and telex it to me? (laughter in Washington)

ROADRUNNER: Duval. I say again, are you still on?

DUVAL: Oh! Roger, Ron. Thank you very much. I've got a rather detailed message concerning the schedule which I will get out to you this evening.

ROADRUNNER: OK. Thank you very much. [*Roadrunner really wasn't concerned about Hangchou. It was a sightseeing stop for the President, and promised to be almost idyllic after the nitty gritty took place in Peking.*]

WATCHDOG: OK. Back to the wall. OK? We said in a special note, "It may be appropriate to keep the party traveling to the Great Wall small. Arrangements will be made so that during the President's trip to China all members of the American party will have the opportunity to visit the Great Wall. All official party members will go to the Great Wall," . . . meaning with the President. "Other

Miss Chang, interpreter for Mrs. Nixon.

persons to accompany the President will be notified." Then on another page, we say that "the President and Mrs. Nixon, Secretary Rogers, and Dr. Kissinger will proceed along the Wall as one group. Other members of the Official Party will follow several yards behind."

ROADRUNNER: OK. That's fine. That's very, very good.

WATCHDOG: OK. By the way, we got this Mrs. Nixon background stuff. Thank you.

ROADRUNNER: Yes, sir.

WATCHDOG: Go ahead with whatever you have. (To the room: "I think we ought to type on the page numbers.")

ROADRUNNER: OK. That's all I've got right now. Hopefully, we'll have a lot of answers tomorrow. I'll give it to Livingood now, he's had a very significant meeting today also.

WATCHDOG: OK. He should know that Duncan's here.

LIVINGOOD: Hi, Dwight, this is Bill. I had a very good meeting today by Mr. You-song, and I sent the results of that meeting to Mr. Taylor. Bill Duncan should have it there.
WATCHDOG: (Have you seen it?) He hasn't seen the traffic yet.
LIVINGOOD: Hmmmm. It's there. They received it about an hour or two ago. I don't know whether you want me to repeat it over the air or not.
WATCHDOG: OK. It's probably here, we just haven't gone down to pick it up.
LIVINGOOD: Do you want me to give it over the air? It concerned the one question that we've had all along.
WATCHDOG: You might as well go ahead and give it over the air.
LIVINGOOD: OK. I read, "Vice Minister Yu stated that the People's Republic of China insists that President Nixon ride in the armored Red Flag limousine and that the PRC concurs that it is necessary that Mr. Taylor also ride in this vehicle in the rear jump seat, along with the interpreter. Thus providing maximum security for the President from both countries. Period." [*The PRC had not wanted an American limousine or an American security person in the Chinese car. It was their job to provide security for the visiting President.*]
WATCHDOG: Thank you.
LIVINGOOD: The narrow dimensions of the front seat will permit room for only the Presidential driver and Mr. Lee, the Chinese security officer, who is actually accompanying our principal and their principal. Mr. Yu further stated, quote, "This will display cooperation between the two countries." So, we think the question has been settled now. He seemed very happy to get it over with.
WATCHDOG: I'm sure he is!
LIVINGOOD: (nervous chuckle) He was most cooperative and said they gave it a lot of thought and they concurred with us and he was very, very friendly about it.
WATCHDOG: I understand. Mr. Yu has always been friendly in all of our discussions. Let me ask, Bill, that puts four in the back part of the car. Is that right?
LIVINGOOD: Yes, sir, that does. He said this came from his government, not from him. They wanted Mr. Taylor to ride in one of the jump seats, it did not matter left or right, and the interpreter to ride in the other jump seat.
ROADRUNNER: (cough, cough)
WATCHDOG: OK. You know better whether it should be the left or the right one.
LIVINGOOD: Yes, sir. Roger.
WATCHDOG: OK, Bill. Thank you. Go ahead with whatever else you have.

LIVINGOOD: That's mainly it. They talked about cooperation. We are really tracking well, and I am most pleased. This has been a big onus on my back. I've been quite concerned about it, as you know, and I'm just glad it's settled. I'm happy and they're happy. So, I feel much better about it.

WATCHDOG: Great. Good. It's good to hear the enthusiasm. I understand that maybe you should go over and play a little basketball now and then. That Chinese food has taken it's toll on you.

LIVINGOOD: You hear correctly, Dwight. (chuckle) You have some good intelligence here also. (laughter) In all seriousness, I think from our standpoint everything is going very well really. We've got people in liaison at every stop now, and they have asked us to help them and we have agreed. So I am very pleased and I appreciate your cooperation on this back seat thing.

WATCHDOG: OK. Very good, Bill, and thank you. Let's move right along.

ROADRUNNER: Roger. I just received a call, and my meeting has been changed from tomorrow morning to quarter of eleven this evening, in about twenty five minutes. So we should have a lot of answers for you.

WATCHDOG: Please call back, huh?

ROADRUNNER: Yes, sir, It's cutting into my sleep time and my health practices, but I will do so.

WATCHDOG: Well, I think you should quit worrying about that. I'm only kidding.

ROADRUNNER: Yes, sir, I think the trip's approaching the point now that health really won't matter. (laughter)

WATCHDOG: That's contrary to what I'm telling everybody over here!

ROADRUNNER: Oh!

WATCHDOG: By the way, did you and Tim talk to your counterparts about the concern with the press corps and the long journey they make that day and the need to get them in the sack early?

ROADRUNNER: No, sir, we have not. As I am sure you understand, I would like to drop that at an appropriate time, and the appropriate time has not happened yet.

WATCHDOG: OK. I . . . OK.

ROADRUNNER: Major Swift has a point. We'll run through that very quickly and that'll wrap it up for us.

WATCHDOG: OK. Move on. (clunk, clunk)

SWIFT: I met with my counterpart today, General Redman, about the mobile radio operations. He informs me that we may commence mobile radio operations when the President arrives and discontinue when he leaves. I explained we had to test that equipment. He stated this was a matter of security, and the way it was going to be. So, I am going to ask Ron to take this up with his counterpart because it's a hard decision to live with, but that's where it stands at the moment.

REDMAN: That's a roger, Swift, and every effort should be made to have the system completely tested before his arrival. Also, when will we be able to come up on the other voice circuits? The total of five?

SWIFT: Well, that is a good question. I called a special meeting just before the banquet, to ask this question. I explained I was under pressure, which is certainly the truth, due to the inability to effectively telephone the United States. With the people in Peking, Shanghai and Hangchou, all depending on one circuit it had become an intolerable situation. And it was very, very difficult to explain why it took eight and ten hours to get a telephone call through. He said he hoped other circuits would be turned up soon and that's the way he left it.

I hope I have an answer on that tomorrow. I really did make an impassioned plea, because tempers are becoming frayed here with the trouble getting a call through. Some of the principals have complained to me and I don't blame them.

In the meantime I propose that we place a limit of thirty minutes per call. I realize some will run over, but perhaps people would attempt to conduct business within the thirty minutes. If they couldn't, they'd stand in line and wait to continue after that.

REDMAN: Swift, Redman. I don't think that's the answer to the problem. I had every reason to believe when I was there with you, that after the fifteenth, six days before the boss arrived, they would allow us to come up to full capacity. I want you to get with the people that we talked to at that time. It's imperative that we get these other circuits up. Maybe another one in the next day or so, but we should be up to full capacity the day before his arrival.

SWIFT: General, everyone here agrees with you, and certainly I do. This is exactly what we've been telling them. I reminded them that Mr. Chu, himself, on the sixth of February, following our return from the Great Wall, had said that our "other communications" would be commencing operation on the fifteenth. I reminded them that we had looked forward to yesterday, the fifteenth, and nothing happened. And today's the sixteenth and nothing happened today.

I don't know what else I can do, General, except bring this to their attention and ask the other principals to bring it to their counterpart's attention, which Mr. Walker has done. I'm sure he'll do it again in the coming meeting. I don't know what else I can do. These circuits have been tested from our switchboard to your switchboard there in the White House. And then the Chinese just turn them off. Frankly, I don't know where the master switch is.

REDMAN: Swift, Redman, that's a roger. We're fully aware of your problem and that you can do nothing more than you've done, but we've got to continue to make it imperative, and I know you are, to get these circuits up as soon as possible.

SWIFT: Yes, sir, I will certainly continue to do so, and Mr. Walker just asked me to pass on to you that he will make this a matter of principle, personally, in his meeting he will go to in a few minutes.

REDMAN: That's a roger, Swift. Another thing, in reducing the number of radios, we want to give longer messages over pageboy. Rather than a cryptic "call the switchboard" when we know this is impossible, we will actually pass information of much greater length than we normally do over pageboys.

SWIFT: Yes, sir. I didn't get into the length of message over pageboys, but I made this matter one of the key points in the memorandum of mobile radio operation which I presented to them today. I explained these were receivers only. We would make maximum use in order to cut transmissions. I assume that transmissions were the problem, and I explained the pageboys would pass information to people who normally carry a radio. I can assure you, sir, I did make this one of the key points.

OPERATOR: Excuse me, gentlemen, Shanghai is now in conference.

REDMAN: That's a roger, Swift. I think other people have information, so we'll be in touch later.

WATCHDOG: Hang on a minute, please. (To the room: "Anybody here have anything?") How's Vern? Vern, how are you feeling?

LIVINGOOD: Vern says he's feeling fine.

WATCHDOG: He just can't talk, huh? How about his fever?

LIVINGOOD: He has some fever, but it's very minor, and he said he feels fine, don't worry about it.

WATCHDOG: How much weight has he lost, Bill?

LIVINGOOD: He says none, zero.

WATCHDOG: Good.

LIVINGOOD: I've just gained it all.

WATCHDOG: Roadrunner?

ROADRUNNER: Yes, sir?

WATCHDOG: When the news summary comes in, when we get there, it's going to have to be retyped. [*Once in China, the President and his aides would count on the White House news summary to keep informed about the outside world.*] We can't pass along a TWX copy. The question becomes who would retype it? It's going to happen three times a day, at 11 A.M., 3 P.M. and 7 A.M. I just want to know if you have any thoughts on that? My thought is Rose. [*Rose Mary Woods, President Nixon's secretary*]

ROADRUNNER: Well, that's an outstanding thought.

WATCHDOG: Ha, ha, the hell it is!

ROADRUNNER: We can attempt to do it in the Advance Office. It might be necessary to call upon Nell's assistance, but we will attempt to do that with Abel and Collins. Let me ask you a question. Is it going to be the news summaries we are receiving, or is it going to be the full Presidential news summaries we receive in the States?

WATCHDOG: It will be summary, probably five pages, three times a day.

ROADRUNNER: I think we can handle that with no problem. Abel and Mac are doing an outstanding job and I think they can do that. They are extremely good typists, and we'll do it in the Advance Office. Let's plan on that right now.

WATCHDOG: OK. Let's try it. Nell can work on it, too. Now, how many typewriters do you have there? You have enough typewriters, obviously.

ROADRUNNER: We have two.

WATCHDOG: OK. So, for every secretary we should bring a typewriter. OK. We're in business. Do you have anything else, Ron?

ROADRUNNER: I have one thing that concerns me greatly. We received a document through Chapin and Henkel, from Whelihan to Elbourne, regarding biographical background information on various individuals. Have you had a chance to see that document yet? [*The document attempted to describe the careers and backgrounds of the various Chinese officials that they thought would be involved in the visit.*]

WATCHDOG: No. Whelihan's telling me that we'll discuss it.

ROADRUNNER: Well . . . You know me. I'm very relaxed and very confident about everything . . . but boy, you better read that mother! [*His tone of voice got everyone's attention.*] Be advised that I presently have it in the most secure place I can and I would hope that if information like that is going to be disseminated that consideration be given to it.

WATCHDOG: Well, obviously . . . (clears throat) I haven't seen it, Ron. I'll look at it, and I hope it hasn't caused any problems.

ROADRUNNER: No, sir, I'm assured that it hasn't. I'm assured that it hasn't. It came through the secure circuits, unclassified.

WATCHDOG: Well, I'll just have to look at it. When's your meeting?

ROADRUNNER: As soon as I finish this phone call.

WATCHDOG: Well, we wish you all the best of luck at that meeting, and why don't we plan on talking as soon as you get out of it.

ROADRUNNER: That's a roger. I'll call you as soon as I get out.
WATCHDOG: OK. Good luck. Ron, tomorrow morning is a busy day here for us, as you know, because we're departing. We'd like to talk to you at 8:00 tomorrow morning our time, which would be 9:00 P.M. your time.
ROADRUNNER: OK, 9 P.M. That's fine. I understand. No problem whatsoever.
WATCHDOG: Good. Take care. Bye, bye. Thank you. Roadrunner? Just hang on about ten seconds. Ron? Roadrunner?
ROADRUNNER: Yes, sir?
WATCHDOG: In regards to the Whelihan cable. This material had been looked over by HAK's [Kissinger's] people here, and General Haig felt that it should be cleared at your end by your Chinese friends prior to being released here. Now, I am not sure this means Haig has approved each of the biographies. Hang on. No, he hasn't! So, I will go to him now and find out if he sees any problems. You obviously do see problems raising it, is that correct?
ROADRUNNER: Yes, sir, I certainly do. I do not feel I could present that and ask for their permission to release that as biographical background.
WATCHDOG: OK. Just from looking at some of this, I can't believe we would either. It's just ridiculous. [The memo contained highly personal yet speculative information about the Chinese officials, including marital status, schools attended, and positions held. While such information is routinely available about American officials, the Chinese would have considered the release of such information to be a serious invasion of privacy.]
ROADRUNNER: Believe me! I have never made that point before, but I would like to go on record right now. Please!
WATCHDOG: Yeah, I agree. Can we get something, from them maybe, on the individuals that are listed by name? In other words, take the name and ask for their description. You ask if there is biographical information we could give to the press corps.
ROADRUNNER: If that subject comes up this evening and I'm in a position to do so, I will make that suggestion. When is Whaleboat looking to release that information?
WATCHDOG: (To the room: "Prior to arrival.") Well, the answer is, whenever we can have it. All this list is, is a list of people, anticipated that the President or Mrs. Nixon would come in contact with during the visit.
ROADRUNNER: I understand that. I understand that loud and clear. I was not sure whether Woodcutter had received additional information at that end. Because I have had no indication at this end, who the people will be.

WATCHDOG: OK. You just keep that thing wherever you have it, until we get back to you. OK?

ROADRUNNER: Yes, sir, it is in the comm center, and that's the best place it can be.

WATCHDOG: Good night, Roadrunner, and thank you. Bye, bye.

ROADRUNNER: Good night, Watchdog. Good night, Steve Bull. Good night, Bill Duncan. (laughter in Washington) Good night, General Redman.

Roadrunner collected his papers and prepared to go right into his meeting with the Chinese. He asked Livingood to go with him, in case they wanted to talk about motorcades. He told Vern to come along also because they might want to talk about ceremonies and banquets. And then he decided that John Thomas might be a good addition for any other activities that just might happen to turn up on the agenda.

It was well after midnight when Roadrunner called Watchdog back. The time was 11:46 A.M. in Washington.

ROADRUNNER: Washington, this is Roadrunner.

SIGNAL: Roadrunner, Washington. Sir, they are trying to reach Mr. Chapin now.

ROADRUNNER: Roger. Can you give me a status on that, please?

SIGNAL: Yes, sir, he should be there momentarily, sir.

ROADRUNNER: Thank you, thank you. (long pause)

SIGNAL: China, Mr. Henkel is on the line.

ROADRUNNER: (cough, cough) Well . . . *good!* Hi, Bill.

HENKEL: Well, hi, Ron!

ROADRUNNER: How are ya?

HENKEL: Oh, good. I've got in my hot little paws all those manifests for you. I'll take them over to the situation room.

ROADRUNNER: OK. I trust that you realized you did not have Redman from Guam to China?

HENKEL: Yes, at 5 A.M. this morning.

ROADRUNNER: Well, as great a job as you've done . . .

HENKEL: I screwed up.

ROADRUNNER: I could hardly believe you lost General Redman and the Chinese had to tell us. Within fifteen minutes we had lost General Redman and picked up two Bill Smalls.

HENKEL: Heh, heh, well, that's a good trade, isn't it?

ROADRUNNER: Yeah, and we went (cough) . . . to 392, but we lost Redman so that brought us back to 391. Then we had an extra Bill Small and ended up with 390. We were missing somebody.

HENKEL: We played that numbers game here for about forty-eight hours and it was one of the most unbelievable exercises. The stuff spread out all over the floor with the girls on their knees matching people . . . it was a scene. We had 394 at one point and that was scary. But it all worked out.

ROADRUNNER: OK. We just got out of a pretty good meeting. Watchdog is not available, so why don't you go ahead. Have you got Julie in there?

HENKEL: Julie? (Tell her to pick up on 241)

JULIE: Hello.

ROADRUNNER: Hi, Julie. I understand you are going to take a trip! [*Julie Rowe was going to Hawaii!*]

JULIE: Yes! I am!

ROADRUNNER: Well, we are really excited for you. That's great. We'd just like to thank you for all you've done. It's very obvious. Let's go through this stuff quickly, OK?

NELL: Mr. Walker? Hello?

ROADRUNNER: Yes?

NELL: Mr. Chapin's talking to HRH. Should we interrupt, or should we just hold the call for another moment? [*Even a call from the People's Republic of China was not important enough to interrupt the Chief of Staff!*]

HENKEL: I'm on it right now, Nell, so I think we're all right.

ROADRUNNER: Nell?

NELL: Yes?

ROADRUNNER: We've got everything set up for you when you get over here.

NELL: OK, ha, ha.

SNAPSHOT: This is Tim. I can't tell you how much we miss ya!

NELL: Hi, Tim. How are you?

ROADRUNNER: We're fine. Thank you for asking. We're looking forward to seeing you. Take care and tell Dwight I'm on the line with Henkel and he can plug in any time he wants to.

NELL: Thank you very much. Bye.

ROADRUNNER: Bye, bye. OK. Let's start off quickly with Mrs. Nixon's schedule. They have agreed to the schedule that we sent to you on February 11, 1972. I assume you have a copy. Don't you?

HENKEL: Yeah, right now I'm going off my summary schedule, Ron. Which has the . . .

ROADRUNNER: OK. Well, they have approved everything on there. We've got the Peking kitchen, the commune, and the glassware factory. I have scratched the university that we saw this afternoon. It is a dead subject, OK?

HENKEL: OK.

ROADRUNNER: We have three options. One is the Summer Palace, two is the Temple of Heavenly Peace, and three is a shopping tour. We will leave those open, and that pretty well locks her schedule in. Be advised that we are TWXing summary sheets that the PRC has prepared for each of these events and the events she and the President will be going to.

HENKEL: OK. Fine, now Ron, you will appreciate that the book will not reflect these changes, but once we are in Hawaii these changes could be reincorporated.

ROADRUNNER: There are no changes, Bill, that is what I'm telling you. There are no changes to the schedule that we have sent you for Mrs. Nixon.

HENKEL: OK, but you said . . .

ROADRUNNER: The point I'm making is that we are sending you additional briefing material, and you can confirm with Watchdog that the schedule has been agreed to with the three options if she wants to do any of the three options. In addition to that, we know . . .

WELCOME: [White House Chief of Staff Bob Haldeman] Roadrunner?

ROADRUNNER: Yes, sir?

WELCOME: Roadrunner, Roadrunner, this is Welcome.

ROADRUNNER: Yes, sir, Welcome, how are you?

WELCOME: Fine. Cancel everything. [Who said Haldeman had no sense of humor?]

ROADRUNNER: OK, sir. Bye. (Sound of phone being set down and a chair being moved) (laughter in Washington)

WELCOME: How is it going, Ron?

ROADRUNNER: Very fine, sir, we are progressing very nicely. We just got out of a meeting with my counterpart and discussed banquets and motorcades and motorcade assignments . . . in a flexible manner. We have the table assignments for the official party and discussed the banquet at some length, and I feel very good right now.

WELCOME: Great. We're looking forward to seeing you.

ROADRUNNER: Thank you, sir. We're looking forward to having you visit the PRC. I know you will enjoy it.

WELCOME: OK.

WATCHDOG: OK. Go ahead guys, I'm listening.

ROADRUNNER: Right, sir.

WATCHDOG: He's left.

ROADRUNNER: Dwight, I was just recapping for Henkel that the memorandum we sent on February 11 has been agreed to by the PRC. WATCHDOG: Great!

HENKEL: Sounds great.

WATCHDOG: Fantastic, Ron.

ROADRUNNER: OK. The next thing is the table assignments for both banquets will be the same with the flip flopping of the two principals. This is an outstanding suggestion as far as I am concerned. They do want all the press covering the event to be a part of that banquet. They will be in an area that will not be disruptive to the banquet.

WATCHDOG: OK.

ROADRUNNER: The tables will run that red carpet, Dwight, in front of the stage in the main banquet hall. At table number one will be Searchlight, Starlight, the Secretary of State, and Woodcutter. At table number three will be Welcome, Whaleboat, and Scowcroft. At table number three is . . .

WATCHDOG: You just said three. You mean two?

ROADRUNNER: Yes, sir, I'm sorry, two.

WATCHDOG: OK.

ROADRUNNER: At three is Green, Watchdog, and Scali. At four is Buchanan, Strawberry, and Jenkins. At table number five is Holdridge and Lord. They have said that we can place our interpreters at these tables. I have said the PRC interpreters are fine, but we will play it by ear.

WATCHDOG: Well, I may come back to you on that.

ROADRUNNER: Roger, I understand. I have left it open, and I am convinced we will have no problem if we want to insert interpreters into those first five tables. Then, we have spotted minimum security. They have most graciously considered to place the military aides and me, with my counterpart, to work and carry on my business during the course of the evening.

WATCHDOG: That's perfect, Ron. Good. That's just sensational. I'm glad to know, because I have had questions from Searchlight as to who would be at his table, and this is very helpful. Extremely helpful.

ROADRUNNER: OK, the President would be escorted on all occasions by the Prime Minister. I asked about Mrs. Nixon's counterpart, and I was told they would get back on that. Same with the Secretary of State, Woodcutter, and Welcome.

WATCHDOG: Well, I think I know a discrepancy there. That would be the Wall, for example. I was under the impression that the Prime Minister would not be going out there.

ROADRUNNER: That's a correction. You're right.

WATCHDOG: The only exception is the Wall and the Ming Tombs.

ROADRUNNER: That is correct, sir.

WATCHDOG: Do we know who will be with him then?

ROADRUNNER: I do not.

WATCHDOG: OK. Thank you.

ROADRUNNER: Next. Be advised they are going to use their card system. It will be a security pass with car number and villa number. We have a motorcade, and this is what it looks like. It would be Searchlight in car number one. Mrs. Nixon with Miss Chang, Secretary of State and his counterpart, Kissinger and his counterpart. In car number five they have Welcome and Watchdog.

WATCHDOG: Perfect!

ROADRUNNER: I have suggested that the communications car be a Red Flag car. And in that car would be Redman, Swift, and I have asked for Colonel Coffey to be in that car, instead of further back where he is currently assigned.

WATCHDOG: Well, now is that car number six?

ROADRUNNER: Well it would be the communications car. It would not necessarily be car number six. Car number six will have Ziegler and Scowcroft in it. So, between five and six, Welcome and Watchdog, you would have the communications car. Then you have car number six, Ziegler and Scowcroft. Then I have asked that they give consideration to putting in the two press cars. The wire cars with the Chinese and U.S., along with Mr. Elbourne and Mr. Ma. In car number seven is Green and Scali. In car number eight is Buchanan and Jenkins. Car number nine is Woods and Holdridge. Car number ten is Walker and Lord. Car number twelve is Higby and Howe.

WATCHDOG: Twelve?

HENKEL: Whoa, whoa, hey, Ron?

ROADRUNNER: Yes?

HENKEL: Would you go back? Ten was Walker and Lord, eleven?

ROADRUNNER: I'm sorry, eleven is Schrauth and Thomas; twelve is Higby and Howe; thirteen is Coffey and Monzon; fourteen is Gwyer and Pineau; fifteen is Yates and DeSantis. Tkach will be in the follow-up car. Platt and Runkle will be in sixteen, and that's it as far as our principal people staying at the villa is concerned. Anyway, be advised that there will be a PRC delegation in Shanghai for Air Force One with their motorcade assignments. Schrauth will be in Shanghai and will pass out the cards for the people on 970.

WATCHDOG: OK.

ROADRUNNER: Then we got into the arrival ceremony at great length . . . at their request. Be advised they have never had one covered by live television before, and I am convinced that they were soliciting advice so they could come up with a plan. We talked about the clean ramp, about the camera locations and the impact that was going to be felt around the world for this one very great moment. Then we talked about positioning for honors, the movement to the motorcade, with people coming off of the rear of the airplane. How we could most expeditiously move to the motorcade. We spent forty-

ARRIVE - CHINA/SHANGHAI - Continued

MONDAY, FEBRUARY 21, 1972

The President and Mrs. Nixon followed by
Secretary Rogers, Dr. Kissinger, Mr. Haldeman,
and Mr. Ziegler are escorted by a PRC delegation into the main terminal building to sitting
room number 2 where tea and snacks will be
served.

OFFICIAL PARTY INSTRUCTIONS

All other members of the official
party will be escorted by a PRC
delegation into the terminal
building to sitting room number 6
for tea and snacks.

UNOFFICIAL PARTY INSTRUCTIONS

Members of the unofficial party disembark from rear ramp and are met by
a PRC delegation and escorted inside
the terminal to sitting rooms 3 and 4
for tea and snacks.

9:20 a.m.	Passengers on 970 reboard the aircraft.
9:30 a.m.	970 departs Shanghai en route Peking.
	Passengers list is the same as on arrival except for the addition of Mr. Schrauth.

9:40 a.m.   The President and Mrs. Nixon, followed by
Chinese guests and passengers on S '76, board
the aircraft.

NOTE: Mr. Roland is manifested on S '76 from
Shanghai to Peking.

TENTATIVE SCHEDULE   - 24 -

A page from the President's schedule book.

five minutes discussing the arrival, and they will get back to us
tomorrow with a complete plan.

WATCHDOG: That's great, Ron, you guys must really be delighted.

ROADRUNNER: Yes, sir. I would say it was an extremely fine
meeting. I was very, very pleased.

WATCHDOG: Well, as we know, they are so efficient and so
thorough in everything they do. It is really a pleasure to get this
worked out this way.

ARRIVE VIA CHINA/SHANGHAI

MONDAY, FEBRUARY 21, 1972

8:40 a.m.   970 arrives Shanghai.

Upon arrival in Shanghai,
passengers (other than press)
will be advised if they are
to proceed into the terminal
for tea, or remain on board.

9:00 a.m.   S '76 arrives Shanghai.
China Time

(11:00 a.m. The President and Mrs. Nixon disembark from the
Guam Time)   front ramp followed by:
Adv.
M. Schrauth   Secretary Rogers
                   Dr. Kissinger
                   Mr. Haldeman
                   Mr. Ziegler
                   Brig. Gen. Scowcroft
                   Asst. Sec. Green
                   Mr. Chapin
                   Mr. Scali
                   Mr. Buchanan
                   Miss Woods
                   Dir. Jenkins
                   Mr. Holdridge
                   Mr. Lord

SPECIAL NOTE

The members of the official party are
requested to move in protocol order
throughout their visit to China.

The President, Mrs. Nixon and the official
party are met at the base of the ramp by a
PRC delegation (From Peking and Shanghai).

TENTATIVE SCHEDULE   - 23 -

The schedule book contained many minute but important details.

ROADRUNNER: Well, I apologize for one thing. I just wish that we could have done it sooner, but I think it will still all work out nicely. It would be nice to have it in the books, but I hope everybody understands.

WATCHDOG: We do, we do. We are not going to run around telling everybody we've got all of this right now.

ROADRUNNER: I understand that, and I won't tell anybody either.

WATCHDOG: Ha, ha, ha . . . go ahead.

ROADRUNNER: OK. Be advised that I ran into considerable flak regarding the Official White House documentary crew. They suggested we incorporate the White House documentary crew and official photographer with the press corps and move them to the hotel. That was the first thing they hit me with tonight in that meeting. So I went into great detail about why there is no way! These people are White House staff; they can't be part of the pool. We have two staying at the guest house and two staying at the hotel to provide maximum flexibility to you. These people work for the White House, they report to you. I think we are OK now. I went into great detail about how this will be used for the archives. It is our historical record and has been discussed on numerous occasions. At this late date, it's very difficult to comprehend why they would be second-guessing what we have put in writing and discussed at great length. I am hopeful that I was successful in selling that.

WATCHDOG: Good job. Very good.

ROADRUNNER: OK. That's all. I immediately came back and picked up the phone and called you, at your request.

WATCHDOG: Ha, ha, ha.

ROADRUNNER: Wait one, please.

WATCHDOG: Yes, sir.

ROADRUNNER: Able just reminded me, they had many, many notes written in English. Are you reading me?

WATCHDOG: Yeah, go ahead.

ROADRUNNER: I was the only one that could see. They had it written in Chinese and in English. I was trying to be very casual and I did see the documentary crew in the motorcade in about car number twenty-one. Now, that is a long way back. I would like those people to be up closer. Hopefully I can sell it.

WATCHDOG: OK.

ROADRUNNER: Ahhhh. Timmie apparently had a meeting this evening that did not go very well. He has got some problems. He is trying to reach Whaleboat or Whelihan right now.

WATCHDOG: How many circuits do we have?

ROADRUNNER: For filing purposes?

WATCHDOG: No. Right now.

ROADRUNNER: One. I made a very urgent plea at the conclusion of our meeting. The burden it is causing us, only having the one circuit. Now that we have the other two stops up and with our TWX traffic, it was requiring our party to stay up late. Since they are so concerned with our health, as I am and you are, another circuit or two would help greatly.

And I also pointed out they had agreed that after the fifteenth of February we would have these channels up. Mr. Chu said he would take care of it. I'm convinced he will and I'm convinced we will have at least two or three circuits up tomorrow.

They are there. They are ready to go. All you have to do is pull some switch, and I know if Fred Swift knew where that switch was he would be out there on his hands and knees trying to find it.

WATCHDOG: Ha! Well, so Timmie hasn't called Ron yet?

ROADRUNNER: No, sir. I had to stop some TWX traffic just to make this call. That's how tight everything is.

WATCHDOG: Ron? Why don't I call Ziegler and have him get on this call?

ROADRUNNER: That would be outstanding. Timmie would appreciate that very much. He is uptight about it.

WATCHDOG: OK. Just hang on. Bill, make sure they don't go off the line.

HENKEL: I'll stay on. Ron?

ROADRUNNER: . . . just a minute. (To Snapshot: "They are calling Ziegler right now. I told them you had a meeting and you were a little concerned and you were going to call Ziegler. I haven't said a word. You don't want to talk to him? OK.")

WATCHDOG: Ron?

HENKEL: He's still on, Dwight, he just stepped away for a second.

WATCHDOG: Ziegler is on his way to my office. Bill, Haldeman gave me stuff on Hawaii and Guam. Make sure I give it to you after this call is over. OK. Walker? Roadrunner, Watchdog.

HENKEL: He's getting Timmie, I believe.

WATCHDOG: OK, good.

ROADRUNNER: Dwight, my counterpart has just brought their menu for the first banquet. I will TWX it to you. Be advised it is not Peking duck.

WATCHDOG: Roger, thank you.

ROADRUNNER: Also be advised, I have made arrangements for you and others who would like to go to the Peking Duck Restaurant to be able to do so. I know that you will enjoy it. It's outstanding.

WATCHDOG: Great!

WHALEBOAT: Thursday night.

WATCHDOG: I've got Fatboat here with me. No . . . uhh . . .

[*Watchdog loved to mess up people's code names deliberately. Here, he is making fun of Ziegler's code name, "Whaleboat."*]

ROADRUNNER: OK. Timmie is right here. Hi, Ron. Nice to hear your voice. Here is Snapshot.

WHALEBOAT: Hello, gang. What's up?

SNAPSHOT: Well, we just got out of a meeting. The PRC is asking some questions, Ron, that I think we should go over. They are principle-type questions; do you want me to proceed with them?

WHALEBOAT: Yes, go ahead.

SNAPSHOT: OK. Regarding the press corps, they realize that you and Mr. Png-hua had an agreement that reporters would be able to talk with third party people and have totally free movement.

WHALEBOAT: Yes.

SNAPSHOT: They would like our suggestion on the place where these meetings should take place. They think both countries should have a mutual agreement regarding meetings of the press corps with third-country parties, while in Peking. Understand that?

WHALEBOAT: By third-country parties, do you mean third-country press or third-country citizens?

SNAPSHOT: Both.

WHALEBOAT: That gets to the question as to whether or not the PRC has granted approval of third-country press using the press facilities.

SNAPSHOT: Yes, of course. They have. As you suggested, they have granted that approval, and third-country press will be using that facility. Incidentally, they told me this evening that they would give me a list very shortly of the third-country press that would be in-country.

WHALEBOAT: Very good.

SNAPSHOT: I think they were most concerned about whether these meetings should take place at the Hotel of the Nationalities, the press hotel. Should it be at the hotel? Should it be another place? Or should it be at the press center? They want our suggestions, and then they will tell us their decision.

WHALEBOAT: Well, my view, Tim, in reference to third-country press, we don't want to have any formal meeting set-up. Seems to me that any contact the U.S. press corps would have with third-country press should not take place in the hotel, but rather in the Palace of the Nationalities press center.

SNAPSHOT: That's a roger. I understand that. I think what they are suggesting is that third-country parties, not press, but parties, not be milling around and, as they put it, "running around the hotel."

WHALEBOAT: I agree with that.

SNAPSHOT: That's fine. OK.

WHALEBOAT: I think we must be very careful, however, on how that appears. We don't want it to appear that we are isolating the U.S. press corps in any way.

SNAPSHOT: That's exactly right, and they figured out that problem. That brings me into another point which dovetails with this. As a result of Mr. Lyon's story where it said that the technicians must go out of the hotel with interpreters at all times. They tried to make it very clear that we are free to move anywhere in this city we want to. The press corps is. With or without interpreters.

WHALEBOAT: I understand.

SNAPSHOT: However, they have brought interpreters from all over China in order to perform a function so the press corps could achieve what they need to achieve in the short time they have here. However, they didn't want the press corps, as a result of that story, to get the wrong idea that an interpreter was needed everywhere they went.

WHALEBOAT: Tim, you can assure them that I understand this fully. We talked about it when I was there, and I have communicated the point to the press here. In relation to the Lyon story, I was asked about that in a briefing yesterday and stated that was not the case. That the People's Republic of China is cooperating fully. That members of the press could move freely, as we agreed. But that interpreters would be available and the U.S. press corps is very pleased with this arrangement. So you can assure them the U.S. press corps have not developed the wrong impression.

SNAPSHOT: OK. That's a roger. I did assure them of this because I knew that you knew the answer. The technicians here independently decided to request interpreters because they were having difficulty without them. There is virtually nobody in this country that speaks English, and it is very difficult to get around without people speaking English.

WHALEBOAT: We understand fully, and I would point out that reporting on the part of technicians should not take place.

SNAPSHOT: That's a roger. They would understand that. Now, this all dovetails in with where third-country people should be met in the overall impression that the U.S. press would get about the freedom. They don't feel that third-country parties, excluding press, should have meetings with reporters in the press center. They would like to do it somewhere else. And they are asking for our thoughts on this and suggestions. (pause) Now do you understand that perspective that I am talking about?

WHALEBOAT: Yes, I do. . . . Let me get back to you on that, Tim.

SNAPSHOT: I understand, Ron. It was a tough one for me, too. They said, "Well, yes, of course, we just want your suggestions and we will be, of course, guided by your suggestions."

WHALEBOAT: What is your feeling?

SNAPSHOT: Well, my feeling on third-country parties residing in Peking, is that it would probably take place with a reporter on a natural basis. In other words, the reporter would probably just talk with that individual or go to that individual's residence. I don't know if they were too excited about that, though.

WHALEBOAT: You see, my concern is that if we place restrictions on a reporter being able to invite a guest up to his room or being able to meet with a third-country person at a restaurant or the press center, then that may pose some misreading of what the intent is. It's my view that this is not that big of a problem because, if a member of the U.S. press corp meets with a party from a third country, he is not going to want to share that with his colleagues.

SNAPSHOT: That's exactly right. I suggested this wouldn't be a major problem, but I did want to talk to you.

WHALEBOAT: My suggestion would be that we let it occur naturally. If we don't let it occur naturally I think a wrong impression as to the intent of the PRC could develop.

SNAPSHOT: That's right.

WHALEBOAT: Let's face it, the U.S. press corps is going to be so busy covering the activities of the President and Mrs. Nixon and the other activities there that they are not going to have that much time to spend with third-country parties.

SNAPSHOT: That's right, that's right. Everything that we have done here has been guided by the agreement in principle between you and Mr. Png-hua, during your last visit. Of course, we have offered many new proposals that were not covered by the original agreement. You are quite aware of what they are, and they have been most gracious in granting these additional things.

WHALEBOAT: Yes, we appreciate that very much.

SNAPSHOT: Yes, we certainly do. I also asked about a come-back copy of what was filed, and they said they do not do that in China, it has never been their practice and they would not like to set a precedent by doing that.

WHALEBOAT: You see the problem, Tim. The wires have to have their copy flow in a more rapid way than the other specials. I am sure you explained that to them. If two lines could be allocated to the wires and if the liaison man could facilitate the movement of their copy, that may be a solution. The only problem with that is cost. I think it should be pointed out that the wire services will be servicing all of the newspapers that do not accompany the President. Therefore, they will be filing substantially more copy and there is a matter of cost involved in this also.

SNAPSHOT: That's a roger. I have pointed out all of these things and they understand our position totally and completely. The way I pointed out the necessity of the wires having full and open access is that they are servicing virtually every newspaper, magazine, television station, and broadcast media in the United States, and could not be held up by a reporter with one newspaper in one city that has the lines tied up.

WHALEBOAT: That's right!

SNAPSHOT: They assured me this wouldn't happen and they would "move the copy with all due expediency." They said, "You can talk to any correspondent in this country. We do it. We are accurate and precise and we have never needed come-back copies." However, they said they would reconsider it again. The allocation idea is a good one.

WHALEBOAT: Perhaps from the standpoint of principle, an allocation could be made and some adjustment in cost to fit with the volume of copy. In other words, the ten-cent tariff per word would be most unfair to the wire services when you take into consideration the network cost.

SNAPSHOT: Well, the ten cents a word is all the way through to New York—ten cents as opposed to a twenty-eight cent-a-word that is the commercial rate, so they figure that they are breaking even on the copy all the way.

WHALEBOAT: I understand that, but you understand the problem that the wires face from a financial standpoint.

SNAPSHOT: Yes, I do understand that.

WHALEBOAT: It's a big hunk. Do you understand that?

SNAPSHOT: Yes, I understand that, Ron. I understand that. Do you want me to present this on a financial basis?

WHALEBOAT: I think that would be your judgment, but that is certainly one of the problems. I mean, you can figure it out for yourself. Think of the volume of copy that the wires will move versus the volume of copy that the individual newspaper reporter will move. Think of the volume.

SNAPSHOT: I understand that. I understand that.

WHALEBOAT: And then add it. Just calculate it and apply ten to fifteen cents to it. You will see the problem, particularly that UPI faces.

SNAPSHOT: Hold on for a minute, Ron. (To the room: "I'm not going to get into this. The wires are going to make a ton of money on this. You see, the more they pump out of here the more money they get from their subscribers, for Christ sake.") Well, OK. (sigh) I'll try to work it out as best I can, Ron. At least it is still under consideration. I am working on it as best I can.

WHALEBOAT: I understand that.

SNAPSHOT: The photo circuit is another problem. We do have our darkroom situation squared away now. Each wire has a darkroom right in the hotel where their pictures will be processed. They are also considering the leases on those. If they lease on those we will be expected to transmit our own pictures. If we do not have a lease the PRC will transmit the pictures. So you understand how important the lease is there.

WHALEBOAT: Yes.

SNAPSHOT: OK. I would like to go into this RCA situation that was released to the press corps going on the trip. I believe it must have been yesterday. Are you aware of that?

WHALEBOAT: I'm aware of it and so is RCA aware that I'm aware of it.

SNAPSHOT: Well, that's good. If I were you, I would think about hitting somebody over at RCA on the side of the head with a board. The People's Republic of China assured me that they have never said anything like that to RCA. We are going to conduct this filing operation, press-wise, the way we described it. It would be the same way in Shanghai and Hangchou as it is in Peking.

WHALEBOAT: Excellent, Tim. I don't operate in the method of hitting people on the side of the heads with boards, but they are aware of my displeasure.

SNAPSHOT: Well, they went out with something they shouldn't have, and I gave the PRC a copy of the statement and they were very surprised and they don't understand it whatsoever. You know we have not gotten into this situation in Shanghai that RCA has been working with the PRC on. But when they come to the White House press corps going on the trip and unilaterally make an announcement that is false, I think we have a major concern about that.

WHALEBOAT: Yes, we do, and it's been dealt with.

SNAPSHOT: OK, I'm saving the best for last.

WHALEBOAT: Right. That's what I thought.

SNAPSHOT: Ha, ha, ha. They have told us there will be no telephones at any of the airports. They say there are phones inside the airport terminals that are available to the press and they may use them. I'm going to need some help on this one. They said, "Mr. Elbow, you have never talked, specifically, about press telephones at the airport." [The Chinese always pronounced Snapshot's name as "Elbow."]

   And I replied, "No, that was a telecommunications matter, and that has been relayed to the telecommunications people." I also indicated that I had never talked about the specific number of telephones in the press center. I've never talked to them about the specific number of broadcast circuits in the press center. I've never talked to them about the specific number of lease lines. That was done, in very great detail, with General Redman on our last trip here. The telephones, however, at the press center appeared. The broadcast circuits appeared in the transmission center. The broadcast circuits appeared in the press room, but the telephones at the airport didn't appear. There was no answer to that.

WHALEBOAT: Do you have any more good news, Tim?

SNAPSHOT: Nope. (sigh) I'm just giving you some of the scope of the problem.

WHALEBOAT: Are we going to have live capability for the independent radios at the airport?

SNAPSHOT: Along with the telephone lines (nervous chuckle) goes the live capability for the independent radio. Now! Let me say this. They said, "Mr. Elbow, we are very busy right now. The press people are not the only people that are busy, but our telecommunications people are very busy."

Major Swift, of course, tells me that it would take, maybe, an hour and a half for his men to string these lines from the transmission center to the airport. In both locations. At the most. At the most, an hour and a half, and there would be absolutely no problem in doing it. So, I asked Mr. Ma if there was a problem other than a technical problem. He again did not answer. Ron, I'm at a loss of where to go right now or what to do.

WHALEBOAT: Hold on a minute, Tim. (muffled discussion in Washington) Tim, I know you understand the problem, but let me just state it so we both agree on the problem we face. With live television and without the ability of anyone else to file immediately, particularly the wires, we're going to begin the visit on a very sour note with everyone other than television. I don't think it's in the interest of either side to allow that to happen. And I think maybe this should be pointed out if you haven't already pointed it out.

SNAPSHOT: I have pointed that out.

WHALEBOAT: Well, where do you go from here?

SNAPSHOT: Well, I just keep working on it some more. They say it is totally my fault, because I didn't bring these specific points up until about a week ago, and it just didn't give them enough time. Even though General Redman talked to them about it in January and somehow, some things happened and other things didn't. I'm asking you what the problem might be and how I might go about solving it.

WHALEBOAT: Well, it's hard for me to assess what the problem is. I can only emphasize to you the necessity of having this available. Now maybe an alternative would be to use some form of linkage for the wires with Air Force One.

SNAPSHOT: I've already thought of that. That's not an assurance when it's on the ground. Let me work on it, Ron. We had a session tonight that lasted a very long time. I think maybe tomorrow morning we can talk again.

WHALEBOAT: OK.

SNAPSHOT: You understand that?

WHALEBOAT: Yes. Anything else?

SNAPSHOT: I hope you got my concern regarding some of the biographical information that Bruce sent here.

WHALEBOAT: Yes, we are well aware of that. I share the concern.

SNAPSHOT: OK. I think, Ron, that's about all I have right now. If we can get these other two problems squared away, we are in excellent shape. They are cooperating magnificently. They've absolutely been marvelous. They want to ensure that the trip goes in the smoothest possible way.

WHALEBOAT: I understand that and appreciate the cooperation. However, I will again emphasize that it is a matter of principle on the wire service.

SNAPSHOT: They understand that, totally and completely.

WATCHDOG: Tim, Dwight, is Ron there?

SNAPSHOT: Yeah. Ron's here, Dwight.

WATCHDOG: ("Are you done, Ziegler?")

WHALEBOAT: Thanks a lot, Tim.

SNAPSHOT: OK, Ron. Sorry for that . . . ha, ha, that blow, but we're working on it.

WHALEBOAT: Right. Thanks, Timmie.

ROADRUNNER: Watchdog, this is Roadrunner.

WATCHDOG: Yeah . . . hi . . . Road. Uh, listen, what do you have on the books for tomorrow morning?

ROADRUNNER: Well, I've been advised that I will not have any meetings with my counterpart. I plan on working on the manifests for the aircraft. The various events in town. We are attempting to put together a flow chart for every event and every movement, and the housing for every individual in the 391 category.

WATCHDOG: (laugh)

HENKEL: Amen.

ROADRUNNER: I think that will take, well, at least an hour or so.

HENKEL: (laugh)

WATCHDOG: Well, Ron, what I'm coming to is, I think it's ridiculous for us to talk at 7:30 your time tomorrow morning. You ought to sleep in, so why don't you call us around ten. Which will be 9:00 tonight our time. And Bill and I can take it from our homes, hopefully.

ROADRUNNER: Well, fine sir, that's fine. Be advised, if I don't get a call from you, I get a call from someone else. So, it's kind of academic really, I think it's a war of nerves. [*The Chinese continued to wake him up several times during the night with questions that needed immediate answers.*]

WATCHDOG: Well, why don't you tell the board not to give you any calls until ten o'clock!

ROADRUNNER: I can do that with the board very easily, but be advised my hotel phone still works.

WATCHDOG: Oh! Ha, ha, ha.

HENKEL: (laughter)

ROADRUNNER: I have two phones in my room. I have a White House phone and a PRC hotel phone.

WATCHDOG: Ha, ha, ha. Well, OK.

ROADRUNNER: One thing that is extremely important. John Thomas met with Mr. Lee about the bank that has been recommended. In the event that it requires cash, there's going to have to be some pretty fast movement on that end. Or it may have to catch up with you either in Hawaii or Guam.

WATCHDOG: I don't know what you are talking about. In other words, more?

ROADRUNNER: Yes, sir.

HENKEL: OK.

ROADRUNNER: That's all I've got. Good talking to you. I had a good meeting. I'm sorry Timmie's went so bad. I don't know that it is *that* bad, I think it may be a feeler.

WATCHDOG: OK, Ron. Well, go to bed, and thank you very much. We're happy you made so much progress.

ROADRUNNER: Roger. Goodnight and you have a pleasant day.

WATCHDOG: Thank you. Thanks for the work!

ROADRUNNER: Bye, bye.

Roadrunner stood up and said, "Come on, let's get the gang together for a nightcap. We don't have many more nights to enjoy our own company before the others arrive. Livingood, do you have any more of that Chinese whiskey?"

"I'll order the ice," Snapshot assured them, as the men prepared to head for the sitting room.

"Get some pijou, too. I haven't had time to buy any more whiskey," Livingood said.

This had become a favorite way to end their long days. The hall attendant still insisted on bringing the ice cubes on a saucer, but they were all getting used to it, just like they had gotten used to lots of other things that they could not seem to change. Perhaps it did not really matter. Sort-of-cold Chinese beer was actually pretty tasty. Hell, Roadrunner couldn't even remember what a frosty cold Coors tasted like anymore. After all, he couldn't get "Colorado Kool-aid" in Washington, D.C., either.

CHAPTER XX

We Came In Peace

February 17, 1972

The halls in the West Wing of the White House were a flurry of activity as briefcases and suitcases were lugged up and down the narrow hallways and staircases. Everybody in Washington was excited about joining their fellow White House staffers in China. It was just after eight in the morning when Watchdog paused to talk to Roadrunner. In China it was 9:05 P.M.

WATCHDOG: Good evening, Roadrunner.
ROADRUNNER: Good morning, Watchdog.
WATCHDOG: OK. We need to be fairly quick today because we have a lot going on here. Everybody's moving in with their luggage. The ceremony out on the lawn is going to be on live national television. Things look good. How's everybody feeling there?
ROADRUNNER: Fine, sir. We're all thinking about this evening, as I am sure you are too. I know everybody must be very pleased that it is about to begin and soon will be over. (laughter)
WATCHDOG: Ha, ha, ha, Oooookay.
ROADRUNNER: Let me go ahead quickly and tell you what transpired in my meeting. One of the first things was the banquet. They want all the official party and members of the unofficial party

not on duty to be with the President when he goes through the receiving line and be there for the official photograph. We may have no Americans in that receiving line, have it be only a PRC receiving line. I made that comment and they picked up on it pretty fast, and they'll get back to me and discuss it at much greater length.

WATCHDOG: OK. What I read you as saying is that we take people over early and pre-position them.

ROADRUNNER: That's correct, sir.

WATCHDOG: The President would start up the stairs, and we feed everybody behind in protocol order. At the top of the stairs there would be a greeting by the Prime Minister and the picture would be taken.

ROADRUNNER: Right.

WATCHDOG: So, you would just basically eliminate the line as far as the Americans are concerned.

ROADRUNNER: That's correct.

WATCHDOG: Well, whatever they want to do, obviously. We want to do what's right.

ROADRUNNER: Yes, sir. They want to keep it small. So, the recommendation would have to be either the entire press corps and nobody else, or the remainder of the 235 people, excluding the official and unofficial parties. And I think that's more than they want to put the Prime Minister through and it's certainly more than I think we want to put the President through.

WATCHDOG: We will take the lead from them, whatever they feel is right. I'll wait for . . .

ROADRUNNER: Roger, be advised, with the date approaching, I find myself being an advisor. They are relying on my advice and counsel and how we do it. So I am simply making some suggestions and hoping that they are the right ones. We will have further discussions.

WATCHDOG: You realize that if you are leading them, it's a complete flip-flop in what they originally wanted to do.

ROADRUNNER: Well, it's not by design on my part. I will attempt to continue to help in any capacity that I can. I have not been pushy at all. I don't want you to misunderstand what I am saying.

WATCHDOG: I don't. I understand. I do not misunderstand you. I understand what you're telling me.

ROADRUNNER: Roger. The bios on the principals are, in my opinion, totally out of the question. I have tried nicely to solicit information regarding their principals, their birthplaces, marriage status, family status, educational status, and positions, and I was advised they do not have this information and it is not their custom.

WATCHDOG: Done! Forget it. Right. You're absolutely right. Just drop it.

ROADRUNNER: OK. I brought up the backgrounder in Hawaii, where we would expand on the information Mr. Ziegler has already released to the press. On background. They understand, but apparently there was some agreement between Whaleboat and Mr. Png-hua stating there would be no backgrounder. So I don't know what answer is going to come out of this. I told them Hawaii would be an ideal time to brief on the facilities and arrangements. We also discussed Elbourne talking by land-line to show the clearness of the communications. I asked for an answer soon, realizing you will be in Hawaii soon.

WATCHDOG: OK, Ron. Whatever they can authorize would be very much appreciated.

REDMAN: Dwight, where will they want to set this background briefing up? At the Ilikai?

WATCHDOG: Who is this, please?

REDMAN: This is Redman.

WATCHDOG: Yeah, we'll talk about it after while, Al.

REDMAN: OK. Fine.

ROADRUNNER: OK. Do you want us to approach it the same way we did last time? Do you want us to write something for them to approve?

WATCHDOG: I am a little confused because I have never asked you for anything. Has Ziegler asked Timmie or something?

ROADRUNNER: Uh . . . the other evening when Ziegler came on the line in your office I was asked specifically to approach the PRC in reference to a background in Hawaii. Is Ziegler there?

WATCHDOG: No, and I sure as hell don't remember him saying that. Was it when he was with me?

ROADRUNNER: That's correct, Dwight, I didn't dream this up.

WATCHDOG: I don't remember it. I may have been over at my desk working, because when Ziegler was talking to Tim I wasn't even listening.

SNAPSHOT: ("No way. I heard him.")

WATCHDOG: What's he yelling about?

SNAPSHOT: Dwight, I never heard of this thing until Ron came back from the meeting this afternoon and told me he had brought up the subject of the backgrounder. I was gone. I wasn't here. I didn't know anything about it and never did know anything about it.

WATCHDOG: Well, Roadrunner?

ROADRUNNER: Yes, Dwight.

WATCHDOG: I'll talk with Ziegler about it on the airplane. But, expanding on what we already know Ron would like to be able to do, I would not burn any bridges in your effort. What can be done, can be done and that's fine. Otherwise, I would just leave it at that.

ROADRUNNER: Dwight, (cough, cough) that's a handful and I do not intend pushing it any harder.

WATCHDOG: Well, you're the best judge on that. I mean, you are right there . . . you know what the temperature is. What is the temperature, by the way? Is it cold?

ROADRUNNER: Uhhhhhhhhh . . . yeah, it's cold. VERY! *[Roadrunner thought the cold was more bitter and penetrating than any he had ever experienced.]*

WATCHDOG: Ha, ha, ha, OK, let me . . .

SIGNAL: Excuse me gentlemen, Shanghai is now in conference.

ROADRUNNER: Dwight, why don't we get a status report and then we will let you get ready to depart.

WATCHDOG: OK. And then we'll talk to Schrauth.

ROADRUNNER: Roger, I understand. OK, here we go.

GIBBONS: General Redman, Colonel Gibbons. We have finished installation of the telephones over at the guest house.

ROADRUNNER: (cough, cough)

REDMAN: Gibbons, that's a roger. What about the situation with RCA down at Shanghai? Have they got the monetary side of this thing squared away yet?

GIBBONS: Roger. Hang on for Swift.

SWIFT: Roger. That is squared away. I had a meeting today with my counterparts and I am proposing that all carriers send a wire to their headquarters which will say the same thing. I drafted it, so that everybody in Washington, all four carriers, will be reading from the same sheet of music. Basically, the Chinese said that procedures established for Peking will apply at the other two stops, so all communications within the PRC will be handled the same. I will get an additional circuit to Shanghai at 1200 hours on the nineteenth and the remaining circuits to Hangchou and Shanghai come up on the twenty-third. And that about covers my meeting with my counterparts today.

REDMAN: I have nothing further, Swift or Gibbons, unless you have something for me.

SWIFT: That's a negative. That about wraps up our activities for the day. I will put on Livingood now for Taylor.

LIVINGOOD: Bob, this is Livingood. We are in real fine shape here. I just sent the survey report to you. It should be in Honolulu when you arrive. It's extremely long, about forty typed pages, but we're here six days. We've looked at security at all sites. We think everything is in pretty good shape. The other two stops are moving slowly based on what decisions are made here. That's about all I have.

TAYLOR: Roger, Bill. It sounds like you've done very well. I'm glad I'm going to get that long report. We've got a meeting scheduled with all hands when we arrive in Honolulu. Everything looks good from our people up to your place and so I've got no problems. That's all I have.

LIVINGOOD: Roger, sir. Thank you very much. Here's Colonel Coffey.

COFFEY: I don't have very much. I spent this afternoon at the villas, and I think the biggest thing I accomplished was actually getting Monzon established. As you know, we still have not cemented how meals are going to be accomplished, and we will work out the details on that after Monzon arrives here. [*Zosimo Monzon was the White House steward responsible for the President's meals*] I will call Ron Jackson in Hawaii and give him additional instructions for the personal comfort of the President. I won't mention that over the phone because I don't want to take up the time of the group. That's all that I have.

SCOWCROFT: Vern, I think Ron Jackson is now on his way to Guam.

COFFEY: We'll track him down one way or another. Sir, while we are on the phone I would like to mention one other thing. We do have a problem here with telephones. It's going to be very austere and in many cases we have to bridge telephones. To provide you a phone and our advance office, we need to bridge your phone with that office. We'll have instruments in both rooms and unless you have any objection we'll go ahead and do that.

SCOWCROFT: No, that's no problem, Vern. We know we are all going to have to be austere. Do whatever you have to do to make the communications satisfactory.

COFFEY: Roger. That's all that I have. I'll turn it back to Ron.

SCOWCROFT: That's all I have, Vern. Thanks very much.

WATCHDOG: Next?

ROADRUNNER: OK, is Whelihan there?

WATCHDOG: No, he's out at Andrews getting ready to depart.

ROADRUNNER: (cough, cough)

WATCHDOG: He's getting on the run to Guam.

ROADRUNNER: All right, sir.

WATCHDOG: I've got an idea. We can have WHCA put the President's departure remarks over the satellite so you guys can hear him as he leaves the South Grounds. He's going to say a few words.

ROADRUNNER: We'd love that, as I am sure you can well imagine.

WATCHDOG: OK. We'll get it worked out here. You can work at your end to get it into Shanghai and Hangchou.

ROADRUNNER: Yes, sir. We'll do everything we can to have both those stops be a party to that departure.
WATCHDOG: Well, great! OK. Everybody that was here has left. Taylor just left. Scowcroft has left. Ha, ha, everybody is trying to get out to the airport. So I think we better shove off, and we will pipe the departure to you guys, and we want you to know we're looking forward to seeing you, and we're glad we're on the way.
ROADRUNNER: That's a roger. OK, sir. Have a good trip. We'll be ready for you.
WATCHDOG: OK, now, listen. When I get to Hawaii what time will it be your time?
SCHRAUTH: There is six hours difference, Dwight.
ROADRUNNER: OK. You initiate the call to me at your convenience and I'll be available.
WATCHDOG: Yeah, I'll just throw one in to you when I get there and we'll see what happens.
ROADRUNNER: OK, sir. We're going to have a general meeting tomorrow afternoon. I don't think it will be a normal countdown meeting, but we'll have a go at it. [A "normal" countdown meeting is held the night before an arrival, during which each participant reports on his area of responsibility. Every minute of the visit, from arrival to departure, would be discussed.]
WATCHDOG: OK. Well, good luck and our best and we'll talk to you later.
ROADRUNNER: Dwight, have a good trip.
WATCHDOG: OK. Hang on a minute. Go ahead, Al.
REDMAN: Yeah, they're all set to broadcast this thing live to them. Our people are already working on it.
WATCHDOG: Great! OK, there you go, Ron.
ROADRUNNER: OK. That's outstanding. OK, Al, have a good trip. That's all we've got, sir.
WATCHDOG: OK. So long!
HENKEL: Good luck, Ron!
WATCHDOG: Bill says good luck.
ROADRUNNER: Schrauth, are you still on the line?
SCHRAUTH: Yep.
ROADRUNNER: Be advised that D'Arcy is going to attempt to fly into your location tomorrow night if you have not gotten word on that.
SCHRAUTH: I had not gotten word on that.
ROADRUNNER: OK. Be advised that I have only been able to get my counterpart to focus on Hangchou and Shanghai remotely. Their concern is Peking at this point, and I know that's tough, but both you

and Mike are going to have to understand that. Duval, are you copying me?

SCHRAUTH: Roadrunner, this is Schrauth. I copy and I understand perfectly. I think we're in pretty good shape here anyway.

DUVAL: This is Duval. Can you copy? Schrauth, this is Duval, can you copy me?

SCHRAUTH: Roger, Duval, I copy.

DUVAL: OK, now, be advised that D'Arcy departs here at 12:40 by PRC aircraft to arrive your location at approximately 1:10 or 1:15. Do you copy?

SCHRAUTH: Yes, sir, I copy.

DUVAL: Roger. He's on a commercial PRC flight. [*One American, going off alone on a CAAC flight, gave everyone cause for concern.*]

SCHRAUTH: OK. We'll take care of it.

SIGNAL: This is Washington, let me interrupt just one second please, sir. Peking, are you on the line?

OPERATOR: Peking is on, sir.

Halfway around the world, the advance team listened intently to the President's live television broadcast as he prepared to begin the long journey to China, a journey made possible by their efforts. It was a very exciting moment, and they marveled at the state-of-the-art technology that allowed them to hear their President.

> *Mr. Vice President, Mr. Speaker, Members of the Congress, and members of the Cabinet:*
>
> I want to express my very deep appreciation to all of you who have come here to send us off on this historic mission, and I particularly want to express appreciation to the bipartisan leadership of the House and Senate who are here.
>
> Their presence and the messages that have poured in from all over the country to the White House over the past few days, wishing us well on this trip, I think, underline the statement that I made on July 15, last year, when I announced the visit.
>
> That statement was, as you will recall, that this would be a journey for peace. We, of course, are under no illusions that twenty years of hostility between the People's Republic of China and the United States of America are going to be swept away by one week of talks that we will have there.
>
> But as Premier Chou En-lai said in a toast that he proposed to Dr. Kissinger and the members of the advance group in October, the American people are a great people. The Chinese people are a great people. The fact that they are

separated by a vast ocean and great differences in philosophy should not prevent them from finding common ground.

As we look to the future, we must recognize that the Government of the People's Republic of China and the Government of the United States have had great differences. We will have differences in the future. But what we must do is to find a way to see that we can have differences without being enemies in war. If we can make progress toward that goal on this trip, the world will be a much safer world and the chance particularly for all of those young children over there to grow up in a world of peace will be infinitely greater.

I would simply say in conclusion that if there is a postscript that I hope might be written with regard to this trip, it would be the words on the plaque which was left on the moon by our first astronauts when they landed there: "We came in peace for all mankind."

Thank you and goodby.

Later that night, Roadrunner recorded on his IBM Dictaphone: "We were very fortunate after our conference call that the White House Communications Agency arranged for an NBC voice feed of the President's departure. In the room with me were Elbourne, Manning, Thomas, Rollins, and Colonel Gibbons. We had a tremendous circuit. It was very clear. We had Hangchou and Shanghai plugged into that audio feed. I don't think any of us here in the PRC really had a true feel for what was transpiring in America. Ed Newman and Robert Gorowlski and Richard Valariani just sent goose bumps and chills up and down our spines. Then to hear Barbara Walters and Herb Kaplow and John Chancellor give their impressions of this very historic trip.

"And then to hear the President (Roadrunner's voice cracked as he quoted the President, and no doubt himself as he looked around his hotel room in Peking, The People's Republic of China), 'We came in Peace.'"

CHAPTER XXI

MASSAGING EGOS IN HAWAII

FEBRUARY 18, 1972

It was almost lunch time, 11:20 A.M., when the call came in from Hawaii. Roadrunner's throat hurt and he wished he still had another packet of Lipton's chicken noodle Cup-O'-Soup. He could not face a table full of Chinese food right now, so he settled for a Lipton tea bag dunked in hot Peking water.

WATCHDOG: Roadrunner?
ROADRUNNER: Yes, sir.
WATCHDOG: Ron, good morning.
ROADRUNNER: Good morning, sir.
WATCHDOG: Who do we have on the line there?
ROADRUNNER: We have Hangchou and Shanghai on the line.
WATCHDOG: OK. We have all the counterparts here. My suggestion would be that we get a report from Duval. Then we go and talk to Shanghai and then switch to you and follow up with what is going to happen at the arrival in Peking. Is that OK?
ROADRUNNER: That's fine. Go ahead, Duval.
DUVAL: Roger, Ron. Dwight, we realize your minds are all on Peking. Everything is tracking here very, very well. We have a great

351

deal of new schedule details. And I am feeding it to Ron. And that's all I've got.

WATCHDOG: OK. Any more basketball games?

DUVAL: Roger. The final score, incidentally was 71 to 26. Favor of Secret Service.

WATCHDOG: That's 71 to 26, Secret Service. Thank you.

DUVAL: Over WHCA.

WATCHDOG: (To the room: "Over WHCA. Ha, ha, ha"). OK! Mike, we got the rooming assignments via Ron Walker, and they look good. We will print all that when we get to Peking.

DUVAL: As Ron knows, we found some excellent quarters at the Hangchou airport. Therefore we've been able to put more people in single rooms.

WATCHDOG: OK. That's sensational. That's good. Do you have anything else, Mike?

DUVAL: No, sir.

WATCHDOG: OK. Let's go to Schrauth. Schrauth, do you hear me?

SCHRAUTH: I can hear you fine. How are you?

WATCHDOG: I can hardly hear you. Whelihan, are you on this phone?

WHELIHAN: That's a roger.

WATCHDOG: We're going to take you off, Bruce. We're bleeding bad here. We'll fill you in later.

WHELIHAN: All right. When you get back to Walker and get rid of Schrauth, ring me back.

WATCHDOG: OK. We'll do that. (click, click) Schrauth, can you talk again, please?

SCHRAUTH: They're gone now. How do you read?

WATCHDOG: You're still weak. I think we ought to drop off Hangchou and see if we can get away with having Shanghai and Peking. Mike, do you mind dropping off? (click, click)

PEKING SIGNAL: Hangchou has dropped off, sir.

WATCHDOG: Thank you. OK, try again, Schrauth.

SCHRAUTH: OK. How do you read me now?

WATCHDOG: Very weak, but go ahead. Why don't you take it through from arrival.

SCHRAUTH: OK. We are set on the arrangements, with one exception: the direction of the aircraft when it docks. We are not certain whether the aircraft will be perpendicular or horizontal to the terminal building. Arrival times are set. The PRC are expecting 970 at 8:40 and 26000 at 9 A.M. Searchlight and Starlight will exit the aircraft and be met by a delegation. We do not have the size of the delegation.

Searchlight, Starlight, HAK, Rogers, Haldeman, and Ziegler will move with their PRC counterparts into gate number three of the terminal, up the steps, and into a sitting room where they will spend the forty-five minutes waiting for departure. Snacks and tea will be available. The rest of the official party will go to the right into sitting room number six. The members of the unofficial party will move to two additional sitting rooms where they will have snacks and tea. Any additional American personnel will go to the area where we had brunch and remain there until time for departure.

WATCHDOG: OK. That's fine. Now, the press corps will be outside for that arrival, right?

SCHRAUTH: That is correct.

WATCHDOG: OK, now, will they allow their official photographer and our documentary people to follow the party through gate three and up the steps into the sitting room?

SCHRAUTH: Roger. But the question is whether or not we will have photography inside the sitting room.

WATCHDOG: Of course that's up to our host, but we request just two or three minutes, upon arrival in that sitting room.

SCHRAUTH: Roger.

SNAPSHOT: Dwight, this is Tim. I think there will be no problem. I'm coming to Shanghai this afternoon with Mr. Ma and I'll talk to him on the airplane. I'm fairly confident we'll get an official photo in that room.

WATCHDOG: Great, Tim. That's sensational. OK. Are you going to meet the press there?

SNAPSHOT: Yeah, that's a roger. I'm going to meet the press planes when they come in and go with the press and our host press staff to Peking.

WATCHDOG: OK, thank you. Let's go back to Schrauth.

SCHRAUTH: Yes, sir?

WATCHDOG: Do we have a number for the people that will be on our plane? The Spirit of '76 flying up?

SCHRAUTH: Yes, sir. I have the manifest.

WATCHDOG: No, I mean do we know the number of Chinese?

SCHRAUTH: Negative, but I think we can guesstimate four or five, in addition to their navigator and radio operator.

WATCHDOG: OK. They will be seated in the lounge of the Spirit of '76, and we will escort them to that area. You may want to inform them of that.

SCHRAUTH: Roger.

WATCHDOG: OK. Schrauth, why don't you listen while we run through this Peking part now with Roadrunner?

SCHRAUTH: Roger.

WATCHDOG: OK, Ron.

ROADRUNNER: Do you want to go through the arrival as it's presently indicated in the schedule? Again?

WATCHDOG: Yes. Go ahead, please.

ROADRUNNER: Dwight, I must advise you that I have had no contact, repeat, no contact, in regard to how the specifics of this arrival are going to transpire. I am still guessing.

WATCHDOG: OK.

ROADRUNNER: To the best of my knowledge, and the others here, this is what we think is going to transpire. Elbourne has requested that the door of the Spirit of '76 open precisely at 11:32, repeat 11:32.

WATCHDOG: OK.

ROADRUNNER: As the door opens, there will be two ramps moved up. One to the rear of the Spirit of '76 and one to the front. There are nineteen steps on each ramp. They will be elevated to where the President and Mrs. Nixon step off. They will be escorted down the ramp by a number yet to be determined, riding on 26000, where, to the best of my knowledge, the Prime Minister will greet them, along with who, I don't know. I am informed there will be additional dignitaries, representing the PRC, assembled approximately fifteen yards away from where Searchlight steps onto Peking soil. At that point, it is my best judge that the Director of Protocol Mr. Han Hsu will introduce the President, in English, to each member of the PRC official delegation. There will be another member of the protocol office doing likewise for Starlight, for the Secretary of State and for Dr. Kissinger. The remainder of the official party disembarking will proceed down the same line, without interruption.

The Prime Minister will join the President for honors. They will be standing to a forty-five degree angle, facing the band, so two camera positions can cover the honors. Mrs. Nixon and her counterpart will be to the rear right of the two principals. The remainder of the official party will be moved in position behind them. The others coming off the rear of 26000 will be held near that ramp to view the arrival ceremony.

Once honors has concluded, and be advised I don't know whether the Prime Minister will stand on the right or the left. I have seen two pictures of heads-of-state's arrivals and both are different. At the conclusion of honors, they will proceed down the Honor Guard, representing the Army, Air Force and Navy, a total of three hundred troops. I do not know the composition of the band or the numbers.

I have suggested that about the time the President reaches his motorcade, we move the unofficial party behind the troops to their motorcade. I have been told that the motorcade will pull up to the position where the President and the Prime Minister board. It will be two or three ranks of cars in numerical sequence. The cards [*giving car number*] will be in the side windows as well as in the front windows. Schrauth and I will be there, to help get our people to the right cars. And I'm sure the PRC will have sufficient people there also helping. So, you got a comment?

WATCHDOG: Well, that sounds . . . sounds fine, Ron. I want to make sure I understand. You feel that the first thing we see happen is the President being introduced to the Prime Minister by Mr. Han Hsu and then the President moving over and starting the rest of the line, while the Prime Minister continues to meet the people coming off the plane. Is that right?

ROADRUNNER: No. Negative. Let me say it again. I am told that the Prime Minister will be at the bottom of the ramp. But, as soon as the President reaches the ground, the other members of the PRC delegation move up and form a single line. They will walk that fifteen yards while the President is greeting the Prime Minister.

WATCHDOG: OK.

ROADRUNNER: I think.

WATCHDOG: Right.

ROADRUNNER: Wait one. (To Snapshot: At this point would you like to add anything?) I'm going to let Elbourne comment on camera positions and coverage and let's see if there's any questions.

SNAPSHOT: OK, I'll be at the rear of the aircraft and take the press pool around toward what you see marked on your diagram there as camera stand number one.

WATCHDOG: Tim, can you hold one minute?

SNAPSHOT: Adjacent to it is a writing press area. Camera stand number one is the one from which we will get the live arrival pictures. There is also a camera up on top of the terminal building which will give an overall view of the entire ceremony. It also catches the aircraft taxiing in. There's a live camera on camera stand number three . . . (To the room: "We've already TWXed it. They've got it.") . . . to catch reviewing the troops and the entrance into the cars. In the meantime I will take the press pool back around the aircraft and into their automobiles for the motorcade.

    The camera on top the terminal building will get the motorcade going out of the airport. There's another camera out in front of the airport, Dwight, which will carry the motorcade down that long road from the airport. You know, the one with the trees painted white. Then the next camera is, of course, in Tienanmen Square. That's basically the coverage areas, and I think we'll have it covered, as well as we've ever done.

WATCHDOG: OK. Tim? Tim?

ROADRUNNER: The thing that concerns me is that in the two pictures I've seen, they have their government photographers preceding the principal by ten to fifteen feet. If they attempt to do this, the live television cameras will have people moving in front of the principals, and that concerns me. However, I have raised the point.

SNAPSHOT: Dwight, I have gone over this subject. They claim that this will not happen. Everybody will be stationary in positions on those camera stands.

WATCHDOG: Let me ask, Timmie, where do you feel our documentary people will be at that point?

SNAPSHOT: They will be on camera platform one. We have room for them on camera platform one. We have another one that wanted to be in Tienanmen Square, so you've only got one camera with you, but you've got the airplane taxiing up, the door opening, President coming out, the first greeting, and a view of them going down the troops. Dwight, if they do need additional film, I'm sure they can get it from the networks on camera stand number three. We just don't have the horses to move these cameras around.

WATCHDOG: Yeah. Are you going to pre-position in the square? With your press?

SNAPSHOT: Dwight, we have three network cameras that have requested to be in the square, along with the documentary crew camera. There's no problem with that.

WATCHDOG: OK. I'm addressing this kind of to Ron, too, because in my cable I had asked if it would be possible to take Byron Schumacher, plus two of our documentary people, on to the square, while the ceremony was in progress. In other words, after the first few minutes, and rush them on ahead, but is that an impossible situation?

ROADRUNNER: Yes. I have raised that question and I have not gotten an answer. But, I did not receive a favorable . . . look . . . when I asked the question. I just don't feel they are going to let those cameramen move. Presently, it is my thought that Hartigan and Gold would be positioned in Tienanmen Square.

WATCHDOG: OK. Well, when Hartigan and when Bert Gold get there, tomorrow, you can talk it over with them. They are with us right now, so they know what you're saying and we'll talk about it after we hang up here. Obviously, if our hosts have any photographers moving on the apron, we would like to request that our official photographers move with them.

ROADRUNNER: Yes, Dwight. I am very much aware of that.

WATCHDOG: OK. Thank you.

ROADRUNNER: Be advised that they have any number of government photographers. They do not plan on moving their photographers like we would like to move ours. I believe that is the problem. I've expressed to them that we are spread very thin and it's important that we do our job. I do not, repeat, do not know what they are going to allow us to do.

WATCHDOG: I understand. I'm not pressing you on that, I'm just asking the questions. OK, shall we pick it up from the point where we get in to the motorcades?

ROADRUNNER: Be advised, I have just been called into a meeting with Mr. Chu at noon. This will be the first time I've met with him in two and a half days. Hopefully, something will come out of it.

WATCHDOG: What time is it there now?

ROADRUNNER: Quarter of noon.

WATCHDOG: We better hurry, huh?

ROADRUNNER: Yes, sir.

WATCHDOG: Well, why don't we cover some other things quickly. We would like to talk to you at 5:00, Peking time, tomorrow. That's right after we get in our hotel [in Guam], and maybe by that time you'll have a clearer perspective on the events for the next day.

ROADRUNNER: Yes, sir. Please be advised that we are all very hopeful that we will.

WATCHDOG: Well, we are, too. It would be most helpful if we got some more direction, because we have many people to notify, as you know. We want to brief them all on the airplanes on the way in.

ROADRUNNER: Yes, sir.

WATCHDOG: Do we agree on 5:00, your time, tomorrow?

ROADRUNNER: Presently, we have Elbourne arriving back here at five. It might be worthwhile to move that to six.

WATCHDOG: OK. Done, done, 6:00 your time.

WHALEBOAT: Dwight?

WATCHDOG: Yeah, Ron.

WHALEBOAT: Yeah, this is Ron. I've been listening. Did Ron have an opportunity to go through the arrival ceremony? I can check with you later.

WATCHDOG: Please check with us later, OK?

WHALEBOAT: Yeah, fine. Is Tim available?

WATCHDOG: In a few minutes. We're going through some questions now. Ron's got to leave there in a second.

WHALEBOAT: Sorry.

WATCHDOG: OK. Ron?

ROADRUNNER: Yes, sir.

WATCHDOG: On that plane on the twenty-third that we wanted to bring into Shanghai?

ROADRUNNER: Yes, sir?

WATCHDOG: It was only approved into Shanghai, is that right? And then we're going to use a courier, or how does that stand?

SNAPSHOT: Yes. The press plane, the film courier plane, which is a Pan Am plane, has been approved in principle. Vern Coffey is working out the details. We have suggested that the aircraft come all the way into Peking, and he's got to work that out.

WATCHDOG: OK. Now . . . there is another need for the same type of a thing on the twenty-fifth. Ziegler is anxious to have film picked up. What's your reading on that, Ron or Tim?

SNAPSHOT: Are you sure you want us to do it right now?

WATCHDOG: No. No, I'm not. I would do it as you men see fit, in consultation with the host at whatever time you feel is best.

SNAPSHOT: Right, all of us have had detailed meetings on new requirements. It's a very sensitive point. Can we study it?

WATCHDOG: OK. Ron?

SNAPSHOT: Dwight, be advised, Ron just rushed out to his meeting.

WATCHDOG: OK. I will call him later tonight, Tim. OK. If you guys don't have anything else, we'll sign off.

WHALEBOAT: Wait a minute, Dwight. I want to talk to Tim.

WATCHDOG: OK.

WHALEBOAT: OK. Tim?

SNAPSHOT: I'm with ya.

WHALEBOAT: Tim, I'd like to talk to you at 6:15, in about ten minutes.

SNAPSHOT: OK. Now, exactly what do you want to go over, Ron?

WHALEBOAT: Tim, look. You've got to understand that we've got some psychological problems to deal with and that's what I want you to do and I don't think I have to explain to you what those problems are and I think if you can sense that you can handle it accordingly.

SNAPSHOT: OK, I understand that. Do you want me to go into the difficulties I'm having here?

WHALEBOAT: No, I don't. I want you to review, just generally, what the filing set up will be. I will cover the problems with them here. OK?

SNAPSHOT: OK.

WHALEBOAT: Do you see what I mean? In other words, give them encouragement, but give them a realistic picture of what they will face.

SNAPSHOT: OK. I will.

WHALEBOAT: Do you see what I mean?

SNAPSHOT: Yeah. Incidentally, Ron, considering that we're in the middle of the People's Republic of China, the filing is gonna be excellent. I'm confident of that.

WHALEBOAT: I'm sure it will be, too. What I'm talking about is special problems that the wire services face and explaining to them how it will develop. OK?

SNAPSHOT: OK!

WHALEBOAT: Do you feel you're prepared to do that?

SNAPSHOT: You know everything I know. I'm prepared to do it, yeah.

WHALEBOAT: OK. The reason I want to do it is just to let them talk to the man they're depending on there, OK?

SNAPSHOT: Thank you. Thank you very much. Ha, ha, ha.

WHALEBOAT: You know what I'm doing here, Tim, so go along with it, huh?

SNAPSHOT: I understand. I will. We track pretty good . . . usually.

WHALEBOAT: OK. I'll call you in ten minutes, huh?

SNAPSHOT: That's a roger.

WHELIHAN: Hey Timmie?

SNAPSHOT: Yeah, Bruce?

WHELIHAN: Tim? Tim?

SNAPSHOT: Yeah, go ahead, Bruce.

WHELIHAN: I'm going to put Jerry on here. He's going to hold you a minute until I get the operator on the other phone so we can switch into this conference, OK? [*Jerry Warren was assistant press secretary.*]

SNAPSHOT: I'd rather do it downstairs. Let me get the switchboard and have them put it . . . OK. I'll hold.

WHELIHAN: All right.

WARREN: Hello, Tim. Tim?

SNAPSHOT: Yes?

WARREN: Bruce is gonna have you switched over to the conference room in just a moment.

SNAPSHOT: OK. Who's all in there, Jerry?

WARREN: It'll be . . . all three of the Associated Press representatives, plus Helen Thomas and Stu Hensley from UPI. [*AP Representatives Frank Cormier, Henry Hartzenbusch, and Hugh Mulligan*]

SNAPSHOT: OK. Am I being quoted on this?

WARREN: Ron will set the ground rules when you talk to him.

SNAPSHOT: OK.

WARREN: So, I wouldn't worry about that. I think it's merely background and information.

SNAPSHOT: OK.

WARREN: All right?

SNAPSHOT: All right. I hope it works.

WARREN: If you get worried about this, ask Ron, if he hasn't already done so, to set ground rules. Did you hear me?

SNAPSHOT: OK.

WARREN: OK. How are you doing otherwise?

SNAPSHOT: Well, we're anticipating the visit. You know how you feel on that.

WARREN: I know how it is close to the arrival. I do indeed. (long pause)

SNAPSHOT: Jerry, are you still there?

WARREN: I'm still on, Tim.

SNAPSHOT: OK. Be advised, I have the names of the third-country news gathering people that are going to be here in China.

WARREN: How many are there, Tim?

SNAPSHOT: Thirteen.

WARREN: Thirteen in addition to the twenty-seven residents?

SNAPSHOT: That's correct. I will send their names to you. I just got them.

WARREN: Good. That would be most helpful.

WHELIHAN: Timmie?

SNAPSHOT: What?

WHELIHAN: We're interrupting you, we're set to go with this conference call if you're ready. Who else is on?

SNAPSHOT: I've got Manning here.

WHELIHAN: OK.

SNAPSHOT: And I'm still on the speaker phone.

WHELIHAN: We're going to put you on the speaker phone. Just a second. OK. Can you get off that speaker phone on your end so we can give these people an indication of how it will sound over a regular hand set?

SNAPSHOT: You'd rather I do it on a hand set?

WHELIHAN: If you can pick one up I think it would be a little better at this end. A little stronger at this end, yeah.

SNAPSHOT: Let me check it with you. (click, click) How does that sound?

WHELIHAN: That's worse.

SNAPSHOT: Worse?

WHELIHAN: Ha, ha, ha . . . Pick up the other one again. (click, click)

SNAPSHOT: OK. Now I'm on the other one.

WHELIHAN: OK. That's great. We're going to put you on conference now.

WHALEBOAT: Tim?

SNAPSHOT: Yes, Ron.

WHALEBOAT: Tim, can you hear us?

SNAPSHOT: Yeah, I can hear you loud and clear. How me?

WHALEBOAT: You sound fine.

SNAPSHOT: Good.

WHALEBOAT: Tim, I've got the wires here. We want to review a couple things with you and then they may have some questions for you.

SNAPSHOT: OK.

WHALEBOAT: First of all, let's cover the wire service photo transmission situation. We have conflicting reports from Lyon and the AP man, as to the exact location of the darkroom for each of the wires and the location of their equipment to transmit over the lease lines. Can you give us the accurate rundown on how that situation stands?

SNAPSHOT: Yes. I can give you an accurate rundown. I have, of course, talked with both Lyon and Achatz, and they seem to be quite happy at this point in time. The darkroom facilities are in the hotel where the press will be staying. The press hotel is approximately fifty yards away from the filing facility. Both Achatz and Lyon have a work room. They also have another room, their darkrooms. I understand Achatz has already transmitted a test photo, and everything went fine. Yesterday we were able to achieve the lease lines, and those are going to be extended up into their working room. After they process the film, it's a matter of maybe ten steps to the transmitter.

WHALEBOAT: Do they have a common processing room, Tim?

SNAPSHOT: That's a negative. They each have their own processing room.

WHALEBOAT: OK. Well, that sounds in good shape. Just a moment, let me see if there are any other questions on that subject. Tim, the question is, is there any prospect of getting wire service photos out of the airport?

SNAPSHOT: Absolutely none. We've gone very hard on that subject and it's absolutely impossible to do.

WHALEBOAT: OK. Now let's move to a description of the telephone facilities available to the wire services at the Peking airport.

SNAPSHOT: OK. There will be, as agreed upon last night with the People's Republic of China, five L.D. [*long distance*] telephones from the airport back through a Chinese switchboard, for tariff purposes, and then through the satellite. The quality should be exactly what it is right now with me. However . . .

WHALEBOAT: Tim?

SNAPSHOT: . . . the phones are going to be located in the press room facility. It's a press resting facility, basically, and not out on the apron. It was impossible for them to put it on the apron.

WHALEBOAT: Tim. I assume you have allocated one of those phones for each wire service.

SNAPSHOT: That's exactly right. They are there for the purposes of the wires and other immediate news that we would have to get back.

WHALEBOAT: OK. So, AP and UPI have an allocated phone in the press room, just off of the runway there, at the airport, right?

SNAPSHOT: That is correct.

WHALEBOAT: At what point, Tim, will they be able to begin use of those phones? Before the President lands?

SNAPSHOT: They will be able to begin using those phones immediately after they get in to Peking on the twentieth.

WHALEBOAT: So, in other words, one of the men . . . one of the representatives from each of the wire services, who will arrive on the twentieth, will be able to go out to the airport, prior to the President's arrival, use the instrument allocated to them to establish contact with his bureau before the President lands and begin to keep the phone open and begin filing. Right?

SNAPSHOT: That is correct.

WHALEBOAT: Recognizing that it is $14.50 for every three minutes.

SNAPSHOT: That is the established tariff from here to there. That's right.

WHALEBOAT: One other question, just a moment Tim. (discussion garbled) At what point will the wires receive their cards?

SNAPSHOT: OK. Let me tell you when all the press will receive their cards. I have made an agreement with the PRC that I will go to Shanghai this afternoon, with representatives of the Information Department here. We will give the press their cards at the Shanghai airport. As soon as they receive their cards, they are accredited members eligible to file from the PRC. Which means you can file as soon as you get to Peking, with no problem whatsoever, and that is agreed upon.

WHALEBOAT: So they can make first use of their allocated phone at the Peking airport tomorrow afternoon when the press arrives. Is that correct?

SNAPSHOT: That is correct.

WHALEBOAT: Now, Tim, obviously, those phones are under the same process as the ones in the press center. No collect calls. They will have to be placed through the PRC switchboard for tariff purposes.

SNAPSHOT: That's correct, but that's the same thing as a collect call. As you know, the revenue must be split up between the PRC and our telephone company, and nobody will pay in cash, anywhere. It will be billed to the individual correspondents, when they get back to the United States, from AT&T.

WHALEBOAT: Right, we understand that. Now, Tim, let's move to the . . . oh, just a minute now, one other question. When will the pool receive their press credentials?

SNAPSHOT: The pool will receive their press credentials from Jack D'Arcy when they arrive with the President in Shanghai. I am carrying those credentials to Shanghai and giving them to D'Arcy.

WHALEBOAT: Thank you. Just a moment. (discussion) Tim, again, the question is, of the five phones at the airport, will one definitely be marked AP and one definitely marked UPI?

SNAPSHOT: Tell Helen [Thomas] that I don't miss too many times and I'll have one marked AP and one marked UPI.

WHALEBOAT: Right, Tim. Now, let's move to the filing facilities at the Palace of the Nationalities. It's my understanding that the wires will not have a leased teletype circuit.

SNAPSHOT: That is correct, and you, I believe, understand some of the background reasons for that.

WHALEBOAT: Correct. Now, the second point is, will they have an allocated telephone at the Palace of the Nationalities?

SNAPSHOT: As of the current time they will not. However, Ron, be advised there are fifteen L.D. circuits coming from the Palace of the Nationalities. I don't think that there will be any problem at all in getting the circuits. That's an awful lot of power for what we've got travelling with us.

WHALEBOAT: Now, Tim, recognizing that they will not have a lease teletype circuit, because of the massive volumes of copy the wire services move, you will want to discuss again in detail with your friends a procedure of close liaison with the wires and a procedure where their copy will be moved in a priority way.

SNAPSHOT: That's a roger. We've discussed that and there will be people to help the wires and their copy will receive priority. I don't like to say that in front of the entire press corps, but that's just for you.

WHALEBOAT: We understand that. The entire press corps is not here . . . as you know. Tim?

SNAPSHOT: Roger.

WHALEBOAT: The other point is, that we should try and make arrangements if the fifteen L.D.s do get tied up, or if there is an overload of calls, to make sure that they will process the AP and UPI call, again, on a priority basis.

SNAPSHOT: The People's Republic of China press officials are very much aware of the importance of the wire services. We've gone through it many times with them, and incidentally, they already knew this before we came in. They are aware that the wire services serve all the publications, broadcast as well as written, in the United States and throughout the world. And they are quite aware of the priority factors involved in that.

WHALEBOAT: Tim, we have one or two other questions.

MALE WIRE: Tim, on this priority list of the so-called PRC, does it recognize the classifications of urgent and fast and double the rate of ordinary press?

SNAPSHOT: No. It's all ordinary press. It's all ordinary press. This ten cents a word for telegram is ordinary press; they do not have another class. This will all go as ordinary press, but believe me, I have seen the facility over there, and it's got twelve punching and sending machines and ten punching machines. Now that's an awful lot of machines. It's more than we've ever used on any trip before, even when we had three and four hundred correspondents along with us.

MALE WIRE: How are they technically, Tim?

SNAPSHOT: Excellent. Very good.

MALE WIRE: (By technically I meant their operators.)

WHALEBOAT: Tim, I was asked a question as to the performance of their operators and what is your impression?

SNAPSHOT: OK. Well, the PRC assured me they have been known worldwide for their speed and accuracy and swiftness in putting out copy, and they assured me they have the finest operators they can get from China to do this task. Believe me, Ron, they want to cooperate and to help in any way possible.

WHALEBOAT: Right, we understand that, we appreciate it. Tim, what is the situation with telephones at any other possible location that may be involved in the visit?

SNAPSHOT: There are no telephones in any other locations. We will have to come back to the press center to do our filing. However, we can call from our rooms at the press hotel by dialing 300. That will put us right into the special switchboard that the Chinese have set up to get us through the satellite. Those calls will be billed to your rooms, and again AT&T will take that billing and split it out when you get back to the United States.

WHALEBOAT: That sounds very good, Tim. In other words, if someone is in their room, they simply dial 300, to the switchboard. So, therefore, they would not have to fill out a phone application on those particular calls. Correct? [*The hotels in China used a form that guests were required to fill out before overseas calls were placed by the switchboard.*]

SNAPSHOT: Well, we're working on that for the wires. I'm not sure about that application business yet. I have pointed out the problems, and they're trying to work this out.

WHALEBOAT: OK. You understand the problem this poses to wires, and whatever you can do will be appreciated at this end.

SNAPSHOT: That's a roger. We are working on that and the PRC is working on that.

WHALEBOAT: Yes, we understand. (discussion) Tim, obviously the particular problem for the wires is having to fill out an application form for each take. That is almost virtually an impossible, time-consuming task.

SNAPSHOT: That's right. We've gone over that. I understand that. They understand that. Ron, believe me, they want to do exactly what is right. I think by the time you get here we are not going to have any major problems at all.

WHALEBOAT: OK. That sounds very good, Tim. Just one other question, just a moment. Tim, now I understand from our previous discussions that incoming messages will be possible.

SNAPSHOT: That is correct. Incoming messages will be possible and they should be slugged to: The People's Republic of China, Palace of the Nationalities, Peking, China, and the name.

WHALEBOAT: The name of the individual.

SNAPSHOT: That's correct, and that also goes for incoming telephone calls. It should be: the Palace of the Nationalities, Peking, China, and the name. Or: The Nationalities Hotel, Peking, China, and the name.

WHALEBOAT: Tim, can you give us a general rundown on the facilities that will be available in Hangchou and Shanghai?

SNAPSHOT: Yes. Let me start off with Hangchou, because there's where we have the real major problem. Ron, they just do not have the facilities in Hangchou to provide the service that we're normally accustomed to. But they have done everything within their power to use the existing facilities to give us what they have.

WHALEBOAT: Well, that's like many cities in the United States where sometimes the facilities are not quite up to standards we receive in the bigger cities. Is that correct?

SNAPSHOT: That's right, that's right. But, they have done everything they can, including putting in telephone booths to cut down outside sound. They've really done a magnificent job. There are going to be, in Hangchou, three L.D. telephones for exclusive press use and seven teletype channels.

WHALEBOAT: And I assume if you work out a priority system in Peking, that this would also apply to Shanghai and Hangchou.

SNAPSHOT: That's right. Let me tell you that anything we establish in Peking is automatically applying to the other cities.

WHALEBOAT: OK, Tim. Just a moment. (discussion) The question is . . . is that address for incoming messages fixed? In other words, is there a way to shorten it?

SNAPSHOT: I'm sorry, I didn't understand you, Ron.

WHALEBOAT: The question is, for incoming messages, is it necessary to put, in all cases, the Palace of the Nationalities, Peking, China, and the name of the individual? [*The wires were even trying to save money on their use of the address!*]

SNAPSHOT: Well, I would think so. I don't know any other way to address it.

WHALEBOAT: Well, I think we'll pass on that one. (To the room: "Any other questions?") Well, now moving to Shanghai. Could you give us a rundown on the facilities there?

SNAPSHOT: Yes. In Shanghai, in the press hotel, there are six L.D. telephones. The teletype was not in when we were there, however, they told us they had been able to meet our requirements in Shanghai. So I assume there's gonna be ten. I'll be there tonight, Ron, and see the facility.

WHALEBOAT: Good. We appreciate that. I am sure if they assured you they were able to meet our requirements that they will be there. I think that's all, Tim. Do you have anything else?

SNAPSHOT: No, except to wish you a good trip and we're really looking forward to seeing you.

WHALEBOAT: Well, we're sure looking forward to seeing you too, Tim. Helen Thomas has a big smile on her face.

SNAPSHOT: Boy, I hope she keeps it for the next eight days! (chuckle)

Snapshot put his head on the table and closed his eyes. That had been quite an exercise in the stroking of hyperactive egos. The wires viewed themselves as the royalty of the press corps and always expected, and often demanded, special privileges and extra attention. He liked them all as individuals (Snapshot liked everybody, actually), but as a group, as a collective body of puffed up personas, they were royal, all right. Royal pains in the ass!

He got up from his chair and rubbed his aching neck. He walked down the hall to his room and threw himself on his bed. He took a huge breath, buried his face in his pillow and screamed as loud as he possibly could. Whew! It wasn't nearly as wonderful as Hawaii would have been, but it made him feel just a little bit better. He climbed wearily off the bed and started packing for the trip to Shanghai. He had just opened his suitcase when Roadrunner knocked at his door.

"Hey Snapshot, is everything OK?" he asked.

"Just super fantastic."

"How was the run-through with all the technicians and their Chinese counterparts? Were they happy with all the equipment we've installed?"

"Correction," Snapshot said sternly. "Equipment that *they* have installed and please don't forget that important detail again."

Roadrunner nodded. It was true. For weeks now, every time an American screwed a screw, connected a connection or nailed a nail, his Chinese counterpart would unscrew, disconnect or remove and re-do on the spot. It was clear. They wanted all the equipment used for the President's visit to be installed by Chinese workers. Everything was done twice. Everything!

Snapshot laughed and said, "When you consider how far we've come since my first meeting with Mr. Png-hua, the press representative, we have made amazing progress. I remember when he asked me how many members of the American press corps would be traveling with the President. I explained that a normal international trip would include a thousand to fifteen hundred press, but since the interest level was so intense for this trip, I would estimate about two thousand would request accreditation for the trip. I thought the man was going to croak on the spot. He was really old anyway, remember?"

Roadrunner certainly did remember.

"He thought about the request for a long time," Snapshot went on. "He just sat there and smoked his cigarette, said nothing and thought about it. He just kept thinking about it, and smoking cigarettes. Forever. Finally the Chinese decided to take a break, and when they came back Mr. Png-hua said, 'Mr. Elbow, we have talked about your requirements. As you know, we do not have the facilities in China to handle so many people. Normally, when a head of state comes here, he travels with maybe five or six press. However, because of the importance of this visit, we are going to allow you something we have never done before. We are going to expand your accredited press to numbers that we have never had before and therefore we will give you twelve people.' And that was our starting point, remember?"

Roadrunner certainly did remember.

"And the way we got it up to more," Snapshot continued, "was when we got home from our advance trip, I chose one news story that would interest them, a major Presidential speech, and then got every newspaper in the United States that we could get our hands on. We compiled a huge book of clippings and showed them how all of these newspapers handled the story in a different way. We convinced them that we needed more people for balance in reporting. This made the difference."

"When you dwell for a moment on where we started, we really have made giant strides," Roadrunner said.

"God, yes." Snapshot was enjoying the opportunity to reminisce. "And we have never seen Mr. Png-hua again."

"Well, he was so old and you were so young, they had to exchange him for Mr. Ma. I think we should be grateful for that," Roadrunner said.

"I'll say. At this same meeting where they said we could have twelve press, my job was to get them to agree to television coverage. I suggested that we bring in a 747 aircraft, configured as a television studio, and park it at the airport. All we needed from the Chinese was to provide us with power. Boeing had a plane coming off the line about that time that they would make available to us. Mr. Png-hua left the meeting again to discuss this in private and when they came back they said, 'Mr. Elbow, we have agreed to this proposal, but you have to sell us this 747.' Remember that one?"

Roadrunner certainly did remember.

"I nearly died," Snapshot said. "I told them that I couldn't sell them a 747, but they just asked, 'You represent your government, don't you?' I told them that's not the way we work, that a private corporation owned that 747 and I couldn't sell one to the Chinese or anybody else. I wanted to remind them that they were on the no-no list, that we didn't have diplomatic relations with each other, let alone the most-favored-nation status required for the purchase of even the most basic technical equipment. But anyway, that's how the idea of the transmission center was born. We got Siegenthaler and the rest of the network people to give us the general guidelines, and we presented our requirements to the PRC. They said that was great, but then they wanted to buy all the television equipment. They wanted to own everything. We were talking literally millions of dollars here. So then we came up with the plan of having them lease all of the television equipment that went over there, and then they leased it back to us to run it.

"But really," Snapshot continued, "with the Chinese insisting on doing everything themselves, it has made everything much harder than it needed to be. The mobile vans are a perfect example of that. Those hummers are so damn huge and complicated and the Chinese are so damn short, but they insisted on knowing how to operate them. Our guys have been letting their counterparts practice driving them out at the airport. It's not exactly Dulles International, so it was the safest place to conduct the training sessions.

"And so today we finally had the preview of all this leased/leased back equipment. We showed them the pictures that every TV camera would make, from every location. We demonstrated the mobile units so they could preview the quality of the coverage. Every American technician and every Chinese counterpart joined in this demonstration. Some things worked and some things didn't.

"When we finished, one of the Americans took his mobile van to fill it up with gas. Have you tried to buy gasoline in the PRC?" Snapshot asked.

"Come to think of it, I don't recall even seeing a gas station," Roadrunner realized.

"Well, there is not exactly an Exxon station every few blocks," Snapshot assured him. "You can't even find them. They are practically camouflaged! But the poor guy finally found a place to buy gas and while he was there a street car ran into the back of the van."

Roadrunner groaned. He hadn't heard about this yet. "Was it bad?"

"Well, not really, when you consider the damage a street car could have done. It broke the tail light cover."

"Well, that's not so bad," Roadrunner said with relief.

"No, it isn't so bad, but the Chinese are saying it would never have happened if the driver had followed the guidelines and had his Chinese counterpart with him. They claim the Chinese counterpart would have shown him how to operate the van properly. The Chinese scheduled a meeting when we got back to the hotel. The American driver kept insisting that the street car ran into his van. The Chinese said the mobile van hit the street car. The driver got so mad that we finally had to take him out in the lobby. I think he had just had it up to here with Chinese counterparts un-doing and re-doing everything and he threw a huge temper tantrum. He yelled, 'Damn it, I didn't do it,' and smashed one of those glass cases where they keep the booze and cigarettes."

Roadrunner groaned again, "Oh dear. Mr. Chu will be calling this to my attention very soon. I imagine they will make a major incident out of this."

"Sure they will," Snapshot agreed as he resumed his packing. "They already have."

"I'll let you get going, but just tell me how the equipment checked out."

"I think everyone was very pleased. The Chinese had a couple of questions when it was all over. They wanted to know if we could improve the red in the Chinese flag. Our engineers assured them they could do that. They thought some of the pictures were a little jiggly, and we explained that we did not yet have all of our tripods in place. The bottom line was that they think they understand the video. They said, 'We understand how all the video works. And we thought we understood all of the audio as well. But could you please clarify one thing? What is *fucking audio*?' They could not find that term explained in any of the zillion manuals they'd translated."

To this day, Snapshot still chuckles at the thought of the Chinese counterparts pouring over countless technical manuals for an explanation of a term that was most likely uttered by more than one frustrated American technician.

CHAPTER XXII

FLEXIBILITY, CENTRALIZATION, AND POINTS OF PRINCIPLE

FEBRUARY 19, 1972

Snapshot and Schrauth had departed for Shanghai to meet the incoming planes. The Chinese were running in every direction. Roadrunner found a quiet moment to collect himself. He picked up his IBM dictaphone and went into his bathroom, sat on the floor, and leaned against the closed door. He turned on the machine and started talking.

"The Chinese had three things that we had to learn and work with from the very beginning. First of all, they had to establish a point of principle. It was a point of principle that the President of the United States would not bring his own car to China; a point of sovereignty that when he came to China he was a Chinese guest and they, in fact, would provide the transportation, including the President's travels inter-theater to Hangchou and to Shanghai. He would travel on Chinese aircraft. I am sure that for many Presidents to come, and many foreign trips to come, Americans will be effected by the decisions that we, the first Presidential advance team in the People's Republic of China, have made.

371

"It was a point of principle, until just recently, that the Secret Service would not ride in the car that was carrying the President and the Prime Minister. It was the responsibility of the Chinese to protect and guarantee the security of the President of the United States.

"So once a point of principle was established, another term was flexibility—we had to be flexible in the execution of that principle. For example, we established a point of principle that the President was going to the Great Wall, but we could not in fact establish a date or a time that he would depart because it might snow. We would make that decision either the night before or the morning of.

"And the last word was centralization. Once we established a point of principle and became flexible in accomplishing that principle, we had to have centralization in order to accomplish it. We have all these units here making up our advance team in China, the normal ones, those that are always with us on an international advance-- Military Aides' Office, White House Communications Agency, Presidential Food Service, Secret Service, State Department, the Press operation--but we also have other ingredients to deal with because we have no embassy, no commercial enterprises and no private industry in this country. We have Comsat, Intelsat, American Tel and Tel, International Telephone and Telegraph, and the network people. To be specific, eighty-five of them are here to help the Chinese in the art of producing and using color television. There are mobile vans, radio technicians, lighting men, sound men, engineers, film editors, guys that do everything!

"The Chinese wanted one person to be the 'responsible person' for all of these people and all that they represent. That person ended up being me.

"I am the centralization, so they wanted every piece of information coming to them, coming from me. And if it didn't, *they* would come to me and say, 'Mr. Walker, we would like to bring to your attention a certain matter.' And then they would explain it to me. And then I would say, 'I'll look into it. Thank you very much for bringing it to my attention.'

"Needless to say, I have lived with this twehty-four hours a day. I know that the Chinese tested me at first, and are probably still testing me. They wake me up every night and ask me questions. They wait until I just reach that deep sleep and then they knock on my door and want to have a meeting. I stagger out of my bed, try to bounce back and be alert. But, I think it worked. I feel relatively calm now. I think the President and Mrs. Nixon will be well received and well taken care of. The Chinese are gracious and hospitable. They want this visit to be a success, just like I do.

"I know I have done a lot of rambling, here in my Chinese bathroom. I wanted to explain my understanding of the flexible centralization of a point of principle while I think I know what it all means. Do you suppose I should be worried that I think I understand it?"

CHAPTER XXIII

SEE YOU TOMORROW

FEBRUARY 20, 1972

Roadrunner walked by the display case with the broken glass. The Chinese still had not fixed it. It was their way of reminding the Americans how unstable they were and how uncivilized their behavior was regarded as being. It worked. Roadrunner was receiving the message loud and clear. The sight of the smashed case always embarrassed him and made him feel very apologetic. He wondered if they were going to leave it that way until the trip was over.

The previous night, they had made a big deal out of presenting the Americans with an orange plastic taillight cover. It was a replica of the one that had been broken on the mobile van. It snapped right in place over the taillight bulb. A perfect fit. It even had "Ford" molded into the plastic. The Americans were astonished. The Chinese had won that round of one-upmanship.

ROADRUNNER: Let's see what the status of everything there is. I have not gotten the status of the press corps. They have not arrived at the hotel yet, so we do not have Elbourne plugged into this conference call.

WATCHDOG: Ziegler, are you on this? (no answer) I guess he's not. Well, why don't we start with Schrauth and see if there's any changes in Shanghai and then come back to you, Ron. OK, Schrauth. We got a pretty good reading from you last night. Has anything changed?

SCHRAUTH: Negative, Watchdog. Nothing has changed. Be advised that I have not received an answer, but I am confident the official photo will take place and we should have no problem moving our official photographers in to take those photos.

ROADRUNNER: Schrauth, is Jenkins present in the conference call?

SCHRAUTH: Roger.

LIVINGOOD: Jenkins, from Livingood. Be advised now, Taylor will ride on the left side, left instead of right. Left side.

JENKINS: Jenkins copy, left side.

SCHRAUTH: OK. That is about all we have to report here. We are awaiting the arrival. We are set. We see no problems.

WATCHDOG: OK. Good, Mike. Thank you. We'll call you from the plane tomorrow and we'll expect things to go just as you gave them to us last night.

SCHRAUTH: Roger. Also be advised that I have talked at great length with my counterpart about the necessity of S'76 departing on time. It's very critical.

WATCHDOG: OK. I understand. You mean for Peking?

SCHRAUTH: Roger, roger.

WATCHDOG: OK. Roadrunner?

ROADRUNNER: Roger, Watchdog. Why don't I go through tomorrow's schedule which has been given to me this afternoon. There are not a lot of changes, but there are some.

The first point: They would like consideration given to have the redwood trees for Hangchou off-loaded in Shanghai. The PRC has expressed concern about the extreme cold weather in Peking damaging those trees. If you don't have a problem we can take them out of the state room when you arrive. They will transport them to Hangchou.

WATCHDOG: OK. I think we should leave one in Shanghai and take two to Hangchou, because right now we do not have a gift for the city of Shanghai. No. Negative, now I find out we have four trees. We'll take all four off in Shanghai, leave two, and send the other two on to Hangchou.

ROADRUNNER: OK. That's fine. You're telling me that you are going to be in a position to present two trees to the city of Shanghai?

WATCHDOG: Well, I think that's what we want to do. I really don't know.

ROADRUNNER: Roger. I'll continue. I have been advised in an official capacity that the PRC will be presenting to the President, and the people of the United States, the gifts that I think you are already aware of. Do you understand what I am saying?

WATCHDOG: Yeah, the . . . are they alive? [*The giant pandas that have become a favorite attraction at the National Zoo.*]

ROADRUNNER: Yes, sir.

WATCHDOG: Yeah. Well, that's a great gift. We're very pleased. That's very nice.

ROADRUNNER: OK. I have the details of the arrival in Peking. I will go slowly. I have the fifteen people in addition to the Prime Minister that will receive the President in Peking. I would like to go through it very slowly and then come back to names so you have a feel of what I'm talking about.

WATCHDOG: Hang on a minute.

ROADRUNNER: As the President and Mrs. Nixon are escorted off the aircraft, they will be met at the bottom of the ramp by Director Han Hsu. Director Han Hsu will introduce the President to the Prime Minister and then he will move down the rank of fifteen PRC officials. Mrs. Nixon will be met by Miss Chang taking her down the line making the introductions.

The Secretary of State will be met by Mr. Chu, C-H-U, who is my counterpart, and Dr. Kissinger will be met by Mr. Kao, K-A-O. At that point, Miss Tong and Miss Wong will be behind the Prime Minister and will make the introductions of the remainder of the official party. As the President moves past the Prime Minister with Director Han Hsu, a group of approximately forty dignitaries from the PRC will start walking toward the end of the official fifteen. The President will continue along with the members of the official party through this additional forty.

When the Prime Minister has concluded receiving the official party he will turn and go to the rear of the airplane and welcome the members of the unofficial party and others. He will move to the position for honors, where he will be met by Director Han Hsu and the President. The President will stand on the Prime Minister's left between the Prime Minister and the band.

To the immediate right rear will be Mrs. Nixon and her escort. Almost directly behind, about a meter, will be Miss Tong, who is the Prime Minister's interpreter, and Colonel Coffey. About three meters behind them will be the Secretary of State and his escort. Dr. Kissinger and his escort will be one rank and then the other rank behind will be the other members of the official party in protocol order. Do you understand up until this point?

WATCHDOG: (To the room: "Got it?")

ROADRUNNER: I'm sorry, are you with me up to this point?

WATCHDOG: Yeah, we're with you. It's very confusing and it's obvious they are going to have to latch on to our people and hold them in place, because we are not that familiar with what you are talking about.

ROADRUNNER: OK. Well, do you want to know this stuff? I'm just trying to explain to you what's going to happen. I realize it's confusing. It's very difficult to talk about on a phone.

WATCHDOG: No, I understand from being there before. For example, when the Prime Minister goes to the back of the plane, he has the President off to the side with Mr. Han Hsu and Mrs. Nixon, is that correct?

ROADRUNNER: No, sir, that's incorrect. The President is continuing to be introduced by Director Han Hsu to an additional forty, repeat four zero, dignitaries who have moved up to join the group of fifteen that are initially receiving the President and Mrs. Nixon. I am sure it will be the Prime Minister who ends up waiting on the President, Dwight.

WATCHDOG: OK. OK.

ROADRUNNER: OK. Is there anything else that you would like to ask before I move on?

WATCHDOG: No. Go ahead.

ROADRUNNER: We go back to the original plan at this point. We pick up where honors transpire. They will play the U.S. National Anthem and the National Anthem of the People's Republic of China. There will be large flags already hoisted, prior to the Spirit of '76 arriving. As the anthems are completed, a military march will be played. There will be approximately five hundred troops to include the band.

As the President and the Prime Minister move down the ranks the First Lady and her escort will follow along with the members of the Official Party. After they have passed the troops and before they reach the motorcade, there will be an additional twenty people representing responsible members from the various ministries in Peking. They will be in a single line. It is their recommendation that the unofficial members getting off of 970 be standing with these twenty PRC representatives and the President and the Prime Minister meet and shake hands with these people on the way to their car.

WATCHDOG: Is that absolutely necessary? We have no desire to do that, unless we have to.

ROADRUNNER: Well, fine. We can knock off our people, but those other people will be there, Dwight.

WATCHDOG: That's fine. That's what I mean, I'm only talking about the 970 people.

ROADRUNNER: Well, it's my feeling that the Prime Minister wants to receive as many guests arriving as possible, sir. He will not have had a chance to do the 970 group unless we do that prior to your arrival.

WATCHDOG: Hold on a minute, Ron.

ROADRUNNER: It will only be a few people. The agents will have moved downtown. It will be General Scowcroft and General Redman and the secretaries who are on 970. I think we're only talking about eight people, but I'll notify the PRC to cancel.

The motorcade will consist of approximately thirty cars, as I have indicated. We are told that along the route there will only be pedestrians. Would you like me to continue?

WATCHDOG: No, I'm back on the twenty people that are in the line, Ron. What did we decide to do with the people off 970?

ROADRUNNER: I'll recommend to the PRC that they not be there.

WATCHDOG: OK. And if that's unacceptable, put them there.

ROADRUNNER: All right, sir, thank you.

WATCHDOG: And then you get in the motorcade and they've got pedestrians along the route and you are headed into town.

ROADRUNNER: Yes, sir. Just let me raise a point, please. I have already indicated that our people are working people, and do not expect that. I was informed that the Prime Minister expects it.

WATCHDOG: I understand. OK. Go ahead then.

ROADRUNNER: Roger, sir. As the President and Mrs. Nixon and members of the official party move down the honor guard, the PRC recommends that we take the remainder of the party and move to the motorcade. Be advised that Mr. Yu and myself, along with Schrauth, will help these people move properly.

WATCHDOG: OK. Then who's gonna concentrate on the official party, the PRC protocol people?

ROADRUNNER: Yes, sir, I've been informed they are to handle it. I've offered my assistance. They've told me the best place I can be is helping the party at the rear of the plane.

WATCHDOG: OK. I understand.

ROADRUNNER: OK. So the motorcade proceeds through town. Upon arriving at the guest house the official party will move into villa number eighteen, to the sitting room. There will not be a formal official photograph, but it looks like an official photograph will be taken. I have gotten concurrence that our representatives from the White House official photograph staff can work that also.

WATCHDOG: OK. But that would just be kind of an informal picture, right? I mean of everybody just kind of sitting around?

ROADRUNNER: That's correct, sir. I have recommended that and they finally agreed. It will only be the official party. Everyone else will be escorted to their villas and rooms.

WATCHDOG: OK, but what I'm asking is when that picture's taken, everybody won't be lined up against the wall, or something, in protocol order. They'll just be sitting around the room. Is that correct?

ROADRUNNER: Yes, sir. To the best of my knowledge, that's exactly what I expect to happen. It would be similar to the other sitting room scenes that you have been a part of. Everyone would simply sit around with their counterparts and the photographers would come in and film.

WATCHDOG: OK, Ron. Going back to the motorcade. What about the Square? Anything? [*An arrival ceremony in Tienanmen Square.*]

ROADRUNNER: Negative. Sir, it looks like it is going to be a zero.

WATCHDOG: Nothing on the way in or through the square except for pedestrians?

ROADRUNNER: That's what we're being informed, sir. That's what the security side is being informed. We don't even know if there is going to be anything . . . colorful . . . along the route. That would probably go up tonight, but when I left today there was nothing up.

WATCHDOG: OK. Very good, go ahead.

ROADRUNNER: The guidelines I've been given are that the principals will decide how long they want to visit. Right now we are tentatively preparing for a meeting at 4:30 at the Great Hall of the People. The two leaders will make that decision once they are together.

WATCHDOG: OK. Go ahead.

ROADRUNNER: They definitely plan to have Searchlight and his party returning to the villa for freshening . . . for some staff time. [*"Staff time" was often a euphemism for rest time.*] I am alerting all U.S. party members to be ready to move to the Great Hall of the People at 6:15. The four groups will begin to arrive at the Great Hall at approximately 6:30. The first group to arrive will be the press, the White House press staff, and our five White House official photographers. They will be received by the Prime Minister and a photo. The next group will be the communications, the ground station people and television technicians to be filmed with the Prime Minister. Are you copying me?

WATCHDOG: Well, Ron, I'm confused. Let's start with . . . what time is dinner? Seven or seven-thirty?

ROADRUNNER: The dinner is at 7:00, sir.

WATCHDOG: Do you think they will hold to that?

ROADRUNNER: Yes, sir. Be advised, the President is arriving at 7:00 for the banquet.

WATCHDOG: OK. But, I mean is this one of those tentative things also, or is this a hard time?

ROADRUNNER: This is a hard time, sir.

WATCHDOG: OK. So, the first thing that happens is at 6:15.

ROADRUNNER: Just let me say it again, please.

WATCHDOG: We're going to have to revise some things, here.

ROADRUNNER: Let me say it again, please. All the party outside of the official and unofficial party, are to be ready to move to the Great Hall at 6:15. At 6:30 the photo sessions will begin, prior to the President's arrival. The Prime Minister will be photographed with the press corps and the staff. The second group will be communications, ground station and TV technicians. The third group will be some security and aircraft crews. Then the last session will be the official photograph of the official and unofficial parties.

WATCHDOG: OK. Are you going to TWX us something on that or is that just it?

ROADRUNNER: No, sir. I am prepared to TWX all this information to you.

WATCHDOG: OK.

ROADRUNNER: When the official photograph is concluded, the President and Mrs. Nixon, along with the official party, will move to the Peking Hall. The remainder of the unofficial party will move into the banquet hall and to the receiving line. They are going to have somewhere between seventy-five and one hundred from their side.

I have a recommendation I would like to discuss with you. What I am recommending is this. That we have sixteen members of the unofficial party, ten from the Secret Service, eight from the White House Communications Agency, the military support would be six. I am recommending that we get a representative group from the press corps of five people. A representative group from the technicians of five people, and then ten members of the White House press staff. This would give us a total of fifty-five people. They did not pick up on the recommendation I made that it was not necessary to have Americans in the line. They want Americans in the line.

WATCHDOG: So we take the unofficial plus all these other people and run them into the banquet hall and put them into line. Is that right?

ROADRUNNER: That's correct, sir.

WATCHDOG: And then does the official party come out and line up also or do they pass through it?

ROADRUNNER: No, sir. They said to me it would be the Prime Minister, the President and Mrs. Nixon, the members of the official party and the PRC officials who would move through the receiving line.

WATCHDOG: The Americans shake hands with Americans?

ROADRUNNER: Yes, sir!

WATCHDOG: So everybody is virtually in a line and one line just runs past the other.

ROADRUNNER: No, it's the U-shaped receiving line, Dwight, that we talked about.

WATCHDOG: OK. Fine!

ROADRUNNER: That's the way it is.

WATCHDOG: If that's the way it's done, that's the way it's done.

ROADRUNNER: Yes, sir. Be advised the experience we had today, I am sure, is going to transpire everyday. We will have a meeting every night with Director Han Hsu and decide the next day's schedule.

WATCHDOG: OK. (pause) That will be enjoyable.

ROADRUNNER: Fine, sir.

WATCHDOG: But I sure would like to see a schedule for the evening with the correct times that we can distribute to our party members once they are in the guest house. Can we do that?

ROADRUNNER: Yes, sir. We can do that.

WATCHDOG: In other words, we'll just take . . . do you have one of our books yet?

ROADRUNNER: No, sir, we do not.

WATCHDOG: Well, that's our mistake. We should have sent them. (pause) Yeah, maybe one of the press staff . . . hang on a minute. Jerry Warren's got one, Ron.

ROADRUNNER: OK.

WATCHDOG: You can get his book and actually what you are talking about is revising pages thirty-five, thirty-six, and thirty-seven, which are the three pages that deal with the banquet.

ROADRUNNER: Yes, but we've just got a lot more information. The only change is the starting time. I anticipated the Prime Minister wanting to have a picture session, as he has on our other visits, but I never could get confirmation. Now we have the confirmation and it will transpire prior to the President's arrival. I have alerted the people here that are responsible for the various groups to alert their people.

WATCHDOG: Well go ahead and run on through it then.

ROADRUNNER: As the President and the Prime Minister and the First Lady and her escort conclude the receiving line, they will move straight to table number one. They are, before anyone is seated, going to play both national anthems. The PRC has no gesture, example hand over the heart, during theirs. They just simply stand at attention.

After the two national anthems are concluded, the people sit down and the meal begins. The toasts will be toward the end of the meal, probably before dessert. From that point on the schedule is the same. They told me that it may run longer, it may run less.

WATCHDOG: OK.

ROADRUNNER: That is the conclusion of our discussion today. We will meet tomorrow night to discuss the next day.

WATCHDOG: OK, Ron, will we do that right after the banquet, do you think?

ROADRUNNER: The timing told to me is between ten and midnight every night for the next day's schedule.

WATCHDOG: OK. Great. When will they get their table assignments?

ROADRUNNER: I am told that table assignments will be made available tomorrow afternoon. We have made arrangements for every group to receive their own table assignments and distribute them.

WATCHDOG: Great. That's it for Monday?

ROADRUNNER: That's it for Monday.

WATCHDOG: OK. Can I ask you some questions now?

ROADRUNNER: Please, go right ahead.

WATCHDOG: How are we doing on the television problem?

ROADRUNNER: Be advised, the technicians have had one of the best days they've had since we've been in China. The financial matters, they have been told, will be resolved. I talked with Siegenthaler and apparently everyone is extremely pleased. They've made good progress today.

WATCHDOG: That's sensational, Ron. Good job. Good work. That's great.

ROADRUNNER: All right. Let me cover one point quickly. I know it will be of some value, in regard to the toasts. My counterpart has said that the Americans can do anything they would like to. "We are not that protocol conscious," the PRC says. He said they could use their juice glass or anything. I sensed that with the Prime Minister, it would be appropriate to take their glass of Mao-tai and symbolically touch the glass and make the gesture of drinking with the Prime Minister.

WATCHDOG: OK.

ROADRUNNER: All right, fine. Those are all the points that I have, presently.

WATCHDOG: Hang on a minute.

BRENNAN: Ron, this is Jack Brennan. I've got a couple of things for Vern Coffey if he's available.

ROADRUNNER: He's right here, Jack. Just a moment.

COFFEY: Go ahead, Jack.

BRENNAN: Vern, in this inspection of the Honor Guard, do they do it the same way we do? Will the President be closest to the troops, walking therefore on the Prime Minister's left?

COFFEY: That's affirmative. The President would be standing closest to the band, with the Prime Minister to his right on the outside. Then to the right rear would be Mrs. Nixon and her escort and to the rear of that formation would be the members of the official party. When the anthems are played, we did raise the point about military, and they agreed that the three Aide de Camps in uniform . . . General Scowcroft, yourself, and myself . . . could render the military hand salute, which I plan on doing. Does that clarify, Jack?

BRENNAN: Yeah, that's fine, Vern, except you went right by the flags. Is that what he does? Nothing at all when he passes the flags?

COFFEY: That's right. These are all organizational flags so there is no reason for him to do anything. He should not acknowledge them at all, just continue along with the Prime Minister. The only national colors or flags that will be present are those that Ron mentioned which will be on two staffs, we are told, in front of the terminal.

BRENNAN: OK, Vern.

COFFEY: Now, again, on this ceremony . . . it's kind of like a box formation. Imagine the terminal is on one side, all right? Then if you draw that line to the left perpendicular to the terminal will be S'76. Then perpendicular to S'76 will be the troop formation, so they've made a U formation with the terminal forming one side, S'76 forming the second side and the troops forming a third side. With everything facing toward the center. Does that clear it up for you?

BRENNAN: Thank you.

COFFEY: There might be some question about the President not saluting in the presence of the U.S. flag, but it will be at a distance. I told them the President would generally do whatever his hosts were going to do and if the Prime Minister did not salute then the President would not salute. So I think that's the guidance that we should try to follow since they will be on camera.

BRENNAN: That's fine. That's what we'll do. OK. Do you guys need any personal gear? We can run to the PX tonight for anything you need.

COFFEY: Hang on one.

WATCHDOG: Vern, Dwight here. He should be wearing an overcoat tomorrow, shouldn't he? [By "he," Watchdog meant the President, who did not want to be wearing an overcoat if the Prime Minister was not.]

COFFEY: We asked that question of the protocol people. They are not really sure what the Prime Minister will wear. I mentioned I'd seen photographs of him on a particularly cold day when their delegation was going to the United Nations and the UN delegation was wearing overcoats but the Prime Minister was not. They said, "Yes, that's right, he may or may not wear an overcoat." So we asked them if they could find out and they said they would attempt to. We then asked how early the Prime Minister would arrive so we might be able to view him and get word to you. So that's what we're working with. Hopefully we will receive some word. If not, we will try to get it to you five or ten minutes prior to landing, Dwight.

WATCHDOG: OK.

COFFEY: The weather was very nice here today. (To the room: "They were asking me what he was going to wear.") It's our guess here, Dwight, that it will be an overcoat. It was nice and sunny, but there was a chill and the same weather is predicted for tomorrow.

WATCHDOG: OK, thanks Vern, thank you very much. Roadrunner?

ROADRUNNER: Yes, Watchdog?

WATCHDOG: Ron, just a minute. Taylor has a question for Livingood.

TAYLOR: Livingood, are you there?

LIVINGOOD: This is Livingood, go ahead.

TAYLOR: The problem for us is coming through the Honor Guard.

LIVINGOOD: Taylor, this is Livingood. I'll take my cue on that from your counterpart. There is no problem. We'll take our cue from them. [*The Chinese head of security had assured Livingood that his President and the entire American party would be perfectly safe; the Chinese Honor Guard would not be armed.*]

TAYLOR: I understand. Thank you.

LIVINGOOD: Bob, also be advised that you are now riding in the left instead of the right. A left jump seat. Searchlight will be in the left seat.

TAYLOR: I understand. I have no other questions. Thank you.

LIVINGOOD: Roger, this is Livingood. Also be advised, I will be changing all of these instructions and stuff. Looks like it is going to be like this many days. [*The Chinese would inform the Americans each night of the schedule for the next day.*]

TAYLOR: Roger.

WATCHDOG: Yeah, we're getting the point on this, Bill.

ROADRUNNER: Yes, sir, and we got the point this afternoon very loud and clear. I think that it's their way of telling us it's their show.

WATCHDOG: That's right, and we know that and I think we've got a good basic framework to fit everything into. And, as you pointed out earlier, what they have added is an expansion of what has previously been given to us.

ROADRUNNER: Yes, sir, and we are prepared. I realize the problems it causes at this late date when people are mentally prepared to have to throw changes at them. Be advised, I am convinced in my own mind that everybody will be handled beautifully tomorrow, and there will be enough people from their side to make sure our people move properly.

WATCHDOG: Got it. Yeah. OK. I've got that. I don't have anything else. So, why don't we sign off, if you don't have anything else, we've got to get started early in the morning.

ROADRUNNER: Yes, sir. I understand that. Have a very good trip and we'll look forward to seeing you at 11:32 tomorrow.

WATCHDOG: Yeah. It's incredible! I can't believe the time flew so fast.

ROADRUNNER: Nor can we. Be advised, we're ready!

WATCHDOG: OK. I know you are. Listen, Ron, any word on Timmie or the press corps yet?

ROADRUNNER: No, sir. That's a negative.

WATCHDOG: Ooooooookay! Has the plane landed?

ROADRUNNER: Yes, it has landed, and Livingood informs me that they are at the hotel now.

WATCHDOG: Good. Well, if there are any problems give me a call.

ROADRUNNER: Roger. I think we've got our answers for tomorrow and we'll look forward to tomorrow night to get our answers for the next day.

WATCHDOG: I guess we'll do that every night.

ROADRUNNER: Yes, sir. It looks that way.

WATCHDOG: OK. Well, thank you. We'll sign off here unless you have anything else.

ROADRUNNER: No, sir. I have nothing else. All of us send our best and *bon voyage*.

WATCHDOG: OK. Thank you. Good night. See you tomorrow.

Roadrunner paused to listen to the echo of Watchdog's "See you tomorrow" ring in his ears. Unbelievable. This historic event was about to happen. The President of the United States was arriving in the People's Republic of China tomorrow. Roadrunner would be going home soon. He would later say that preparing for the President's trip to China had been the toughest thing he had ever done in his life.

CHAPTER XXIV

"THE WEEK THAT CHANGED THE WORLD"

FEBRUARY 21, 1972

In the end, it is always the reporters, pundits, editors, and photographers who judge how well a Presidential visit comes off. Evidently Roadrunner, Snapshot, and their colleagues had done their work well, because most of the news accounts, as the following excerpts show, bubbled with ebullience. The correspondents probably wouldn't have been so happy had there not been enough telephone lines in Shanghai!

*   *   *

THE WASHINGTON POST
Monday, February 21, 1972

PRESIDENT IN CHINA FOR SUMMIT
Chou Greets Nixon Amid Prospects of A Historic New Era
by Stanley Karnow

PEKING, Feb. 21 (Monday) – President Nixon landed here today to open a summit meeting that promises to herald a new era in relations between the United States and the People's Republic of China.

Mr. Nixon was greeted by Premier Chou En-lai and other senior Chinese leaders as he descended from the presidential aircraft, the Spirit of '76. Following the President off the airplane were Mrs. Nixon, Secretary of State William P. Rogers, White House National Security Adviser Henry Kissinger, Presidential Assistant H. R. Haldeman and other members of the official party.

Mao Tse-tung was not present. The aged Chinese Communist Party Chairman is expected to meet the President late this week in Peking and possibly again in Hangchou, the resort city in central China.

Cordial, Austere Welcome

The welcome accorded the President by Chou and his associates was cordial yet austere.

After his arrival at 11:40 A.M. Peking time (10:40 P.M. Sunday EST), Mr. Nixon was escorted by Chou to a position of honor to hear a Chinese military band play the Star-Spangled Banner and China's national anthem.

With Mrs. Nixon and the official party behind them, the President and Chou then reviewed a contingent of Chinese troops. Mr. Nixon and the Premier thereupon climbed into a large black Chinese-made Red Flag limousine. The ceremony lasted less than 20 minutes.

In accordance with Chinese practice there were no speeches. The only slogans present were prominent airport placards bearing such aphorisms as "Long Live the People's Republic of China" and "The Basic Theory That Guides Our Thought is Marxism-Leninism."

Peking's foreign diplomatic representatives were advised last night that they would be excluded from the airport reception. They have also been told that they would not be invited to the state dinner being held for Mr. Nixon this evening in the Great Hall of the People, the site of banquets for foreign dignitaries.

This suggests that the Chinese plan to treat the President's visit as a strictly bilateral Sino–American encounter, rather than a lavish ceremonial occasion.

The lack of extravagant attention was also likely to be visible as the President's motorcade—which was to include buses for nearly 100 newsmen—made the 40-minute drive from the airport through Peking to a special compound of guest houses on the city's western outskirts.

Street Slogans

The drive from the airport was to follow an avenue of trees bordering rice fields and orchards. This leads into a gray landscape of factories and work-

President Nixon's arrival in China.

ers' tenements, a district where slogans like 'Grasp the Revolution to Promote Production' adorn street corners and buildings. From the suburbs, the route of the President's motorcade was to take him into downtown Peking along Chang An Chih—the Street of Perpetual Peace—which emerges into the celebrated Tienanmen Square, the Plaza of the Gate of Celestial Peace.

The square, an area nearly 100 acres in size, is the scene of gigantic rallies and parades marking such occasions as China's National day and May Day. It was also the site of huge demonstrations during Mao's tumultuous Cultural Revolution, which faded three years ago.

Anti-American slogans were on display in the square today despite the President's imminent arrival. One read, 'We Warmly Hail the Great Victories of the Three Indochinese Peoples in Their War Against U.S. Imperialism and for National Salvation.'

Support for Arabs

Another slogan decorating the red Tienanmen Gate, atop which Mao usually appears on holidays, expressed support for the Arabs 'in their struggle against U.S. imperialism and Zionism.'

Mr. Nixon's route was to take him past such buildings as the Museum of the Chinese Revolution and the Great Hall of the People. The Great Hall, constructed in socialist-realist style, was built by more than 14,000 people in 11 months during the 1958-1959 period known as the Great Leap Forward.

By 1 P.M. (midnight EST) the President and his party were scheduled to reach their compound of guest houses, modern two- and three-story buildings originally built for Soviet aid technicians in the 1950s and set in a sector called Jade Abyss Pool Park.

Pakistani President Zulfiqar Ali Bhutto stayed in one of the guest houses during his visit here earlier this month. Another visitor who stayed there was North Vietnamese Premier Pham Van Dong, who came to Peking in the fall.

The park is a maximum-security area surrounded by electrified wire fencing. Several Chinese leaders also reside in a sector of the park, some distance from where Mr. Nixon will stay.

First Talks

The U.S. and Chinese groups are scheduled to begin their first round of talks this afternoon. The discussions will take place in the Great Hall of the People, where Chou En-lai maintains his office.

Speaking to newsmen aboard the Spirit of '76 yesterday, the President stressed that he and the Chinese leaders were meeting as total strangers without any clear philosophical understanding of each other.

Mr. Nixon explained that this contrasts with his encounters with such other world leaders as Japanese Prime Minister Eisaku Sato and British Prime Minister Edward Heath. 'Because of a lack of communication we are as much a mystery to them as they are a mystery to us,' he said.

The President voiced the hope that he would find a common basis for discussing the practical problems which may arise in his talks with the Chinese, adding: 'It would (be) useful on the part of both sides to discuss our philosophical backgrounds, differences and some similarities.'

Continuing his analysis of the Chinese, Mr. Nixon said that 'they take the long view.' He explained that his own approach to world problems 'is not tactical.'

The President disclosed that his daily sessions with the Chinese will last two hours in the afternoon. He will reserve his mornings for White House work.

Could Last Longer

Mr. Nixon went on to say that the meetings could last longer. 'We are leaving it totally flexible,' he said. 'If we get into productive talks, we are perfectly free to continue. I am prepared to participate in the talks as long as our hosts want to participate in them.'

Referring to the likelihood that long sessions will feature lots of tea, the President said that he likes tea.

According to Western diplomatic sources here, the President is apt to find himself confronted with profound philosophical discussions when he meets with Mao. In recent meetings with foreigners, these sources say, Mao has asked his guests such abstract questions as whether they believe in God.

In other conversations with foreigners lately, these sources recall, Mao has also ranged over subjects like the historical relations of peoples and their destinies.

Chou En-lai, on the other hand, will probably get down to practical matters. Or, as one diplomat here described the difference between the two leaders, 'Mao is a philosopher of history and Chou is making history.'

Western diplomats attuned to current Chinese thinking believe that Chou will make it clear to the President that Peking fully supports the Vietnamese Communists, and will in no way show any sympathy for the administration's Indochina policy.

These diplomats suggest that the premier may take the line

that the unification of Vietnam is a long way off, and that a U.S. withdrawal from the South would not necessarily augur a 'Communist takeover in Saigon.'

Speculation on Offensive

One subject of speculation here is whether the North Vietnamese will trigger an offensive in the South to coincide with the Peking summit. Such an offensive, it is thought, would inevitably provoke U.S. bombing of the North and embarrass both Mr. Nixon and Chou.

Signaling China's concern about a possible intensification of U.S. bombing, the Chinese Foreign Ministry issued a formal statement on Saturday denouncing the American air raids against North Vietnam last week.

The statement said that the bombings 'have completely shed the disguise of sham peace and laid bare the aggressive features of the U.S. aggressors.'

There is some indication here that the North Vietnamese and other Indochinese Communist movements are planning to hold a meeting with the former Cambodian chief of state Prince Norodom Sihanouk, who has been living in Peking since his ouster in March, 1970.

Sihanouk is at present in Hanoi, but he reportedly hinted that he would be willing to meet with Mr. Nixon and would return to Peking to do so.

There is no confirmation of reports that North Vietnamese

politburo member Le Duc Tho
is now in Peking to see the
President. Some sources believe, however, that Chou En-lai
would be receptive to arranging
an encounter between Mr. Nixon and the Hanoi leader.

Cooperating With Press

Even though they are giving
the President relatively low-key
treatment domestically, the
Chinese are cooperating in
extraordinary fashion with the
nearly 200 American newsmen
and technicians here to cover
the visit.

Reporters are being given
interpreters and automobiles,
and they have been invited to
visit a number of sights in the
Peking area. These include
schools, universities, factories,
collective farms and hospitals,
many of which are never seen
by resident foreign correspondents and diplomats.

The newsmen accompanying
the President are working out of
a special press sector in the
Palace of Nationalities, which is
normally used for meetings of
China's minority peoples like
Tibetans, Uighurs and Kazakhs.

The palace is equipped for
the visit with long-distance telephones, teletype machines and
luxurious sound booths for
broadcasters.

With all their cooperation,
however, the Chinese are making it plain both to newsmen
and U.S. government officials
that they are guests of the People's Republic of China and
should take nothing for granted.

In a welcoming speech last
night, a Chinese spokesman said
that if U.S. press officials wanted to use the press room for
briefings, they should submit
their requests and the Foreign
Ministry 'will consider the matter.'

Shanghai Stopover

Flying aboard two chartered
Pan American Boeing 707s, the
press corps preceded its arrival
in Peking yesterday with a stop-
over at Shanghai airport. There
was a perceptible mood of excitement aboard the aircraft as
it carried the first large contingent of American newsmen to
visit China since Communists
took power in 1949.

Summing up the general
mood, one Washington reporter
exclaimed: 'History, here I am!'

American reporters and the
airplane crews were tendered a
lunch at the airport restaurant
by a group of Shanghai editors.
There was much drinking of
convivial toasts in a fiery sor-
ghum liquor called maotai as
well as a sweet grape wine that
might have been labeled Mani-
schewitz.

But the Chinese editors, despite their cordiality, drew the
line at revelations. When a
reporter asked about the fate of
Marshal Lin Piao, Mao's former
heir who has been purged, an
editor replied, 'Have some more
duck.'

THE EVENING STAR
Washington, D.C.
Monday, February 21, 1972

NIXON, MAO TALK FRANKLY
By Henry S. Bradsher, Star Staff Writer

PEKING- President Nixon had 'serious and frank discussions' with Chairman Mao Tse-tung 3½ hours after he arrived in Peking and then, after a meeting with Premier Chou En-lai, asked the Chinese to 'start a long march' with the United States toward peace.

The quickness of the hour-long meeting with Mao at his capital residence, following the turn out of Chou and other top Chinese leaders at the airport, emphasized the attention the People's Republic was giving the Nixon visit.

In his toast at the banquet in the Great Hall of the People, Premier Chou said that although fundamental differences existed between the U.S. and China, these differences 'should not hinder the countries from establishing normal state relations on the basis of five principles— mutual respect for sovereignty and territorial integrity, mutual non-aggression, non-interference in internal affairs, equality and mutual benefits and peaceful coexistence.

Nixon, in his response suggesting the 'long march together,' said the two countries should march 'not in lockstep but on different roads toward the same goal' of justice and equality.

The meeting of Mao with Nixon had not been announced on the President's schedule. It delayed the announced beginning of Nixon's talks with Chou.

The premier is expected to handle detailed talks with Nixon on Sino-American relations and world problems, but in China Mao sets the line.

Following his talks with Chou, Nixon and the Americans accompanying him here were guests at the state banquet in the Great Hall.

Presidential Press Secretary Ronald Ziegler announced Nixon's meeting with Mao. He refused to elaborate on his description of 'serious and frank discussions' or disclose subjects.

In normal Chinese Communist terminology, 'serious and frank' indicates that the two sides disagreed on their points of view— which is only to be expected under the circumstances. There was no hint of unpleasantness.

Mao was seconded by Chou at the meeting and Nixon was accompanied by Henry A. Kissinger, his National Security Adviser. Pressed by reporters, Ziegler said Secretary of State William P. Rogers was not present.

Rogers accompanied the President and Kissinger to the later meeting with Chou, which opened one hour and 25 minutes late at the Great Hall of the People.

Also with Mao at his meeting with Nixon was a deputy protocol officer who had met Nixon in Shanghai this morning and flew to Peking with him. She is Wang Ha-jung, who is rumored to be Mao's niece. She also sat in on Mao's recent talks with Pakistani Zulfikar Ali-Bhutto.

The Premier turned out an impressive showing of his top government leaders for the airport reception that gave full honors to the visiting President, but was nonetheless brisk and brief. The public was not invited to the airport.

Along the 10-mile route into the city, spectators seemed to be just people caught by the halting of normal traffic.

They watched the presidential motorcade with polite curiosity, but no enthusiasm—as the Peking public watches most official visitors.

Neither was the diplomatic corps invited to the airport. There had been intense speculation among Peking's resident diplomats how the Chinese would handle the problem of some of their friends such as North Vietnam having no relations with the United States. The government simply avoided the problem by leaving diplomats out.

Aside from 42 officially identified government officials at the airport, 17 of whom Nixon met personally, there was only a large military honor guard and security and press officials.

A military band gave a well-rehearsed version of the Star Spangled Banner before playing China's own anthem, 'March of the Volunteers.'

Neither Mao nor his wife, Chiang Ching, appeared at the airport, to the surprise of none of the American officials. With them missing and with two Shanghai-based members of the Communist party Politburo also not at the airport, although reported in Shanghai to be in Peking now, the main leaders of China's overlapping government and party high command met Nixon.

Next to Chou was Yeh Chien-ying, who seems to have been acting as defense minister since Lin Piao was purged from that job and the position of Mao's heir apparent last September. Yeh, 74, and Chou negotiated as a team with Chiang Kai-shek's Nationalist government during the 1940s when George Marshall and other Americans tried to stave off China's civil war.

This was, so far as anyone at the airport could remember, the first time high American officials, and especially anyone in a U.S. military uniform like some presidential aides, had been back in Peking to meet with

Communist officials.

Chou's right-hand man in the civil government, Deputy Premier Li Hsien-nien, was next in the receiving line. With him was his wife, Lin Chia-mei, who is reported to be an official in the finance and trade staff office which Li supervises.

Working wives in China, including those of senior officials, are usually important figures in their own right who earned their positions. The common case of a top man's wife holding a good job is a sign of involvement of Chinese Communist wives rather than a matter of nepotism.

Next was Kuo Mo-jo, an 80-year-old intellectual who is vice chairman of the standing committee for China's inactive National Peoples Congress or parliament.

Then came Chi Peng-fei, who recently became foreign minister after years as deputy foreign minister. He was accompanied by his wife, Hsu Han-ping, the only other woman in the top group greeting President and Mrs. Nixon.

The acting mayor of Peking, Wu Teh; a soldier who recently became minister of foreign trade, Pai Hsing-kuo; and the only service chief to escape being purged with Lin Piao, navy commander Hsiao Chin-kuang, stood ahead of other officials.

It was a sizeable turnout in honor of the American President, who smiled and shook hands with each as a translator helped another official to introduce them.

Nixon drove to the state guest house in the western part of the city. The house, known as Angling Terrace for Fishing Possibilities in Peking Lakes, housed ousted Cambodian Prince Norodom Sihanouk until the Chinese government gave him a more prominent exile home here.

Sihanouk flew last week to Hanoi. There is no indication he will return during Nixon's visit—in fact he seems to have deliberately absented himself for the occasion.

Cambodia and the whole Indochina situation are likely to be among the topics Nixon and Chou will discuss. But Chou made it plain that he cannot arrange an end to the Indochina war and Nixon has said he does not expect to achieve such a result here.

In fact just what result might be achieved other than some 'ongoing communications' that the White House has spoken about was unclear as the cool dusk that settled over Peking.

But the full protocol honors that the Chinese government gave Nixon seemed to bode well for an atmosphere in which fruitful results could be sought.

UNITED PRESS INTERNATIONAL
February 21, 1972

EVEN THE CHOPSTICKS, CHOU BANQUET A HIT
By Stewart Hensley

PEKING — Pat and Richard Nixon wielded chopsticks like old pros tonight at a banquet thrown by Chou En-lai.

The American guests ate with obvious gusto, and the trim Chinese waiters and waitresses were hard pressed to keep the wine goblets filled, so vigorously and frequently did the Nixons toast their hosts.

The dinner lasted almost three hours. The supping was leisurely, the sipping unrestrained.

An ebullient Nixon, after formally toasting Chou from the rostrum in front of the immense Great Hall of the People, stepped down and meandered from table to table among lesser officials, lifting his glass, clicking it, taking a tiny nip, nodding his head smartly, moving on to the next guest. He appeared to miss no one.

Chou was an exemplary host, apparently conversing at times in English with his American guests at the big round table where he sat between the President and Mrs. Nixon.

Once, Chou served Mrs. Nixon a bit of food from a dish. Another time the tiny, slender Chinese premier rose from his seat and reached as far as he could across the table to spear with his chopsticks what appeared to be a shrimp.

Aside from the serious, long formal toasts by Chou and Nixon, an air of joviality marked the first meal. The Nixons enjoyed the food and seemed to relish the company.

Chou, 73, though ramrod straight in his leather chair, several times allowed a look of enjoyment to flit across his normally severe mien.

Through the dinner, fragile, traditional Chinese music gave way first to what the Chinese described as 'revolutionary themes,' then the large orchestra broke into 'Home on the Range' and then 'America the Beautiful.'

The main table at the banquet was huge and round. A bower of flowers, several feet in diameter, highlighted the circular table. Chou and an interpreter sat between the Nixons.

They all spoke animatedly as white-coated Chinese waiters flitted unobtrusively throughout the immense hall, serving the guests.

Mrs. Nixon was splendidly coiffed and wore a severe black dress with a tight white collar.

When the guests entered the hall, the Nixons and Chou stood at attention in front of the flags of their respective countries as a band played first, 'The Star Spangled Banner,' then the Chinese anthem, 'March of the Volunteers.'

At one point while Nixon and Chou were dining, Henry A. Kissinger, the President's national security adviser, leaned over to talk with both men. Chou and Kissinger appeared to exchange light-hearted humor.

At several times in the dinner, Chou and Nixon appeared to converse in English.

Smaller tables were placed in neat rows throughout the hall. Hundreds of lesser officials sat at these tables, as well as visiting newsmen and technicians. The tables were about half the size of the main banquet table.

THE WEEK THAT CHANGED THE WORLD
by David C. Whitney

As part of his plan to bring about a 'generation of peace,' President Richard Nixon culminated a period of careful diplomatic preparation in February 1972 by flying to Communist China for an eight-day visit to open the way toward normalization of relations, cultural exchanges and trade with the world's largest nation. For more than two decades, the United States had refused official recognition of the Communist government of China. As Senator, Vice-President, and presidential candidate, Nixon himself had been one of the foremost advocates of containing Communist China. Therefore, the Policy reversal had almost as many personal overtones as it did international implications and warranted the President's own assessment that 'This was the week that changed the world.'

THE LOS ANGELES TIMES
February 28, 1972

NIXON IN CHINA

It was not 'the week that changed the world, but the President can be forgiven some exaggeration in the enthusiasm of a mission accomplished. The record suggests that it was a stroke of statesmanship, intelligently conceived, carefully executed.

TIME MAGAZINE
March 6, 1972

[COVER: Four pictures, separated by a large Chinese character: A
black and white of President Nixon shaking hands with Chairman
Mao; and three color photos: The President and the Premier; The
Nixon party at the Great Wall; and a scene from "The Red Detachment of Women."]

In *A Letter from the Publisher*, Henry Luce wrote, "'There is a
kaleidoscopic quality about the events and the trip,' White House
Correspondent Jerrold Schecter cabled from Peking last week. 'Each
moment fixed, then whirling on to a new sensation. This has been a
week of sights and sounds.'"

The Nation. Diplomacy/Cover Story
RICHARD NIXON'S LONG MARCH
TO SHANGHAI

What, if anything, did Richard
Nixon bring back from Peking?
Above all, the event itself, the
fact that it took place. Rarely
had a U.S. President spent so
long a time—a full week—in a
foreign land. The visit, moreover, was to a country with
which the U.S. did not even
have diplomatic relations and
which for two decades had been
a virtual enemy. That paradox
was obscured by the pageantry
and (most of the time) by the
warm atmosphere. As summits
go, the meeting was a glittering
technical success, stage-managed
with precision.

Time Essay
PEKING IS WORTH A BALLET

The scene in Peking's Great
Hall of the People last week
certainly had to be one of history's great ironies. There,
while a Chinese army band
played America, the Beautiful, a
U.S. President merrily clinked
mao-tai glasses with his Chinese
hosts, long considered the true
'baddies' of the Communist
world. Nor was it just any
American President either; it
was a conservative Republican
who has long had a reputation
as being the perfect cold war-
rior. The American public
could be excused if it found its
neck wrenched and its equilibri-
um upset by the surprising spectacle of Nixon chumming it up
with his former enemies and
sitting patiently through a revolutionary ballet in Peking.

LIFE MAGAZINE
March 3, 1972

[COVER: A black and white photo of Chairman Mao in his study, with a red and white banner across it, "Nixon in the land of Mao."]

NIXON'S GREAT LEAP INTO CHINA

Rotund and jovial, the great revolutionary welcomed Richard Nixon to his private study as if the United States and China had been warm friends for the last quarter century, instead of bitter enemies. It was the extraordinary beginning of the most extraordinary week in the history of personal presidential diplomacy.

Only an hour or two later, Nixon was locked in intense discussion with Chairman Mao Tse-tung's chief associate, Premier Chou En-lai. While the President was occupied with matters of state, Pat Nixon seized the opportunity to have a good look at China - and let the Chinese have a good look at her. There was a visit to the Peking Zoo, where she saw a panda, and to a commune, where she struck up a tentative acquaintance with a pig. And in the kitchen of the Peking Hotel she talked to workers and received a chrysanthemum with a grasshopper on it - carved out of a big radish.

A PRESIDENT WRAPPED IN AN ENIGMA
by Hugh Sidey

Nothing has swallowed up the presidency like China. Richard Nixon is linked to America by his electronic umbilical and an occasional courier plane carefully shepherded up from Shanghai, but those TV pictures America gets with the morning eggs are deceptive. Nixon is farther away than he seems, in a realm less accessible than any of us thought. There is so much meaning in what he is doing that for the moment there is almost no meaning.

He came in vast silence. It was the only such welcome for a President in history, and it was stunning. We stood under a cloudless sky hearing only the sound of each other's voices and an occasional truck in the distance. The Spirit of '76 split the hush, snarled up to the small figure of Chou En-lai. Then the silence again. One could hear the Nixons' voices 30 yards away. The panoply of presidential power that has brought whole cities into the street cheering was shrunken to a few people, a little uncertain and no more impressive than the rest of us. France's Andre Malraux said it would take 50 years to figure out what happened in China in the last week of February 1972. At least, I'd say.

LIFE EDITORIAL

The real success or failure of the Peking mission may not be visible for months or years, when it will be manifest in responses to events yet unforeseen. A long march has indeed begun.

U.S. NEWS & WORLD REPORT
February 28, 1972

NIXON IN CHINA,
WHO STANDS TO GAIN MOST
THE HARD BARGAINERS FACING NIXON

Waiting in Peking for Richard Nixon were two of the toughest —and most ruthless—Communist revolutionaries of the century. Mao Tse-tung, Chairman of China's communist party, is the largely self-educated son of a Chinese peasant. At 78, he is still No. 1 man.

Premier Chou En-lai is No. 2, a well-educated and self-styled member of a 'bourgeois' family. He is 73. One is the brain, the other is the mouth. It is Mao who speaks to China, but it is Chou who speaks for China to the rest of the world. What this means to Mr. Nixon is that almost all substantive talks are scheduled with the Premier—but always within the framework of what Mao wants.

NEWSWEEK
March 6, 1972

[COVER: Colored picture of President Nixon and Premier Chou En-lai toasting at the banquet.]

As he headed home from China this week, Richard Nixon had ample reason for satisfaction. His historic seven days in the People's Republic, which included a visit with Chairman Mao, had not only opened a new door to China; they ushered in a new age of diplomatic pragmatism that is sure to have a global influence.

1ST STEPS OF LONG MARCH

As 'The Spirit of '76' approached Peking airport, the chief U.S. security man on board radioed to an agent on the ground. 'What about the crowd?' he asked. Back came the answer, 'There is no crowd.' Incredulous, the Secret Service man in the plane tried again: 'Did you say no crowd?' 'That is affirmative—no crowd.'

Richard Nixon had barely arrived at the spacious State Guest House in Peking to prepare for his first substantive talks with Chinese Premier Chou En-lai. Suddenly the telephone rang. 'Chairman Mao Tse-tung,' said the polite voice on the other end of the phone, 'would be pleased to receive the President of the United States at his residence, at Mr. Nixon's convenience.'

The formal toasts were over and in the Chinese fashion, the President was beginning to stroll from table to table to salute his hosts with a glass of mao tai. Chou En-lai appeared at Mr. Nixon's side and whispered: 'Mr. President, I know that they played 'America the Beautiful' at your inauguration. That is why I have asked the band to play it for you now.

From its very beginning, Richard Nixon's mission to China was a mosaic of surprises. No Presidential trip in history had been so meticulously planned, yet the expected often did not happen and the unexpected frequently did. The President's party hoped that the airport reception would include some hoopla and pageantry, but that was conspicuously missing. Everyone knew that a meeting with Mao was somewhere on the schedule, but no one dared to dream that it would come within three hours of Mr. Nixon's arrival. And while few doubted that the visitors would be treated with courtesy and care, Chou En-lai's thoughtfulness and special grace surpassed all hopes. But most surprising of all was how the leaders of the U.S. and China—whose nations have been locked in bitter hostility for 22 years—met in an atmosphere like that of a grand reunion. Mr. Nixon himself captured the mood when he proposed in his toast at the opening banquet that the two countries 'start a long March together.' And in a way, it seemed they already had.

Throughout the week, all Peking was a stage across which Richard Nixon strode like the hero in a Chinese opera. He had done his homework; he knew all the television camera positions on the Great Wall. He had learned his lines: he quoted Mao Tse-tung's poetry at the opening banquet and greeted Chou before one session with a lusty Ni hau ('How are you?'). And yet if Mr. Nixon was the star of the show, there was no doubt that the drama had been produced and directed by Chou. From its inception, the visit was orchestrated by the Chinese, with a unique mixture of elegance and simplicity, propriety and warmth.

The tone struck at the opening of Mr. Nixon's first substantive discussion with Chou also seemed a good omen. As the two sides sat in a reception room of the Great Hall of the People beneath a landscaped mural of the Long March, Chou bantered about the youthfulness of several White House staffers. 'We have too many elderly people in our government,' he said, 'so on this point we should learn from you.' And the Premier seemed even more good-natured at that night's nine-course banquet when he hailed Mr. Nixon's journey to Peking as a 'positive move,' and exclaimed that 'the gates to friendly contact have finally been opened.'

Mrs. Nixon, dressed in a scarlet cloth coat, made the rounds of Peking from a commune to a hotel kitchen to the zoo. It was she who announced that the Chinese were giving the U.S. two giant pandas in return for two musk oxen.

As Mr. Nixon toured the old Imperial Palace, known to the Chinese as the Forbidden City, his escort, China's military chieftain Yeh Chien-ying, was asked his view of the Nixon journey. Yeh replied that the President had brought with him 'peace and good harvests.' And again that evening, at an American-hosted banquet featuring grapefruit, oranges and champagne flown in from the U.S., the cordiality still continued.

As one student of foreign affairs suggested: 'The talks in Peking could turn out to be one of the hinges of postwar history.'

GIRL FROM WEST 11TH ST.

Whenever President Nixon and Premier Chou had something to say to each other last week, a slim, bespectacled young Chinese woman was present to help them bridge the language gap. Many in the U.S. who watched her in action were startled to find that her English came across with a distinctly American accent—until they also learned that Nancy Tang was born in New York City and spent her first years there.

A CHINESE DIARY
by Mel Elfin

Monday, Feb. 21 — New York Times man Max Frankel and I go shopping. As we walk up one of the large commercial streets, we realize we are as much an object of curiosity to the Chinese as they are to us. After buying a few things, Max and I sit down for a luncheon snack at a primitive neighborhood cafeteria and between us spend 7 cents. Now, what accountant in the U.S. is going to believe that expense-account item: 'Lunch, 3.5 cents'?

Friday, Feb. 25. Looking back over my stay in Peking, I realize that I have walked the darkest streets by night unafraid and left my hotel rooms unlocked without fearing for my possessions. I have not tipped a hotel employee or seen a beggar, a drunkard or a litterbug in the streets. But neither have I seen an attractively dressed citizen, or a dog, or heard an animated conversation.

Saturday, Feb 26. Can Maoism survive Mao? I think not. As people as imaginative as the Chinese cannot live permanently in drab regimentation. This was brought home to me at the ballet in Peking when a Western woman journalist entered, dressed in a dazzling silk blouse of ancient Chinese design. I saw the eyes of the women in the Mao jackets focus upon her until the curtain went up. That told me more about modern China than almost anything else.

CHINA MEETS THE PRESS

Aside from its lack of copy paper (and wastebaskets), the press center constructed by the Chinese Government for the U.S. news corps exceeded all expectations. In addition to elaborate working facilities, it was equipped with a basketball court, a bowling alley and dozens of pigtailed waitresses dispensing cups of green tea.

The language gap also proved less of a problem than expected. The Chinese managed to supply every two reporters with their own interpreter—who was also happy to act as a guide, or watchdog, for his journalistic charges. 'It's like having a possessive wife,' grumbled old China hand Theodore H. (Thunder Out of China) White. Sooner or later, nearly all of White's colleagues asked him the same question: How has China changed? His invariable reply: 'Completely.'

TV: AN EYEFUL OF CHINA,
A THIMBLEFUL OF INSIGHT

U.S. television had gone to the moon; now it was China's turn. Newsweek Contributing Editor Joseph Morganstern watched the network coverage of President Nixon's visit and wrote these impressions: It was billed as an official visit, which implied pomp, circumstance and plenty of background briefings from friendly White House news sources. The networks, therefore, assigned their White House correspondents, and also their most experienced anchor men, the ones who'd performed so well at public events from President Kennedy's funeral to moonshots at Cape Kennedy. They made up standard news teams to cover a spectacular in standard American terms. Not a single network seat on the press plane went to a specialist in Chinese languages or Chinese culture. Each network had its own Sinologist, to be sure, and very impressive they were—articulate, attractive, knowledgeable. But the Sinologists were in New York. There was little they could do to help their colleagues in Peking once the interpreters proved reticent or inadequate, the personality pieces wore thin, the logistical problems piled up and the White House news sources turned out to be as tight-lipped as their Chinese counterparts. With hours of air time to fill and easy access to little but trivia and carefully guided tours, the networks were thrown back on their own resources. The Sinologists were 7,000 miles from the scene.

THE LITTLE THINGS THAT COUNT
by Sydney Liu

To the millions of Americans watching President Nixon's televised arrival in Peking, the welcome must have seemed frosty indeed. No cymbals or gongs rang out in greeting. No children came forward to present Mrs. Nixon with flowers. It was all very official—Chou En-lai and a galaxy of China's top leaders standing stiffly in a receiving line. Yet to a China watcher like myself, the airport reception seemed downright friendly, the warmest reception that Chou could possibly arrange for someone whom Peking only a year ago was calling 'the most ferocious and cruel chieftain of imperialism.'

In watching Chinese ceremonies, it is important to remember that it is the small, subtle gestures that count. A smile or frown can tell more than a page of pleasantries. The protocol-minded Chinese do not do anything just for diplomatic courtesy. Everything they do has its meaning. Thus it was highly significant that the People's Liberation Army guard of honor was at the airport. Not only was the 500-man guard of honor the biggest that China watchers can remember, but the entire practice of having a guard of honor for visiting heads of state was done away with several years ago and restored only this year. To provide such an impressive guard of honor for Mr. Nixon's arrival—and to raise the Stars and Stripes at Peking airport—were truly remarkable gestures of welcome to the President.

Yet another significant sign of respect was the fact that not just one or two, but nearly all of China's senior leaders appeared at the airfield and again at the banquet Monday night. Neither Emperor Haile Selassie of Ethiopia nor President Zulfikar Ali Bhutto of Pakistan received such honors in their recent state visits to Peking. Yet both Ethiopia and Pakistan have formal diplomatic relations with China.

To give additional honor to Mr. Nixon, Chairman Mao broke his practice of seeing visiting dignitaries at the end rather than at the beginning of their trips to China. The smile on Mao's face was an unmistak-

able indicator that the Nixon–Mao talks were in fact cordial.

Equally fascinating was the unprecedented coverage in the Chinese press of the trip. China's most important newspaper, Peking's People's Daily, gave the event continuous front-page banner-headline treatment, with photos and numerous stories in its regular six-page issue. Radio Peking and provincial radio stations broadcast reports of the visit, and all over China people gathered before loudspeakers to hear the news.

There is little doubt in my mind that meticulous planning and thorough rehearsal by both sides enabled Mr. Nixon to start his 'Long March' with Chou En-lai so favorably and so fast. In his banquet speech, the President was ready with a quotation from one of Mao's poems. Moreover, the President proved extremely apt at making those little gestures the Chinese believe to be important—such as helping Chou En-lai off with his coat when the Premier came to visit him at the State Guest House. And, if my personal impressions as a Chinese are any gauge, Pat Nixon will leave behind her in China a deep impression of an American First Lady who talked to every Chinese she met as an equal and showed an intense interest in learning about China.

Mr. Nixon's Chinese hosts, for their part, were extremely gracious. Even such a small thing

Roadrunner comes home.

as playing 'Home on the Range' at the first banquet was not without its significance. Certainly it has never happened before at the Great Hall of the People. Supposedly, all 'bourgeois' music—as well as all Russian music—is now banned because it is considered decadent.

And in his speech at the opening Banquet, Chou went out of his way to express his wishes for the 'normalization' of relations between China and the United States. This, in itself, was a major step, and a well-planned one. For all the Chinese leaders, and especially Chou En-lai, are masters at the specific use of words, and he would not have chosen such words unless he believed that a formal, friendly relationship with Washington was a distinct possibility in the near future.

In my opinion, that opening is destined to grow much larger. After the pandas and the musk oxen are exchanged, journalists and scholars, athletes and cultural groups, tourists and trade officials will almost certainly follow across the Pacific. Possibly there is an element of wishful thinking on my part, but I am convinced that a decade from now the Nixon visit to China will be seen for what it is—the beginning of a rapprochement between two major Pacific powers and, as such, a landmark in modern diplomatic history.

And Roadrunner came home. And so did Watchdog and Snapshot and Schrauth and all the men who had played a role in making history in the People's Republic of China. They gathered up their families and they accepted an invitation to go to Disney World and christen a Chinese junk destined to sail the man-made waters of Walt Disney's magic kingdom. Roadrunner said that it was quite a contrast to go from the land of wintry cold and Chairman Mao to the warm, make-believe fairyland of Mickey Mouse. "But some days, none of those hectic weeks in China seemed real, either," he decided.

EPILOGUE

Roadrunner returned to the People's Republic of China in 1978, at the invitation of Han Hsu, then Deputy Chief of Mission at the PRC Liaison Office in Washington. A visa was required for travel to the PRC, and they were still relatively hard to obtain. Han Hsu adroitly cut through the red tape. He also insisted that Roadrunner and Watchdog bring their wives and spend some time in China.

By the 1978 trip, Roadrunner had served as President Nixon's Director of the National Park Service. While the group was in Hangchou, they visited the Botanical Gardens, where Director P.Y. Tan told them that one of the Redwood trees planted by the President, *Sequoia sempervirens Endl*, had done very well. He proudly pointed out many, smaller trees in the surrounding area, young redwoods that had come from the original tree. Over five thousand additional redwood trees had been generated, many of them sent to the provinces for replanting. Unfortunately, the other tree, *Sequoiadendron giganteum Bucholz* (Giant Redwood) had not fared as well. "It was hit by worms in its second year of growth," Director Tan explained, adding, "From a book, we learned about the differences in climates. There is more moisture and fog during the summers in California. Summer in Hangchou is dry. We have installed sprinklers. We must struggle hard every day to find the answer to this problem."

When Roadrunner returned home, he was able to get the National Park Service and the U.S. Forest Service involved in restoring the Giant Redwood tree to health.

Signs at the base of the original trees read, "Presented by

409

President Richard Nixon of the United States during his visit in 1972." The Chinese like to tell visitors that Chairman Mao visited the trees and Premier Chou En-lai stopped there on many occasions as well. The Premier had made a point of telling Director Tan, "The Redwood trees were a symbol of the friendship between the people of America and China. As the trees grow stronger, so will the friendship and understanding."

The trees are a symbol, yes, but the roots grow stronger and deeper each day, bringing hope of peace everlasting for both Americans and Chinese. Roadrunner and Watchdog are proud of that. So is President Nixon, who wrote from La Casa Pacifica on July 19, 1978, "Dear Ron: I was delighted to get the report on our China Redwoods. I hope the symbolism they (the Chinese) spoke about becomes reality as the trees grow to maturity."

With the wisdom of hindsight, and the incredible collapse of communism in many parts of the world, today we dare also to hope that the tiniest seeds of democracy were planted in the People's Republic of China by President Richard Nixon in February of 1972. Roadrunner is very proud of the part he played in the week that really did change the world.

Appendix

February 14, 1972

<u>ORDER OF PRECEDENCE</u>
<u>U. S. PARTY</u>

1. THE PRESIDENT
2. Mrs. Nixon
3. Secretary of State William P. Rogers   Official
4. Dr. Henry A. Kissinger   Official
5. Mr. H. R. Haldeman   Official
6. Mr. Ronald L. Ziegler   Official
7. B/Gen Brent Scowcroft   Official
8. Asst Sec Marshall Green   Official
9. Mr. Dwight L. Chapin   Official
10. Mr. John A. Scali   Official
11. Mr. Patrick J. Buchanan   Official
12. Miss Rose Mary Woods   Official
13. Director Alfred Le S. Jenkins   Official
14. Mr. John Holdridge   Official
15. Mr. Winston Lord   Official
16. Mr. Ronald H. Walker   Unofficial
17. Mr. Gerald L. Warren   Press Staff
18. Dr. Walter R. Tkach   Unofficial
19. Mr. Timothy G. Elbourne   Press Staff
20. Mr. Michael R. Schrauth   Unofficial
21. Mr. Michael Raoul-Duval   Unofficial
22. Mr. John Thomas   Unofficial
23. Mr. Jonathan T. Howe   Unofficial
24. Mr. Lilburn E. Boggs   Security
25. Mr. Robert H. Taylor   Security
26. Mr. Wilson Livingood   Security
27. Mr. William L. Duncan   Security
28. Mr. William E. Hudson   Security
29. B/Gen Albert Redman, Jr.   Communications
30. Dr. William M. Lukash   Support
31. Col Ralph D. Albertazzie   Aircrew
32. LTC Vernon C. Coffey, Jr.   Support
33. Major John V. Brennan   Support

34.	Mr. Lawrence M. Higby	Unofficial
35.	Mrs. Florence Gwyer	Unofficial
36.	Miss Julienne L. Pineau	Unofficial
37.	Mrs. Nellie L. Yates	Unofficial
38.	Mr. Nicholas Platt	Unofficial
39.	Mr. Charles W. Freeman, Jr.	Unofficial
40.	Mr. Calvin E. Mehlert	Unofficial
41.	Mr. Paul E. Kovenock	Unofficial
42.	Mrs. Maggie C. Runkle	Unofficial
43.	Dr. Kenneth Riland	Unofficial
44.	Mr. Oliver T. Atkins	Unofficial
45.	Mr. Fritz Roland	Unofficial
46.	Mr. William Boyd Hartigan	Unofficial
47.	Mr. Bertram Gold	Unofficial
48.	Mr. David Michael Ronne	Unofficial
49.	Mrs. Rita De Santis	Unofficial
50.	Miss Diane Sawyer	Press Staff
51.	Mr. John P. D'Arcy	Press Staff
52.	Mr. Ray Zook	Press Staff
53.	Mr. Robert Manning	Press Staff
54.	Miss Constance Gerrard	Press Staff
55.	Mr. Byron Schumaker	Press Staff
56.	Mr. William Dale	Press Staff
57.	Mr. Ron Pontius	Press Staff
58.	Mrs. Geraldine Rudolph Breier	Press Staff
59.	Miss Mickey Copeland	Press Staff
60.	Mr. Roy Andres	WUI Ground Station
61.	Mr. Don Bacon	Newhouse
62.	Mr. Chuck Bailey	Minneapolis Tribune
63.	Mr. Aldo Beckman	Chicago Tribune
64.	Mr. Paul Benson	AT&T
65.	Mr. Bob Boyd	Knight
66.	Mr. Forrest Boyd	Mutual
67.	Mr. Henry Bradsher	Washington Star
68.	Mr. William F. Buckley, Jr.	Star Syndicate
69.	Mr. David Buksbaum	ABC Producer/Director
70.	Anthony Brunton	CBS Producer
71.	Mr. Stan Carter	NY Daily News
72.	Mr. Jim Cary	Copley
73.	Mr. John Chancellor	NBC
74.	Mr. Bob Considine	Hearst
75.	Mr. Frank Cormier	AP
76.	Mr. Walter Cronkite	CBS
77.	Mr. Lester Crystal	NBC Producer

78.	Mr. Marshall Davidson	CBS Vice Chairman
79.	Mr. Rolf Drucker	ABC Technical Director
80.	Mr. Dick Dudman	St Louis Post Dispatch
81.	Mr. Mel Elfin	Newsweek
82.	Mr. Edward Fouhy	CBS Producer
83.	Mr. Max Frankel	NY Times
84.	Mr. Don Fulsom	UPI Audio
85.	Mr. Joseph Gancie	ITT
86.	Mr. James Hargreaves	CBS Technical Director
87.	Mr. Henry Hartzenbusch	AP
88.	Mr. Stewart Hensley	UPI
89.	Mr. Tom Jarriel	ABC
90.	Mr. Bernard Kalb	CBS
91.	Mr. Stan Karnow	Washington Post
92.	Mr. Herb Kaplow	NBC
93.	Mr. Joseph Keating	ABC Producer
94.	Mr. Robert Keatley	Wall Street
95.	Mr. Norman Kempster	UPI
96.	Mr. James Kitchell	NBC Vice Chairman
97.	Mr. Ted Koppel	ABC
98.	Mr. Joseph Kraft	Pub. Hall Syndicate
99.	Mr. Dave Kraslow	Los Angeles Times
100.	Mr. Peter Lisagor	Chicago Daily News
101.	Mr. Raymond Lockhart	NBC Producer
102.	Mr. Jim McManus	Westinghouse
103.	Mr. Gordon Manning	CBS Producer
104.	Mr. Robert Martin	US News/ World Report
105.	Mr. Chester Mazurek	ABC Technical Director
106.	Mr. Don Meaney	NBC
107.	Mr. James Michener	Reader's Digest
108.	Mr. Hugh Mulligan	AP
109.	Mr. Tom O'Brien	ABC
110.	Mr. Larry O'Rourke	Philadelphia Bulletin
111.	Mr. Bernard Osborne	ABC Business Manager
112.	Mr. John Osborne	New Republic
113.	Mr. Walter Pfister	ABC Executive Producer
114.	Mr. Phil Potter	Baltimore Sun
115.	Mr. Dan Rather	CBS
116.	Mr. Harry Reasoner	ABC
117.	Mr. Jack Reynolds	NBC Radio Producer
118.	Mr. John Rich	NBC
119.	Mr. Bill Ringle	Gannett
120.	Mr. Tom Ross	Chicago Sun Times
121.	Mr. Jerry Schecter	Time Magazine

122.	Mr. Eric Sevareid	CBS
123.	Mr. R. H. Schackford	Scripps-Howard
124.	Mr. William Sheehan	ABC Producer
125.	Mr. Courtney Sheldon	Christian Science Mon
126.	Mr. Hugh Sidey	Life Magazine
127.	Mr. Bob Siegenthaler	ABC Chairman
128.	Mr. William Small	CBS Pool Producer
129.	Mr. Bill Sprague	Voice of America
130.	Mr. Jerry terHorst	Detroit News
131.	Miss Helen Thomas	UPI
132.	Mr. Howard Tuckner	ABC
133.	Mr. Robert Vitarelli	CBS Producer/Director
134.	Mr. Robert Voss	RCA Global Communic.
135.	Miss Barbara Walters (Guber)	NBC
136.	Miss Fay Wells	Storer
137.	Mr. Av Westin	ABC
138.	Mr. Theodore White	Public Broadcasting
139.	Mr. Richard Wilson	Des Moines Register
140.	Mr. Robert Wussler	CBS Executive Producer
141.	Mr. Murray Alvey	ABC Cameraman
142.	Mr. Isadore Bleckman	CBS Cameraman
143.	Mr. Frank Cancellare	UPI Photographer
144.	Mr. Bob Daugherty	AP Photographer
145.	Mr. John Dominis	Life Mag. Pool Photo
146.	Mr. Horst Faas	AP Photographer
147.	Mr. Dirck Halstead	UPI Photographer
148.	Mr. Bruce Hoertel	Pool Cameraman
149.	Mr. James Kartes	CBS Cameraman
150.	Mr. George Lawler	Communic. Satellite
151.	Mr. Wally McNamee	Newsweek Pool Photo
152.	Mr. Fred Montague	NBC Cameraman
153.	Mr. George Romilly	ABC Cameraman
154.	Mr. Masaaki Shiihara	NBC Cameraman
155.	Mr. Thomas Kelly	Security
156.	Mr. Alford Wong	Security
157.	Mr. Garry M. Jenkins	Security
158.	Mr. Dennis P. Shaw	Security
159.	Mr. Richard E. Keiser	Security
160.	Mr. John D. Ready	Security
161.	Mr. Charles T. Zboril	Security
162.	Mr. Harold G. Thomas	Security
163.	LTC James H. Gibbons	Communications
164.	LTC Lester C. McClelland	Aircrew
165.	LTC Carl A. Peden	Aircrew

166.	LTC Leonard C. Gulig	Aircrew
167.	LTC Laurence W. Donoho	Aircrew
168.	LTC Robert W. Rawlins	Aircraft support
169.	Maj Frederick W. Swift	Communications
170.	Maj Charles H. Freed	Communications
171.	Maj Reginald W. Bruff	Communications
172.	Maj Donald F. McKeown	Aircrew
173.	Maj John G. Schutes	Aircrew
174.	Maj Andrew A. Radel	Aircraft Support
175.	Maj Clark R. Morgan	Aircraft Support
176.	Maj James T. Morrow	Aircrew
177.	Maj Robert R. Mease	Aircrew
178.	Maj Robert R. Duke	Aircrew
179.	Capt Bruce A. Garrity	Aircrew
180.	Capt Kenneth R. Weber	Aircrew
181.	Mr. Mario Lilla	Communications
182.	CWO Orpheus E. Deaver	Communications
183.	CWO Ralph M. Douglas	Communications
184.	CWO Leonard C. Stephens	Communications
185.	SGM Richard J. McCoy	Communications
186.	CMSgt William J. Chappell	Aircrew
187.	CMSgt James W. Daniel	Aircrew
188.	CNSgt William H. Justice	Aircrew
189.	CMSgt Jose R. Lopez	Aircrew
190.	MSG Leon T. Moore	Communications
191.	ETCS Raymond C. Medbury	Communications
192.	SMSgt James H. Brown	Aircrew
193.	SMSgt Kenneth Dixon	Aircraft Support
194.	SMSgt Joseph Kuchinsky, Jr.	Aircrew
195.	SMSgt Louis G. Maughon	Aircrew
196.	SMSgt Tedd D. Wright	Aircrew
197.	Mr. William E. Kingsley	Communications
198.	Mr. Freeman Thibault	Communications
199.	Mr. William Achatz	AP Photo Technician
200.	Mr. Daniel Acker	Projectionist
201.	TSgt Earl D. Ainsworth	Communications
202.	SFC Dean E. Allen	Communications
203.	Mr. Joseph L. Angeletti	Ground Station
204.	MSgt Abel Araiza	Support
205.	Mr. Aldo Argentieri	Engineer
206.	Mr. Richard Aronson	Engineer
207.	Mr. Harold Bailey	VTR
208.	Mr. Peter Bates	Audio
209.	SSgt William J. Baldridge,Jr.	Aircrew

210.	Mr. Robert Bates	Security
211.	Mr. James M. Beary, Jr.	Security
212.	Mr. Walter T. Benedict	Security
213.	TSgt James K. Bloom	Aircrew
214.	SFC Hershal H. Braswell	Communications
215.	Mr. Alphonso Bressan	Audio
216.	Mr. Joe H. Brown	Ground Station
217.	Mr. Wesley A. Brown	Ground Station
218.	Mr. Willis Brown	CBS Soundman
219.	Mr. Charles Buchage	Cameraman
220.	Mr. Charles Brunner	Microwave Specialist
221.	Mr. Leslie Buntin	Power Gen. Mechanic
222.	SP5 Richard M. Burke	Communications
223.	Mr. Bernard F. Burns, Jr.	Ground Station
224.	SP5 Robert O. Burre	Communications
225.	SSgt John L. Burson	Aircrew
226.	SSgt Donald L. Cammel	Communications
227.	Mr. Alfred Camoin	Cameraman
228.	Mr. John E. Carrell	Security
229.	Mr. Robert W. Caughey	Security
230.	Sgt Brian A. Chamberlain	Communications
231.	Mr. Richard O. Cheadle	Security
232.	Sgt Henry Chimeno	Communications
233.	SSgt William A. Clark	Aircrew
234.	Mr. Bobby A. Coates	Security
235.	SP4 Lanny P. Cobb	Communications
236.	GySgt M. A. Collins	Support
237.	Sgt Anthony J. Coppola	Communications
238.	SP4 Herman W. Cordray	Communications
239.	Mr. Donald E. Crowl	Security
240.	TSgt James R. Czzowitz	Aircrew
241.	TSgt Raymond H. Dabney	Communications
242.	Mr. Robert Decker	Microwave Specialist
243.	SP5 James A. Dexter	Communications
244.	Mr. Joseph Di Giovanna	Engineer
245.	Mr. Leon Dobbin	Cameraman
246.	MSgt George O. Dowling	Aircrew
247.	HMC Robert J. Dunn	Support
248.	Mr. Thomas Dunphy	Film Processor
249.	SP5 Donald F. Eickhorst	Communications
250.	Mr. Edwin Einarsen	Film
251.	Mr. Don Farnham	Cameraman
252.	Mr. John Fernandez	VTR
253.	Mr. Eddie N. Findley	Security

254.	Mr. Richard Fischer	Comm Spec
255.	Mr. Patrick J. Finnerty	Security
256.	Mr. Fred Flamenhaft	Film Editor
257.	Sgt Steven R. Fletcher	Communications
258.	Mr. John D. Flinn	Security
259.	MSgt Harry L. Formby	Aircrew
260.	Mr. Steven Frankel	Film Editor
261.	Mr. Robert Gaff	Microwave Tech
262.	Mr. John Gardiner	VTR
263.	TSgt William R. Garman	Aircrew
264.	Mr. Lowell Gayman	Engineer
265.	Sgt Terry W. Geiser	Communications
266.	Mr. Eugene Gerlach	Soundman
267.	Sgt Garland L. Gifford	Communications
268.	Mr. John Gillen	VTR
269.	Mr. William Goetz	Cameraman
270.	SSgt Stanley J. Goodwin	Aircrew
271.	Mr. Stanhope Gould	Productions/operations
272.	Mr. Louis A. Greenbaum	Ground Station
273.	CT2 Douglas A. Griffiths	Communications
274.	Mr. Peter Groom	VTR
275.	Sgt Norman R. Groves, Jr.	Communications
276.	TSgt John T. Hames	Aircrew
277.	SP5 Harry C. Harbin	Communications
278.	Mr. Walter R. Hartwig	Security
279.	Mr. James Harvey	Microwave
280.	SSG Williard L. Hausenfluck	Communications
281.	TSgt Woodrow W. Hayes	Communications
282.	Mr. Henry Heustis	VTR
283.	Sgt Harris C. Hinley, Jr.	Communications
284.	Mr. Francis Hodnett	VTR
285.	SP5 William W. Holloway	Communications
286.	Mr. James C. Holt	Security
287.	SSgt David B. Hostetler	Communications
288.	SFC Richard W. Housewright	Communications
289.	Mr. Richard Hyde	Supervising
290.	MSgt William H. Jablonski	Aircrew
291.	SSG Robert S. Johnson	Communications
292.	SP5 Malcomb S. Jones	Communications
293.	SFC Donald C. Jourdain	Communications
294.	SSgt Mays F. Joyner	Communications
295.	SP5 Gordon E. Jurgensen	Communications
296.	SP5 Grant E. Jurgensen	Communications
297.	Mr. Abraham Kabak	Audio

298.	Mr. Raymond C. Kalinowski	Security
299.	TSgt William S. Kemmer	Aircrew
300.	MSgt John J. Keough	Aircrew
301.	SFC Charles E. King	Communications
302.	SP5 Richard J. Klesch	Communications
303.	Mr. George Klimscak	Cameraman
304.	Mr. Albert Koury	Asst. Ground Station
305.	SFC George T. Kranich	Communications
306.	ET3 Douglas R. Kunze	Communications
307.	Sgt Douglas L. Laubach	Communications
308.	Mr. Gerald E. Lewis	Ground Station
309.	SSgt William W. Lisenby	Aircrew
310.	Mr. William Lord	Radio Engineer
311.	TSgt William R. Lucas	Communications
312.	Mr. Walter Lupinsky	Projectionist
313.	TSgt Leslie Luther	Aircrew
314.	SSgt Francis Lynch	Aircrew
315.	Mr. Fred W. Lyon, Jr.	UPI Photo Tech
316.	SSG David W. Lytle	Communications
317.	Mr. Daniel McAvoy	Operator
318.	Mr. Charles W. McCaffrey	Security
319.	Mr. Richard A. McCann	Security
320.	Mr. Dennis McCarthy	Security
321.	Robert McEwan	Lighting
322.	Patrick E. McFarland	Security
323.	Mr. Daniel McKinney	Cameraman
324.	Mr. Patrick Malik	VTR
325.	Sgt Charles A. Marshall	Communications
326.	Mr. Richard Martinez	Engineer
327.	MSgt Robert C. Maurice	Aircrew
328.	Mr. Stephenson C. Miller	Security
329.	SP4 Raymond H. Mills	Communications
330.	Mr. Stanley Mitchell	Video
331.	Mr. Phillip Mollica	Transmission
332.	SP5 Kenneth W. Monroe	Communications
333.	SDC Zosimo Monzon	Support
334.	Mr. John R. Morgan	Security
335.	Mr. Randolf W. Nelson	Security
336.	SP7 Herbert G. Oldenburg	Support
337.	TSgt Charles K. O'Quinn	Communications
338.	SSgt John F. Palmer	Aircrew
339.	TSgt Harold R. Paulsen	Aircraft Support
340.	ET1 Carman L. Peltzer	Communications
341.	Mr. Anthony Piwowar	Transmission

342.	Mr. Donald Pike	Engineer
343.	SSgt Robert V. Planck	Communications
344.	Sgt David E. Poecker	Communications
345.	Mr. Frank Pollick	Projectionist
346.	Mr. Carl Prince	Engineer
347.	Sgt Gary F. Quint	Communications
348.	Mr. Leonard Raff	VTR
349.	TSgt Charles E. Rasmussen	Communications
350.	TSgt David E. Read	Communications
351.	MSgt Winfred B. Reid	Aircrew
352.	TSgt Richard J. Richardson	Aircraft Support
353.	Mr. Garfield Ricketts	VTR
354.	TSgt James W. Rierson	Communications
355.	Mr. Charles W. Rochner	Security
356.	Mr. George Romansky	Video
357.	Mr. Charles Roppolo	Soundman
358.	Mr. Dennis G. Rosdahl	Security
359.	Mr. Norman Rosensheim	VTR
360.	Mr. Cleveland Ryan	Lighting
361.	RMC Aaron B. Salter	Communications
362.	SFC Ronald D. Sanders	Communications
363.	TSgt William S. Scalf	Aircrew
364.	ETC Daniel Schoettlekotte	Communications
365.	Donald R. Schwartz	Security
366.	Carl D. Shawver	Security
367.	TSgt Lee F. Simmons	Aircrew
368.	Lawrence Sine	Operation
369.	Donald Smith	Film Editor
370.	Harry Smith	Projectionist
371.	SP5 Donald W. Spicer	Communications
372.	Herbert Starbird	Operator
373.	MSG Hazen F. Stevens	Communications
374.	Tom Tate	Microwave Spec
375.	John J. Taylor	Security
376.	Harlan Thiede	Ground Station
377.	Galen Tustison	Ground Station
378.	Vincent Vacca	Satellite Coordinator
379.	MSgt Ernesto Vasquez	Aircrew
380.	MSgt Buddie L. Vise	Aircrew
381.	William Walls	Ground Station
382.	James Watt	Soundman
383.	Sgt Billie W. Warren	Communications
384.	Douglas A. Weaver	Security
385.	Norman Weinhouse	Project Engineer

386. David P. Welch   Security
387. Walter Werner   Video
388. Carl M. Williams   Security
389. MSG George D. Williams   Communications
390. Sgt David A. Winkelman   Communications
391. Wayne Wright   Microwave

INDEX

421